Rolf Kreyer

The Nature of Rules, Regularities and Units in Language

Cognitive Linguistics Research

Volume 51

Rolf Kreyer

The Nature of Rules, Regularities and Units in Language

A Network Model of the Language System and of Language Use

DE GRUYTER
MOUTON

ISBN 978-3-11-031832-6
e-ISBN 978-3-11-031871-5
ISSN 1861-4132

Library of Congress Cataloging-in-Publication Data
A CIP catalog record for this book has been applied for at the Library of Congress

Bibliographic information published by the Deutsche Nationalbibliothek
The Deutsche Nationalbibliothek lists this publication in the Deutsche Nationalbibliografie; detailed bibliographic data are available in the Internet at http://dnb.dnb.de.

Printing: Hubert & Co. GmbH & Co. KG, Göttingen
♾ Printed on acid-free paper
Printed in Germany

www.degruyter.com

to Anna

Acknowledgements

There are numerous people from whom this book has greatly benefited. I am indebted to them for their help and comments and I am glad to have the opportunity to thank some of them in particular. First and foremost, I would like to thank Jürgen Esser who read earlier versions of the manuscript and provided detailed comments and most invaluable advice. Without him this book would never have been completed.

I would also like to thank Hannes Kniffka, Manfred Kohrt, Karl Reichl, Klaus Peter Schneider and three anonymous reviewers who read an earlier draft and provided me with very helpful and detailed feedback. For insightful comments and stimulating discussions on individual aspects I am grateful to Barbara Güldenring and Steffen Schaub. To the former special thanks are also due for proof-reading the whole manuscript. I would also like to express my gratitude to the series editor, Dirk Geeraerts, for including this book in *Cognitive Linguistics Research*. Naturally, I am responsible for all remaining errors and infelicities.

Finally, I would like to express my deepest gratitude to my beloved wife, Anna, for her unfailing and continuous support and love. To her this book is dedicated.

Content

Acknowledgements — vii

1 **Introduction — 1**

2 **A cognitively plausible network model of the language system — 8**
2.1 A cognitively plausible model — **8**
2.1.1 A usage-based model — **8**
2.1.2 A redundant-storage model — **9**
2.1.3 A frequency-based model — **11**
2.1.4 A comprehensive model — **12**
2.1.5 An integrative model — **13**
2.1.6 A hierarchical model — **14**
2.1.7 A rank-permeability model — **15**
2.2 A network model — **16**
2.2.1 Network models in psychology and linguistics — **16**
2.2.2 The present network model — **24**
2.2.2.1 A glance at neurophysiological aspects — **25**
2.2.2.2 Frequency — **28**
2.2.2.3 Spreading activation — **30**
2.2.2.4 *If-then* relations in the network — **33**
2.2.2.5 Competition — **34**
2.2.2.6 Distributed or local — **44**
2.2.2.7 To be or not to be – ISA and other relations in the network — **46**
2.2.2.8 The inheritance of features — **52**
2.2.2.9 The representation of sequence — **59**
2.2.2.10 Learning - changing network structures — **63**
2.2.3 Notational conventions — **67**

3 **Units, classes, structures and rules – language data and linguistic modelling — 73**
3.1 From data to description — **73**
3.2 From description to grammatical rules — **91**

4 'Traditional' concepts and their representation in the network model — 95
4.1 Traditional descriptive and early generative concepts — 95
4.2 Applying the model to rules and units of grammar — 106
4.2.1 The formation and representation of classes — 108
4.2.2 Gradience in the network model — 116
4.2.3 Ambiguity, vagueness and polysemy — 134
4.2.4 The formation and representation of sequences and structures — 142
4.2.5 The representation of rules — 158
4.2.6 Rules and their instantiations: redundancy and related issues — 167
4.2.7 A network view on morphological productivity — 177

5 Cognitive schemas — 181
5.1 Schemas in psychology and linguistics — 181
5.2 Cognitive schemas in the network model — 188
5.2.1 Regular clausal constructions — 188
5.2.2 Idiosyncratic constructions and patterns — 199
5.3 Recurrent item strings — 205
5.4 Recurrent item strings in the network model — 212
5.4.1 Concrete fillers with no intervening material — 213
5.4.2 Abstract fillers in continuous strings — 217
5.4.3 Concrete and abstract fillers with intervening material — 219
5.4.4 The interaction of idiomaticity and productivity — 222
5.5 Frequency and other causes for entrenchment in the present network model — 226

6 Beyond grammar: language use and the network — 228
6.1 The nature of categories and its relevance for processing — 228
6.2 The exploitation of expectation — 233
6.3 Processing principles — 245
6.4 A note on garden paths and related issues — 262

7 Outlook and conclusion — 265

References — 269
Index — 290

1 Introduction

Richard Hudson, in his many publications within the field of Word Grammar, formulates what he refers to as:

> **The Network Postulate**
> Language is a conceptual network (Hudson 2007a: 1, among others).

This view, as Hudson claims, can be regarded as a "commonplace of modern linguistics" (1) if we take into consideration the structuralist idea of language as a system in which each element obtains its value from its relation to other elements in the system: "Any system of interconnected entities is a network under the normal everyday meaning of this word" (1).

Uncontroversial as this claim may appear at first sight, problems may arise if the claim is taken seriously, i.e. "language is **nothing but** a network – there are no rules, principles, or parameters to complement the network. Everything in language can be described formally in terms of nodes and their relations" (1; Hudson's emphasis). Such a view of language, although in line with cognitive approaches and psycholinguistic models of language, runs counter to basic tenets of traditional linguistic schools, such as a strict division between lexis and grammar or, more generally, between the fully regular and the idiosyncratic in language. Network models do away with this neat bipartition: "The claim that language is a network therefore conflicts with the claim that information is divided between the grammar and the lexicon. In a network analysis, the same network includes the most general facts ('the grammar') and the least general ('the lexicon'), but there is no division between the two" (Hudson 2007a: 3). This example illustrates a very important point: "[T]he conceptual-network idea is not merely a matter of our choice of metaphors for thinking about language or what kinds of diagram we draw. It also has important consequences for the theory of language structure [...]". (Hudson 2007a: 4)

The model of language suggested in the present study is in line with the general claims underlying the models suggested by Hudson and others. It follows the Network Postulate, in that it understands language to be a network and nothing but a network. However, the present study wants to take the network idea one step further. The appeal of network models lies in the fact that the brain itself consists of a network of nerve cells and links between these nerve cells. Network models seem to be inherently closer to a possible psychological or neurophysiological reality and, hence, more cognitively plausible. However, existing network models of language (apart, perhaps, from purely connectionist models of the kind illustrated in MacWhinney et al. 1989) make use of a descriptive apparatus which goes beyond what brain cells and neurophysiology have to offer, e.g. different kinds of links between nodes (such as ISA or relation nodes, e.g. 'giver' or 'receiver'; Hudson 2007a among others), numbered links to represent sequence of elements (Roelofs 1997) or different classes of nodes to represent concepts like AND or OR (Lamb 1998). The present study, therefore, is an attempt to meet what could be referred to as:

> **The Neurophysiological Challenge**
> Language is nothing but a network. This network mirrors the neurophysiology of the brain in that the nodes and the connections are closely modelled on what we know from nerve cells and their connections.

The 'ingredients' of the network are, thus, significantly reduced: the network consists of nodes, which represent sounds, morphemes, syntactic structures, etc. These nodes can be activated to different extents. If this activation meets a certain threshold level, the node will pass on activation to all the nodes to which it is connected. A higher degree of activation may lead to a faster passing on of activation. Activation is passed on through links between nodes. These links do not represent relations; rather they are of an associative kind. Links just serve as conduits through which activation can be transferred. They always start in a node but they may end in a node as well as in another link. In line with basic neurophysiology, links are of two kinds: 1) excitatory links increase the activation of the target, while 2) inhibitory links decrease or block the activation of the target (see also Lamb 1998).

That is the basic machinery underlying the present network. In addition to these ingredients, network structures may change in different ways, thus implementing the view advocated in Bybee (2010: 2; among others): "language can be seen as a complex adaptive system [...], as being more like sand dunes than like a planned structure, such as a building". The frequent activation of a node will lead to a lowering of the activation threshold that this node has. That is, frequently 'used' nodes will be accessed and activated more easily in future. Similarly, links that are used more frequently will become stronger, so that they pass activation on more quickly. In general, portions of the network that are used a lot become trained so that future use is facilitated. In this way, the network implements the cognitive notion of entrenchment (e.g. Langacker 2008). In addition, nodes grow links between one another if they are co-activated frequently. This is the network correlate of association of previously unrelated

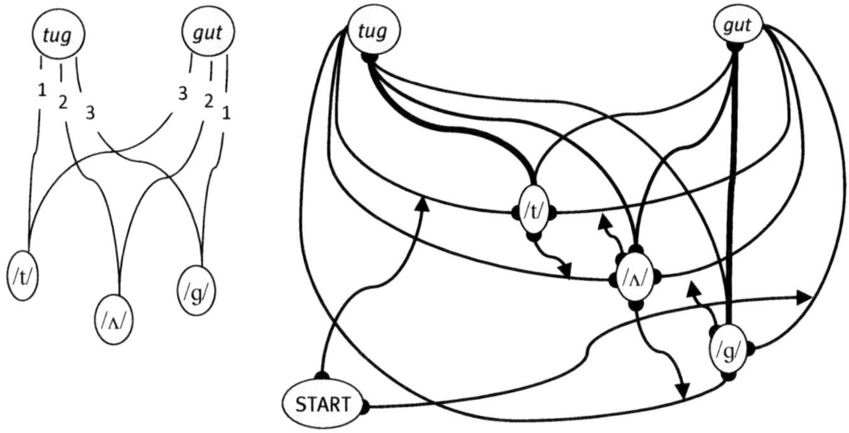

Figure 1.1: Sequences in a network model with ranked (left) and purely associative links (right).

events; it explains well-documented phenomena like priming and important concepts like collocation or colligation. Finally, the network may 'grow' new nodes as the result of new experiences or the result of categorization.

In following these neurophysiological restrictions the present model is in line with the idea of 'cognitive commitment', i.e. "a commitment to make one's account of human language accord with what is generally known about the mind and brain, from other disciplines" Lakoff (1990: 40). This commitment has far-reaching consequences for the network model. For instance, simple linguistic facts, like the order in which, say, phonemes appear in a word, are extremely easy to represent in a network model that allows for links that express ranks. To achieve the same is a lot more difficult in a network that is based on neurophysiological facts. Instead of ranked links, such a model has to apply links of different strengths, the notion of word beginnings and an intricate pattern of excitatory connections (see figure 1.1).

The obvious question, then, is: 'What is the advantage of a significantly more complicated way of representation in the present model?' The first answer is that this way of representation is more accurate in that it follows what we know from neurophysiology. If in the brain we do not have axons (the connection leading from a neuron to another neuron) that can represent ranks, a network model should try to make do without such a kind of connection. The second answer is related to that. The model presented in this study, similar to the suggestions made by Hudson or Lamb (among others), is of the hard-wired type. It is not self-organising but it is the researcher that decides on the number and kind of nodes and on the connections that exist between these nodes. In connectionist circles, this approach has been dismissed as being of little value, since it is assumed that more or less everything can be hard-wired. This would, then, make models like those presented by Hudson or Lamb and the present model little more than mere presentational variants of other, more traditional kinds of representation. There is no need, here, to go into further detail regarding this aspect. Let it suffice to say that, as we have seen above, existing network models, by their very nature, do make claims about language structure that go far beyond or even contradict traditional models. Again, the present study would like to take this development one step further. It is not only concerned with how particular facts of language are represented in a network but it also tries to account for the processes that are going on in the network as soon as particular nodes are activated. Following Langacker (1987: 382), language in the present network model "is not something a speaker *has*, but rather what he *does*." This is an additional challenge and leads to problems that are far from trivial. For instance, it is fairly easy to describe an activation pattern that represents the fact that in the sentence *John reads books* the finite verb inherits or copies person and number features from the subject *John* and not from the patient *books*. But it is fairly difficult to design a network structure which leads to the correct activation pattern as soon as the network 'knows' that *John* is the agent of the action of reading. In particular, how can we make sure that the plurality of the patient does not interfere with this process? Without going into further detail at this point (see section 4.2.4 for a detailed discussion), the structure that solves this problem is shown in figure 1.2.

The present study, thus, not only presents an alternative to network models like those of Hudson or Lamb, it also tries to provide a model that explains how network structures interact in the production and the comprehension of language. The model is a model of the static language system but, at the same time, accounts for the system in action. In this, the present study follows Lamb's (2000: 95) dictum that a model of the language system "must represent a competence to perform". Which nodes to include and which connections to establish depends on the question whether such changes increase the performance of the whole system or not. Finally, the present study seeks to explain how network structures evolve on the basis of two fundamental cognitive processes, namely association and categorization. Association is a very basic process that underlies many cognitive operations. As mentioned above, it refers to the fact that events (or rather: stimuli) that co-occur frequently come to be seen as related and interdependent in the cognitive system of the organism that experiences these events. Association lies at the heart of categorization, since categories are

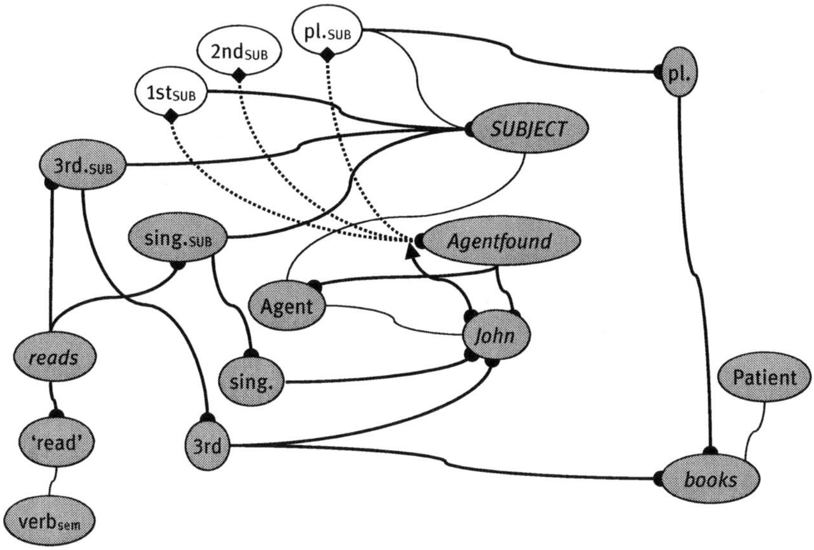

Figure 1.2: Choosing the right verb form if the agent *John* is the subject of the clause *John reads books*. (details omitted).

understood as an accumulation of features that co-occur frequently. A semantic category, for instance, is described as a set of co-occurring semantic features. This view of categories makes it very easy to implement what Langacker (2000b: 4) refers to as 'schematization', the "capacity to operate at varying levels of 'granularity' (or 'resolution')." Different degrees of abstractness or specificity can be represented and accessed simply by manipulating the number of features that are seen as relevant for membership in a given category. This kind of flexibility is indispensable given the enormous diversity of categories in language. Categories are highly useful in interpreting and organising new data, since they can help to make apparent patterns that otherwise would remain hidden: the two sentences *I like books* and *The boy kissed the girl* are as distinct from each other as they can be. It is only through viewing them with regard to functional categories that it is revealed that both sentences are instantiations of the same clause pattern, namely SVO. From this example it becomes apparent that the language system unfolds through an iterative process of association, which leads to categorization, which leads to new kinds of association, which leads to new categories and so on.

This process is fundamental to the description of any language system. The aim of the present study is not merely to show that language systems (in this case the English language system) can be described by the present network model. One of its other major aims is to show that the iterative process described above is a consequence that follows from the nature of the network and the processes going on in the network. The network model, therefore, has a high degree of explanatory power: the structures that we find in the network are the result of the nature of the network itself, i.e. they are the result of elements and processes that are similar to the elements and processes that are found in the human brain. Similarly, it follows from the nature of the network that basic-level categories are optimal for processing. As a consequence, from a network point of view, abstract notions like 'XP', although they may increase the elegance of academic descriptions of language, do not seem to be relevant. Other aspects that can be derived from the nature of the network include redundancy of storage, i.e. the fact that complex forms are stored if they are frequent enough or the fact that the language system contains structures at different levels of abstraction and specificity that transcend rank boundaries. Similarly, the nature of the network itself suggests that the model is both local and distributed at the same time. That is, some concepts are represented by a single node in the network, while others are represented by the co-activation of a number of different nodes. In this way, the present model does not fall prey to the exclusionary fallacy that networks either have to be distributed or local, or, for that matter, that they have to be real-copying or virtual copying – the nature of the network suggests that both kinds of information-inheritance co-exist. Finally, in some cases the network suggests answers to problems of linguistic description. An example is the problem of gerunds in English. Without going into detail at this point (see section 4.2.2), the present network would rule out a solution where an *–ing* form is classified as a verb and a noun at the same time. In cases like these, the study (or its author) does not choose a particular representation of a linguistic feature but the study shows what solutions are possible if we consider the assumptions underlying the network as valid.

On the whole, the present study suggests a network model of language that restricts itself to elements and processes known from the human brain. The model should not be understood as a presentational variant of other models of language – network or other. Rather, the study wants to show how a system that is based on neurophysiological 'ingredients' can create structures that represent units and structures of language; at the same time, the study wants to show how these structures, when in operation, lead to activation patterns that represent the outcome of processes of language production and comprehension as described over the last few decades. This way, the present study hopes to make a contribution to the cognitive linguistic enterprise.

The study is organized in six chapters. After the introductory remarks in this chapter, chapter 2 discusses a number of standards that have to be met for a model of language to be regarded as cognitively plausible and it introduces the basic features of the network model advocated in this study. Chapter 3 discusses the steps of any linguistic theory from data to description and from description to the formulation of rules and shows how these steps are represented in the evolution of network structures. The following three chapters explore the implementation of a wide range of linguistic phenomena in the network model. Chapter 4 focuses on the description of traditional concepts and notions in the present model including the representation of sequences, structures and rules. It also discusses aspects like gradience, redundancy and ambiguity. Chapter 5 looks at more recent concepts discussed in cognitive and corpus-linguistic circles, namely cognitive schemas (including aspects of construction grammar) and various kinds of multi-word units. Chapter 6 focuses on language use. It explores how the nature of categories and aspects like expectancies are exploited during processing and how the network structures relate to claims made in research on processing principles such as the end-weight principle.

2 A cognitively plausible network model of the language system

This chapter introduces, in the first part, a number of requirements that have to be fulfilled for any language model to be cognitively plausible and that the present model is aiming for. In part, these requirements are based on considerations of a more general kind. Some requirements, however, are formulated envisaging the vast array of linguistic concepts and phenomena that a comprehensive model has to encompass. In this sense, the first part of this chapter can also be understood as a preview of chapters 3 to 6. The second part develops a network model of the language system that meets all of these demands.

2.1 A cognitively plausible model

2.1.1 A usage-based model

'Usage-based' can be understood in two ways, namely as relating to quantities that are found in language use and their representation in a model of language or as relating to an empiricist view. Although throughout this study there will be references to frequencies and statistical associations, 'usage-based' is primarily interpreted in an empiricist way: all the structures and elements that are described in this model are understood as being based on language data that the language user has encountered. Every structure that will be described in the remaining chapters is thought of as resulting from the application of general cognitive mechanisms to these language data. More specifically, the model is informed by Langacker's (1988a) 'content requirement' and thus ensures that all the elements in the description can be traced back to word forms or strings of word forms that actually occur in language data. That is, the model only contains elements that are of one of the following kinds: 1) elements that are direct representations of overtly occurring language strings, i.e. representations of word forms and of strings of word forms. 2) abstractions or schemas that results from generalizations of these (strings of) word forms. A category like 'past tense', for example, is the result of schematization on the basis of a set of actually occurring past tense forms like *kissed, begged, loved, hugged* and so on. 3) relations that exist between overtly occurring language strings, between abstractions and overtly occurring strings, or between abstractions and abstractions. An example of the first kind of relation is that of collocation, e.g. the co-occurrence of the two word forms *naked* and *eye*. Relations between abstractions and overtly occurring strings are exemplified by the class 'regular past tense verbs' and all of its instantiations. Finally, an example of relations between abstractions and abstractions is the instantiation relation between clause types such as the mono-transitive clause and its instantiating patterns SVO and OSV. It is clear that the general usage-basedness of the present model rules out the concepts developed in more recent approaches in the generative-transformational paradigm, since "[t]he notion of grammatical construction is eliminated" (Chomsky 1995: 170) in these theories (see section 4.1).

2.1.2 A redundant-storage model

Given the usage-basedness it makes sense to assume that the model stores information redundantly. This is in line with many cognitive accounts of language (and also other network models, e.g. Hudson 2007a) and is suggested by findings from different areas of language research. One of these is language acquisition. For instance, Tomasello and his co-workers find that child language acquisition starts off with "specific item-based constructions" (Tomasello 2006: 285) which only later become more abstract. It is important to note, though, that "as children create more general constructions, they do not throw away their more item-based and local constructions" (Tomasello 2003b: 11). In this way, rules or abstract constructions and concrete instantiations are supposed to co-exist, at least in the mental grammar of the child during language acquisition.

In a similar vein, Langacker (1987: 28) argues against what he calls the 'exclusionary fallacy', an assumption which wrongly suggests "that one analysis, motivation, categorization, cause, function, or explanation for a linguistic phenomenon necessarily precludes another." A special instance of the exclusionary fallacy is the 'rule/list fallacy', i.e.:

> the assumption, on grounds of simplicity, that particular statements (i.e. lists) must be excised from the grammar of a language if general statements (i.e. rules) that subsume them

> can be established. Given the general N + -s noun-pluralizing rule of English, for instance, specific plural forms following that rule (*beads, shoes, toes, walls*) would not be listed in an optimal grammar. (Langacker 1987: 29)

Recent research rejects such a view on the basis of its lack of psychological plausibility, as Dabrowska (2004: 27) points out: "[h]uman brains are relatively slow processors, but have enormous storage capacity. From a psychological point of view, therefore, retrieval from memory is the preferred strategy". Langacker (2000b) integrates storage as well as rules in the following "viable alternative" to the 'rule vs. list' approach, namely:

> to include in the grammar both rules and instantiating expressions. This option allows any valid generalizations to be captured (by means of rules), and while the descriptions it affords may not be maximally economical, they have to be preferred on grounds of psychological accuracy to the extent that specific expressions do in fact become established as well-rehearsed units. Such units are cognitive entities in their own right whose existence is not reducible to that of the general patterns they instantiate. (Langacker 2000b: 2)

Another reason for such a redundant representation arises from findings in the field of corpus linguistics. The study of vast amounts of language-use data shows that many collocations and colligations do not depend on lexemes but on individual word forms, as can, for instance, be seen in Sinclair's (1996: 84) statement that "*blue* and *brown* collocate only with *eyes*", not with *eye* or any of the other forms of the lexical unit (see section 5.3). It therefore makes sense that the word form *eyes* needs to have its own representation in the network (not just as a product of the general rule of plural formation) to do justice to that fact.

On the other hand, not all word forms of a lexeme are equally frequent with respect to their potentiality of use. A case in point is Esser's (2000a) observation that one meaning of TREE, namely 'drawing', has a strong tendency to occur with the singular form only, while such restrictions are not observable with the 'plant' meaning of TREE. Such facts are best represented if word forms are integrated in the network even though they are completely regular and thus may be generated by a grammatical rule. This redundancy is not restricted to the lexical level but may be found at any level of description.

Finally, redundant storage seems to be licensed by experimental data that suggest a strong influence of frequency in language use and the shape of the language system (see section 4.2.6). A case in point is the observation that highly frequent instantiations of regular phenomena are stored even though they could be generated on the basis of the underlying rule they instantiate (see, among others, Stemberger and MacWhinney 1988; Baayen et al. 1997; Gordon and Alegre 1999). As Bybee and Thompson (1997) remark: "[t]he effects of frequency have important implications for our notions of mental representation. There is not necessarily just one representation per construction; rather, a specific instance of a construction, with specific lexical items in it, can have its own representation in memory if it is of high frequency" (Bybee and Thompson 1997: 386).

On the basis of this overview of facts and previous findings it seems reasonable to demand of any theory of language that it is able to implement redundancy on any level of the language system.

2.1.3 A frequency-based model

Frequency, in addition to redundant storage, figures prominently in other areas of linguistic description. Over the last one or two decades the importance of frequency in the shaping of the language system has been underlined by many researchers (see section 4.2.6 for a more detailed account). According to some, frequency effects are all-pervasive and can be found in any area of language processing and production. Ellis (2002), for instance, claims that there are "frequency effects in the processing of phonology, phonotactics, reading, spelling, lexis, morphosyntax, formulaic language, language comprehension, grammaticality, sentence production, and syntax" (Ellis 2002: 143).[1]

Corpus-linguistic and cognitive linguistic research has emphasised the role that frequency and statistical associations play in the shaping of the language system. Firstly, we witness many, usually frequency-based, patterns of co-occurrence that are characteristic of language use, such as collocations, idioms, or lexical phrases. Secondly, the combinatorial potential of the language system is not exploited to its full extent in language use: For instance, the different meanings of polysemous items often differ significantly in the frequency of realization, frequencies of words and constructions change in dependence of the genre. These differences in frequency influence the processing of language and the shape of the language system itself (see section 6.2). Highly frequent units and strings are more deeply entrenched in the language system[2]: highly frequent items are retrieved faster and more accurately than less frequent items, and highly frequent strings are reported to coalesce over time and to be stored

---

1 See, for instance, the edited volume by Bybee and Hopper (2001), which documents frequency effects on many levels of linguistic description.

2 Of course, frequency is not the only source of entrenchment. Other possible sources include (partial) opacity of meaning or a particular pragmatic function (see section 5.5).

as one unit even if they are fully regular and thus analysable into their component parts. A plausible model of the language system will need to take these aspects into account. The present model meets this requirement, albeit in a fairly rudimentary fashion by implementing different degrees of entrenchment of nodes and connections. These are designed to capture crude differences but are not meant to mirror correlations or conditional probabilities precisely.

2.1.4 A comprehensive model

Previous attempts at modelling the language system have often been restricted by focusing on some levels of linguistic description only, while at the same time ignoring others. This can be witnessed in the large number of dichotomies and distinctions usually drawn in traditional linguistics, such as those between lexis and grammar, between decontextualized and contextualized units, or between the semantics of sentences and the pragmatics of utterances. Drawing these distinctions, no doubt, has been useful and has led to many important insights. Yet, although a number of aspects concerning the language system can be studied in isolation from other areas of language description, this should not lead us to ignore the fact that many aspects of the language system show interdependencies transcending borders that are usually drawn. This becomes most obvious with regard to the distinction of lexis and grammar, which, according to more recent corpus-linguistic and cognitive research, can no longer be upheld (see the discussion of patterns and pattern grammar in section 5.1[3]).

Other points become apparent as soon as we take seriously the assumption that "[t]he mental system [...] is not some kind of abstract 'competence' divorced from performance, but a competence to perform" (Lamb 2000: 94). That is, we may assume that the language system is based on and shaped by language use. It, therefore, seems reasonable to additionally include in a description of the language system those aspects that are usually relegated to the study of language use and that are mostly regarded as being (at best) only indirectly relevant for the study of the language system. One consequence that arises from the consideration of competence as "a competence to perform" concerns efficiency of language processing and production. It is safe to assume that a model of the language system should be geared towards efficiency (see also the discussion in 6.3), and an efficiency-driven processor will make use of any bit of information available to ensure smooth and accurate interpretation of language data. For

3 In this respect also see Hasan (1987) and her notion of lexis as most delicate grammar.

instance, we are all aware of the effect of genre on the interpretation of utterances and on the disambiguation of word senses, since some word senses are more frequently used in particular genres or discourse types. It stands to reason that a processor will make use of such information. Hence, a plausible model of the language system should integrate contextual information where possible.

Since the envisaged model tries to be comprehensive with regard to these, usually isolated, areas of linguistic description, it will show a wide range of 'elements' that are included in the descriptive apparatus: The model is based on actually occurring strings of word forms, but it will also include information that can be abstracted from these strings of word forms (see the discussion of 'a usage-based model' above). Such pieces of information, for instance, may be a particular semantic feature, it may by a syntactic function like subject or direct object or structures like that of phrases or clauses. The model will also incorporate elements that make reference to the situation of use, such as spontaneous speech or edited writing, and the genre, such as written academic or prose fiction. In short, the envisaged model is comprehensive in that it takes into consideration all aspects of language system and language use simultaneously.

2.1.5 An integrative model

Related to the above is the problem that linguistic description, for decades of research, has upheld the distinction between what is regular and irregular, between productive rules and repeated idiomatic formulae, or between core and periphery. Such distinctions are usually not easy to draw: the division between the regular and the irregular is often a highly subjective one – when is the proportion of regular items large enough to justify the stating of a rule? Also, research by Eleanor Rosch and her colleagues (e.g. 1975) points out that the categories of linguistics are not Aristotelian but rather of a prototypical kind that exhibit what has been referred to as fuzziness, gradience or indeterminacy. The distinction of the productive versus the idiomatic is similarly problematic. The number of completely fixed idioms is rather small, while the largest share of idiomatic expressions show productive variation (see Barlow 2000 for examples). On the other hand, recent corpus linguistic research has made clear that what traditionally has been assumed to be the result of productive application of rules, to a large extent, is based on the use of prefabs or formulae and other kinds of more idiomatic strings or units. Erman and Warren (2000), for instance, claim that more than half of a given text consists of prefabricated phrases. On the whole, there is no language-inherent way of drawing a clear distinction between a core characterized by full generality, productivity and regularity and a periphery of completely particular, idiomatic and irregular items and strings. Rather, we are dealing with a continuum of different degrees of 'coreness' or 'peripherality', which suggests one descriptive apparatus to account for all phenomena found in the study of language (see also the discussion of cognitive schemas in section 5.2).

2.1.6 A hierarchical model

No model of language can dispense with different levels of hierarchy in its descriptive apparatus. One reason for this is the phenomenon of 'constituency', i.e. the observation that a particular linguistic item uses items on a lower level at its building blocks. In many cases, linguistic rules are nothing but a formulation and description of different relations of constituency in language data. In addition, hierarchies are demanded by the fact that we can make use of different degrees of detail in our description of linguistic phenomena.[4] Different degrees of detail automatically lead to a hierarchical structure where a superordinate and less differentiated class encompasses a number of subordinate and more differentiated classes. A similar intuition also becomes apparent in Rosch et al.'s (1976) distinction of 'superordinate', 'basic-level', and 'subordinate' categories (see section 6.1). The advantage of such a system lies in the fact that it enhances processing by enabling the language system to work with those amounts of information that are needed at a particular point in time and not burden itself with additional information that would be useless at that particular moment (see also the discussion of schemas in section 5.1). This feature can be witnessed in many different areas of cognition. Consider, for instance, people at a ball. If a new song begins, dancers might at first only be interested in the rhythm in order to determine whether they should dance a waltz, a rumba or a tango. In this situation more detailed information on the song being played (such as the instruments being used, the language in which the singers sing, etc.) might actually impede the recognition of the style of music. When crossing a street, processing on a very low level of delicacy also seems to have its advantages. The most important information is already carried by fairly large and unspecific categories such as 'pedestrian', 'bicycle', 'motorbike', and 'car', since these tell us something about the speed and the potential to harm us when

4 In this respect, see Halliday's (1961: 272) notion of 'delicacy', i.e. "the scale of differentiation, or depth in detail".

crossing the street. More detailed information (brand of car or motorbike, colour, etc.) might make it difficult for us to process the relevant pieces of information as fast as necessary. If we want to buy a car, in contrast, a far more detailed level of scrutiny is appropriate. The cognitive system thus seems to be fitted with the ability to 'zoom in and out' of objects, dependent on the amount of information that is needed in a particular situation and for a particular purpose; Langacker's (2000b) idea of 'schematization' (see section 5.1).

A similar ability is also useful in the processing of language structures. Often the processor does not need all the information contained in a linguistic element to draw relevant conclusions and make useful predictions. A case in point is the occurrence of the definite article in a string of words. On the basis of the definite article alone the processor can tell that the structure about to being processed is an NP (see Kimball's 1973 parsing principle 'New Nodes'). This bit of information will lead to expectations regarding certain other features that are relevant for processing. At the beginning of the clause, this NP is very likely to function as the subject; at least in written English. In spontaneous conversation the mere fact that the processor has encountered the beginning of a full NP is a fairly reliable cue for the fact that the NP is not the subject of the clause, since these are mostly realized by pronouns. In both cases, the processor will be fairly safe to assume that the whole NP makes reference to generic entities or entities already given in the previous discourse, since this is what the definite article signals. This makes clear that the very general category 'definite NP' already enables the processor to draw highly relevant conclusions about the general nature of the linguistic string being processed. In the light of principles like Hawkins' (2004) 'Maximize On-line Processing' (see section 6.3), which suggest that the human parser will ascribe ultimate properties of the language string as early as possible, it makes sense to assume that the language system, similar to other cognitive systems, makes use of different degrees of delicacy or granularity during processing. These degrees can be expressed in a hierarchic system.

2.1.7 A rank-permeability model

Having emphasised the importance of hierarchies in any model of language description, it is also important to stress the interaction between elements on different levels of hierarchy. Obviously, any model of language needs to have a certain degree of permeability between adjacent ranks; otherwise, it could not do justice to the phenomenon of constituency that we find in any traditional model of grammar. However, and more importantly, we also witness interdependencies between levels of grammatical description beyond constituency relations (see section 2.1.1). This becomes clear if we take into consideration cognitive schemas or recent corpus-linguistic concepts (sections 5.2 and 5.3, respectively). Cognitive schemas, as exemplified in Fillmore et al.'s (1988) notion of construction or Hunston and Francis' (2000) concept of pattern show a high degree of inter-rank dependencies. Similarly, the notions of semantic preference and semantic prosody (e.g. Sinclair 1991) combine word forms with semantic features, e.g. the string *naked eye* co-occurs frequently with word forms that make reference to visibility and word forms that contain a semantic aspect of difficulty. In summary, a cognitively plausible model of the language system should allow for associations between any kind of element on all conceivable ranks of linguistic description.

The next section will show how a network model of language is able to meet all of the seven standards discussed above.

2.2 A network model

2.2.1 Network models in psychology and linguistics

The idea of using networks to model cognitive and linguistic processes is not new. In particular, network models have been employed in psychology to account for experimental findings regarding the understanding of sentences or the effect of priming on word form recognition. For instance, Collins and Quillian (1969) suggest a hierarchical network model of semantic memory. Their network encodes properties of objects and classes, and the superset-subset relations between them, i.e. the network is primarily organised on the basis of ISA-relations (a 'subset' is a (kind of) 'superset'), e.g. A canary ISA bird and a bird ISA animal. In addition to the ISA-links, the model also has feature links. A canary, for instance, shows the property 'can sing' and 'is yellow'. Superordinate classes also show distinctive features, such as 'can fly' for *BIRD* or 'has skin' for *ANIMAL*. The model largely is what has been called a 'virtual copying' model (see Goldberg 1995: 74), i.e. the information for subordinate items is only stored in the superordinate nodes[5]. The property 'can fly' is, thus, directly con-

---

5 Note that this is only the simplest case. Collins and Quillian (1969: 242) make clear "that people surely store certain properties at more than one level in the hierarchy". See also Collins and Loftus (1975: 409) for a discussion of this point.

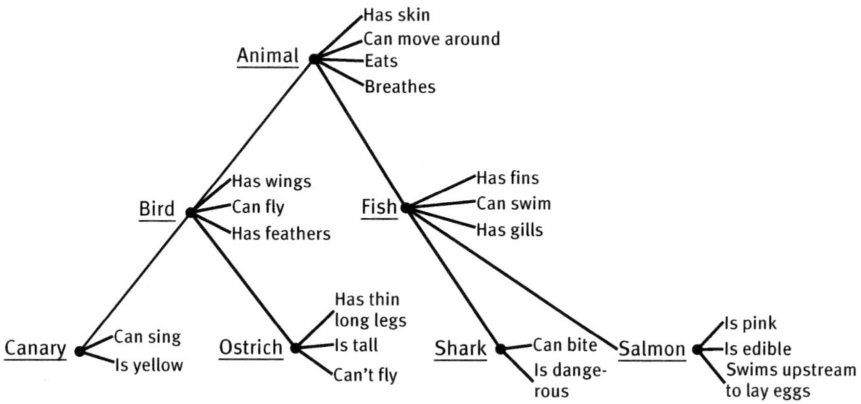

Figure 2.1: The network model of Collins and Quillian (1969: 241) (with kind permission of Elsevier).

nected only to the class *BIRD* but not to the class *CANARY*, and the property 'has skin' is connected to *ANIMAL* but neither to *BIRD* nor *CANARY*. In Collins and Quillian's approach the respective network appears as shown in figure 2.1.

According to this model, it should be easier to verify a sentence like 'a canary can sing' than a sentence like 'a canary has skin', since in the first case the relevant information is directly attached to the 'canary' node, whereas in the second case the relevant information is two nodes away from the 'canary' node. This is exactly what is borne out by Collins and Quillian's data, i.e. sentences of the first kind were verified faster than those of the second kind.

A less strictly hierarchical network model is the one suggested by Collins and Loftus (1975). Their model is based on similarity: "The more properties two concepts have in common, the more links there are between the two nodes via these properties and the more closely related are the concepts" (411). Relatedness, in this model, is expressed by proximity of nodes, as figure 2.2 shows. The different kinds of vehicles in the upper portion of the network are closely related, since they share a number of features. In contrast, 'fire engine' and 'cherries' are not closely related, since they only share the singular feature 'red' and no other features.

Most of the network accounts have focused on restricted aspects of language, such as the mental lexicon (see above and, among others, Beckwith et al. 1991; Fellbaum 1998; Miller and Fellbaum 1991, 1992; Steyvers and Tenenbaum 2005), morphological processes like past tense formation (Rumelhart and

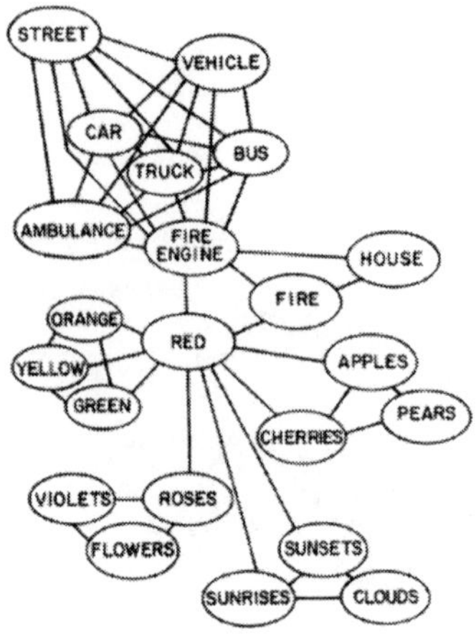

Figure 2.2: The network model of Collins and Loftus (1975: 412) (with kind permission of the American Psychological Association).

McClelland 1986; MacWhinney and Leinbach 1991), or the acquisition of syntactic categories (Gasser and Smith 1998). The only comprehensive network models of the English language, to my knowledge, are provided by Sidney Lamb (1998)[6] and Richard Hudson (2007a, 2007b and 2008). In contrast to the approaches by Collins and Quillian or Collins and Loftus as sketched out above, Lamb makes use of a fairly elaborate system of different kinds of nodes which "differ from one another according to three dimensions of contrast: (1) *UPWARD* vs. *DOWNWARD* orientation, (2) *AND* vs. *OR*, (3) *ORDERED* vs. *UNORDERED*" (Lamb 1998: 66). According to Lamb, the whole language system consists of a network of such nodes related to one another (see figure 2.3).

An upward unordered AND node is shown in the triangle that links 'GO' and 'Verb' to the line next to '*go*'. This means that the activation of this line will activate both 'GO' and 'Verb' and, conversely, that '*go*' will be activated if both 'GO' and 'Verb' are activated. The symbols in the bottom line of figure 2.3 show upward unordered OR links. This means that the phoneme[7] /g/ spreads its activation to all the nodes to which it is connected, i.e. all the forms that contain this phoneme. Conversely, all forms that contain this phoneme will activate the

6 See also Lamb's (1966) first outline of 'stratificational grammar' and Sampson's (1970), Lockwood's (1972) and Schreyer's (1977) introductions to the theory, as well as Makkai and Lockwood (eds.) (1973) for an early collection of papers following Lamb's approach.
7 Despite Lamb's highly idiosyncratic terminology, I will here stick to the traditional terms.

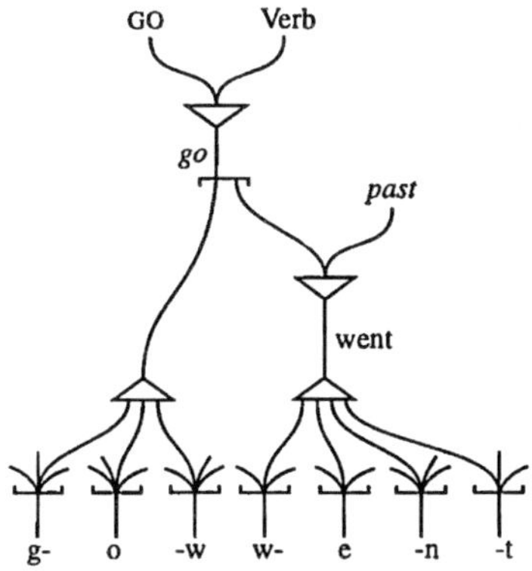

Figure 2.3: A network portion for GO in Lamb's (1998: 60) network (with kind permission of John Benjamins Publishing Company, Amsterdam/Philadelphia).

node representing /g/. As a final example consider the triangle that connects the three phonemes /g/, /o/ and /w/. This triangle denotes a downward ordered AND node: only if the three phonemes are activated in the order in which they are represented in the figure will the node *go* be activated, and, again, the activation of the latter will activate the phoneme nodes in this particular order

Another important point of divergence from the two approaches discussed before resides in the fact that Lamb explicitly denies the necessity of any symbols in the network:

> If the relationships of linguistic units are fully analyzed, these 'units' turn out not to be objects at all, but just points of interconnection of relationships. We may conclude that the linguistic system (unlike its external manifestations) is not in itself a symbol system after all, but a network of relationships, a purely connectional system, in which all of the information is in its connectivity. (Lamb 1998: 65)

This is also exemplified in figure 2.3 above. As can be seen, the symbols '*go*' and 'went' are written at the sides of the connecting lines and are not part of the network structure. In Lamb's view, an integration of these symbols would be superfluous, since all the information about the form *go* is already given in the connectivity of the network, namely that it has a particular meaning (here represented by GO), that it belongs to the syntactic class of verbs, and that it is realized by the three phonemes on the left of the bottom line of the figure. That is, the information about the form *go* lies in the connection of these particular parts of the network. Similarly, *went* is superfluous in this network, since this form is represented by all those parts of the network that lead up from the four phonemes on the right-hand side of the bottom line in figure 2.3.

At the basis of Richard Hudson's (1984, 1990, 2007a, 2007b, 2010) Word Grammar is the Network Postulate which states that "language is a conceptual network" (2007a: 1; see chapter 1). Figure 2.4 illustrates the main components of Hudson's model. The lines with the triangular base signify ISA-relations. As in the model by Collins and Quillian, these relations are fundamental, since they guarantee that properties of a category are inherited by every member of that category and by every member of every sub-category (unless they are overridden). In the figure above b ISA a, which means that b inherits all features from a. The arrows in the model relate two nodes in such a way that the node at the endpoint of the arrow is the function of the starting point of the arrow, i.e. "the e of a is c", e.g. the/a property of a bird is that it can sing. Hudson claims "that this notation applies throughout language, from phonology through morphology and syntax to semantics and sociolinguistics" (2007b: 511). The network model to be advocated in this study is similar to Hudson's model in that it tries to account for the vast range of linguistic phenomena by a fairly simple notational apparatus.

Hudson follows Lamb (1998) when he claims that "the nodes are defined *only* by their links to other nodes; [...] No two nodes have exactly the same links to exactly the same range of other nodes, because if they did they would by definition be the same node" (Hudson 2007b: 520). That is, all the information is contained in the network itself, labels are a mere representational device and, therefore, redundant.

As can be seen from figure 2.4, some of the links in the network model are labelled. These labels are essential, because Hudson's network is not a mere associative network, as is the one suggested by Collins and Loftus (1975: 412) (see figure 2.2). However, just like nodes, links are also organized in a network

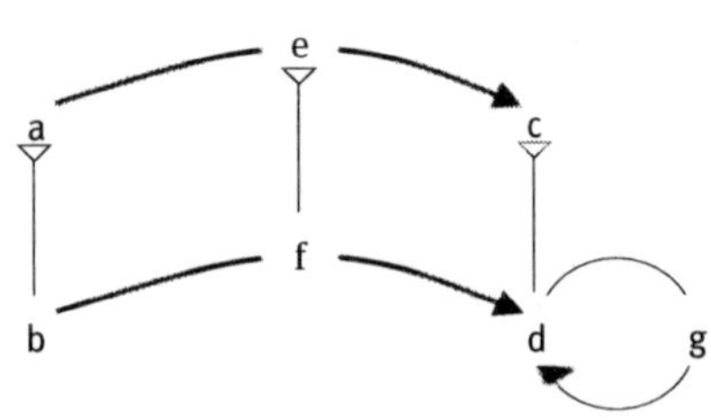

Figure 2.4: Notation in Hudson's Word Grammar (2007b: 512) (with kind permission of Richard Hudson).

of hierarchical classification, which means that they can simply be identified by their relation to other links. Again, the label is a mere representational device. We will leave it at that for the moment and discuss Hudson's model at greater length at different points in this chapter when we contrast it to the network model developed in this study.

All of the models so far are what is called 'hard-wired', i.e. it is the researcher who determines which nodes in the network should be connected to each other and how strong the connections should be. In this way, it is possible to model any aspect of a given language despite such networks not being able to learn. A cognitively plausible model, in addition to dispensing with symbols (as Lamb's and Hudson's models do), should also be self-organizing, as MacWhinney (2000: 123) makes clear. However, "[w]hen the prohibition against symbol passing is combined with the demand for self-organization, the class of potential models of language learning becomes extremely limited" (MacWhinney 2000: 124). As a consequence such models are usually confined to highly restricted aspects of the language system only, such as past tense morphology (Rumelhart and McClelland 1986; MacWhinney and Leinbach 1991, Plunkett and Marchman 1993), spelling (Bullinaria 1997), reading (Bullinaria 1997) or acquisition of syntactic categories like *NOUN* and *ADJECTIVE* (Gasser and Smith 1998).

Without going into too much detail, many models of the self-organizing kind all have a similar architecture consisting of a layer of input nodes[8], a layer of output nodes and one or more intermediate layers of hidden nodes. Let us consider an example of a network that 'learns' the assignment of the correct form of the direct article to German nouns (MacWhinney et al. 1989). The network is shown in figure 2.5 below.

As can be seen from this figure, the network consists of a total of 66 (=11+5+15+16+2+17) input nodes (we will discuss presently what these nodes represent). Each of these input nodes is connected to a first layer of hidden nodes. More specifically, 49 of the input nodes are connected to 20 gender/number nodes and 19 of the input nodes are connected to 10 case nodes. The 30 nodes in first layer of hidden nodes are connected to 7 nodes on a second hidden layer. These are connected to 6 output nodes, which represent the six possible forms of the German definite article. The layers of hidden nodes can be understood as representing those parts of the language system that contain the knowledge relevant for the choice of the definite article; MacWhinney et al. (1989) write: "We can think of these internal layers as forming a useful internal

8 I will use the term 'node' instead of 'unit' here.

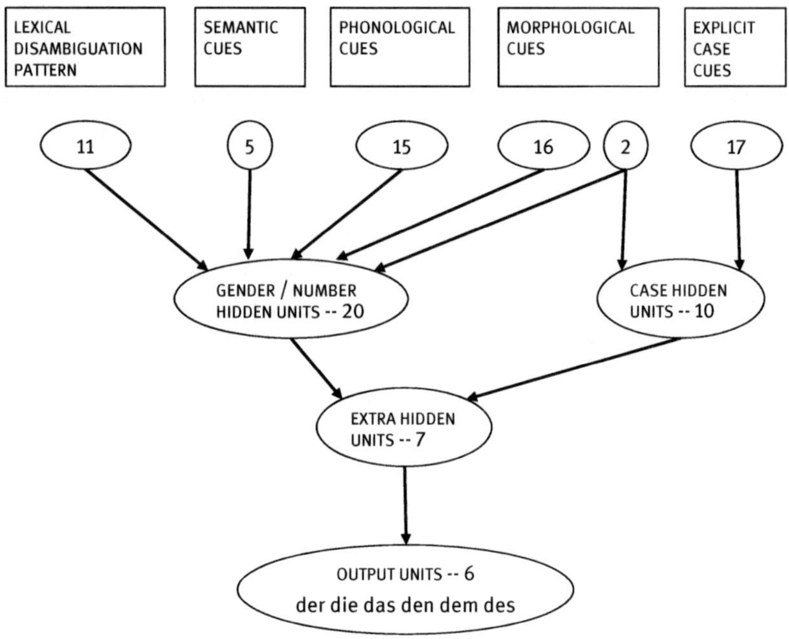

Figure 2.5: MacWhinney et al.'s (1989: 264) network model for the acquisition of the German definite article (with kind permission of Elsevier).

representation of the input. [...] we would expect these to correspond to the grammatical categories that describe the German nouns presented to the network" (MacWhinney et al. 1989: 263).

How does this network 'learn' to assign the correct form of the definite article to a given noun? The choice of the German article depends on three parameters, namely the gender, the number and the case of the noun form. However, the network model does not have any specific information on these three parameters i.e. it does not know that the German noun form *Junge* (*boy*) is nominative singular and has masculine gender. Rather, like a child acquiring the German language, the network has to find the correct form of the definite article solely on the basis of features associated with a particular noun form.

In the case of case of *Junge*, for instance, such features would be the natural masculine gender, the ending of the word in <-e>, the beginning of the word with a consonant immediately followed by a vowel, etc. These features are represented by the 66 input nodes in the network. By way of illustration, let us look at the assignment of gender in more detail. With regard to gender, three kinds of cues are relevant, namely semantic, phonological and morphological cues. As to the first kind, one of the five semantic cues for gender assignment is the natural gender of the noun at issue. A natural male gender, as for the form *Sohn* (*son*), is a good indicator of a male form of the definite article, whereas what the authors describe as 'young being' is a cue to neuter gender, as in *das Kind* (*the child*). Examples of morphological cues are the diminutive endings *–lein* or *–chen*, as in *Fräulein* and *Mädchen*; these predict neuter gender. As to the 15 phonological cues, an *umlaut* in the noun stem usually indicates masculine gender, as in German *der Ärger* (*anger*), and so does the sequence of consonant and vowel at the beginning of the noun. As these examples make clear, some cues are fully reliable (e.g. the diminutive endings), whereas others are probabilistic and only show tendencies, like the *umlaut*. In a similar fashion, cues like the ones above also yield information on the number and the case of the noun form[9].

Each noun that is fed into the network is represented by a configuration of activated and non-activated input nodes, which represent the cues discussed above. For instance, the noun *Mädchen* would be represented by an activation of the nodes 'natural female gender', 'ending *–chen*', '*umlaut*', etc., whereas nodes like 'natural masculine gender' or 'ending *–lein*' would not be activated. All the active nodes will spread their activation to the first level of hidden nodes, dependent on the strength of connection between the respective nodes. This will lead to a particular configuration of activated and non-activated hidden nodes on the first layer, which will result in a particular activation pattern in the second layer of hidden nodes, which will in turn lead to an activation of the output nodes. The most strongly activated output node is the network's 'suggestion' for a definite article corresponding to the noun form represented by the activation pattern among the input nodes. This suggestion is compared to the correct definite article, and the network is given feedback on the correctness of the output[10].

This feedback will lead to slight changes in the network, more particularly, to changes in the connectivity in the network. As in the models by Lamb (1998) and Hudson (2007a), the information about how to use the definite article is contained in the connections within the network and the weights between these

9 The 11 nodes covered by the box 'lexical disambiguation patterns', are used to disambiguate individual noun forms, since two different noun forms may be identical with regard to the 55 nodes representing the semantic, the phonological, the morphological and the explicit case cues.

10 This feedback is provided with the help of what is called the 'back-propagation algorithm'. I will here dispense with the technicalities; the interested reader is referred to Rumelhart et al. (1986).

connections. In the beginning of the learning process, all connections are assigned a small random weight. These weights are adjusted after each training cycle, which will lead to differences in the way that the activation spreads from the input to the output nodes. Eventually, the network will be able to assign the correct form of the definite article to the nouns in the training set and also to nouns not encountered before. The network has learned the use of the definite article. It is important to note that this learning, i.e. the adjustment of connection weights, does not include any intervention of the researcher but is solely based on the feedback that the network gets after each training cycle. The network is self-organizing.

2.2.2 The present network model

The aim of this section is to introduce the network model advocated in this study on a very general and basic level, i.e. it will describe the major features of the network and the processes that go on in this network. For purposes of illustration this section might sometimes make reference to linguistic phenomena, but the real discussion of how the present network described and accounts for language will begin with chapter 3.

Like the model by Lamb (1998) and Hudson (2007a) and in contrast to the one advocated by MacWhinney et al. (1989), the present model is of the 'hard-wired' type. But, as will be made clear in section 4.2 below, the structures in the network are understood as resulting from the application of two basic cognitive mechanisms, namely categorization and association, to language data. All of the network structures presented in the following can, thus, be accounted for by basic human learning mechanisms.

One focus throughout the study will lie on describing how the development of network structures can be explained by these mechanisms. That is, the network advocated here does not stand in contrast to self-organizing connectivist models advocated by MacWhinney (2000). The model, therefore, is cognitively plausible in that it evolves in a fashion that is similar to processes that might be going on during language acquisition.

Similar to Lamb (1998), Hudson (2007a) and MacWhinney et al. (1989), the present model is non-algorithmic, i.e. all the information in the system is in the connection between the individual nodes and the weights of these connections. Still, the model will make use of 'symbols' to describe a given node for the sake of presentational clarity. Nevertheless, this description does not add information to the system.

After these general preliminaries, we can now turn to a discussion of the architecture of the network itself.

2.2.2.1 A glance at neurophysiological aspects

One of the appeals of network models is the fact that the brain is organised in a network of nerve cells. While, to my knowledge, it is not possible at present to describe the neurophysiological correlates of, say, a word or a syntactic category, it is nonetheless appealing to describe language in ways that are similar to what we know about the neurophysiology of the brain and the characteristics of neurons and of the processes between neurons. Obviously, the description here will be on a very basic and general level.

Although neurons may have many different forms, their general layout is identical. A typical neuron consists of a body, or *soma*, a number of dendrites (incoming connections) and one axon (outgoing connection). The axon connects the neuron to other neurons. However, two nerve cells do not have a direct contact. Any axon is separated from the target cell through what is called the synaptic cleft. The connections between neurons, accordingly, are called synapses. Three types of synapses can be distinguished: between axon and dendrite, between axon and soma and between axon and axon. The first two are the more common type, the third is fairly rare. Neurons pass a signal that, typically, is received through the dendrites or the soma on to other neurons via the axon. These signals can be excitatory or inhibitory, i.e. they can contribute to the activation of the target neurons or inhibit the target neuron. Within the cell, signals are of an electric kind. Yet, electricity cannot travel over the synaptic cleft, which is why the electric signal within the cell is transmitted to the target cell with the help of neuro-transmitters. These chemicals lead to a change in the electric potential of the target cell, which, as soon as a certain threshold has been reached, will result in the action potential, an electric signal that will travel through the neuron to those neurons to which the axon and its branches connect. Summing up, and in a more schematic way, we can say that a neuron receives activation from other neurons. If this activation passes a certain threshold, the neuron will pass its activation on through the axon to other neurons. The activation of a neuron is binary, i.e. the threshold level is reached or it is not reached. Still, the spreading of activation is not binary, since a neuron can fire with different speeds: intensity translates into impulses per second. This is relevant for the present network model. The same node is understood to fire more rapidly if it receives activation from many sources than if it receives activation from fewer sources.

The network will follow the schematics of neurons to a certain extent. A distinction will be made between nodes and links that connect nodes, representing body plus dendrites and axon, respectively, as shown in figure 2.6 below.

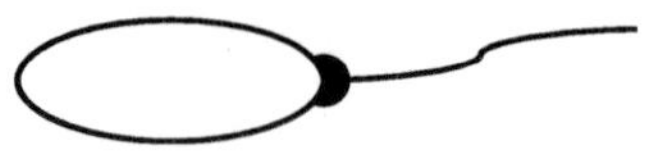

Figure 2.6: A node in the network.

Typically, a node will receive activation from more than one node and it will send activation to more than one node (even though each neuron only has one axon, each axon usually has a large number of different branches). In the network, connections will be represented by solid lines. To distinguish outgoing connections from incoming ones, outgoing connections will (usually) be connected to the source node by a filled half-circle. As mentioned above, an axon can also be linked to another axon. This is represented by the line on the bottom right that is connected to one of the axons (figure 2.7).

The present model also tries to do justice to insights from neurophysiology with regard to the ways in which neurons are likely to react to new experience, i.e. learning. Following Rosenzweig and Leiman (1982), Birbaumer and Schmidt ([2]1991: 542-3) formulate a couple of hypotheses about synaptic changes that might form the basis of learning. These changes either concern the number of neurotransmitters that a (pre-synaptic, i.e. before the synaptic cleft) axon releases into the synaptic cleft, or they concern the way in which the postsynaptic cell reacts to neurotransmitters. As to the first, other things being equal, an increase in the number of neurotransmitters will increase the speed with which the action potential in the target cell is reached. As a consequence the signal will be passed on faster from one cell to the other cell. Conversely, a decrease in the number of neurotransmitters will lessen the speed of signal transmission. Regarding the second kind of change, given the same amount of neurotransmit-

Figure 2.7: Incoming (on the left) and outgoing connections (on the right) in a node.

ters, changes in the postsynaptic cell can result in a stronger reaction and, hence, an increase in the speed with which the action potential is reached, or a weaker reaction and a decrease in speed. In addition, we also find that new synaptic contacts are created and that contacts can wither away.

In the present network model these effects will be represented by the strength of outgoing connections (representing axons), by the strength of the nodes (representing the soma and the dendrites, i.e. those parts of the neuron that receive activation), and by the number of connections between nodes. With regard to the strength of outgoing connections two cases will be considered. An outgoing connection may pass on the signal faster because it has been trained. This is one possible network representation of the cognitive notion of 'entrenchment', i.e. processes that are used a lot are executed faster (see Langacker 2000a: 103). This is usually a long-lasting effect. In the present model this will be depicted by a thicker outgoing connection, as shown in figure 2.8.

Figure 2.8: Permanent effects of learning on outgoing connections.

A similar effect can be achieved if an outgoing connection receives additional activation from an incoming connection (the network representation of an axon-axon synapse). This is the network representation of the psychological notion of 'priming', an effect that is not permanent. Figure 2.9 depicts this situation.

The influence of changes in the postsynaptic cell is indicated through ellipses marked by lines of different strengths. The thicker the ellipsis the faster the

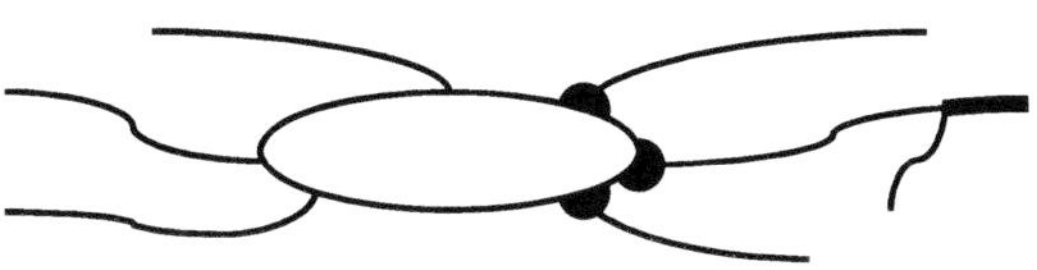

Figure 2.9: Temporary effects of learning on outgoing connections.

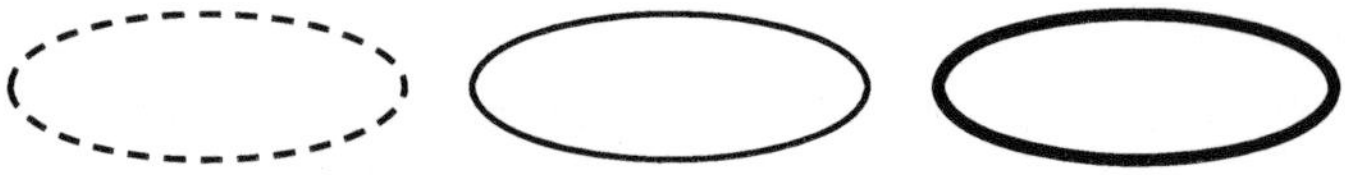

Figure 2.10: The representation of degrees of entrenchment of elements in the network model.

node it represents is activated. This is the second way to implement the cognitive concept of entrenchment into the network model. Figure 2.10 shows three degrees of entrenchment, with an increase from left to right.

2.2.2.2 Frequency

The importance of frequency for a model of language has been emphasized again and again in cognitive research (see section 4.2.6 for further detail), and the following claim by Bod et al. (2003: 3) can be taken as representative: "Frequency affects language processes, and so it must be represented somewhere. The language-processing system tracks, records, and exploits frequencies of various kinds of events."[11] Network models are a prime means to represent such frequencies. In particular, two aspects are of relevance. The first has to do with the frequency of individual elements of description, such as frequency differences in realizations of lexemes, word forms, constructions, etc. In the envisaged network model these frequency differences will be mirrored by the strengths of the nodes that represent the individual elements, as shown in figure 2.10 above. For instance, the word form *kin* is far more frequent than the word form *kith*, and accordingly the first will be more deeply entrenched in the cognitive system. More important for the present purpose is the second aspect, namely the influence that frequency of occurrence has on the connections between the individual nodes. Differences in connection strength capture the degree to which the occurrence of one element in the language data predicts or primes the occurrence of another element of the language system. Therefore, the role of frequency attributed in the present model comes close to what we find in probabilistic approaches to language. Bod (1998: 145), for instance, claims that "the knowledge of a speaker/hearer cannot be understood as a grammar, but as a statistical ensemble of language experiences that changes slightly every time a new utterance is perceived or produced." Such probabili-

11 Also see the discussion of Herdan's (1956: 79) claim that "language is the collective term for linguistic engrams (phonemes, word-engrams, metric form engrams) together with their particular probabilities of occurrence" in section 6.2.

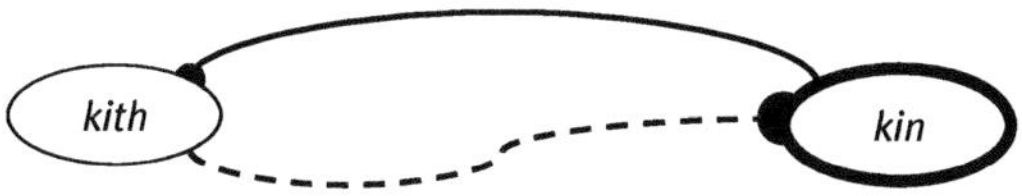

Figure 2.11: Uni-directional connections in the network.

ties in the language system are exploited in production and comprehension, as Jurafsky (2003) points out:

> the probability of a word given the previous or following word plays a role in comprehension and production. Words with a high joint or conditional probability given preceding or following words have shorter durations in production. In comprehension, any ambiguous words in a high-frequency word-pair are likely to be disambiguated consistently with the category of the word-pair itself. (Jurafsky 2003: 53)

In a similar vein, Halliday (1991: 31) claims that "the linguistic *system* [... is] inherently probabilistic, and that frequency in text [... is] the instantiation of probability in the grammar" (see also Halliday 1992: 65).[12]

A case in point is the word form *kith*. The occurrence of this form is a very good predictor of the occurrence of the word form *kin*. On the other hand, *kin* is not a very good predictor of the word form *kith*. This example makes clear that two elements, A and B, need to have two separate unidirectional connections, one leading from A to B, the other leading from B to A. Both aspects of frequency are represented in figure 2.11 through a thick line leading from the word form node |*kith*| to the node |*kin*|, and a thin line leading from |*kin*| to |*kith*|. Note that figure 2.11 is not to be interpreted sequentially, but rather it merely states that if a text contains the form *kith*, it is fairly likely that somewhere in the vicinity we also find the form *kin*, but not vice versa.

The intuition mirrored in the figure above is also captured by collocation-metrics: a search for collocates of *kith* in the BNC shows *kin* to be the strongest collocate. In contrast, *kith* only ranks as eleventh collocate of *kin*, with *next*, *of*, *support*, etc. being stronger collocates. From the viewpoint of the individual nodes, the relative strength of connection is what counts: although the absolute contingency value is the same, namely a log-likelihood value of almost 301, the relative strengths of connection differ, since 301 is the highest log-likelihood value for *kith* but only the eleventh highest for *kin* - the highest being 932 for the

12 See Newmeyer (2003) for a critical account of stochastic grammars, and see Clark (2005) for a reply to Newmeyer (2003).

word form *of*, followed by *next* with a value of 675 and *and* with 608, and so on. This situation is depicted in figure 2.12 (note that this figure focuses on the strength of the connections between nodes and not on the frequencies of the individual word forms).

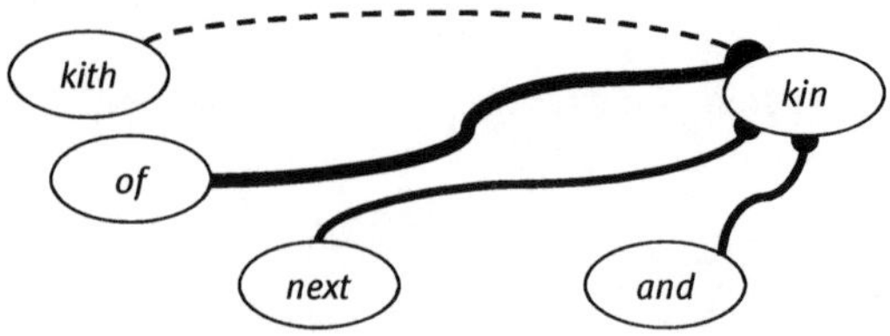

Figure 2.12: Relative connection strengths of the node |*kin*|.

In summary, the envisaged network model represents aspects of frequency by differences in strength of individual nodes and by differences in strength of unidirectional connections between individual nodes; the latter aspect represents degrees of association between individual nodes. It is important to note, though, that the strengths of lines in the network figures are usually not supposed to be an exact representation of frequencies and strengths of association as they, for instance, can be found in corpora. Rather, they serve to indicate relative degrees of entrenchment and association of individual elements within one figure in a more-or-less fashion.

2.2.2.3 Spreading activation

Spreading activation is a central mechanism in all network models, but it seems that the minutiae of this phenomenon have not been worked out quite yet for linguistic models. The present study hopes to provide a satisfying account of spreading activation and to show how this concept together with Langacker's (e.g. 2000a) notion of entrenchment can explain how learning takes place in the network. I will basically stick to the notion of activation used by Dell (1986), although I will introduce some minor modifications that can be found in other approaches (e.g. Lamb 1998). Dell (1986: 287) claims that "[t]he defining components of spreading activation are *spreading*, *summation*, and *decay*." The first refers to the idea that an activated node will spread this activation towards neighbouring nodes in dependence on the strength of the connection between

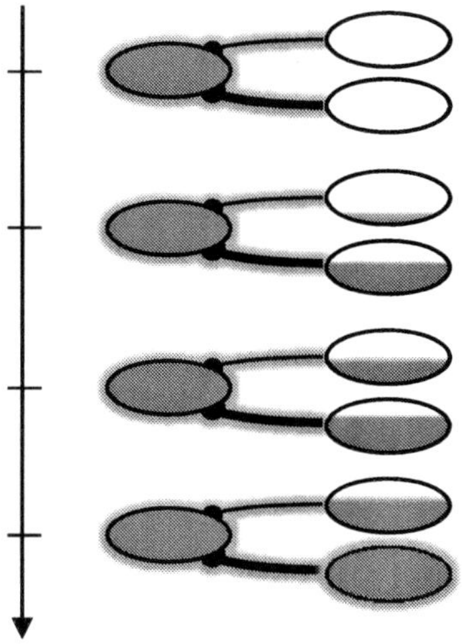

Figure 2.13: Activation spreading through connections of different strength at four successive points in time (the amount of filling in the ellipses represents the amount of activation of the nodes; the 'glow' represents the activation of a node and the passing on of activation through a link).

individual nodes. In the present model, the strength of connection (indicated by the thickness of the lines between boxes) influences the time it takes for a particular amount of activation to spread from one node to another node (see also Lamb 1998: 206 for an essentially identical suggestion). In this way, the present model mirrors the idea of entrenchment advocated in cognitive approaches to language (e.g. Langacker 2000b). Consider figure 2.13, where the process of activation spreading from the source node to the target nodes is depicted for four successive points in time (the order of magnitude, here, would be milliseconds, since figure 2.13 depicts cognitive processes in the mind of the hearer/speaker). The node to the left (the source node) is fully activated, which is represented by the 'glow' around the ellipsis. The node spreads activation through the two links to the two nodes on the right to which it is connected (the target nodes). Since the connection to the bottom target node is more deeply entrenched (indicated by the thicker line) than that to the top target node, the activation from the source node will spread faster to the bottom target node. As becomes clear from the above, a deeply entrenched connection between two nodes (indicated by a thick line) will lead to a faster spreading of activation from the source node (on the left) to the target node (on the right).

Figure 2.13 might suggest that spreading activation is similar to water in a bucket (the nodes to the left) that is transported to neighbouring buckets (the nodes to the right) through a system of hoses until the source bucket is empty. This analogy is not entirely correct. A more appropriate one would be to regard the source node as a water-tap which is connected to a system of buckets. This water-tap remains open as long as the activation threshold is satisfied, i.e. more water flows through the hoses if the water-tap is turned on for a longer time[13].

The second aspect of relevance to the concepts of spreading activation concerns the fact that a node which is partly activated will become more activated if it receives further activation from other nodes, and activation from more than one node add up in the target node. As a consequence, a node that is already active to a certain degree will become fully activated faster than a node that is not pre-activated. This is a very important characteristic of the network that is exploited during language processing, as we will see in chapter 6.

Thirdly, "[i]t is necessary [...] to include a passive decay of activation over time to keep levels down" (Dell 1986: 287), otherwise all nodes in the network would eventually become fully activated and remain that way. It is important to note, though, that the activation of the node is kept up for a certain amount of time before it decays, as is shown in figure 2.14.

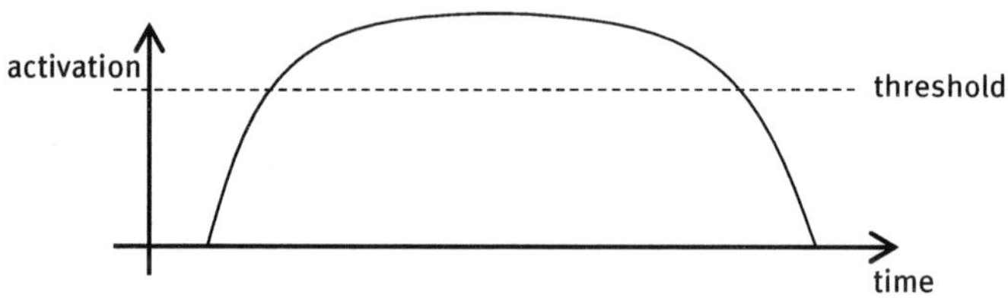

Figure 2.14: The typical temporal activation profile of a node in the network.

This feature of activation in a node is fundamental, because it helps us to understand the association of phenomena that do not occur simultaneously, e.g. the association of two words in a collocation.

13 Lamb (1998: 81), in line with neurophysiological findings, understands the activation to "consist [...] of a series of pulses, not just one, and [...] it takes a certain number of them [...] to satisfy whatever threshold will be encountered farther down the line." Thus the spreading of activation is of an inherent temporal nature.

In contrast to Dell (1986), the present network model makes use of two further concepts that are often found with network models (e.g. Lamb 1998) and that are in line with what was said about neurophysiological aspects in section 2.2.2.1. The first is that of an activation threshold. A node will only spread activation to its neighbouring nodes if its activation threshold is satisfied. The 'height' of these thresholds is the way in which different degrees of entrenchment of the nodes are implemented in the network. A strongly entrenched node will have a low threshold, indicating that this node will be activated fairly quickly, while a node that is not deeply entrenched has a high threshold and, consequently, will not be fully activated as fast. If the threshold level of activation is not reached the spreading of activation will stop at this node. The binary nature of the threshold notwithstanding, the same node can send out pulses of activation with different frequencies. This will usually depend on the amount of activation that a node receives from incoming links.

Together with decay, this mechanism is one possible way of solving what has been termed the 'heat death' problem, i.e. "the danger that too many nodes in the network are overactive at the same time" (Berg and Schade 1992: 405). Secondly, connections between nodes may be excitatory and inhibitory. That is, activation spreading through an excitatory connection will add to the activation level of the target node, while inhibitory connections will diminish the activation level. This concept is useful to implement the competition aspect to be discussed below.

2.2.2.4 *If-then* relations in the network

The need for a way to implement *if-then* relations in the network becomes obvious as soon as we become aware of the pervasiveness of this relation in language models. For instance, the phoneme(s) /t/, /d/ or /ɪd/ should usually be considered as indicators of past tense in verbs, but only if they occur at the end of a word form. Similarly, concept-related features like 3rd person and singular for the concept *Peter* should be transferred to the finite verb-form of the clause, but only if the concept at issue is the subject of the clause, not if it is the object.

The basic 'logic' behind *if-then*, from a network perspective, is the following: 'send activation from node |a| to node |b|, if node |c| is activated'. This is achieved with the help of a very weak link leading from |a| to |b|. The node |a| may be able to spread a tiny amount of activation to the node |b|, but it will not be enough to activate the target node to a sufficient extent. This is only possible if the link is boosted, which happens when the node |c| is activated at the same time. *If-then* in the network looks as follows.

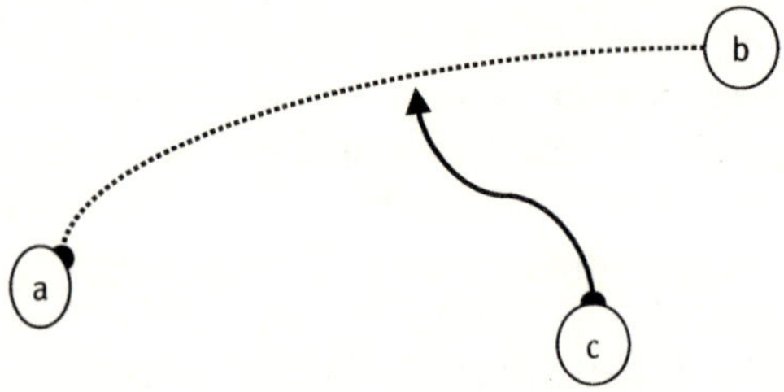

Figure 2.15: *If-then* in the network: |b| only receives sufficient activation from |a| if |c| is activated.

A similar relation is *if not–then*, e.g. 'interpret *Peter* as the patient of the clause if no other patient has yet been specified'. This relation looks almost identical in the network with the exception that the link from |a| to |b| is of 'normal' strength and an active node |a| would send sufficient amounts of activation to fully activate the node |b|. This spreading of activation can be blocked by an active node |c|, since an inhibitory link originates from |c| and blocks the connection between |a| and |b|. That is, 'send activation from node |a| to node |b|, if node |c| is not activated'.

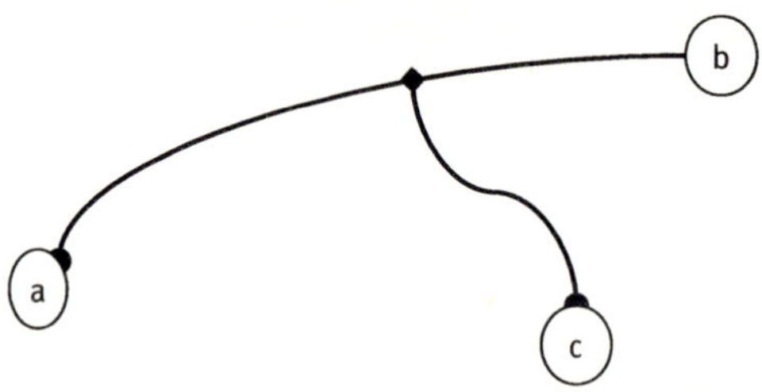

Figure 2.16: *If not-then* in the network: |b| only receives sufficient activation from |a| if |c| is not activated.

Both patterns will occur frequently in the present network model.

2.2.2.5 Competition

Competition is part of many network models and the concept has also been used to explain processes going on during morphological processing. In the present network model, competition is a consequence of the connectivity within the model and the notion of spreading activation. The 'problem' in this respect is that there is no governing authority in the network which tells the activation which way to go; as soon as a node is activated this activation spreads to all nodes to which it is connected. Let us assume that the system is 'searching' for a form of READ that expresses progressive aspect. How does the network know which word form is the correct one?

In the network model advocated here the situation just described is equivalent to the activation of two nodes, namely |M(read)| denoting the meaning or conceptual node, and the node |progressive|. The first node will spread its activation to all nodes to which it is connected, i.e. to all the word forms of READ. The second node is connected to all *–ing* forms and will activate these. In the present model, all of these nodes compete for realization in a spoken or written word form. Among these there is one node that receives activation from two nodes, namely |*reading*|, as it conveys the meaning M(read), and the progressive aspect. The node |*reading*| thus is the first node to be fully activated. It is this form that would be realized through speaking or writing. However, the other forms of READ and also other *–ing* forms might still become fully activated. If that was the case, the respective forms would also be realized, which is undesirable. To prevent this from happening, it makes sense to introduce inhibitory connections (represented in figure 2.17 by lines ending in squares). These would link all nodes representing word forms to all of their possible competitors. Of all nodes that are competing for realization, that node which is fully activated first will spread activation through inhibitory connections to all competing nodes, thereby keeping their activation below the

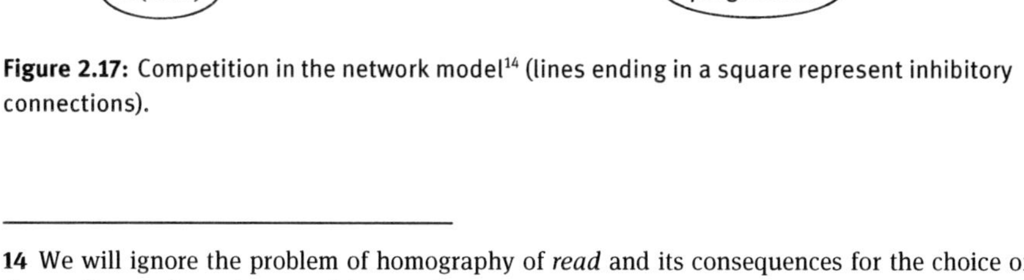

Figure 2.17: Competition in the network model[14] (lines ending in a square represent inhibitory connections).

---

14 We will ignore the problem of homography of *read* and its consequences for the choice of the medium-independent word form at the moment.

threshold. As a result, only one form out of a set of competing forms will be realized at one point in the production process. In the present example, as soon as the node |*reading*| is fully activated, this word form will be realized and, at the same time, the node will send activation through inhibitory connections to all other forms of READ and to all other *–ing* forms, thereby suppressing the realization of any of these forms.

The above kind of competition takes place everywhere in the network and the number of inhibitory connections between nodes is potentially very large. With the help of this system it is possible to keep many nodes of the same kind, e.g. nodes representing word forms, activated to a more or less medial extent. The respective word forms, this way, are prepared for realization, even though it is not clear yet which word form will finally be realised. However, even a medially activated node will pass on activation to related nodes. For instance, such a node might pass on activation to a semantically related concept. Let us take as an example a well-known cross-modal priming experiment discussed in Marslen-Wilson (1987) (see section 4.2.4 for details), where subjects were presented with segments of words, e.g. [kæpt]. Since this segment is shared by both *captain* and *captive*, both nodes are equally strongly activated in the network. Even though none of them is yet fully active and none of them fires at their highest possible frequency, they already spread activation to the semantically related nodes |*boat*| and *guard*|. These also become activated to some extent (figure 2.18).

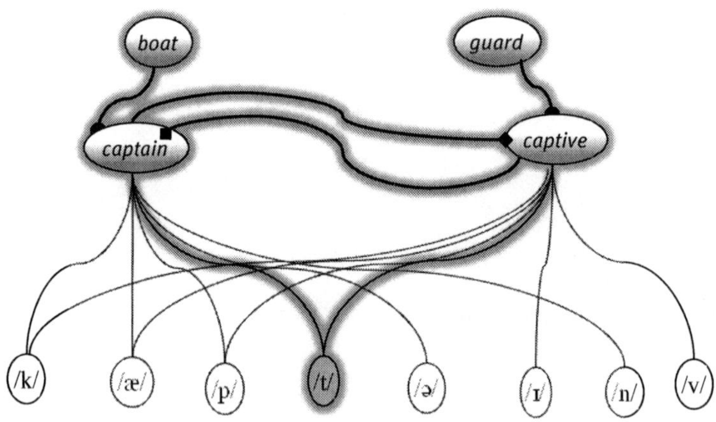

Figure 2.18: The nodes |*captain*| and |*captive*| after the activation of the phoneme node |/t/|.

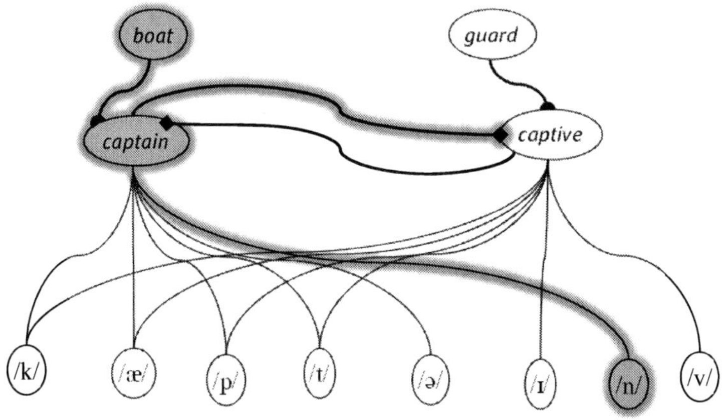

Figure 2.19: The nodes |*captain*| and |*captive*| after the activation of the phoneme node |/n/|.

Since both |*captain*| and |*captive*| are equally strongly activated, their respective inhibitory links fire with the same intensity, i.e. the two nodes supress each other to a certain extent. The whole system is in limbo, as it were. The situation changes drastically when the end of the word *captain* is reached. The node |*captive*| does not receive any further activation which will lead to a gradual reduction of its activation and the speed with which it sends impulses of activation through the network. That is, |*captive*| will not increase the activation of |*guard*| any longer and it will stop inhibiting its competitor |*captain*|. |*captain*| on the other hand will become fully activated, thereby activating |*boat*| more strongly and supressing its competitor |*captive*| completely. This situation is shown in figure 2.19. The central notion of competition and the use of inhibitory links help to implement the idea that in the network (and through mental processing) many alternatives are held ready for a certain period of time until further data allow to select one of these alternatives. The point of decision has been reached when one node is fully activated, thereby supressing all the competitor nodes to the strongest extent possible. This way, the present model can explain common characteristics of processing that show up in experiments, e.g. priming (see section 4.2.4).

In addition, the idea of competition and the use of inhibitory connections also help to explain the well-known phenomenon of knowing what word is meant even though we have not yet heard the complete word, e.g. the word *hippopotamus*. This happens when the competitors of a word do not receive any further activation: they will stop inhibiting the word that is being uttered. Competitors of *hippopotamus* are *Hippocrates* of *Hippocratic* (*oath*). Until the phoneme /ɒ/ is processed, all three words are still possible and the three respective nodes will be activated to a similar (medial) extent. The next phoneme, /p/ will only further activate |*hippopotamus*| but not the other two nodes. Already at that point in the processing of the auditory data, only one competitor is left. The respective node will be activated further and it is no longer inhibited by the competitor nodes. These, in contrast, do not receive further activation and still are (and even more strongly) inhibited by the node |*hippopotamus*|.

The kind of competition described above is of a fairly simple kind, in that the network merely has to 'single out' the one competitor that finally receives full activation. More complicated is competition when it involves the correct connections between a set of different nodes. For instance, the distinction between the two sentences *John hit Paul* and *Paul hit John* lies in the fact that the mapping of concept nodes and semantic role nodes is reversed. The network representation of the two sentences (as far as the mapping of concepts to semantic roles is concerned) looks as shown in figure 2.20.

It is one thing to describe sentences or propositions in a network representation, but unfortunately, it is a completely different thing to explain how a network arrives at this particular state that is shown in the representation. In the example at issue, the problem lies in the fact that both *Paul* and *John* are eligible for the semantic roles of agent and patient. The network implementation of this is the simple fact that both nodes are connected to both semantic-role nodes (as shown in figure 2.20). As we have seen in the previous discussion, an active node will spread activation to all the nodes to which it is connected. As soon as the human starts to 'think' PAUL the relevant node will be activated and activation will spread to both the nodes |Agent| and |Patient|.

How does the network 'decide' where the activation has to go? This involves a somewhat intricate pattern of excitatory and inhibitory links, but it is possible

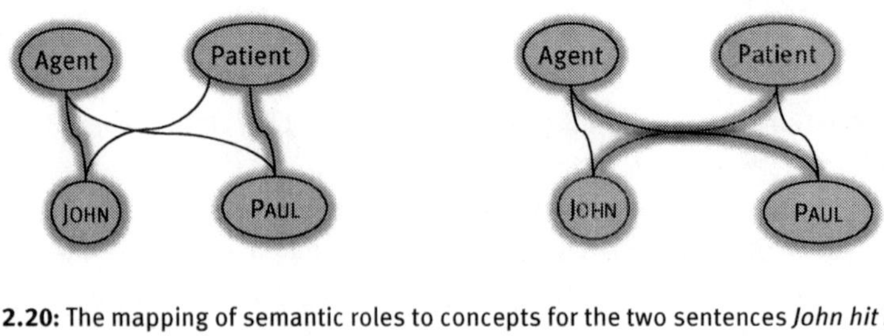

Figure 2.20: The mapping of semantic roles to concepts for the two sentences *John hit Paul* and *Paul hit John*.

to account for this process on the basis of very simple network that restricts itself to mechanisms that we know are at work in the brain.

The sentence *John hit Paul* is an instantiation of the proposition HIT(John, Paul). Although it makes sense to assume that this thought is represented through a particular activation pattern which involves the simultaneous activation of all the relevant nodes (similar to a picture that is a simultaneous representation of the whole event), it is also reasonable to assume that in the 'thinking' or the 'creation' of the proposition the different aspects of the event come into being one after the other (similar to changing figures and grounds when looking at the picture). Let us assume that the first aspect of the whole proposition is the information that John is the agent of the action (we could also start with Paul being the patient, it would not make any difference). Thinking this part of the proposition would lead to the simultaneous activation of the nodes |JOHN| and |Agent|. Both nodes would start spreading activation to all neighbouring nodes. As a consequence, activation passes between the two activated nodes (which is a desired outcome), but activation would also spread from |JOHN| to |Patient| and from |Agent| to |PAUL| (an undesired outcome). This problem can be solved by taking the idea of competition seriously. As stated above, competition happens everywhere in the network. More specifically, nodes that are similar in a certain respect compete with each other. With the example of *reading* we have seen that the activation of the nodes |M(read)| and |progressive| leads all nodes that express either of the two meanings to compete for realization. In a similar fashion, once the node |Agent| is activated it competes for all possible concept nodes with nodes that represent other semantic roles, e.g. |Patient| or |Recipient|. With regard to the present example, the node |Agent| competes with |Patient| for the concept nodes |JOHN| and |PAUL|. The outcome of this competition depends on which pair is activated first and can be accounted for by the intricate use of inhibitory and excitatory connections between nodes and links. We will develop the network step by step. Figure 2.21 represents the fact that within the network each node competes with every other node on the same level.

The fact that the node |Agent| competes with the node |Patient| can be represented by two inhibitory links leading from |Agent| to all those connections that lead to |Patient|. Similarly, |Patient| sends out inhibitory links to all potential candidates that qualify as agents. The same accounts for the two concept nodes at the bottom: |JOHN| inhibits any connections leading from |PAUL| to the semantic-role nodes and vice versa.

The network so far (as shown in figure 2.21) makes sure that |JOHN| and |Agent| are connected (if they are activated first) but they prevent the establish-

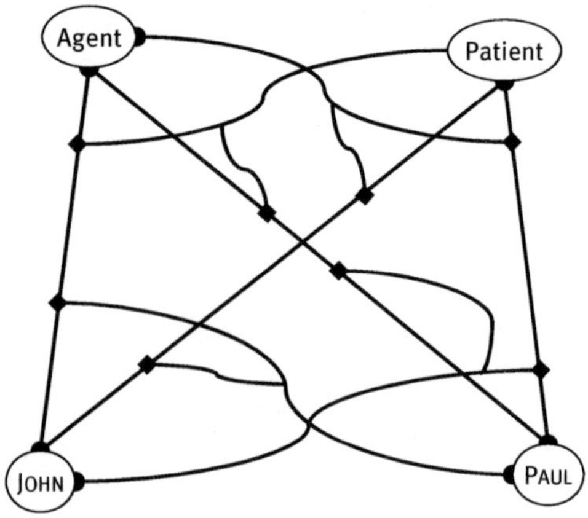

Figure 2.21: John competing for agenthood.

ing of any further connections. In particular, the connection between |PAUL| and |Patient| cannot be established, since it is blocked by two inhibitory connections, one from the node |Agent|, the other from the node |JOHN|. To prevent this from happening we have to find a way to 'tell' the network the following: 'If |JOHN| is connected to the node |Agent|, stop blocking connections to or from |PAUL| and |Patient|.' This kind of *if-then* is difficult to realise in the network, but it can be done, as we can see in figure 2.22 (note that the inhibitory links originating in |Patient| have been ignored for reasons of presentational clarity).

In figure 2.22, a new node |*AGENTfound*| has been introduced. This node becomes activated whenever the node |Agent| and a possible conceptual node, in this case: |JOHN|, are activated together. The node |*AGENTfound*| has an inhibitory connection (1) that inhibits the inhibitory link that leads from |Agent| to the connections leading from |Patient| to possible conceptual nodes - in this case, only |PAUL| (2). This means, as soon as the |Agent| node is satisfied, i.e. as soon as it is connected to a conceptual node, the node |Agent| stops competing for possible conceptual nodes – |PAUL| is now open to become connected to the node |Patient|. The only obstacle for Paul to be conceptualised as the patient of the given action lies in the fact that the node |JOHN| still blocks the link connecting |PAUL| and |Patient|. This block is inhibited by another inhibitory connection (3) that originates in |*AGENTfound*|. As a consequence, Paul can now 'become' the patient.

This kind of connection pattern works in an *if-then* fashion, more specifically: *if John is the agent, then* ... This is due to the fact that the inhibitory links

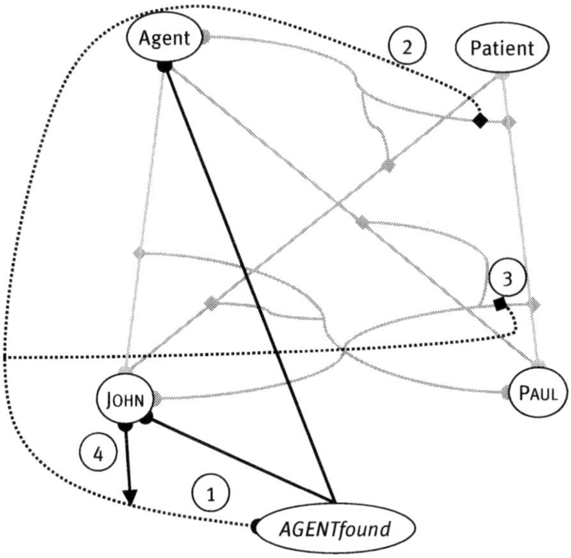

Figure 2.22: Allowing Paul to become patient.

leading from |*AGENTfound*| are very weak (represented by the dotted line) and need supplementary activation from other nodes. In the present case, this activation comes through an excitatory link originating in the node |JOHN| (4). The activation pattern can be translated as follows: 'if John is the agent (which it is at the moment), stop blocking the patient role and stop blocking other conceptual nodes'. The two inhibitions that were in the way of a potential active connection between |PAUL| and |Patient| are 'switched off'. To sum up so far: the two nodes |Agent| and |JOHN| and the connection between them are active. This represents the thought that John is the agent of whatever action is described. In the next step, the two nodes |Patient| and |PAUL| are activated simultaneously. The network has to make sure that the connection between these two nodes can be established and that, at the same time, the connection between |Agent| and |JOHN| remains intact. Figure 2.23 shows how this can be achieved.

As soon as the node |PAUL| is activated it will spread this activation through the links that originate in that node. Since |PAUL| competes with any other node on the same level, the node inhibits the connection between |JOHN| and |Agent| (1) since the node |PAUL| competes with any other conceptual node for any of the semantic-role nodes. Eventually, this would lead to a complete inhibition of the

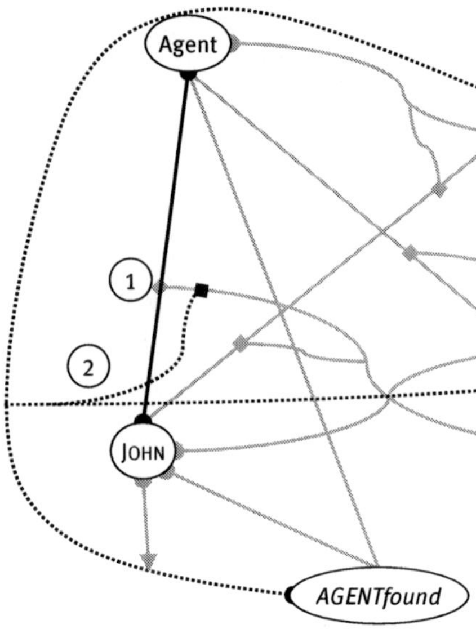

Figure 2.23: John as agent and Paul as patient.

activation traveling through the link between |JOHN| and |Agent|. To prevent this from happening, we have to introduce a new inhibitory link (2) that suppresses the inhibitory link originating in |PAUL|. This way, the activation from |PAUL| does not interfere with the active connection |JOHN|–|Agent|, in those cases when John is the agent. Note that the new inhibitory link branches off from the connection that starts in |*AGENTfound*| and is boosted by the node |JOHN| . The same connection, as already mentioned above, suppresses the two inhibitions that block the connection between |PAUL| and |Patient| (3) and (4), so that the activation can travel freely between the two nodes. As a result, we now have the activation pattern that we wanted to achieve: A simultaneous activation of the four nodes |Agent|, |Patient|, |JOHN| and |PAUL| together with an active connection between |JOHN| and |Agent|, and |PAUL| and |Patient|.

A final problem still has to be taken care of. So far, the network model explains how the semantic role of agent is mapped onto John and how that of patient is mapped onto Paul. It is not yet able to explain, though, how the reverse mapping is implemented. To account for that we need to have a mirror image of those connections leading away from |JOHN|. This is shown in figure 2.24.

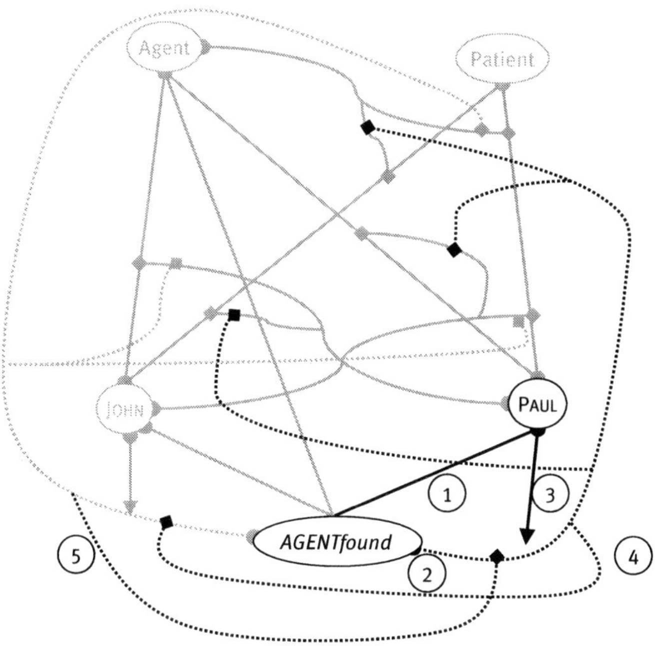

Figure 2.24: The network portion that ensures the correct mapping of agents and patients to conceptual nodes.

Since Paul also competes for the semantic role agent it is also a possible contributor to the activation of the node |*AGENTfound*| through the link number 1. Originating from this node is a weak inhibitory link with several branches (2) that needs to receive supplementary activation from the node |PAUL| through link number 3. This pattern of connectivity represents the mechanism 'if John is Agent (which it is at the moment), stop blocking the patient role and stop blocking other conceptual nodes'. We have to make sure, of course, that this *if-then* routine only works for one agent at a time. This is achieved with the help of connections number 4 and 5 in figure 2.24. Let us assume that Paul has been singled out as the agent. As soon as the second mapping – John as patient – is 'thought', the node |JOHN| will become fully activated as well. And it will send supplementary activation to the link that leaves |*AGENTfound*| on the left-hand side, which would result in the routine 'if John is agent ...'. This will be prevented by link number 4. It is active as soon as Paul has been identified as the agent and it blocks any activation leaving the node |*AGENTfound*| on the left before this activation can be boosted by the node |JOHN|. In the same way link number 5 makes sure that the *if-then* routine only applies to |JOHN| if John is the agent.

On the whole, it has been shown that although it is easy to represent a state of affairs in a network model, it can be very difficult to describe how this state of affairs is arrived at through the traveling of activation in the network. It is in this sense that the present model is more than a mere representational variant of other linguistic models, network or traditional. It manages to explain how language processes work with a very simple machinery of nodes, links and passing on of activation, i.e. language is regarded "not [as] something a speaker *has*, but rather [... as] he *does*" Langacker (1987: 382).

The two examples of competition discussed so far refer to what could be called 'static' competition, in that it asks how the network needs to be wired to arrive at particular activation patterns. A second kind of competition concerns the temporal aspect of activation spreading. Sometimes an identical result, for instance the activation of one particular node in the network, can be achieved in two (or more) ways. That is, there are two routes leading from an initial activation state in the network to the desired end-state. An example is the production of regular word forms. Highly frequent regular word forms are stored as holistic units in the cognitive system, although they are predictable on the basis of general rules. This situation translates into two routes through the network. One, the composition route, represents the application of the general rule, the other, the whole-word route, represents the storage of the form as a holistic unit. The production of this kind of word forms leads to a competition between composing the word form on the basis of its individual components and retrieving the holistic word form in the cognitive system (see section 4.2.6 for details). Such a competition view of language processing also seems psychologically plausible: "If we interpret efficiency in terms of speed of processing, the brain may be wise to follow more routes simultaneously and see which is fastest" (Nooteboom et al. 2002: 5). As we will see in chapter 4, the second kind of competition has huge effects on the language system.

2.2.2.6 Distributed or local

Network models, as an attempt to achieve psychological and cognitive plausibility, do not know 'rules' in the traditional sense; consider the quote from Lamb (1998):

> It would make no sense to suppose that within that system [the human information system] are symbols occurring in linear arrangement as in ordinary writing or as in symbolic

> notation. [...] The mind does not have little pencils and paper, nor chalk and blackboard, with which to write such strings of symbols; nor does it have eyes to read them if they could be written. (Lamb 1998: 71)

Rather, the whole language system is represented by nodes and connections between nodes only. What traditionally is described as a linguistic rule is here represented by the connections in the network and by activation spreading from node to node. Rules, thus, are not located as an algorithmic string somewhere in the network but they are distributed over a (probably) large portion of the network.[15] Complex concepts like word classes or structures consist in activation patterns in the network. Learning and language acquisition consist in establishing nodes, establishing links between nodes and in strengthening (or weakening) existing connections and nodes.[16] In this sense, the present network can be regarded as a distributed network. At the same time the network is also symbolic or local. Not in the sense that little symbols are passed on in the network, but in the sense that nodes in the network usually are of a symbolic kind. Here I follow Hudson (2007a: 9), who claims that "the network is symbolic rather than distributed; in other words, one node represents the word *dog*, another node represents each sound, and so on." The present model is both, symbolic and distributed, since a distributed representation has some advantages. Firstly, in section 3.1, it will be made clear that there is no *a priori* way of categorising language data; the possibility for multiple analyses will be seen as a prerequisite for any model of language, since different analyses might be preferable under different circumstances. If the network was fully symbolic a decision would have to be made which category would be represented by a node and which category would not, i.e. it would have to discard one or more options in favour of another option. In addition, for any category the network would have to make a decision about the exact number and kinds of subcategories. For instance, given the category *PRONOUN*, a strictly symbolic network would have to include in its description a node of any conceivable subclass of pronoun, e.g. *SINGULAR PERSONAL PRONOUN* as opposed to *PLURAL PERSONAL PRONOUN*.

---

15 For attempts to model regular and irregular processes see, among many others, the much debated model of Rumelhart and McClelland (1986), and Lee and Gasser (1991), or Li (2006). See Pinker and Prince (1988) for an extensive discussion of the Rumelhart-McClelland model and Pinker (2001) for an overview of rule-based and connectionist accounts in the past tense debate.

16 See, however, Hulstijn (2002), Prasada and Pinker (1993), Pinker and Prince (1994), Pinker (1998), or Say and Clahsen (2002) who argue for the co-existence of symbolic rules and associative networks.

In addition, such a network will have to make a decision regarding the hierarchies of subcategories; which is more basic: the class *PERSONAL PRONOUN* or the class *SINGULAR PRONOUN*? The present network model does not have to make this decision. While large general categories are represented by nodes in the network, small subcategories are usually represented by the co-activation of the general-category node and nodes that represent additional features (see section 4.2.1). Secondly, a fully local symbolic network lacks the flexibility we need to explain the establishment of new categories, represented by their own nodes. These nodes would be licensed on the basis of a frequent co-activation of a more general node and additional-feature nodes.

2.2.2.7 To be or not to be – ISA and other relations in the network

In Hudson's (2007a) model the ISA-relation is regarded as the basic relation between elements/nodes; it "stands out from all the others as particularly fundamental" (10). The word form *attempt*, for instance, stands in multiple ISA-relation, namely as being a verb, an English word and a formal word (13). Another relation between nodes is that of part and whole, e.g. the beak is a part of bird. The problem here, of course, is how to represent relations between nodes in the network. In Hudson's model nodes can be linked by connections of different types, i.e. ISA-links, part-links, etc. However, if we take seriously the neurophysiological aspects that were discussed above we have to admit that this solution is not optimal because it introduces an 'artificial' element into the network. After all, the brain only knows cells and connections between the cells. Ideally, relations between nodes would be expressed by these very simple means only. If I understand Hudson correctly, he claims that his way of dealing with relations is a mere notational variant: relations between elements could, in principle, also be treated as nodes if, in addition to the ISA-link, new primitive links were introduced, namely 'argument' and 'value' (16). These links are needed to express the directionality involved in many relations: the beak is part of a bird but not vice versa. According to Hudson "[d]ecomposing every non-primitive relation into a node plus primitive relations may provide a satisfying theory, but it multiplies the problems of diagramming" (17), which is why he prefers to allow non-primitive relations between nodes. As will be seen later, the present network model does not follow a strict representation of the network in terms of 'simple' nodes and links only, since the "problems of diagramming" that Hudson mentions would multiply to such an extent that a network representation becomes unreadable. However, before we can use non-primitive nodes (i.e. nodes that represent features, categories, meanings, etc.) as a representational device we have to show that it is possible to base any network structure on simple nodes and simple associative links alone. Even a small set of primitive relations or links makes assumptions which, in my view, are not warranted by what we know from brain physiology: the brain is a network of nerve cells that are linked to each other, and all links are of a similar kind. In particular, there are no connections between nerve cells that represent relations like 'ISA', 'argument' or 'value'. This is a big challenge to any network model of language.

Is it possible to represent relations between nodes just on the basis of unspecified directed associative links between nodes? What would relations look like in such a network? By way of illustration let us first look at the 'part-of' relation; ISA will be discussed later. The 'thought' or the piece of information that a blossom is part of a flower, for instance, would involve the activation of the nodes |FLOWER|, |BLOSSOM|, |PART|, and |WHOLE|. In addition, the link between |FLOWER| and |WHOLE| and the link between |BLOSSOM| and |PART| should be active. That is, in the present network model relations are not expressed as links between nodes but instead through 'assigning' particular nodes to particular roles in that relation. The pattern of co-activation shown in figure 2.25 represents the state of affairs that the flower is a whole and the blossom is a part, which together express the proposition 'a blossom is a part of a flower'.

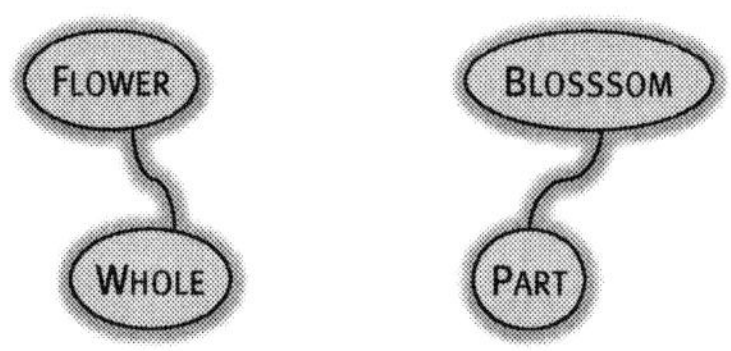

Figure 2.25: The proposition 'a blossom is a part of a flower' in the present network model.

The problem, here, is that the individual nodes of course are not isolated in the way it is shown in the figure. A blossom is a whole to the part 'petal', for instance, and a flower is a part to the whole 'bouquet'. That is, a flower can be a whole but it can also be a part and likewise for a blossom. The situation is a little more complicated, as figure 2.26 shows.

Obviously, in a purely associative network activation will spread from |FLOWER| to both, the nodes |WHOLE| and |PART| as soon as the node |FLOWER| is activated. The same holds for the node |BLOSSOM|. How then can we represent in

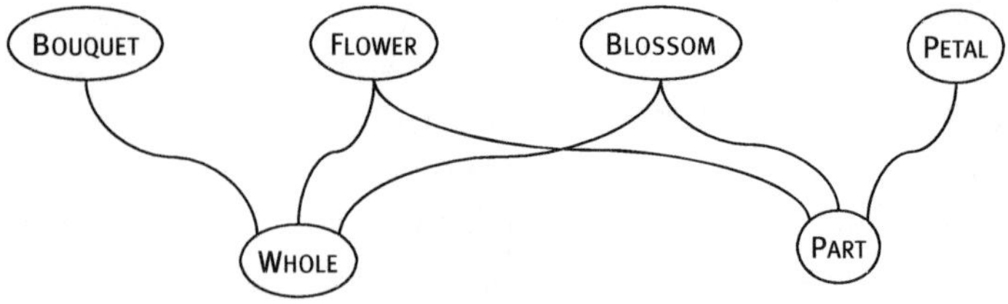

Figure 2.26: Wholes, parts, bouquets, flowers, blossoms and petals in the network.

the network that with the pair |FLOWER| and |BLOSSOM| the first will be assigned the status 'whole', while the second will be the 'part' and not vice versa? A solution to that problem lies in the use of inhibitory connections. The node |BOUQUET|, for instance, would inhibit all the connections from the other entity nodes to the node |WHOLE|, i.e. |FLOWER|-|WHOLE| and |BLOSSOM|-|WHOLE|. The node |FLOWER|, in addition, would inhibit the connection |BLOSSOM|-|WHOLE|. Conversely, |PETAL| has inhibitory connections to |BLOSSOM|-|PART| and |FLOWER|-|PART|, and the node |BLOSSOM| inhibits the connection |FLOWER|-|PART|. This situation is depicted in figure 2.27.

What happens when |FLOWER| and |BLOSSOM| are activated? The activation of the two nodes will start spreading through the network. The activation of |FLOWER| will lead to an activation of the node |WHOLE|, because the spreading of activation in that direction is not inhibited, since |BOUQUET| is not activated. The node |BLOSSOM| will also spread its activation to the node |WHOLE|. However, the connection between these two nodes is inhibited because of the inhibitory connection coming from |FLOWER|. As a consequence, the node |FLOWER|, the node |WHOLE| and the connection between these two are activated, which, in the pre-

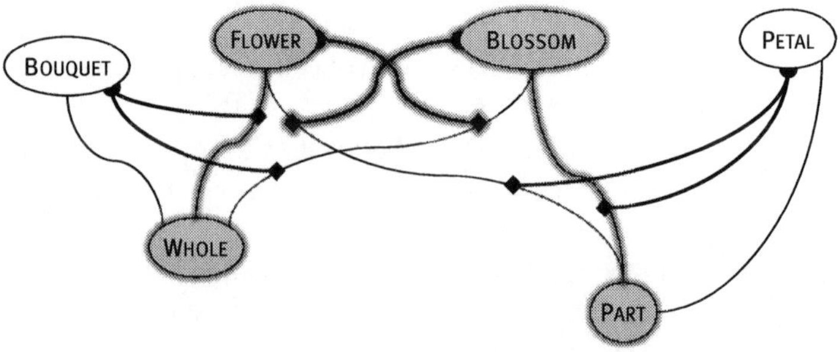

Figure 2.27: The proposition 'a blossom is a part of a flower' in the present network model.

sent network model, represents the proposition 'a flower is a whole'. The node |Blossom| also spreads activation to |Part|. The only way to prevent this from happening would be by activation of |Petal|, because this node has an inhibitory link to the connection blossom-part. Since that is not the case, the activation of |Blossom| will, eventually, activate the node |Part|. At the same time, the node |Blossom| inhibits the spreading of activation from the node |Flower| to the node |Part| (note that the activation from |Flower| would also spread to the node |Part|, because the two are linked). As a result we have a co-activation of the nodes |Blossom| and |Part| through the connection between the two nodes; this expresses the proposition 'a blossom is a part'. Together with the other activation pattern, this is understood as the representation of the part-of relationship between flower and blossom. In the same way the network captures any kind of two-argument relations. For instance, the relation 'bigger-than' is expressed by two nodes |Big| and |Small|, and the relation 'feature-of' requires the nodes |category| and |feature|.

So far, we have only looked at relations on one level of hierarchy. Often the same entity can fill different argument slots in the same relation, depending on the other entities to which it is related. By way of example let us look at the way in which the present network represents taxonomic hierarchies, i.e. what others (e.g. Collins and Quillian 1969 or Hudson 2007a) call the ISA-relation. Being a two-argument relation, ISA is implemented with the help of two additional nodes which I will refer to as |category| and |member|. Let us consider the category *BIRD*. This category has as members the robin, the sparrow and the owl.

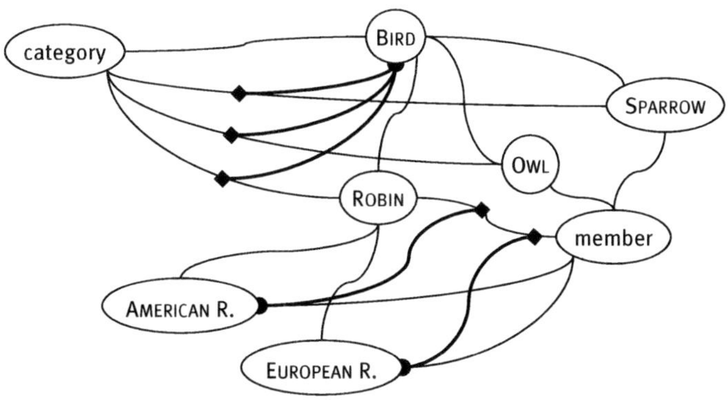

Figure 2.28: The representation of taxonomic information in the network (note that the network is only fully elaborated for the nodes |Bird|, |Robin|, |European Robin|, and |American Robin|).

Each of these members is a category of its own. With robins, for instance, we can distinguish between the American robin and the European robin. Figure 2.28 shows how this taxonomy is represented in the present network.

How, in the network, are we able to tell that a robin is a member of the category *BIRD*? Let us assume, the two nodes |BIRD| and |ROBIN| are activated (figure 2.29). This activation will spread through the network. In particular, |BIRD| will spread its activation to the node |category| and the nodes |ROBIN|, |OWL| and |SPARROW|, whereas |ROBIN| will spread its activation to the nodes |category|, |member|, |EUROPEAN ROBIN| and |AMERICAN ROBIN|. A potential problem is that |ROBIN| might spread its activation to the |category| node, which would mean that |ROBIN| and not |BIRD| is given the category value. To prevent that from happening, an inhibitory link connects the node |BIRD| and the connection |category|-|ROBIN|. Any activation travelling from |ROBIN| to |category| will therefore be suppressed, guaranteeing that the |BIRD| node will have an active connection to |category|. While this is happening, activation will spread from the |ROBIN| node to the |member| node, expressing that the robin is a member relative to the category *BIRD*.

What has been sketched out above is a model of the thought process that is triggered by a question like 'how does robin relate to bird?'. The mere activation of the node |BIRD|, e.g. as a result of thinking about birds, will also lead to an active connection to the |category| node. In addition, activation will also spread to the nodes |ROBIN|, |OWL| and |SPARROW|. From here activation will travel to the node |member|. This activation pattern expresses the state of affairs that robins, owls and sparrows are members of the category *BIRD*.

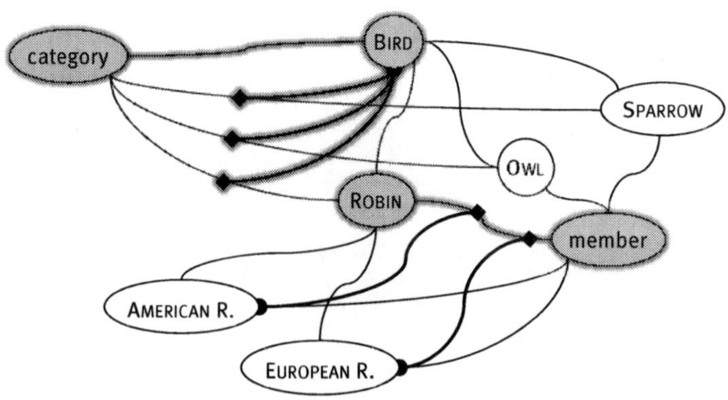

Figure 2.29: 'A robin is a bird' (note that the network is only fully elaborated for the nodes |BIRD|, |ROBIN|, |EUROPEAN ROBIN|, and |AMERICAN ROBIN|).

Often, members of a category themselves can be grouped into different subcategories. Robin, as a member of the category *BIRD*, is also the name for a subcategory that contains two groups of members, namely the European robin and the American robin. That is why the node |ROBIN| is also linked to the node |category|. Let us assume that the nodes |ROBIN| and |EUROPEAN ROBIN| are activated. The activation of |ROBIN| will be passed on to the |category| node, representing that relative to the European robin, the robin is superordinate. Note that this connection is not inhibited because the node |BIRD| is not active. While activation travels to the |category| node, it also travels to the |member| node, since |ROBIN| is connected to both nodes. However, the activation of |EUROPEAN ROBIN| leads to an inhibition of the connection |ROBIN|-|member|, while at the same time activating the |member| node through the connection |EUROPEAN ROBIN|-|member|. Note also, that the transitivity that is given in a taxonomy is also realised in the present model: the activation of |BIRD| and |EUROPEAN ROBIN| will result in an activation pattern that represents the state of affairs 'bird is a category and European robin is a member'.

The present way of representing taxonomies has one disadvantage over models that make use of specific connections like ISA or 'part-of'. In Hudson's (2007a) model, for instance, the node |ROBIN| would be related to |BIRD| via an ISA-link, and the node |EUROPEAN ROBIN| would be connected to |ROBIN| in the same way. Because of that all the information that a taxonomy entails is simultaneously available in Hudson's network. That is, a look at the network will reveal taxonomic and other relations in an instance. In the present network model this is not the case. Hierarchies only become apparent if we imagine the activation of nodes and the way this activation travels. This is in line with Langacker (1987: 382) who claims that "a schematic network is a set of cognitive routines, entrenched to varying degrees: [...] it is not something a speaker *has*, but rather what he *does*."

We see that the network is able to represent hierarchical relations even without links that express particular relations. This is an extremely important point, because it lends further credibility to the model advocated here: just like the brain, that merely consists of neurons and links that pass on activation between them, the present model merely consists of nodes and links that pass on activation between them. Still, as was mentioned above, in the following I will regularly make use of a simplified representation of network structures with different kinds of nodes, e.g. category nodes or feature nodes (see section 2.2.3 for details), which makes apparent the kind of relation that exists between nodes. This simplified representation, however, is only a presentational variant, since it was shown that any kind of relation can be expressed with the simple machinery that the present model exploits.

2.2.2.8 The inheritance of features

Two general problems with any kind of hierarchical network are 1) the question how a network should deal with cases where features of the subordinate category contradict features of the superordinate one, and 2) the question whether information about a subordinate category is stored if this information is also true for the superordinate category. As to the first problem, Goldberg (1995: 67 – 119) distinguishes two kinds of inheritance, namely 'normal' and 'complete'. In the former:

> information is inherited from dominant nodes transitively as long as that information does not conflict with information specified by nodes lower in the inheritance hierarchy. Normal inheritance is simply a way of stating partial generalizations. (1995: 73-74)

Normal inheritance accommodates "the fact that much of what we know about a category is not true of every instance of a category" (Croft & Cruse 2004: 275-276). For instance, one feature of the category *BIRD* is 'can fly', and most of the instances of this category share this feature, with the exception of birds like penguins and ostriches. This situation can conveniently be captured through normal inheritance: in the default case, we assume that an instance of the category *BIRD* can fly provided that we do not have any additional information to the contrary, as in the cases of penguin and ostrich. In a normal-inheritance network, these bits of information would be attached to the nodes that represent the exceptions. By contrast, in complete inheritance models "all information specific to every node which directly or indirectly dominates a given node is inherited. Information from one node may not conflict with that of a dominant node without resulting in ill-formedness" (Goldberg 1995: 74). With regard to the bird example above, we find that a complete inheritance model demands at least two further nodes immediately dominated by the |BIRD| node, namely |CANNOT FLY| and |CAN FLY|, under which the individual birds can then be grouped.

Related to inheritance is the question as to where the information of dominating nodes is stored in a network. Again, two ways are possible. A network may be aiming for storage parsimony, which means that inherited and therefore redundant information is only stored in the highest-ranking node or construction. Goldberg refers to such models as "virtual copying" (1995: 74) models, since the information inherited from dominating nodes is not stored in the dominated node but can be inferred from dominating node. It is clear that storage parsimony thus leads to an increase in online processing. In 'real copying' models, by contrast, inherited information is also stored in every dominated node, that is, the amount of processing is minimized. Such models aim at processing parsimony at the expense of storage parsimony.

As will be shown below, the present network model is a normal inheritance model with a special way of dealing with conflicting features of subordinate categories. It will also be shown that the present model does not have to decide whether the copying of information is virtual or real. Instead, virtual copying is seen as the default case, but real copying can emerge for particular subcategories.

In the present network model features are linked to the node that represents the category, in this case |BIRD|, and a |feature| node. Consider figure 2.30 below, which extends figures 2.28 and 2.29 above by including some features typical of birds.

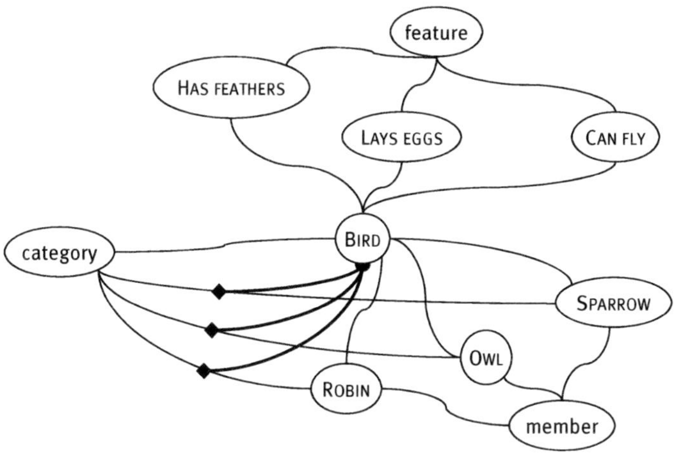

Figure 2.30: Birds and their features.

One of the advantages of organising entities with regard to categories and their members is that members inherit properties of the category to which they belong, e.g. the above figure expresses that all of the features that are true for the category *BIRD* are also true for its members.

According to Hudson, the ISA relation is so vital because it is involved in all processes of generalization:

> [...] anything we know about Bird generalises to anything which isa Bird - in other words, to any particular bird or type of bird. This process of generalisation is 'inheritance' [...]. Inheritance plays such a fundamental part in all conceptual networks that I shall call these networks 'inheritance networks'. In short, these networks allow generalisations thanks to the links which are labelled ‘isa’. (Hudson 2007a: 10-11)

In Hudson's model the inheritance of features is modelled by expanding the network. If two superordinate categories A and B stand in a relation R (e.g. flying as a means of locomotion for birds), then a copy of that relation, R’, is created in the network for a given instance A’ of A, and the relevant instance B’ of B, as shown in figure 2.31 below.

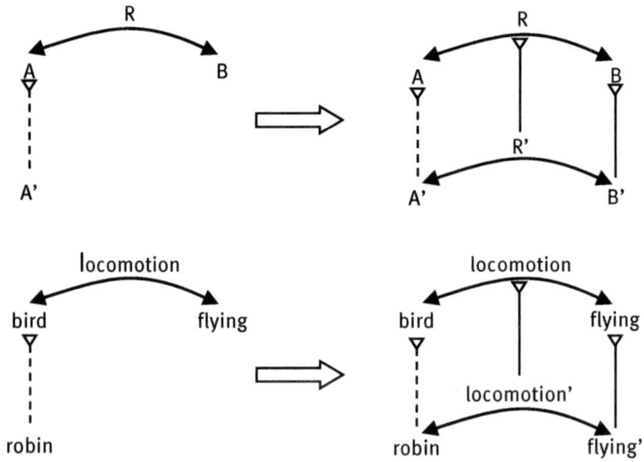

Figure 2.31: Inheriting features in Hudson's (2007a: 24) model (with kind permission of Richard Hudson).

In the example above the nodes |bird| and |flying| are linked through the relation ‘locomotion’, which expresses that birds can fly. Every single bird, in Hudson's network, is related through an ISA-connection to the |bird| node, as is shown for |robin| in the bottom left part of the figure. In general, everything that is true for the superordinate category is also true for each of its members, i.e. if |bird| stands in a locomotion relation to |flying|, then each bird stands in the same relation. This is what we see in the bottom right part of figure 2.31: |robin|, being an instance of |bird|, stands in a particular locomotion relation of one particular instance of the category |flying|. As can be seen, Hudson's model makes use of real copying.

In the present, fully associative, network, inheritance of features has to be accounted for in a different way, since the network does not know connections of a particular kind, such as 'locomotion'. Similar to the model by Collins and Quillian (1969) inheritance will here be explained by the spreading of activation. The node |BIRD| is connected via associative links to nodes that represent features of birds, such as |HAS FEATHERS|, |LAYS EGGS|, |CAN FLY|, etc. In the present model, learning that a robin is a bird is identical to connecting the |ROBIN| node to the |BIRD| node. An activation of the |ROBIN| node will spread to the |BIRD| node, which will become fully activated. From there activation will spread to the features that birds have, e.g. the ability to fly. Since the |ROBIN| node and the nodes that represent the features of a bird are only one node away from each other, the |ROBIN| node and the individual feature nodes will be activated almost simultaneously, and all of these nodes will be co-activated for some time. This is how the present model implements the fact that information that is true for the superordinate category is also true for subordinate categories and sub-subordinate categories.

A fundamental problem with inheritance, as mentioned above, is overriding features which are true for the general category but which are not true for one of its members, e.g. a penguin, which cannot fly, to name a notorious example. In Hudson's approach (figure 2.33) this problem is solved by assuming that an

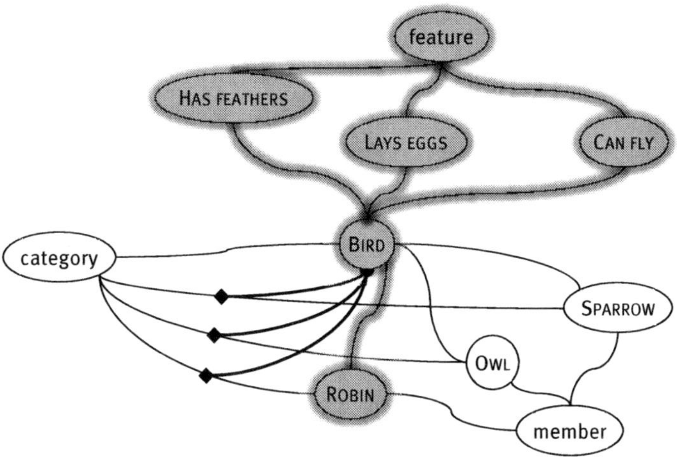

Figure 2.32: The node |ROBIN| inheriting all the features that are relevant for birds.

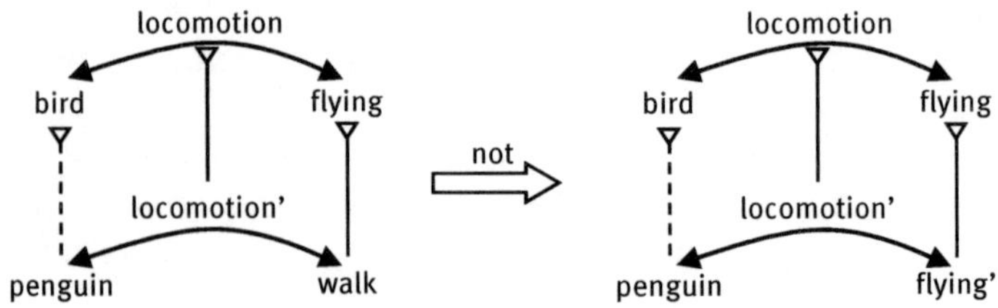

Figure 2.33: Overriding features in Hudson's (2007a: 24) model (with kind permission of Richard Hudson).

already existing proposition about a node will block the inheritance of elements that belong to the same relation. That is, a given exemplar of a category can keep its features even if they are not in line with the features of the category in general, e.g. a three-legged cat or a bird that walks or runs. This is in line with normal inheritance.

The present network is also a normal inheritance model but overriding features works differently. Let us assume that a child sees a penguin for the first time and he or she will categorise the penguin as a bird. This will mean, as sketched out above, that the node |PENGUIN| in the child's mental grammar will be connected to the node |BIRD|. As a consequence, the child will assume that the penguin can fly because birds can fly. However, the fact that the child will never see a penguin fly, or the fact that the child is told that penguins cannot fly, will create an immediate link of the node |PENGUIN| to the node |CANNOT FLY|

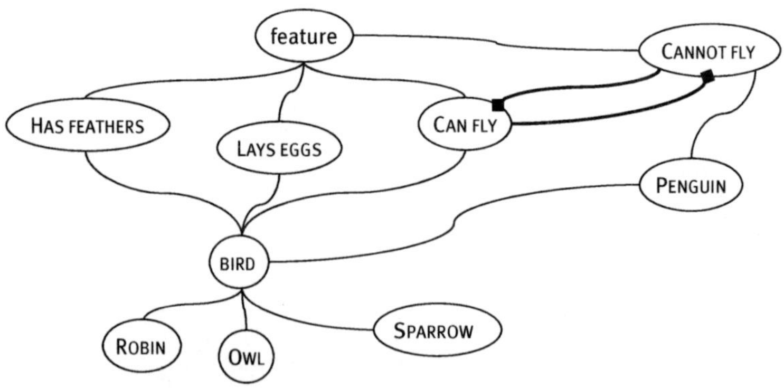

Figure 2.34: Opposite features inhibiting each other in the network (some details have been omitted for reasons of presentational clarity).

(or something like that). Obviously, the two nodes |CAN FLY| and |CANNOT FLY| cannot be active at the same time because they are contradictory. In the present network model, and in line with knowledge about the neurophysiology of the brain, this problem is resolved by inhibitory connections: the activation of a node will inhibit the activation of the node that expresses the opposite, as shown in figure 2.34.

The question then is: which node is activated first when the node |PENGUIN| is activated? In the present network (see figure 2.35), activation will spread from the |PENGUIN| node to the node |CANNOT FLY|. At the same time, activation will spread from |PENGUIN| to |BIRD| from where activation will spread to the |CAN FLY| node. However, since |CANNOT FLY| is already activated, the |CAN FLY| node cannot be activated any longer because its activation is inhibited by the |CANNOT FLY| node, and the activation pattern looks as shown in figure 2.35. Note that |CAN FLY| is not activated even though it receives activation from other nodes. This is the way in which the network implements the override of default inheritance in case of conflicting features. Note that those features that are not in conflict with our experience of penguins are still valid, i.e. a penguin is a bird that cannot fly but, being a bird, it has feathers, lays eggs and so on.

Above it was claimed that the present model is a virtual as well as a real copying model. How can that be? Obviously, the model is virtual copying because the features of a robin or an owl are arrived at through the activation of the superordinate node |BIRD|, which then leads to the activation of the respective features. To some extent this seems to run against the fundamental cognitive creed of processing parsimony and the idea of massive redundant storage (as, for instance, in Hudson's model). In the present model virtual copying is the

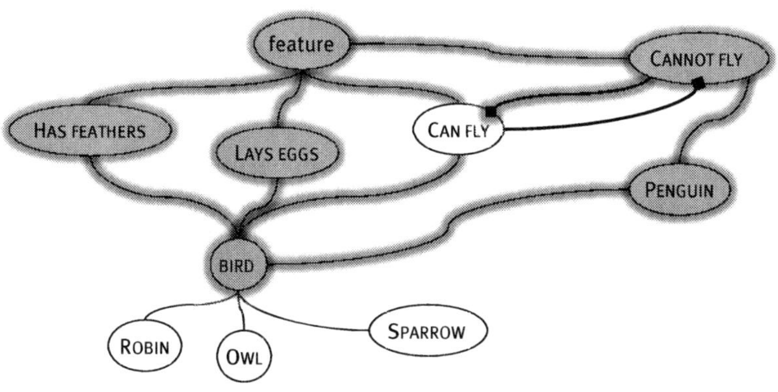

Figure 2.35: The network's representation of 'a penguin is a bird that cannot fly'.

default case. However, the model is flexible enough to also store features directly with a subordinate category. This would be expressed by a direct link between a node like |ROBIN| and the node |CAN FLY|. For that particular subcategory the model represents inherited features in a real-copying way. For other subcategories the same features might be copied virtually. Which way features are associated with a category does not depend on an *a priori* decision in favour of real or virtual copying. Real or virtual copying are understood as results of learning processes.

Another problem is related to the use of 'negative' features, as Luger and Stubblefield (1993: 388; quoted from Hudson 2007a: 25) point out: "If we define a penguin as a bird that does not fly, what is to prevent us from asserting that a block of wood is a bird that does not fly, does not have feathers, and does not lay eggs?" Hudson (2007a) claims that this classification is unlikely because it would be unlearnable on the basis of the best-fit principle, "which provides the best global fit between the token's observed properties and the existing network. How could a block of wood qualify as a bird in this scenario?" (25) Although I agree with the general description of how the best-fit principle is instantiated in Hudson's network, i.e. by letting "activation spread from the observed properties and converge on the node [at issue]" (43-55), the question why some negative features are represented in the network, while others are not, is not trivial and deserves a somewhat detailed discussion. Most importantly, there must be a way in the model to restrict the proliferation of negative features. In the present model, this is possible and, what is more, it follows from the general nature of the network. Let us go back to the example of penguin. Why does it make sense to assume a negative feature like 'cannot fly' but no feature like 'cannot talk', although both negative features are equally true? The answer to this, in my view, lies in the notion of spreading activation. Any time the learner sees a penguin the |BIRD| node will be activated and, as a consequence of spreading activation, the feature node |CAN FLY| will also be activated. The co-activation of the node |PENGUIN| and of the node |CAN FLY| contradicts the learner's experience with penguins. It is this experience of contradiction which will lead to establishing the node |CANNOT FLY| and connecting it to the node |PENGUIN|. If such a contradiction is not experienced a negative node will not be established. This explains why we do not have a connection between the |PENGUIN| node and the |CANNOT TALK| node: somewhere in the network there is a node |CAN TALK| but it is not in the vicinity of |PENGUIN| or |BIRD|. As a consequence, there is no co-activation of the |PENGUIN| node and the node |CAN TALK|, which means that there is no experience of contradiction and, therefore, no need to establish that particular bit of knowledge about penguins. The fact that there is no proliferation of negative features follows from the nature of the network.

2.2.2.9 The representation of sequence

Halliday (1961: 255) defines 'structure' as "arrangement of elements ordered in 'places'", and any account of language must be able to account for sequences. The representation of sequence is not trivial in a fully associative network model. Some approaches seem to take the ability of the organism to somehow detect and keep track of sequence for granted. Consequently, in some models questions of sequence are not discussed even though the representations are of a sequential type. An example would be Bybee's (2001: 24) network representation of the emergence of the *–ing* suffix. (see figure 2.36).

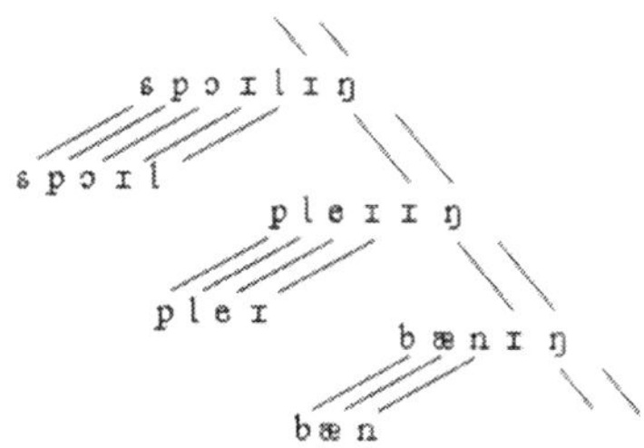

Figure 2.36: The suffix *–ing* in Bybee's (2001: 24) exemplar model (with kind permission of Cambridge University Press).

Other approaches make use of numbering. In Roelofs' (1997) model, illustrated in figure 2.37, numbered links are used to express the order of elements for a

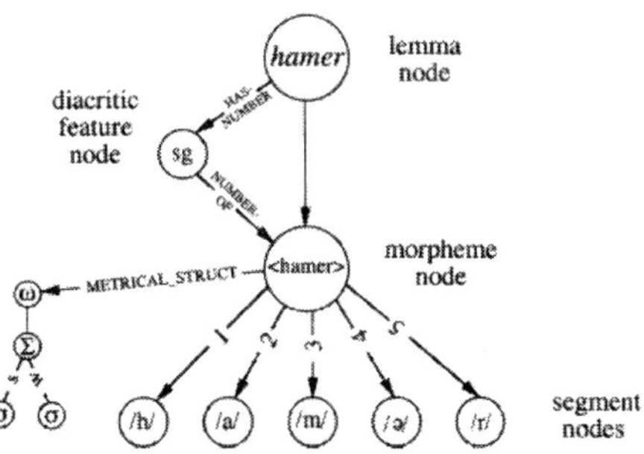

Figure 2.37: Sequence in Roelofs (1997: 258) (with kind permission of Elsevier).

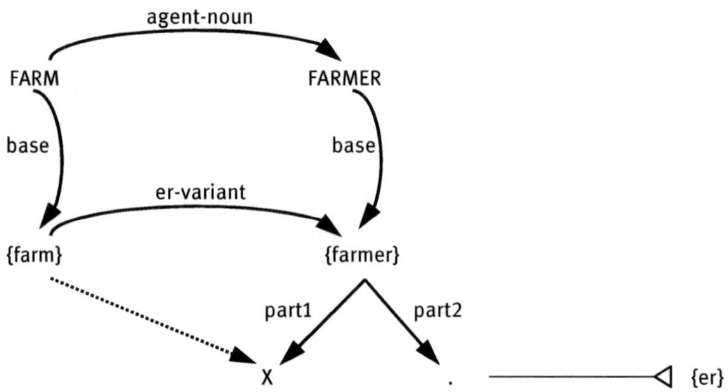

Figure 2.38: The derivational morphology of *farmer* in Hudson's (2007a: 65) model (with kind permission of Richard Hudson).

given word form. A similar approach is pursued by Hudson (2007a: 65) when, for instance, he describes the derivational morphology of *farmer*, where he makes use of arrows 'named' *part1* and *part2* to ensure that the elements end up in the right places.

Solutions of this kind, in my view, are problematic for two reasons. Firstly, as already discussed in section 2.2.2.7, it does not seem reasonable to assume that the brain contains connections between nerve cells that express relations like 'first', 'second', 'third', etc. Secondly, it does not seem plausible, as in Roelofs' model, to assume that we have a representation of where exactly an element occurs in a sequence. We are not able to answer the question 'what is the tenth letter in the word *interrogation*?'. This shows that such pieces of information are not stored in the mind. A network that works with numbered connections to express sequence makes predictions that are too strong. However, it is not difficult for us to provide the answers to questions relating to the sequence in which letters or phonemes occur in a word. All of us are able to answer the question 'which letter follows 'a' in *interrogation*?', and this knowledge needs to be represented in the model.

As a final suggestion to the representation of sequence, consider figure 2.39 taken from Lamb (1998): In his model, sequence resides in what he calls 'ordered AND links'. These provide the necessary 'machinery' to represent any kind of sequence. It remains unclear, however, how such a link can be realised with the 'tools' and 'materials' that accumulations of connected nerve cells provide.

In the present model I try to dispense with any kind of 'artificial machinery' or second order elements. And even with such rudimentary means it is possible

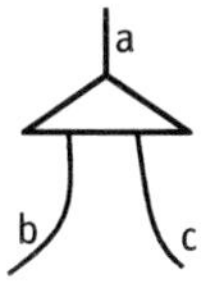

"Downward activation from **a** goes to **b** *and later* to **c**.
Upward activation from **b** *and later* from **c** goes to **a**.

Figure 2.39: The ordered AND link in Lamb's (1998: 67) framework (with kind permission of John Benjamins Publishing Company, Amsterdam/Philadelphia).

to represent sequences. Two problems need to be solved: firstly, how can we make sure that the activation of a node that consists of elements in a particular sequence leads to the activation of the constituent elements in the right order? This kind of sequence could be referred to as 'top-down' sequence. Secondly, how can we make sure that the activation of all nodes that represent constituent elements leads to the activation of the correct 'parent' node, if there are other 'parent' nodes that have the same elements but in a different order; e.g. how can we make sure that *pan* gets activated and not *nap*? This could be referred to as 'bottom-up sequence'.

The problem of top-down sequence is easily solved with the help of links of different strengths. Let us assume a node represents an entity *abc* that consists of the elements *a*, *b*, *c* in this particular order. The connections from the parent node to the element nodes differ in strength, which will lead to differences in the speed with which activation passes from the parent to its elements. The three elements will be activated depending on the strength of their connection to the parent node, resulting in the correct order of activation (and realization) in the case of |*abc*| as well as |*cba*|.

The second problem is a little more difficult. Let us assume that the same links also go from the constituent elements to the parent nodes. If the organism

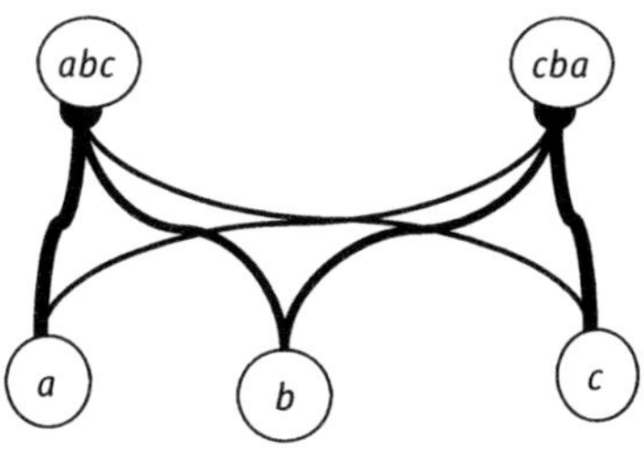

Figure 2.40: The realization of top-down sequence.

encounters the first element, *a*, this will lead to a much higher activation of the node |*abc*| than |*cba*|, which is what we would hope for. If then the element *b* is encountered, the top left node keeps its lead relative to the top right node, because in both cases the links are equally strong. At this point in time, then, the top left node is already highly activated, the top right node is considerably less so. However, as soon as the node representing element *c* is activated, the top right node receives a lot of additional activation in a very short period of time, which eventually will result in the simultaneous full activation of both parent nodes. Obviously, another solution has to be found.

To solve this problem we have to make sure that the node |a| is only activated when it occurs at the beginning of the sequence; |b| should only be activated when |a| has been activated before and so on. The *if-then* mechanism discussed in 2.2.2.4 is useful in that respect as is shown in figure 2.41.

Note that the links that lead from the element nodes to the parent nodes are fairly weak. That is, the activation of the node |a|, for instance, will only spread very slowly to the two parents nodes. However, the |START| node on the bottom left boosts this weak connection. The co-activation of the nodes |START| and |a| will lead to a quick spreading of activation to the node |*abc*|; the node |*cba*|, in contrast, will almost not be activated at all. The node |a| supports the spreading

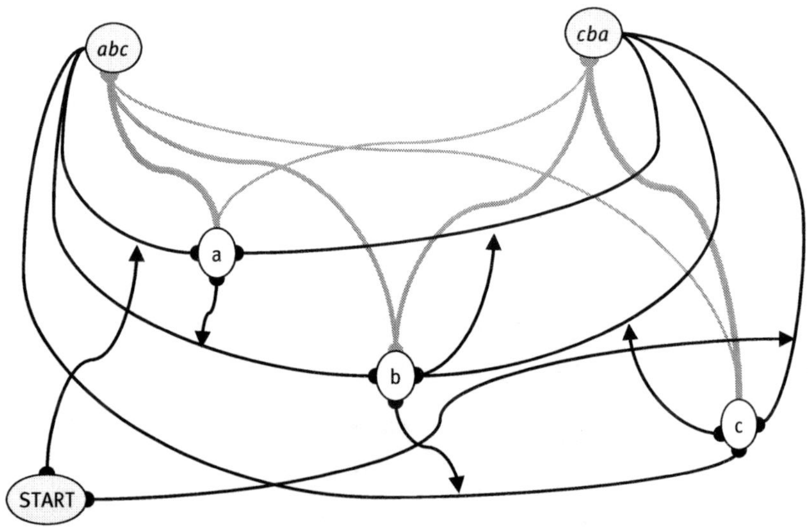

Figure 2.41: The realization of top-down and bottom-up sequence.

of activation from the node |b| to |*abc*|. The activation of |b| will, therefore, strongly contribute to |*abc*| but not to |*cba*|. Finally, the activated node |b| amplifies activation going from |c| to |*abc*|, but not the activation spreading from |c| to |*cba*|. As a consequence of these supporting or boosting links, the node |*abc*| will be fully activated if the constituent elements are encountered in that order but not the node |*cba*|. As was shown, sequence can be represented in the present network model with its very rudimentary machinery.

2.2.2.10 Learning - changing network structures

To conclude this section on the general mechanics of the network model we explore the ways in which learning takes place in the network. Keeping in mind that the network solely consists of nodes and links between nodes, 'learning' can only refer to a change in existing nodes and existing links (see the short discussion of that aspect in 2.2.2.1) or the creation of new nodes and new links (see also Hudson 2007a or Lamb 1998). With regard to the former, nodes and links can either become more deeply entrenched in the cognitive system or they become less deeply entrenched. The cognitive concept of 'entrenchment', in the present model, is linked to the way in which a network portion reacts to activation spreading. A node that represents something that is deeply entrenched in the system will have a low activation threshold, i.e. it will be activated faster than nodes that are less deeply entrenched. For instance, a node that represents a highly frequent and, therefore, deeply entrenched word form will have a low activation threshold and will be activated quickly. In this way the present model implements the fact that highly frequent word forms are retrieved more quickly than rare word forms. With regard to links between nodes, 'learning' changes the speed with which a link transmits activation from the source node to the target node. An entrenched link, usually a link that has been used regularly (but see section 5.5 for other sources of entrenchment), will pass activation on more quickly than a link that is less entrenched. For instance, the degree of prototypicality of members of a category correlates with the speed with which humans are able to verify that a given entity is a member of that category. In the current network model this phenomenon would be represented by different strengths of links leading from category nodes to member nodes.

One reason for the creation of new nodes can be a new experience, e.g. a newly learnt word or a novel kind of perception. Often, this kind of learning involves an abstraction, i.e. focusing on a (sometimes very small) number of features, while disregarding other features, such as the creation of the category 'male' or 'female' on the basis of repeated exposition to male and female exemplars of the category 'human'. More interesting is the creation of new nodes that happens as a result of a frequent repetition of activation patterns within the network. An example is the formation of the linguistic sign as a pairing of a particular form with a particular meaning. Each time the organism encounters a particular sign, this will lead to the co-activation of a form node together with its respective meaning node, which eventually results in the creation of a new node that represents the sign at hand.

Of course, this kind of learning also entails the creation of new links, since frequent co-activation of nodes results in an association, which is expressed by an associative link between the nodes: "any two things that consistently occur together are likely to become associated" (Lamb 1998: 271). Association is based on distinctively frequent co-occurrence/co-activation, not just frequent co-occurrence/co-activation. For instance, although all birds breathe, breathing is not associated (in the sense it is used here) with birds, since breathing co-occurs equally frequently with a large number of other species. In contrast, the feature 'wings' is associated with birds. Association, as understood here, is thus always related to the idea of predictability, that is, the occurrence of an event A predicts the occurrence of event B in some way or other and to a certain extent.

It seems reasonable to distinguish between two kinds of association, namely 'direct association' and 'indirect association'. In the first case, the nodes in question are actually co-activated for a certain amount of time. Direct association deals with the more or less simultaneous co-occurrence of two (or more) features, as illustrated by any linguistic sign. For instance, the 'discovery' that the formal feature 'verb ending in [-ɪd]' frequently co-occurs with the semantic feature 'in the past' is represented by the creation of two links between the two respective nodes in the network (see section 4.2.5).

While in the example above the two features do actually co-occur simultaneously and, accordingly, the two nodes will be activated at the same time, this is not a prerequisite for the establishing of simultaneous prediction. Association phenomena like collocation or colligation, for instance, are also understood as instances of this kind of relation even though the elements that take part in such relationships never actually co-occur, despite one of them occurring slightly before the other. How can the present network model explain that the two still become associated? The solution to that problem lies in the nature of the activation of nodes in the network. As seen in section 2.2.2.3, an active node remains active for a particular extent of time. So, while this node is still active, other nodes can become activated, so that they are co-activated for a certain amount of time, even though the individual nodes are not activated for the entire period of time. This difference is shown in figure 2.42 below: the left-hand

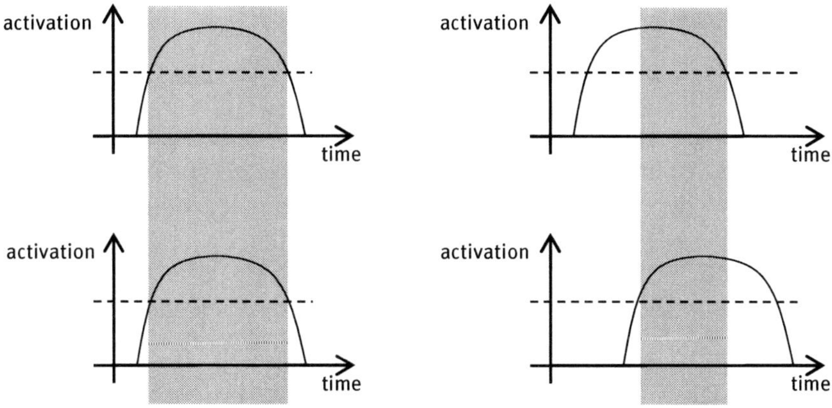

Figure 2.42: Different extents of co-activation.

side shows two nodes that are activated at the same time, whereas the right-hand side shows two nodes that have been activated one shortly after the other.

Direct association is a rather simple kind of association, since in these cases we do actually have a co-activation of nodes. However, our linguistic knowledge also entails the association of features, even though they are never realised at the same point in time, for instance the fact that adjectives can be used attributively and also predicatively. Both features are associated with one another (after all, they characterise the same formal class[17]) even though they never co-occur. How can the model account for such cases? Aarts (2007: 106) suggests that adjectives can be described with regard to five central properties, as shown in example (1) below[18,19,20]:

(1)	a happy woman	(attributive position)
	she is happy	(predicative position)
	very happy	(intensification)

---

17 I am aware of the fact that these features are not restricted to the category *ADJECTIVE*. See section 4.2.2 for discussion of that point.

18 I am aware of the fact that there are other features that are characteristic of adjectives but we will ignore these, since the aim at present is to illustrate the mechanisms that are at work in the formation of the network.

19 More precisely, the first two properties are actually properties of adjective phrases.

20 See also Quirk et al. (1985: 402-404), for a similar descriptive framework.

happy/happier/happiest (gradability)
unhappy (*un*- prefixation) (cf. Aarts 2007: 106)

As is obvious from these examples, attributive and predicative position are mutually exclusive, and so are intensification and comparative or superlative (i.e. gradability). Still, the five features together serve as a description of adjectives. How, then, can the present model explain the formation of classes on the basis of co-activation if some features rule out other features? The answer to this problem lies in the fact that nodes may become activated not only through language data that are processed at a particular point in time but also through past experience associated with a particular set of data. Let us assume that the processor has encountered the adjectives HAPPY and FRIENDLY and their related forms in the uses exemplified above for a number of times. This experience is captured in the network shown in figure 2.43.

Note that the individual features are not yet connected to each other. This is due to the fact that the two adjectives *happy* and *friendly* on their own do not occur frequently enough to licence such connections. However, each (prototypical) adjective will strengthen the experience that the organism has had with the adjective *happy*. Namely that some of the features of adjectives can occur together, e.g. *the very unhappy girl* or *he looked unhappier than before*, while others rule each other out, e.g. **the very happier girl*. The experience that the organism makes with HAPPY and other (prototypical) adjectives will, eventually, result in a distinctive pattern of connections among the feature nodes, as de-

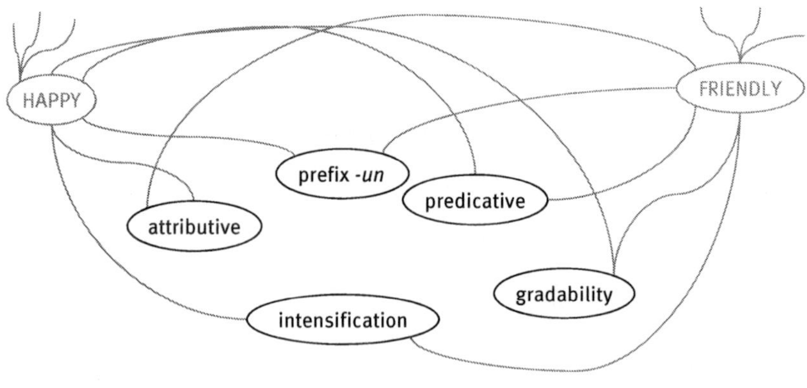

Figure 2.43: Features of the adjectives HAPPY and FRIENDLY.

picted in figure 2.44. As can be seen, this pattern of connectivity involves associative links between features that can co-occur and inhibitory links between features that rule each other out. However, even though the features 'intensification' and 'gradability' never actually co-occur, they are still indirectly related through three other nodes in the network. The same holds true for the two nodes |attributive| and |predicative|. The pattern of connectivity that we see in the above figure is the representation of the organism's experience with the adjectives like *happy*, which eventually will lead to the formation of the category *ADJECTIVE* (see section 4.2.1 for details).

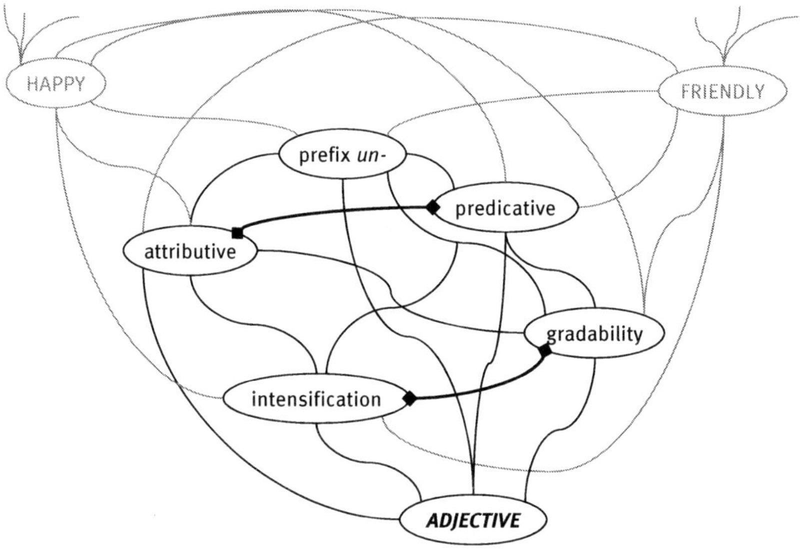

Figure 2.44: Features and instantiations of the class *ADJECTIVE*.

2.2.3 Notational conventions

Some of the symbols applied in the network model have already been used in the previous section. The present section provides a comprehensive overview of all the notational conventions that will be relevant for the remaining study.

The network consists of nodes and connections. Nodes are represented by ellipses. These can be of different strengths, which indicates the degree of entrenchment of a particular item in the cognitive system. Low degrees of entrenchment are represented by broken lines, high degrees of entrenchment by thick solid lines[21].

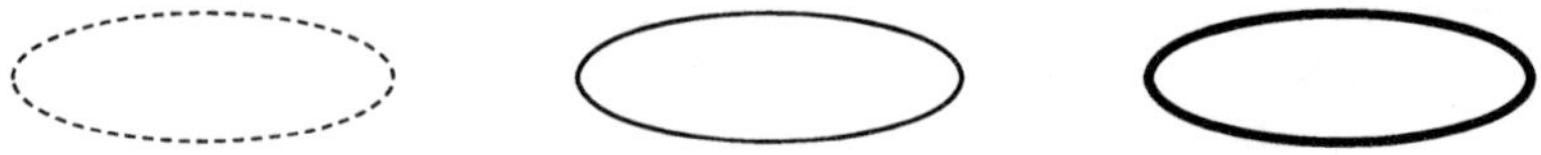

Figure 2.45: The representation of degrees of entrenchment of elements in the network model. (= Figure 2.9; repeated here for convenience)

As was already hinted at above, the degree of entrenchment is more important for the connections that exist between two nodes. In this case the thickness of the lines represent predictability in the language system. Consider figure 2.46 for convenience.

Figure 2.46: The representation of degrees of entrenchment of connections in the network model. (= Figure 2.10; repeated here for convenience).

Figure 2.46 makes explicit two aspects: it shows that the word form *kin* is more strongly entrenched them the word form *kith*, i.e. the former will be produced and retrieved faster than the latter. In addition, figure 2.46 shows what has been called a 'uni-directional link'. These connections express to what extent the word form or item represented in the source node (the node form which the connection starts) predicts the occurrence of the item in the target node (the node where the connection leads)[22]. With regard to *kith* and *kin*, the former is a very good predictor of the latter. Even though the word form |*kith*| is not particularly deeply entrenched in the cognitive system, once the node is activated it

21 As mentioned in section 2.2.2.2, the strengths of the lines are simply meant to allow for comparisons of degrees of entrenchment and strengths of association. They are not designed to represent corpus-based differences in frequencies or associations.

22 It is important to note that uni-directional links are not a representation of sequence in the present network model.

will spread this activation very quickly to the node |*kin*|. Conversely, activation will spread very slowly from |*kin*| to |*kith*|.

In some cases we are not particularly interested in the strength or direction of the individual links. Sometimes it suffices to merely state that two nodes have become associated, i.e. connected through links. In this case, two nodes are just connected through one line, as indicated in figure 2.47 below, which represents the association of the ending /-d/ with the meaning 'in the past'.

Figure 2.47: (Non-directional) association of two elements.

Sometimes in the discussion, particular portions of a network are in focus, while others are of secondary importance only. In this case, the less important parts are marked in grey, while black is reserved for those parts of the network that are central for the discussion at this point.

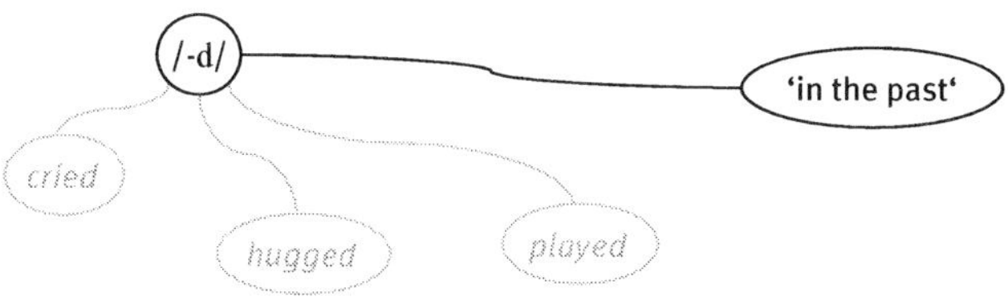

Figure 2.48: Focal and non-focal areas in the network model.

So far, we have been dealing with the representation of static network structures. The concept of spreading activation, however, calls for ways of presenting activation potentials and the spreading of activation through the network. The former is mirrored by a grey filling of ellipses. A completely filled ellipses represents a node which will spreads activation to neighbouring nodes in the strongest possible way. Ellipses that are not completely filled represent nodes that are not yet fully active. Still, these can also spread activation to neighbouring nodes but not as much as a fully active node (other things being equal). The spreading of activation will be symbolised by a 'glowing' node and the link through which activation spreads also 'glows', like the nodes and the connections on the left

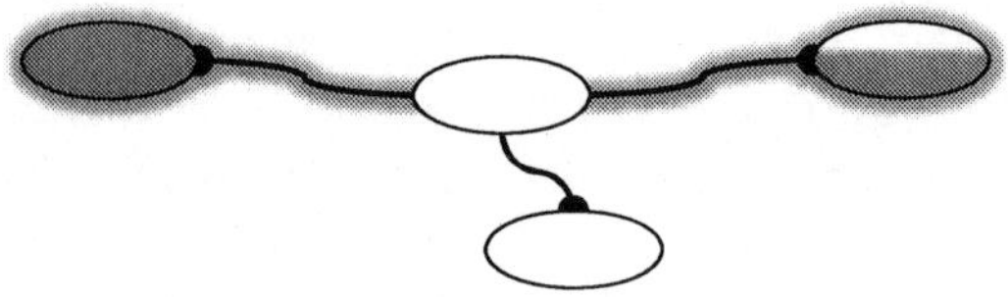

Figure 2.49: A fully activated node (on the left) and a partially activated node (on the right) spreading activation. The bottom ellipsis represents a node whose activation threshold has not been met; it does not spread activation.

and right of figure 2.49 below. A node whose activation threshold has not been met is represented by an unfilled ellipses. These nodes do not spread activation.

A last type of link is that between a node and a connection. That is, an active node may strengthen or weaken a connection (i.e. an association) between nodes. As an example consider the way genres influence collocations. Hoey (2005: 10) points to the fact that *recent* and *research* are collocates only in academic writing and news reports on research. In that case, the activation of the node |academic| would spread to the connection between |*recent*| and |*research*|, thereby strengthening it. Connections of this kind are represented as follows in the network:

Figure 2.50: A node-connection link.

Finally, the present model distinguishes between excitatory and inhibitory connections, as exemplified on the left-hand side and the right-hand side of figure 2.51, respectively.

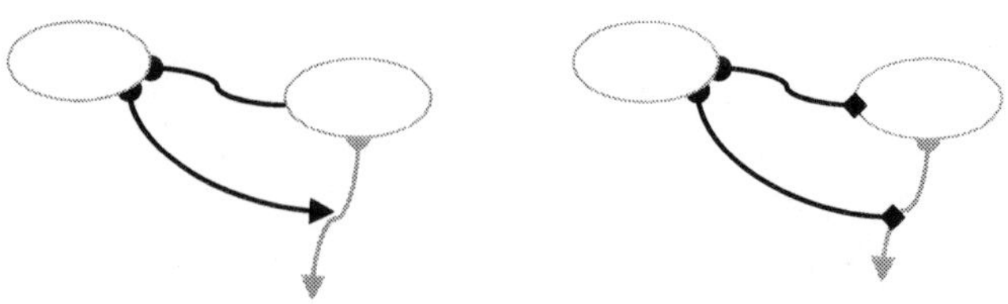

Figure 2.51: Excitatory (left) and inhibitory (right) connections in the network.

The introduction to this study has emphasised that one goal is to design a network model that is restricted to elements that are of a basic neurological kind. More specifically, the present model cannot distinguish between nodes of different kinds, e.g. nodes representing word classes or nodes representing features, etc. Neither can the present network distinguish between different kinds of relations between nodes, i.e. all connections are of a simple associative kind. However, to keep "the problems of diagramming" (Hudson 2007a: 17) at bay, the figures, in the following, will make use of non-primitive nodes, e.g. nodes that represent categories and nodes that represent members. This is only shorthand for a much more complicated way of representation. The present network model meets the neurophysiological challenge described in the introduction, since section 2.2.2 has shown how it is able to represent non-primitive nodes in a fashion that is in line with that challenge.

Nodes in the network represent a variety of linguistically relevant aspects and elements. I will stick to the usual conventions where possible. Meaning is represented in two ways in the network. The meaning of DOG, for instance, could be represented conventionally as 'a furry barking animal' and in a more abstract fashion as 'M(dog)'. The second kind is used in those cases where meaning paraphrases are too long to be given in the small boxes used in the network figures. Table 2.1 provides an overview of the conventions used in the followings chapters.

Table 2.1: Notational conventions used in the network description.

Linguistic aspect/element	**Representation**	**Example**
word form	*abcde*	*show*, *houses*
morpheme	{___}	{bird}, {un-}
phonemes	/___/	/bird}, {un-}/
semantic features	[+___], [-___]	[+ male], [- difficult]
meaning	'___', M(___)	'furry barking animal', M(dog)
word classes, syntactic functions	*ABCDE*	*NOUN*, *ADJECTIVE*, *SUBJECT*
lexical unit, lexeme	ABCDE	TABLE, WATER, JOHN
clause-level constructions, argument roles	Abcde	Ditransitive, Agent, Patient
'cognitive' concepts	ABCDE (small caps)	FLOWER, BIRD, WHOLE, PART (small caps)
miscellaneous (genres, grammatical categories, ...)	abcde	academic writing, perfective, hander, ...

To conclude, the same conventions will mostly be used in the text of the following two chapters. Reference to nodes (represented as ellipses in the diagrams) is made by the use of vertical slashes on the left and right in the text. For instance, I will talk about the meaning node |M(dog) |or the word form node |*bird*|.

In this chapter I have discussed on a fairly general basis a number of requirements that any model of language needs to meet and I have sketched out the basics of a network model of language with a focus on the mechanics of the network and the processes going on in the network. The remaining chapters are devoted to language in a more 'linguistic' sense. Each of these chapters will discuss a particular aspect of language and will present how these aspects can be implemented in and accounted for by the present network model. Chapter 3 deals with the general relation of language data and linguistic modelling and discusses how this is reflected in the model. Chapter 4 is concerned with rather traditional descriptive approaches to grammatical description. Chapter 5 focuses on the more recent cognitive notion of 'schema' and a number of corpus-linguistic concepts and investigates their place in the current network model. Chapter 6, then, moves away from the description of static network structures and, following Lamb's (2000: 95) dictum that a model of the language system "must represent a competence to perform", explores how the present network model is able to explain how the shape of the language system is exploited during language use.

3 Units, classes, structures and rules – language data and linguistic modelling

This chapter describes in some detail how the linguists' grammatical system gradually emerges from successive steps of abstraction and generalization from language data. Capitalizing on taxonomic structuralism and on Halliday's (1961) 'scales-and-categories' model, I show how grammatical units, structures and categories are at the basis of any grammatical description of language and how they emerge when studying the patterns that occur in language data. This will give us an idea of the demands that any theory of language has to fulfil, and it will provide us with a linguistic standard against which the present network model can be measured. The following description is deliberately kept at a highly general level to show that the procedures adopted by and the results obtained through the structuralist methods of 'segmentation' and 'classification' are largely theory-neutral.

3.1 From data to description

It is useful to imagine in the following the role of a linguist that is confronted with a language that he or she does not have any knowledge of, or to imagine an infant at the earliest stages of language acquisition. This person is presented with language events that are perceived as holistic, i.e. unanalysable, entities. It is mainly on the basis of repetitions of parts of one language event in other language events that holistic structures begin to be understood as analysable. This is the well-known view expressed in taxonomic structuralism, with a basic two-step procedure to arrive at a description of the language data, as for instance, described in Harris (1951: 6): "the setting up of elements, and the statement of the distribution of these elements relative to each other."

The identification of elements in the first place, rests on the discovery of repetition. For instance, the element, or phoneme, /k/ is discovered if we witness utterances like [kæt], [kæn] and [kɔːl], where the user will discover that the initial element is repeated in all three instances. 'Repetition', in this case, does not capture the facts fully accurately, since it is well-known that no two utterances and no two elements that are pronounced are actually identical from an acoustic point of view. However, substituting each of the [k]'s for one of its counterparts would show that they do not change "the response from native speakers who hear the utterance before and after the substitution" (Harris 1951: 20). In linguistic terms, the substitution does not involve functional contrast; it does not lead to a distinction in meaning. It is at this stage that the first abstraction and, along with it, the first step away from the data in the direction of description are actually made. Minimal differences between individual events are ignored and abstracted away from. To put it more technically, allophones, or perhaps better: phones, are grouped together under the more abstract phonemes.

Having identified the elements that occur in utterances, a further step towards description is the statement of their distribution, "the freedom of occurrence of portions of an utterance relatively to each other" (Harris 1951: 5). The description of the phonemic distribution suggests the inclusion of another, higher-level, unit into the description of language, namely the morpheme:

> [...] when the distribution of phonemes is considered over longer stretches of speech they are found to be highly restricted; [...] we can best state these limitations by setting up new (morphemic) elements in which the phonemes will have stated positions, the elements being so selected that we can easily state their distribution within long stretches of speech. (Harris 1951: 156)

Morphemes, as is well known, are identified basically with the help of substitution or deletion tests, and there is no need here to go into any further detail. What accounts for phonemes in relation to morphemes is also true for morphemes themselves: these, too, are restricted and these restrictions also are best stated in terms of higher elements, the lexemes, lexical units and word forms, which again pattern to form yet higher elements and so on. On the whole, the language system can quite conveniently be described as a multi-tiered system, with each tier consisting of a set of elements or units (abstracted from the actual data) that combine according to particular rules to form units of the next higher level. A fairly technical description of the nature and the needs of such a system is provided by Halliday's (1961) 'scales-and-categories model', developed in his paper "Categories of the Theory of Grammar" (see Halliday/McIntosh/Strevens 1964 for a more accessible description of this model). In the following I discuss some of what I regard the most important aspects of Halliday's model, modifying it where necessary. This will serve as a descriptive framework that will help to describe a range of linguistic phenomena, which will be discussed in the later chapters.

Halliday (1961: 247) claims that a theory of grammar needs four fundamental categories, namely 'unit', 'structure', 'class' and 'system'[23]. Within the category 'unit' Halliday distinguishes five different ranks, namely 'sentence', 'clause', 'group' (or 'phrase'), 'word', and 'morpheme'. Halliday does not say much about these units or about why these are needed to describe the English language. It is easy to see, though, that some of the facts that are witnessed with regard to the morpheme are best described by positing a higher unit, i.e. the word. The patterns of occurrences of words are best described with reference to phrases, and so on. The same accounts for the description of the structure of higher-level units. Clauses, for instance, are not (in the first place) described as strings of words. Rather, we are aware of another level of organization, i.e. the level of groups or phrases.

The second category, 'structure' is defined by Halliday (1961) as "an arrangement of elements ordered in 'places'" (255), where "[e]ach place and element in the structure of a given unit is defined with reference to the unit next below" (256). Elements, in this understanding, are the abstract components that make up a given structure. The English clause, for instance, can be conceived of as consisting of the four elements: subject, predicator, complement and adjunct (according to Halliday 1961). These elements are instantiated by members of those units that are one level below clause-level, i.e. groups or phrases. How do we arrive at these abstract components? The answer provided by Halliday lies in the concept of 'class'.

The analysis of structures shows that elements at particular places may not be instantiated by any arbitrary unit of the level below, rather "at each element operates one grouping of members of the unit next below" (259). Here we find the traditional distinction of syntagmatic and paradigmatic relations: A 'place' in a structure can be conceived of as a 'slot' in a syntagm, while the notion of 'element' can be interpreted as designating a particular paradigm of possible fillers for this slot. Halliday (1961) speaks of 'class' in this context:

> [...] there will be certain groupings of members of each unit identified by restriction on their operation in structure. The fact that it is not true that anything can go anywhere in

23 The last component, the system, is not of relevance in this context. It accounts for "the occurrence of one rather than another from a number of like events" (Halliday 1961: 264), i.e. it deals with choices between units, structures and classes. Here, we focus on how these units, structures and classes are established in the first place. Accordingly, the concept 'system' will not be discussed any further.

> the structure of the unit above itself is another aspect of linguistic patterning, and the category set up to account for it is the "class". (Halliday 1961: 260)

In Harris' (1951) terms, members of one class share the same "freedom of occurrence."

The progression from data to description so far can be sketched as follows: starting off from the grammatical level of morphemes, we find patterns which suggest the introduction of a unit of a higher level, which would be the (grammatical) word. These units again pattern to form higher-ranking units until eventually we arrive at the level of the clause complex as the highest unit of grammatical description. All of these units (apart from morphemes) exhibit structure, that is, they can be described as arrangements of elements in a particular order. Such structure may give rise to the formation of further classes (see below for examples).

Within this progression from holistic utterance to the most abstract entities of the language system we find several steps of abstraction. All of these steps include two basic processes. The first process is best understood as an abstraction away from irrelevant features of a number of entities and an emphasis on shared relevant features among entities. Individual entities are thus grouped together to form classes or categories and are treated as essentially identical, although there are aspects in which they are dissimilar. Underlying this process is Aristotle's fundamental distinction of 'essence' versus 'accident'. All members of the category 'man', for instance, share essential features like [two-footed] or [with speech] but show differences in non-essential features, such as colour of hair and skin. The same process also underlies the formation of linguistic categories. Lyons (1977: 587), for instance, speaks of 'standardization': "What the linguist does, in practice, is to discount all but the major systematic variations in the language-behaviour of the community whose language he is describing". A similar intuition is captured by Daneš' (1964: 22) distinction of 'utterance-event', i.e. the "[s]entence as a singular and individual speech-event" as opposed to 'utterance', the "[s]entence as one of all possible different minimal communicative units [...] of a given language". Since no two events or entities in the extralinguistic world are identical in the strict sense of the word, this first kind of abstraction is a fundamental prerequisite for the formation of classes of units at different levels of description. This accounts for phonemes as an abstraction from phones and allophones but also for higher-ranking units and for the setting up of classes where non-identical units are grouped together on the basis of similarities in the way they operate in structures. This classification always entails the setting up of 'ISA', 'type-token', 'instantiate' or 're-write as' relations: as soon as a class has been identified and defined, all of the entities from which this class has been abstracted can be regarded as instantiations of this particular class.

The second process is the description of data in terms of the classes obtained through abstraction. These classes allow us to describe language patterns in a new way. We are not dealing with raw language data any more but we start to describe patterns of segments and classes that are already the result of abstractions. The process of abstraction provides a vocabulary which enables the researcher to translate the language data into more abstract secondary data. These, in turn, can be made subject to another step of segmenting and classifying, thus yielding still more abstract classes, which can be used to describe still more abstract tertiary data, and so on. Figure 3.1 illustrates the whole process of abstraction and description through abstract classes.

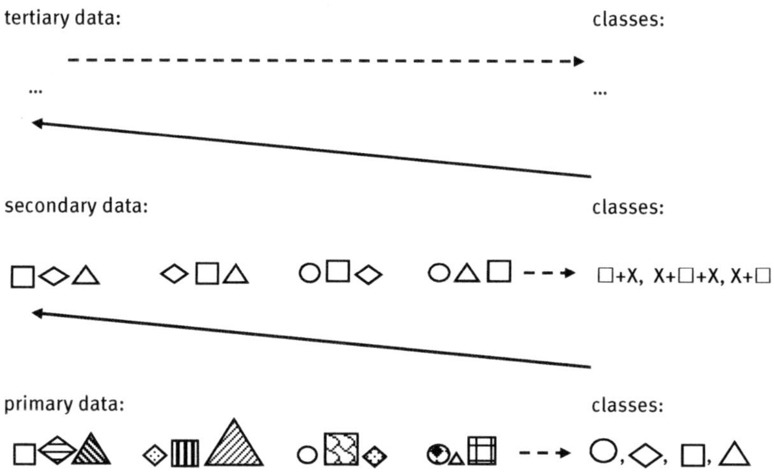

Figure 3.1: 'Abstraction away from data' and 'description of data through classes'.

This figure has to be read from bottom to top. The primary data are four strings of geometrical symbols of different size and patterning. The first process, 'abstraction away from data' (represented by the broken arrow), disregards size and surface pattern and reduces the individual items within the strings to classes. In the bottom row of figure 3.1 we can distinguish four basic classes of geometrical objects, namely 'circle', 'diamond', 'square' and 'triangle'. These are represented on the right by the respective geometrical shapes all scaled to one size without patterns. As said above, each of the broken arrows can be understood as representing an (inversed) relation of instantiation or of type versus token: For instance, each of the squares one the left-hand side of figure 3.1 is a token of the more abstract type depicted on the right.

The second process, 'description of data through classes' (represented by the solid arrow), enables us to view data from a different perspective, or through a different pair of glasses, as it were, yielding secondary data (in the middle row of figure 3.1). The set of primary data in the bottom row can now be described in terms of the classes represented on the right-hand side in the bottom row, resulting in the more abstract strings in the middle row (secondary data). This allows us to find further patterns in the data, which leads to the establishment of new classes. The different sizes and patterns of the individual squares on the lowest data level may divert the attention of the observer and thus keep him or her from realizing the three patterns that emerge more clearly if each of the tokens on the left-hand side of the bottom row are substituted by the types they represent. These patterns can be defined with regard to the position of the square, □,i.e. initial, medial or final and thus lead to further classes (or classes of strings of classes), namely '□+X', 'X+□+X', and 'X+□'. These classes might then be applied to new data, leading to a set of tertiary data, and so on.

A linguistic example is the following:

(1) Tom hit Paul.
(2) Did Peter read the book?
(3) I drove to Paris.
(4) Did you go to London?

The four clauses above do not bear much resemblance at first sight. The patterned behaviour in these examples becomes apparent only with the help of abstract classes like S, V, O and A[24]. That is, a 'translation' of the primary data under (1) to (4) into these classes yields a set of secondary and more abstract data, showing clear patterns which remain hidden in the primary data:

24 Note that this is not the only way of establishing more abstract classes. A more thorough discussion of the question as to where the process of abstraction starts is given below (see the discussion of figure 3.3).

(1') SVO
(2') VSVO
(3') SVA
(4') VSVA

This set of data can be subjected to a process of abstraction identical to the one that yielded the classes S, V, O and A, that is, ignoring differences while stressing similarities. In this case, emphasizing the nature of the first two segments and ignoring the last would lead us to form two groups, namely (1') and (3'), and (2') and (4'), which eventually might be labelled 'declarative' and 'interrogative' clauses[25]. These classes can then be used to describe data from a yet different (and more abstract) perspective, thus yielding a set of tertiary data, and so on.

It is fairly safe to assume that the process described above is at the basis of linguistic reasoning and theory. Exactly the same process is at work in the present network model, and, most importantly, it follows as a consequence of the nature of the model and the processes at work in the network (see section 2.2.2).

Let us assume that an organism frequently encounters the three phenomena *A*, *B*, and *C*. Each of these three is characterised by a number of features from the set {u, v, w, x, y, z}, as shown in the following figure.

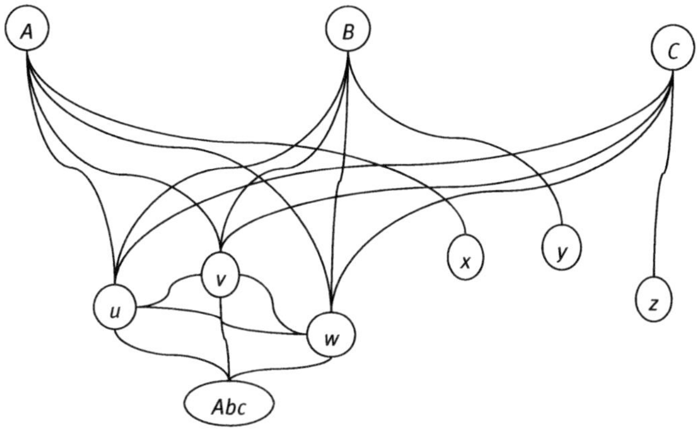

Figure 3.2: Phenomena, their features and the rise of new categories.

25 Of course, this set of data could just as well be grouped into 'monotransitive' (1' and 2') and 'copulative' (3' and 4'). There is no inherent way of classification; see below for more details on that point.

Since all three phenomena share the features u, v, and w, any occurrence of *A*, *B*, or *C* will lead to a co-activation of the three features. As described in section 2.2.2.10 this frequent co-activation results in the establishment of connections between these three features. Once the three features are linked to each other, a category has been formed. In the network, this will be expressed by the introduction of an additional node in the network, let us call it |*Abc*|, which is connected to the three feature nodes. The abstraction involved in categorization, i.e. the fact that some features are ignored, is a consequence of the nature of the network which includes that only frequent co-activation leads to association; since the features *x*, *y*, and *z* do not co-occur as frequently as the other three features, they do not become part of the newly formed category *Abc*.

The second process, the description of data in terms of the classes obtained through abstraction, also derives from the nature of the network and the processes therein. Let us assume that in addition to the category *Abc* shown in figure 3.2 the network has also established a category *Def* as a result of the frequent co-occurrence of features related to the phenomena *D*, *E* and *F*, e.g. the features *r*, *s* and *t*. Let us further assume that phenomena of the group *A*, *B*, and *C* are frequently followed by a phenomenon of the group *D*, *E* and *F*. However, none of the individual sequences (e.g. *at* or *bs*) are frequent enough to lead to a change in the network. Still, any sequence of an element from the first group followed by an element from the second will trigger a particular activation pattern in the higher-level nodes |*Abc*| and |*Def*|, namely that the activation of the node |*Abc*| is often followed by an activation of |*Def*|. This might very well lead to a change in the network.

A linguistic example is Altenberg and Eeg-Olofsson's (1990) notion of 'collocation in the stricter sense', which

> goes beyond [... the] notion of textual co-occurrence and emphasizes the relationship between *lexical items in language* [...and] cuts across word classes (cf. *drink heavily, heavy drinker, heavy drinking*), applies to discontinuous items (*he drinks pretty heavily*), and presupposes lemmatization (*drink/drinks/drank/drinking heavily*). (Altenberg and Eeg-Olofsson 1990: 3-4)

Although the individual instantiations (*drink heavily* or *heavy drinker*) might not occur with sufficient frequency to warrant associations between individual word forms, each of these instantiations strengthens the link between two more abstract representations involved, namely a representation of the lexemes DRINK and a representation of the adjective HEAVY with all their respective inflections and derivations (see section 5.4.3 for details).

In sum, the identification and classification of units provides the linguist with a descriptive apparatus which enables him or her to identify further patterns, further similarities and thus establish further units and classes. This view is expressed nicely in the following quotation from Harris (1951):

> Once the elements are defined, any occurrence of speech in the language in question can be represented by a combination of these elements [...]. It is possible to perform upon the elements various operations, such as classification or substitution, which do not obliterate the identifiability of the elements but reduce their number or make the statement of interrelations simpler. [...] It is this that underlies the usefulness of descriptive linguistics: the elements can be manipulated[26] in ways in which records or descriptions of speech can not be; and as a result regularities of speech are discovered which would be far more difficult to find without the translation into linguistic symbols. (Harris 1951: 17-18)

This also shows that the progression from low-level units to higher-level ones is usually accompanied by an increase in abstraction. A higher-level unit is usually not described by reference to individual lower-level units. For instance, clause structure is described not in terms of individual phrases but in terms of classes of phrases, i.e. abstractions from actual phrases: in the structural description of the monotransitive clause, the S refers to a class of phrases and so do the V and the O. Similarly, to describe the nature of the head of an NP we do not list all possible words that may occupy this position but we describe the head as being realized by members of a class of words, namely nouns. In this manner, units of one level are described with regard to classes of units of the next-lower level and not with regard to individual units of this level. But such classes themselves are abstractions already. It follows that a higher-level unit is an abstraction on the basis of an abstraction which again is the result of another process of abstraction, and so on (consider figure 3.1 above). Consequently, low-level units (or units of a lower rank in Halliday's (1961) terminology) are usually less abstract than those of higher ranks. It is in this sense that the rank scale, according to Halliday, can be understood as a scale of abstraction.

Another scale of abstraction in the theory of language, although of a different kind (see below for details), is that of delicacy, i.e. "the scale of differentiation, or depth in detail" (Halliday 1961: 272). In terms of what was said above we can describe delicacy as being related to the willingness to regard instantiations or classes of units at a particular rank as identical or not. At a very low level of delicacy a large number of features of individual units would be treated as irrelevant, resulting in one large set of units, all treated as essentially the same. A

26 'Manipulated' here seems to refer to the discovery procedures of taxonomic structuralism.

high level of delicacy would increase the number of features that are treated as relevant and would thus cluster units into a larger number of smaller classes.

Let us consider the highest rank, the clause complex, first. At a low level of delicacy we would maybe only distinguish clause complexes on the basis of the kinds of relations that obtain between the individual clauses, namely coordination, subordination or both. Only at a more delicate level would we consider the number of clauses that occur in the clause complex and the structural arrangement of these clauses. 'Structural arrangement', here, refers to coordination (clause + clause), subordination (clause > clause), superordination (clause < clause) and to hierarchies (clause + (clause > clause)). Delicacy at clause rank is illustrated in examples (1') to (4'). At the lowest level of delicacy all four examples would be treated as essentially the same, namely as instances of the category 'clause'. A higher degree of delicacy would make a distinction between interrogative and declarative clause (VSX as opposed to SVX), not taking into consideration the final elements in the clauses. These would be considered at the most delicate level of description, where each of the clauses would be taken as representative of its own class, i.e. 'monotransitive declarative', 'monotransitive interrogative', and so on. A still more delicate description would make reference to optional adverbials and thus distinguish patterns like SVO, ASVO, SVOA, ASVOA, etc. The description can still become more delicate. The term 'SVO', i.e. a simple monotransitive clause without any optional adverbials, represents various more delicate sub-patterns, e.g. SVO in its unmarked order and its 'allo-sentences' (see Daneš 1964, Esser 1984 and Lambrecht 1994 for more details on this term) like the fronted variant OSV but also the cleft, pseudo-cleft or passive sentence. Similarly, with phrases of, say, the 'prem.+Head' kind, a more delicate description would distinguish different structures on the basis of the premodifying items that occur, such as 'Det + Head' or 'Det + Adj + Head'. On the rank 'word', the most delicate description would list individual word forms, e.g. *tree*, *trees*, *tree's* and *trees'*. These are regarded as instantiations of lexical units in the sense of Cruse (1986), i.e. as "the union of a lexical form and a single sense" (78), where 'lexical form' refers to a set of word forms that only differ with regard to inflection[27] (see below for a discussion of the necessary distinction of word forms and lexical units on this rank). Examples of such lexical units are $TREE_1$ ('plant') and $TREE_2$ ('drawing'). These lexical units, again, can be understood as instantiating a lexeme TREE, which following Cruse (1986:

27 I refrain from using the term 'lemma' here, since this term is purely form-based and does not take meaning into account.

76) is understood as "a family of lexical units". The scale of delicacy, in my view, can also quite conveniently account for the relations of a given instance of a unit and its 'allo-realizations', such as one morpheme and its allomorphs or one lexical unit and its word forms. This understanding of delicacy, however, is not in line with Halliday's model and will be described in more detail below.

Rank and delicacy can thus be interpreted as two interacting scales of abstraction, one in a vertical, the other in a horizontal dimension, as figure 3.3 below shows. Note that this figure is only used for illustrative purposes; it is not supposed to give an exhaustive description of the different degrees of delicacy on any of the ranks. Note also that this figure does not include realization in substance as we want to keep the description independent of the medium of realization. The figure makes reference to 'medium-independent' forms of words and morphemes.

On the left-hand side we have the units ranking from morphemes to clause complexes. This scale makes reference to a 'constituency' relation, in that the lower units are the building blocks of the units of the next-higher level. In contrast to this relation, the scale of delicacy is structured in terms of an 'instantiation' relation: The classes or units further to the right are instantiations of the class or unit immediately to the left. Clause complexes may be instantiated by coordinated or subordinated clauses or by a combination of both. The class 'clause', for instance, can be instantiated by a clause of the type 'SVX', 'VSX' or 'VX'. The class 'SVX' can be broken down into the seven major clause patterns suggested by Quirk et al. (1985) and so on. As has already be pointed out above, the instantiation relation can also be interpreted in terms of type and token, e.g. clause complexes with co- and subordination are two tokens of the type 'clause complex'. Similarly, the type 'lexeme TREE' has two tokens, namely the lexical units $TREE_1$ and $TREE_2$. These, in turn, are types on a higher level of delicacy and have as their tokens the individual word forms *tree, trees, tree's, trees'*. Each of these can be understood as types with regard to their actual realizations in text, i.e. the word form type *tree* in figure 3.3 has as its instantiations each actual occurrence of the word form *tree* in a text or a text corpus.

A further difference between the scales of rank and delicacy also deserves mention. While the former is completely de-contextualized and understands 'unit' from a more generic perspective, distinctions on the latter are partly due to contextualization. This becomes obvious if we follow the delicacy scale to the right, i.e. to the level of 'allo-realizations'. The step from abstract clause pattern to allo-sentence (inversion, fronting, etc.) involves an increase in contextualization, since the choice of the many allo-sentences depends on (linguistic and non-linguistic) context. The consequences of contextualization can be witnessed on all levels of description. On phrase rank, for instance, the choice of genitive vs. *of*-construction can be regarded as being dependent on contextualization if we take into consideration the influence of the weight of the respective constituents (i.e. 'possessor' and 'possessed') (see Gries 2002, Kreyer 2003, Ros-

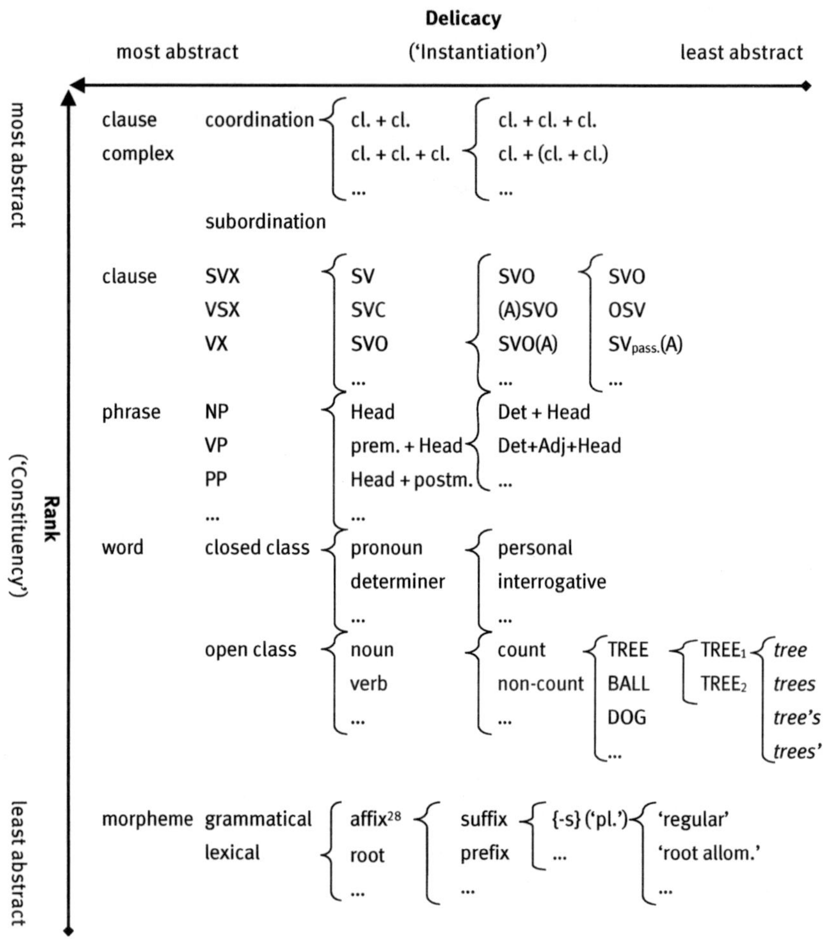

Figure 3.3: The interaction of rank and delicacy.

---

28 In contrast to other approaches that talk of free grammatical morphemes (e.g. {the} or {and}; Kastovsky 1982: 72-73) I only consider affixes as possible candidates for grammatical morphemes.

enbach 2003 and 2005, Hinrichs & Szmrecsanyi 2007 and Szmrecsanyi & Hinrichs 2008). While the influence of context on clause and phrase rank is usually related to decoder-orientation (and thus a matter of 'presentation'; see Esser 2006 for details), contextualization on word and morpheme rank makes reference to the language system itself: Allo-units on word rank, i.e. the word-forms of a lexical unit, are determined by the rules of syntax. The choice of allomorphs depends on rules that make reference to phonological and morphological context. Still, on all rank levels the most delicate descriptions make reference to the contextualization of de-contextualized units.

Another important point needs to be mentioned here. Figure 3.3 shows the distinction of clauses into 'declarative', 'interrogative' and 'imperative' to be the most fundamental or the least delicate one. This is an arbitrary choice, although it might be the most suitable from the perspective of structuralism. If semantic arguments were taken into account we would want to start off from the semantic roles or cases that are warranted by different classes of verbs. At the least delicate level, we then might have a distinction between 'monotransitive', 'ditransitive', 'intensive', etc. verbs and their related clause patterns; examples of this approach are Halliday's later writings (for instance 1967) with a focus on systems like transitivity, mood and theme. From this point of view, 'SVO' would be at a low level of delicacy and the actual declarative, interrogative and imperative structures 'SVO', 'VSO' and 'VO', respectively, would be regarded as more delicate descriptions.

This is an extremely important point that has been hinted at above already but nevertheless warrants a more thorough discussion. In a set of data there is no intrinsic way of describing these data. Groups or categories can be formed on the basis of any feature or set of features found in the data: "language can be structured in respect to various independent features" (Harris 1954: 146), leading to different ways of categorising the same data. A case in point is the variation in the numbers and kinds of parts of speech that grammarians have posited for the English language (Fries 1952: 65-66). Extreme cases can be found in tagged corpora, where often over fifty part-of-speech tags are applied.

New possibilities for categorization arise if we dispense with a strict dividing line of lexis and grammar, as can be seen in more recent cognitive accounts. In this case, a description of syntax, for instance, may well take constructions related to particular lexical items or semantic groups of lexical items as a starting point. At the least delicate level of description we might have something like 'constructions that contain the lexical item X'. Only at a more delicate level would we distinguish between, say, '*that*-clause containing lexical item X' and '*to*-infinitive clause containing lexical item X'. Instead of forming categories on the basis of traditional clause distinction, categories on the basis of lexical items might be more appropriate for the English language. Hunston and Francis' (2000) Pattern Grammar is but one example of this kind of approach. Also, such lexically driven approaches may call the traditional distinction of different ranks into question: lexical items are no longer regarded as mere fillers for slots provided by syntactic constructions but both are regarded as being co-selected, thus forming a complex unit with 'constituents' of different rank.

Finally, from a psycholinguistic perspective even phonetic detail may serve as basis for categorization of larger units. Apparently, the human brain builds groups of items with regard to similarity in sound. The influence of so-called 'gangs' in psycholinguistic experiments on morphological processing and production bears witness to the importance of such groups (see, for instance, Stemberger & MacWhinney 1988 and Alegre & Gordon 1999). The more traditional concept of 'analogical change' (see, among others, Bloomfield 1933) bears witness to this influence as well.

It is clear, then, that there is no *a priori* way in which data should be categorized and classified; different approaches or paradigms find different solutions to this problem, as will be discussed in more detail further below. Which categories are actually chosen depends on criteria that are external to the data, such as computational elegance or processing parsimony, minimization of storage, and so on. The model advocated in this study tries to dispense with theory-internal restrictions (e.g. the idea of consistent binary branching in many generative approaches). Instead, it is guided by psychological and cognitive plausibility and the assumption that a model of language "must represent a competence to perform" (Lamb 2000: 95). As a consequence, the present model will embrace categorizations of all kinds as long as the resulting categories make sense from a cognitive perspective. In addition, the model relieves us from the need to discard one plausible analysis or way of categorization in favour of another which is neither more nor less plausible; we can eat our cake and have it too, as it were. One of the major advantages of the model lies in its flexibility that allows different analyses and different ways of categorization to coexist alongside each other. In this, I follow Quirk et al. (1985: 90) who claim: "[t]here are occasions [...] when [...] alternative analyses seem to be needed, on the grounds that some of the generalizations that have to be made require one analysis, and some require another." This 'multiple analysis' is inherent in the present model and follows as a consequence from the nature of the processes that are involved in the evolution and the functioning of the network. The present study will show how this openness is beneficial with regard to online processing (see, for instance, section 4.2.1).

A second problem is the question as to how delicate a description can get. What are the limits of delicacy on each rank level? According to Halliday (1961: 272-3) "[t]he endpoint set to grammar on the delicacy scale is where differentiation ceases [...]." This criterion is not always easy to apply. Particularly problematic, in my view, is delicacy at the rank of words. Traditionally, classes on this level are formed on the basis of paradigms, i.e. sets of words that are interchangeable at one slot in a syntagm. Corpus-linguistic studies suggest that this conception of language in terms of slots and fillers needs revising. The question where to separate grammar from lexis is not one that is easily answered. One problematic example is given by Esser (2000a), who shows how the two meanings of the lexeme TREE, i.e. 'plant' and 'drawing', exhibit strong tendencies with regard to their instantiation in word forms: "there is a strong association between the meaning 'drawing' and the singular form tree" (97). Consequently, realizations of TREE in the meaning of 'drawing', i.e. realizations of the lexical unit $TREE_2$, are not likely to occur in 'frames' like 'these ... are X'. Numerous other examples are provided by the many cases of what corpus linguistics calls 'colligation', i.e. the association of a lexical item with a particular syntactic structure (see section 5.3 for details). Lexis seems to be more grammatical than has been assumed traditionally, and, hence, delicacy on the word level should perhaps be extended down to lexical items, and even down to individual medium-independent word forms (see Esser 1998, 2000b and 2006 for more information on this concept). This leads to a certain degree of redundancy a word form like *trees* is treated as an instance of most delicate description on word rank although it is clearly decomposable, consisting of a root morpheme and an inflectional morpheme, the first of which is realized by {tree}, the second by {-s}. It could be argued that in treating *trees* as a holistic item on the word rank, we have "throw[n...] up the grammatical sponge and move[d...] out to lexis while this [was] still avoidable" (Halliday 1961: 271). But that this move is unavoidable was seen in the above discussion of the fact that we often find syntactic restrictions only for some word forms of one lexical unit, but not for all. In the case of the lexical unit $TREE_2$, i.e. in the meaning 'drawing', it is not all of its word forms that are restricted. Therefore, generalizations cannot be made for the complete lexical unit, i.e. for all word forms with the root morpheme {tree} = 'drawing', since the singular form *tree* does occur frequently in corpora, while the plural forms are rare. Neither can this particular behaviour of *trees* be explained through the plural morpheme alone. It is the combination of this particular root with the plural suffix that leads to rare occurrences. Accordingly, on word level we sometimes have to make reference to individual word forms since they are grammatically relevant. Note that even at higher ranks lexis needs to be taken into account. This is unavoidable in those cases where a unit is more than the sum of its parts, such as idiomatic expressions like *from the frying pan into the fire* or *it ain't over till the fat lady sings*. With these and similar items, a decomposition into their constituent parts is of no use; they have to be treated holistically. A similar view is expressed in Halliday's (1985b) later writings:

> grammar cannot be modelled as new sentences made out of old words – a fixed stock of vocabulary in never-to-be-repeated combinations. [...] we process and store **entire groups, phrases, clauses, clause complexes and even texts** [my emphasis]. (Halliday 1985b: 8)

This, then, is yet another piece of evidence which makes clear that the traditional strict division between lexis and grammar cannot be upheld in all cases. As will be shown in the next chapter the present network model is flexible enough to do justice to these facts.

With regard to the description of actual language data, Halliday (1961) introduces a third scale, exponence, that is supposed to bring "the categories of the theory together, relating them to each other and to the linguistic data they are set up to account for" (Butler 1985: 27). For instance, NPs are possible exponents of the element 'S' (subject) in clause structure; in this way, a particular class ('NP') is related to an element in a structure ('S' in, say, 'SVO'). In addition, the structure 'det + noun' is a possible exponent of the class 'NP' and the element 'S', and so on. This is what is meant when Butler above talks of relating the categories of the theory. The end-point of the scale of exponence is reached in the description of a linguistic phenomenon in terms of lexical items or morphemes (the linguistic data), e.g. the string *the man* as an exponent of the class 'NP' or of the element 'S' in the structure of clauses. Therefore, the scale of exponence can be interpreted as accounting for the realization of units and structures. Although such a third scale might be motivated on theory-internal grounds (see Halliday 1961: 270 and 281-2), I think the description of language data can dispense with it. In lieu of exponence, I advocate that the basis of linguistic description is the 'instantiation' relation, as will become clear presently.

In the description of data, the scales of rank and delicacy work hand in hand. Let us consider the clause *big dogs chase cats*. We could describe this string merely as a clause and leave it at that, or we could be more delicate and state that it is a declarative clause, or still more delicate, has the structure SVO (which in this case would also refer to the contextualized clause pattern). These successive steps show an increase in delicacy on the rank level 'clause'. Note, that there is not more to say, with regard to the structure of the clause as a whole. A more thorough description would need to move to a description of each of the elements of the SVO structure. Here we shift from the rank of 'clause' to the rank of 'phrase' and describe the S and O as realized by an NP, and the V as realized by a VP[29]. At this point we might want to get more delicate and describe the subject as an NP of the kind 'prem.+Head' and the object and verb as an NP or VP of the 'Head'-type. Moving further down the rank scale we arrive at the level of words. Note that, since the phrases were described in some detail, the description at word level does not treat the NPs holistically but in terms of their structure. That is, at word level we do not describe the realization of, say, the subject NP as one holistic unit that is realized by the word string *big dogs*. Rather, we analyse the realization of the premodifying part and the head of the NP. Each is described as being instantiated by one word each, namely *big* and *dogs*. Even if we choose not to be more delicate in our description at word rank, it still provides information, namely that the premodifying part of the subject NP is realized through one word only. Each of the words that make up the individual phrases can be analysed as strings of morphemes, and at this stage we could get more delicate again by stating the kind of morpheme, i.e. lexical or grammatical. This way of describing the string *big dogs chase cats* is portrayed in figure 3.4; the broken arrows represent descriptive steps on the basis of delicacy, the solid ones descriptions that exploit rank relations.

Above we have made a distinction of description with regard to rank and description with regard to delicacy, i.e. with regard to the two fundamental relations 'constituency' and 'instantiation'. The more important, or the more pervasive, of the two is the 'instantiation' relation. It is involved in those parts of the description that are characterized by increases in delicacy. This is obvious since the delicacy scale was characterized as being defined on the basis of 'instantiation' relations. The same also holds true in those instances where the description moves down the rank scale. The only difference being that the 'instantiation' relation does not obtain between the complete unit of the higher rank and its constituent units of lower rank but between the parts of a structure and units of lower rank. For instance, in the description of the SVO structure, the 'instantiation' relation obtains between S, V, and O and the unit 'phrase', and not between the whole clause and the phrase. That is, both the S and the O are instantiated by an NP and the V is instantiated by a VP. But if these parts are added up, we can still conceive of the 'sum', i.e. 'NP+VP+NP', as instantiating the structure SVO. Similarly, although in the strict sense it is the three individu-

29 Note that 'VP', here, is not used in the generative but in the traditional structuralist understanding of the term.

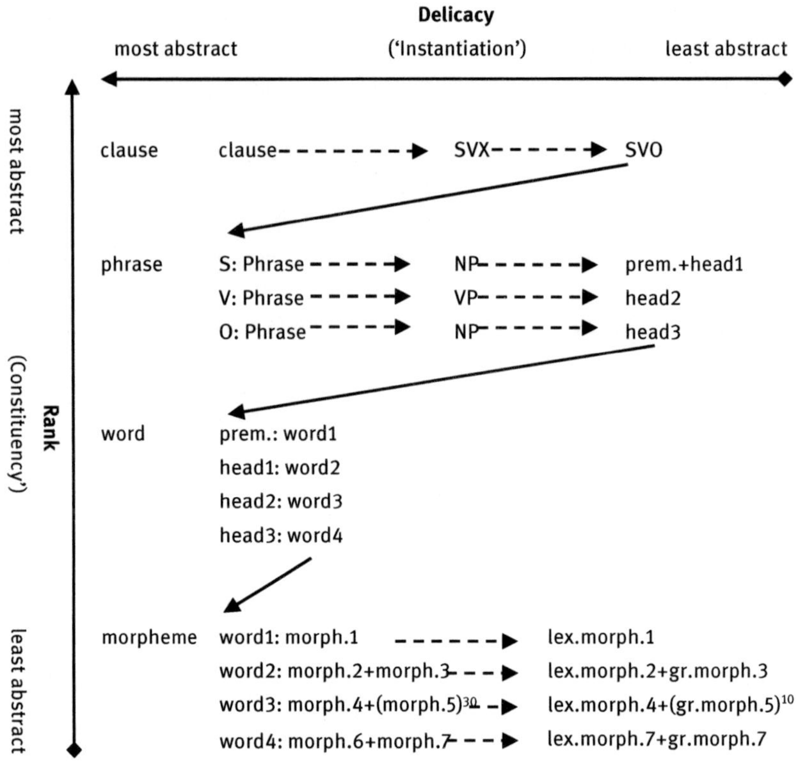

Figure 3.4: A possible description of the structure *big dogs chase cats*.

al phrases that are instantiated by (strings of) word classes or words, for instance Adj+N, V, and N or *big dogs*, *chase* and *cats*, respectively, we can interpret the 'sum' of these strings, i.e. 'Adj+N+V+N' or 'big dogs chase cats', as instantiating the whole SVO pattern. In this sense, then, we can understand the 'instantiation' relation as being the most fundamental one in the description of data.

This strong focus on instantiation also helps us to do justice to recent corpus-linguistic findings that defy the division between lexis and syntax, such as the concept of 'lexicalized sentence stem', illustrated by the example 'np be-tense sorry to keep-tense you waiting' (Pawley and Syder 1983: 210). Patterns

30 Positing 'morpheme 5' and 'grammatical morpheme 5' obviously only makes sense if we assume that the concept 'zero morpheme' is valid.

like these make clear that the language user does not necessarily stick to the rigid categories and ranks that linguistic theory comes up with. What is called for is a model that allows for a high degree of permeability between the individual ranks and the individual degrees of delicacy of more traditional descriptions. It will be shown in this study that a network model meets such a requirement.

In summary, the present section has shown how through two processes of abstraction, namely 'abstraction away from data' and 'description through classes', the units, structures and classes of a theory of grammar are obtained. It has also been shown how these units, structures and classes are connected through two fundamental relations, i.e. a 'constituency' relation which accounts for the different ranks, and an 'instantiation' relation which underlies the different degrees of delicacy found in the description of units on one rank level. Also, we have seen that the latter relation is granted a special status in the description of actual language data.

3.2 From description to grammatical rules

So far, the procedures shown were of the inductive type, i.e. from the patterned behaviour of language to general statements about these patterns. A theory of grammar cannot stop here but has to move on, since the ultimate aim is not to merely describe instances of language encountered up to a particular point in time, but also to make predictions about possible future utterances. This 'generative' view is emphasized by Hjelmslev (^{2}1961 [1943]) in the following quote:

> [...] by using the tools of linguistic theory, we can draw from this selection of texts a fund of knowledge to be used again on other texts. This knowledge concerns, not merely or essentially the processes or texts from which it is abstracted, but the system or language on which all texts of the same premised nature are constructed, and with the help of which we can construct new texts. With the linguistic information we have thus obtained, we shall be able to construct any conceivable or theoretically possible texts in the same language. (Hjelmslev ^{2}1961 [1943]: 16 – 17; see also Hockett 1954: 212)

While the progression from data to description is essentially concerned with the classification of language events and parts thereof, a grammatical theory rather focuses on relevant features that have been abstracted from the observed units, structures and classes. The progression from description to theory can thus be understood in terms of extensionally and intensionally defined classes, i.e. with regard to describing classes in terms of their members or in terms of the features that are shared by all members. Harris (1951) writes:

> For the linguist, analyzing a limited corpus consisting of just so many bits of talking which he has heard, the element X is thus associated with an extensionally defined class consisting of so many features in so many of the speech utterances in his corpus. However, when the linguist offers his results as a system representing the language as a whole, he is predicting that the elements set up for his corpus will satisfy all other bits of talking in that language. The element X then becomes associated with an intensionally defined class consisting of such features of any utterance as differ from other features, or relate to other features, in such and such a way. (Harris 1951: 17)

To give one illustrative example, consider the realizations of the past tense morpheme {-d}. Let us assume that the linguist is confronted with a corpus of past tense forms:

(5) [hændɪd], [kraɪd], [mendɪd], [mæpt], [leɪd], [pækt], [rɪskt], [brɪdʒd], [bɒkst], [pʊʃt], [krɒst], [pi:kt], [lændɪd], ...

The first step of segmenting leads to the identification of the forms of the past tense morpheme and the stems:

(6) [hænd-ɪd], [kraɪ-d], [mend-ɪd], [mæp-t], [leɪ-d], [pæk-t], [rɪsk-t], [brɪdʒ-d], [bɒks-t], [pʊʃ-t], [lænd-ɪd], ...

The classification of these forms yields three (well-known) classes:

(7) [hænd-ɪd], [mend-ɪd], [lænd-ɪd],
[kraɪ-d], [leɪ-d], [brɪdʒ-d]
[mæp-t], [pæk-t], [rɪsk-t], [bɒks-t], [pʊʃ-t]

The result of this classification procedure are three classes of stems that occur with the past tense allomorph [-ɪd], [-d], and [-t], respectively. These classes are described extensionally, i.e. by listing all their members. The step from description to theory begins when we abstract away from the individual members of the classes and focus on shared features of these members; in this case, the phonetic features of the stem-final sounds, i.e.:

(8) [hænd-ɪd], [mend-ɪd], [lænd-ɪd], [pet-ɪd]	> [alveolar plosive]
[kraɪ-d], [leɪ-d], [brɪdʒ-d]	> [+voice, -[alveolar plosive]]
[mæp-t], [pæk-t], [rɪsk-t], [bɒks-t], [pʊʃ-t]	> [-voice, -[alveolar plosive]]

Instead of an extensional description of the three classes, those classes are defined intensionally, i.e. by listing relevant attributes of their members. It is thus no longer particular members of a set or class that occur with particular forms of the past tense morpheme but features of members that result in particular forms of the past tense morpheme.

(9) *stem ending in*	*past tense morpheme realized as*
[alveolar plosive]	[-ɪd]
[+voice, -[alveolar plosive]]	[-d]
[-voice, -[alveolar plosive]]	[-t]

It is at this point that we cross the border from description to prediction and enter the realm of grammar or linguistic theory. The configuration under (9), resulting out of successive steps of abstraction and generalization, is no longer a mere description of the data but, in its transition from extension to intension still captures what is relevant in the data given under (5) but at the same time states hypotheses that transcend the given data and can be tested against new data. The statement under (9) above, thus, is a rule of grammar based on the description of a corpus of data.

In the present network model the question of description and rule basically boils down to the question in which direction activation travels. Figure 3.5 shows the realization of the category *ADJECTIVE* in the network. Without going into too much detail at this point (see section 4.2.1), the category has evolved on the basis of repeated co-occurrence of features in individual adjectives, e.g. *happy* and *friendly*, as described above. This network is the result of a description of language data. It describes features of the use of these adjectives and shows possible patterns of co-occurrence of these features which, eventually, leads to the formation of a new category *ADJECTIVE* and to a link between the two adjective nodes and the category node. This way, the network captures regularities found in language data, i.e. the network is a description of language use.

The same network that provides the description also provides the rules. Let us assume that the organism has encountered the word form *healthy* used attributively, predicatively, intensified by *very* and in its various graded forms. Any use of the adjective in that way will have contributed to establishing a direct link between the word form node |HEALTHY| and the node |*ADJECTIVE*|, eventually leading to a direct link between the two nodes. Once this link is established, the word *healthy* falls under the rules that hold for adjectives. More specifically,

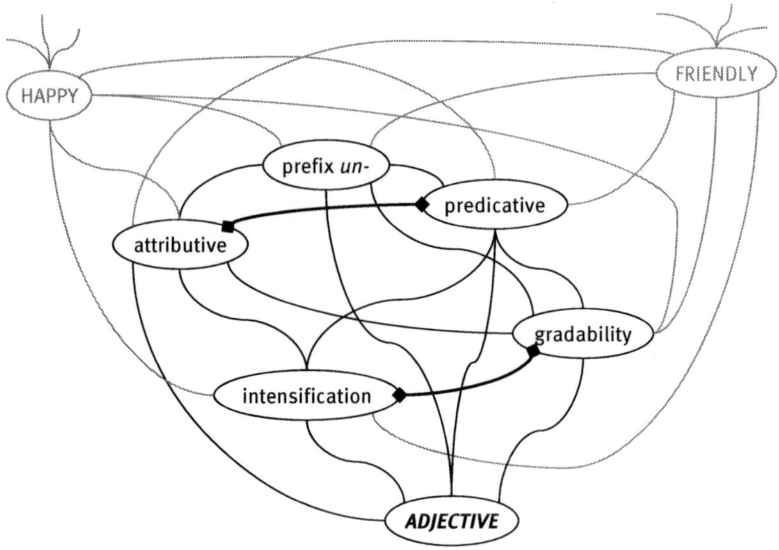

Figure 3.5: An example of a category, its features and its members.

the organism will have learnt that *healthy* can also be used with the prefix *un-* even though the organism has never seen it used that way.

The network, thus, provides a summarizing statement about all members of a given class (its extension) and a summarizing statement about the defining features of this class (its intension). The network represents both a description of language data and a set of rules that accounts for the creative use (in the technical Chomskyan sense) of language.

4 'Traditional' concepts and their representation in the network model

In the previous chapter it has been shown how, from a very general point of view, a theory of a language emerges from the study of language data. More specifically, it was shown how theoretical categories emerge from an iterative process of abstracting away from the data. The resulting model showed several ranks of linguistic units, which are connected through a 'constituency' relation on a vertical dimension. The horizontal dimension distinguished different degrees of delicacy, and accordingly, was concerned with regarding different realizations of units as essentially similar or dissimilar. The fundamental relation between objects along this dimension was that of 'instantiation.

On the basis of this general discussion in chapter 3, the present chapter shows how ideas and concepts discussed in traditional descriptive grammar and in approaches in the generative-transformational framework can be represented in the network model advocated in the present study.

4.1 Traditional descriptive and early generative concepts

The following discussion is held at a fairly general level and will not go into any detail as regards the intricacies of the different grammatical approaches (in the strict sense). I will first discuss some general aspects of rules in grammar and linguistics that are considered largely uncontroversial, and will then proceed to portray some characteristics of descriptive rules, in particular as they are presented in Quirk et al.'s (1985) monumental description of the English language. Descriptions of this kind will be compared with models in the generative-transformational framework.

We have seen in section 3.1 that a theory of language generally makes use of three different categories, namely units, classes and structures. Put most simply, the aim of descriptive grammars, and hence descriptive rules, can be understood as providing an inventory of all units, classes and structures at different levels of delicacy and as describing the way these are interrelated (also at different levels of delicacy). In this way they spell out the relations of constituency and instantiation that can be observed among the elements of linguistic description. Although the aim of descriptive rules can be stated in a very simple way, it is not achieved easily. This is due to three major problems that are met with any attempt to describe any natural system: 1) the problem of generalization, 2) the problem of (ir)regularity, and 3) the problem of gradience or fuzziness.

It is commonly accepted that descriptive rules are concerned with a correct and objective description of empirical observations, i.e. "a statement expressing a generalization about the facts of a language" (Trask 1999: 264). The term 'generalization' is crucial here: usually, linguistic description draws a distinction between those aspects of language that are regular and thus generalizable and those that are rather idiosyncratic, i.e. lack regularity and thus generalizability. It is only the first kinds of facts that are described as a part of grammar, whereas the latter kind of facts usually is confined to the lexicon of a language:

> Most modern theories of grammar draw a sharp distinction in principle between generalizations, which are expressed by rules, and non-general facts, which are expressed by other means, notably by lexical entries in the lexicon. (Trask 1993: 245)

This view is not new (see, for instance, the discussion of Halliday 1961 above) and also underlies most of the reference works of grammar. *The Comprehensive Grammar of the English Language* states:

> Our general principle will be to regard grammar as accounting for constructions where greatest generalization is possible, assigning to lexicology (and hence beyond the scope of this book) constructions on which least generalization can be formulated. In applying this principle we will necessarily make arbitrary decisions along the gradient from greatest to least generalization. (Quirk et al. 1985: 15)

The quote above makes explicit the important point that we can draw no neat distinction between 'general' and 'non-general'. Rather, we are dealing with a cline on which we find different degrees of generalization. This ties in well with what has been discussed in the previous chapter. Generalization is closely connected to the instantiation relation that was found to be fundamental with regard to the description of the language system. Each time a descriptive statement makes reference to this fundamental relation we walk down the generalization gradient. Instead of one highly general class, i.e. a class that contains a large number of members, we are left with a larger number of less general classes, i.e. classes that contain a smaller number of members. The question of the endpoint of generalization in the last resort is a question of the minimum number of members that a given framework allows classes of linguistic objects to have. If the number of members of a potential class becomes too small, we refrain from establishing this class but rather provide the same information in the lexicon, as stated in the quotes above.

This situation is depicted in figure 4.1 below. At the highest degree of generalization we have large classes that represent a large set of objects, for instance, the class 'declarative clause'. Within such a large class further smaller subclasses can be distinguished, such as SVO and SVC clauses. Each member of the smaller subclasses is also an instantiation of the larger class 'declarative' clause. This process can be reiterated until we arrive at single-element classes which cannot be divided any further. At some point on our way to single-element classes the classes will become so small, i.e. the degree of generalization will become so low, that there is no point in making any further distinctions. Where exactly to draw the line is very difficult to decide, and any decision of that kind will involve an arbitrary element (see the quotation from Quirk et al. 1985 above). In my opinion, it seems more satisfactory to provide a model of grammar that is flexible with regard to the number and kinds of categories that are established. It will be shown in section 4.2 that the model advocated here provides that flexibility.

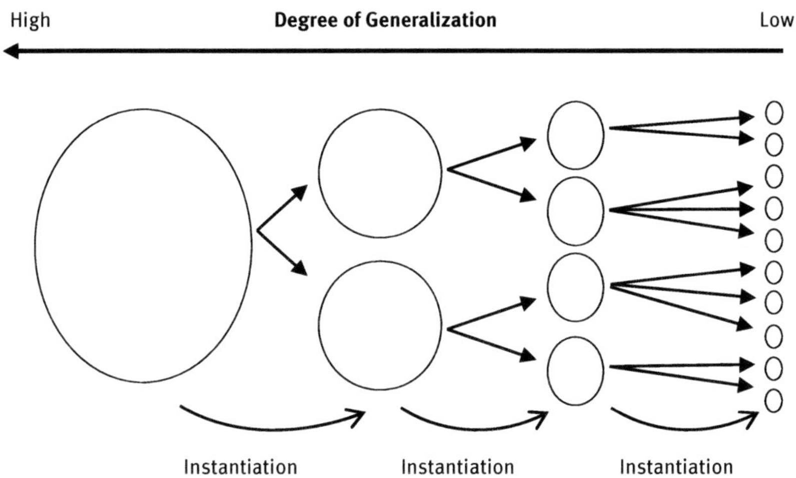

Figure 4.1: Generalization and instantiation.

The problem of generalization also touches on a more fundamental one, namely the validity of rules. Many researchers distinguish between 'categorial' and 'variable' rules; if the former are disobeyed, the result will be an ungrammatical string, i.e. categorial rules must always be applied, while variable rules only apply in particular contexts or in a particular percentage of the cases to which, in principle, they might be applied (see, for instance, Matthews 1997: 325). Generally, then, there may be exceptions to rules:

> A rule need not be exceptionless. For example, the rule of English that says that a noun forms its plural by adding <-s> is genuine, and it applies to most new nouns entering the language, but there are some well-known exceptions, like feet, children and radii. (Trask 1999: 264)

Again, exceptions to rules can conveniently be described with reference to the notion of instantiation. If we consider a class with at least two subclasses, we would talk about exceptions to a rule if one of the subclasses, the one that contains the 'regular' tokens, was very large while the other, the one with the 'irregular' tokens, was very small. With regard to the formation of the past tense, for instance, the situation could be depicted as follows: of all the past tense word forms in English a very large subset is realized by adding [-ɪd], [-d], or [-t] to the stem, while only a small subset is realized in another way. This subset is regarded as an exception to the more general realization.

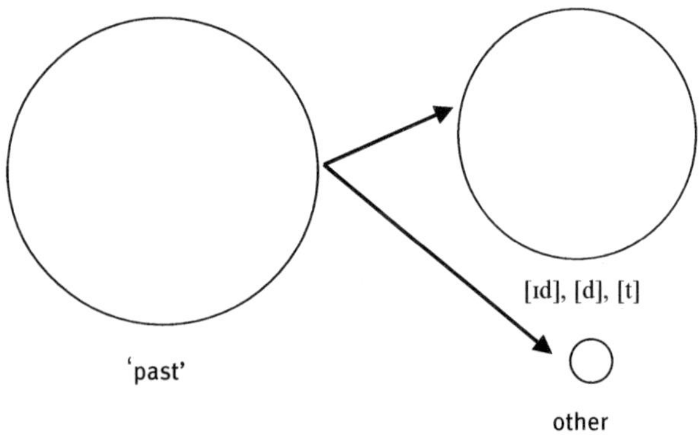

Figure 4.2: Regularity and irregularity in the formation of past tenses in English.

We thus witness two problems: firstly, the question of how 'general' a set of facts has to be to warrant the formulation of a descriptive rule, and, related to this, the question of the number of exceptions that a rule can bear until it is no longer valid. As might be guessed, no principled answer can be given. Usually, cases have to be decided individually and often the criteria involved in the decision process are not hard-and-fast but make reference to vague notions like 'simplicity' or 'elegance'. These criteria, again, may be counteracted by the urge to state general facts if these show in the data, i.e. aspects of informativity. As an example, consider the following instance of "'failure' of allophonic rules" (Lass 1984: 34-35): many English dialects have an allophonic rule for the realization of /æ/ which states that /æ/ is lengthened in front of fricatives, voiced stops and non-velar nasals. However, exceptions do exist: while, as expected, we find [hæ:v] (*halve*) and [k^hæ:n] ((*tin*) *can*) we also find the unexpected [hæv] (*have*) and [k^hæn] ((auxiliary) *can*). A completely unproblematic solution would be to consider the examples above as minimal pairs and hence posit that we are dealing with two phonemes instead of allophones, i.e. /æ:/ and /æ/. This solution would result in a highly elegant (because exceptionless) description, but at the same time, it would also discard the considerable amount of information that is captured in the allophonic rule. A less clear solution would be to regard the two realizations as allophones of one phoneme and admit that the allophonic rule has exceptions. Although this rule would then no longer be 'true' but only be 'largely true', it would still describe regularities that occur in a considerable amount of data.

Another problem grammars face is that of 'gradience' or 'indeterminacy', i.e. the fact that "[c]ategories and structures [...] often do not have neat boundaries" (Quirk et al. 1985: 90). While generalization and (ir-)regularity are concerned with sets of data and their subsets, gradience has to do with the boundaries of classes on one level of generalization and with the representativity of their members. The classical understanding of classes and their definition rests on the identification of necessary and jointly sufficient features that are supposedly exhibited by each member of the given class. It follows from this that each member of a class is as good a representative of this class as any other member (for instance, there is no even number that is a 'better' or 'worse' representative of the class than any other even number). This view on categorization came under heavy criticism in the early seventies of the last century, when it was shown that this idea of classification and categorization cannot be brought in line with experimental and empirical data on human categorization. Instead, it has been suggested to treat classes and categories as having a prototype structure. Without going into too much detail at this point (see section 6.1 for a more thorough discussion), we can distinguish three kinds of indeterminacy: 1) one member of a class exhibits more features than another member of the same class, i.e. members show different 'degrees of representativity', 2) the classes themselves may not be clearly defined, i.e. class boundaries are fuzzy and clas-

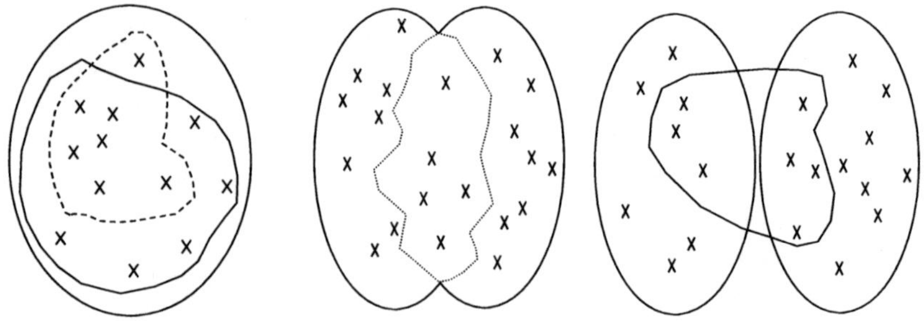

Figure 4.3: Gradience in linguistics: more and less representative members, fuzzy category boundaries and multiple membership.

ses shade into one another, and 3) items may show features of two distinct classes, i.e. items may show multiple or indeterminate class membership[31]. These three situations are depicted in figure 4.3 below. The circles, this time, represent sets of features, not sets of linguistic objects. Each feature is represented by a little cross. The areas encircled by the hand-drawn lines on the left and the right-hand side of figure 4.3 represent linguistic items, interpreted as bundles of features.

Illustrative with respect to degrees of representativity is Ross' (1973 [2004]) 'Nouniness Squish', which hierarchically orders grammatical constructions from least to most 'nouny'. *That*-clauses, for instance, are at the lowest end of the hierarchy and nouns (naturally) at the other end, with derived nominals (*Max's gift of the letters to Frieda*) and action nominals (*Max's giving of the letters to Frieda*) in between. He finds that a subset of features that typically are associated with nouns are also associated with derived nominals. Of this set, again, a subset also holds for action nominals, and so on for categories that are less nouny than action nominals. The smallest subset of features is found with the bottom end of the hierarchy, i.e. *that*-clauses. From the perspective of form classes, in this case a class that contains forms that behave similarly to nouns, Ross' 'nouniness squish' can be interpreted as a class where the members show

31 Note that a recent study on the nature of gradience, i.e. Aarts (2007), denies the existence of the fuzziness of categories. Essentially, he would treat this as a special case of what he calls 'intersective gradience', which is identical to the notion of multiple or indeterminate membership discussed here. We will leave it at that for the moment and discuss this point in more detail in section 4.2.2.

differing degrees of representativity. Nouns would be regarded as highly representative of this class, whereas nominals would be regarded as being representative to a smaller extent. Items at the bottom of the 'nouniness squish' would hardly be treated as representing the class, although they share one or two of the defining features. The question is what to do with this kind of indeterminacy. Ross proposes "that what is necessary is a relaxation of the claim that sequences of elements either are or are not members of some constituent class, like NP, V, S, etc." (387). Instead, he argues that category membership should be a matter of degree, so that a linguistic item is, for instance, a sentence to a degree of 60%, 85% or 100%. Rules and conditions of grammar would then not work in an either-or-way, but instead would have thresholds, ranging from 0% to 100%, to state to which kinds of objects they apply and to which kinds they do not apply. In the model advocated here, different degrees of category membership evolve as a consequence of the underlying nature of the model itself.

The second kind of indeterminacy, fuzzy boundaries are, for instance, found with the classes 'noun' and 'adjective'. Although each of the classes shows a number of features that are not shared by the other (e.g. plural marking vs. gradability) they also exhibit common features: for instance, both adjectives and nouns can serve to premodify the head of a noun phrase, and both can fill the complement slot in an SVC clause.

An example of multiple membership, the third kind of indeterminacy, can be found in Jackson's ([2]1982: 126-127) discussion of the preposition *off*. While in the clause *Jim jumped off the bus*, *off* would be classified as a preposition, *off* in *The meeting is off* would be regarded as an adverb. In between these two fairly clear cases, we find examples like *Jim jumped off* where the word at issue is used as an adverb but is also at least a potential preposition.

Related to the problem of multiple membership is what Quirk et al. (1985) refer to as 'gradients':

> A gradient is a scale which relates two categories of description (for example two word classes) in terms of degrees of similarity and contrast. At the ends of the scale are items which belong clearly to one category or to another; intermediate positions on the scale are taken by 'in-between' cases – items which fail, in different degrees, to satisfy the criteria for one or the other category. (Quirk et al. 1985: 90)

The distinction between subordinating and coordinating conjunctions is a gradient in Quirk et al.'s sense. While *and* is a clear case of coordinator, and *if* clearly counts as a subordinator, the conjunction *for* sits somewhere in the middle between these unproblematic cases just like the form *the* is in between clear cases of the categories 'word' and 'affix'.

To sum up, descriptive grammars and descriptive rules are best understood as attempts to spell out the relations of constituency and instantiation that are found in language data. This involves the identification of units, structures and classes and, thus, rests on the identification of categories on different levels of description. This process of categorization entails a number of problems that have been discussed in some detail, namely the question of the degree of generalization, the question of regularity and exception and the question of indeterminacy or variance.

To some extent, the rules formulated in generative-transformational grammar are highly similar to those in traditional descriptive approaches. In fact, Newmeyer (1996) writes:

> the first decade of generative syntax was a highly rule-oriented one. More and more in this period, descriptive goals came to outweigh explanatory ones. In much of the work in this period – perhaps outside of the MIT mainstream, but nevertheless numerically significant – transformational grammar has become little more than descriptive linguistics with a transformational veneer. (47)

In particular, this holds for phrase-structure rules. They can be interpreted as a formalization of the various constituency relations that exist between units of different ranks. Consider one of Chomsky's (1957: 26) earliest examples as an illustration of a grammar with phrase-structure rules:

(1) (i) *Sentence* → *NP* + *VP*
(ii) *NP* → *T* + *N*
(iii) *VP* → *Verb* + *NP*
(iv) *T* → *the*
(v) *N* → *man, ball, etc.*
(vi) *Verb* → *hit, took, etc.*

Through successive rewriting of the different elements to the left of each rule this grammar generates sentences like *the man hit the ball* or *the man took the ball.*

Rewrite rules can conveniently be described by reference to the notion of constituency and instantiation. As stated above, rewrite rules make explicit the relations of constituency that exist between units of different ranks. At the same time, they state possible ways of generating all the instantiations of a particular linguistic item, i.e. rewrite rules provide algorithms for creating the extension of classes. In this respect, rewrite rules of the earlier models of generative-transformational grammar are actually not that much different from the rules that are found in descriptive grammars. We are dealing with a shift of focus that by and large can be accounted for by a mere change in the 'wording' of descriptive rules. For instance, instead of the descriptive statement 'An NP may be instantiated by the sequence of a determiner followed by a noun' we may formulate the generative statement 'To generate/create an NP take a determiner and let it be followed by a noun'. By and large, we can understand rewrite rules as reformulations of descriptive rules; the former can be mapped onto the latter[32].

This also holds true for newer kinds of rewrite rules formulated in X'-Theory, instigated by Chomsky's influential 1970 paper "Remarks on Nominalization" and further developed in Jackendoff's (1977) monograph *X' Syntax. A Study of Phrase Structure* and has since then been subject to major revisions by other researchers. The following account of X'-Theory is based on Haegeman's (^{2}1994) *Introduction to Government and Binding Theory*. The description will dispense with unnecessary technicalities but nevertheless hopes to provide information on the basic claims and underlying arguments of X'-Theory.

The major achievement of X'-Theory is that it has shown that all phrases in English grammar[33] can be described by a set of three phrase structure rules, as follows (Haegeman ^{2}1994: 104):

XP → Spec; X'
X' → X'; YP*
X' → X; YP,

where X refers to any lexical category, YP to complement phrases and Spec to the so-called specifier; the asterisk in the second rewrite rule shows that more than one X' of this kind can occur in one XP.

---

32 As is well known, there are major differences as regards the content of the rules in, say, the standard version of generative-transformational grammar and the rules as they are found, for instance, in the descriptive *Comprehensive Grammar of the English Language* by Quirk et al. (1985). An example would be the consistent binary branching in the former as opposed to the 'flatter' tree structures in the latter. But such differences do not undermine the general fact that both kinds of rules can be mapped onto each other.

33 This set of phrase structure rules actually seems to be universal, but we are only interested in its relevance for the English language.

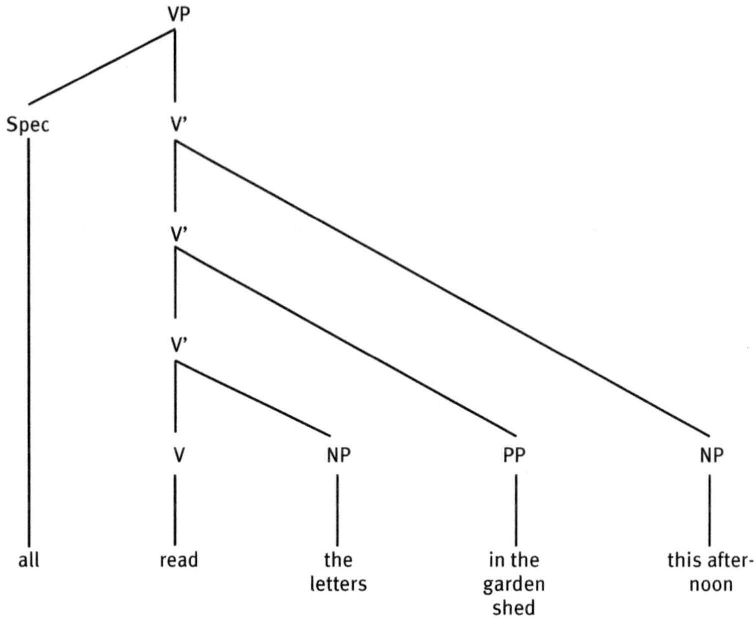

Figure 4.4: The X'-schema for *all read the letters in the garden shed this afternoon* (Haegeman [2]1994: 92) (with kind permission of Wiley publishers).

As an example consider the English VP in the sentence *The detectives have all read the letters in the garden shed this afternoon* (see Haegeman [2]1994: 87-95).

The same basic structural description can be used for NPs, APs and PPs. In addition, X'-Theory can also be applied to sentence structure. Main clauses are assumed to consist of a subject NP, an inflectional element that carries tense and agreement distinctions and a VP. In a similar fashion, subordinate clauses can be accommodated in the same schema (see Haegeman [2]1994: 116-123) so that X'-Theory allows the description of all phrases and clauses with regard to a very small set of three rewrite rules. As I have said above, X'-Theory is an extension of the traditional part of the base component, that is, it is another version of the rewrite rules of grammar (cf. Ouhalla 1994: 3). Also, it was claimed above that rewrite rules essentially are a mere reformulation of descriptive statements about the possible instantiations of a class of linguistic objects. In principle, it should thus be possible to describe the more complex rewrite rules of X'-Theory with the help of the model developed in chapter 2.

The major difference between the rewrite rules of the Standard Model and X'-Theory lies in the degree of abstraction that the two models apply. In the previous chapter I have claimed that the categories of linguistic theory are the outcome of an iterative process of two alternating processes of abstraction: 1) 'abstraction away from data', and 2) 'description of data through classes'. From this perspective, the difference between the rewrite rules of the Standard Model and those captured in X'-Theory can simply be regarded as the result of a further step in this iterative process of abstraction: The different classes of phrases are the result of abstracting away from the individual head words and define phrases with regard to the kind of head word that is used, i.e. noun, verb, adjective and preposition. As a result we arrive at 'new' classes of objects, namely NP, VP, AP, and PP, i.e. classes that are more or less similar to the ones that are found in traditional descriptive grammars. In X'-Theory, these new structures, again, are submitted to a further step of 'abstraction away from the data'. The study of the new phrases reveals that all of them show the same basic structure: the head is preceded by the specifier and followed by the complement (at least in English). The next (and the new) step of abstraction, ignores the different classes of possible heads, specifiers, and complements and groups them together under the highly general class of XP. Note that this new class 'XP' also allows a new view on the data: Structures that hitherto have not been treated as phrases are now treated as such. Main and subordinate clauses apparently can be accounted for by the same descriptive apparatus. Here we find the second step of abstraction in operation, 'description of data through classes'. To conclude, we can state that to a large extent the description provided by X'-Theory does not differ in kind from the accounts found in descriptive grammar. The difference lies in the degree of abstraction away from the data, but even the highly abstract X'-descriptions follow Langacker's content requirement. Section 6.1 will discuss whether descriptions of such a high level of abstractness make sense in a model that aims for cognitive plausibility.

Different in that respect are transformations in generative-transformational grammar, since they do not described language structures but relations between language structures. Such relations do not serve to describe a string of data and do not follow the content requirement. Therefore, they are not relevant for the present usage-based model of language. The same holds for more recent approaches in the transformational-generative paradigm, which show a decisive shift away from constructions (which eventually can be related to instantiations in actual language) to a description of abstract processes that are assumed to be part of the native speaker's competence: "the notion of construction type has quite disappeared, being atomized into the various subtheories" (Brown

1991: 493; see also Cook & Newson [2]1996: 48). Among these subtheories we find X'-Theory, which accounts for the phrase structure of the deep structure representation, Theta theory, which regulates the assignment of case, the transformational component, which explains how constituents may move, the Case Filter, which may provide reasons why constituents will have to move, and so on.[34] Such kinds of abstraction are entirely different from the abstractions we find in traditional descriptive grammars.

4.2 Applying the model to rules and units of grammar

This chapter explores how the phenomena discussed in the previous section can conveniently be described with the help of the network. It will be shown how the model accommodates aspects of the language system that are completely regular, while at the same time, with the same descriptive apparatus, being able to capture the less regular aspects of language, those areas that traditionally are conceived of as being fuzzy, indeterminate, and gradient.

Section 2.2.2.10 has shown how the network evolves and changes by the introduction of new nodes, new links and by adapting the degree to which nodes and links are entrenched in the cognitive system. The present section will discuss how network structures of language are formed on the basis of an analysis of natural language data. In section 2.2.2 it was emphasized that we aim at a model of the language system which is cognitively plausible in that it evolves in a fashion that is similar to processes that might be at work in language acquisition. That is, when in the following I speak of the formation of classes, structures and rules, these formation processes can be understood as statements about language acquisition, though not very detailed ones. The focus lies in showing that the present network model evolves on the basis of processes that are in consonance with basic human cognitive mechanisms. The fact that these processes can be related to language acquisition merely lends further credibility to the claim that the present network model is plausible from a cognitive point of view.

All the aspects that show up in the network model can be traced back to the application of basic cognitive mechanisms to strings of word forms. It is important to note that these mechanisms are in no way specific to language but

34 Note that the Minimalist Program tries, at least to some extent, to dispense with some of these modules (see Cook & Newson [2]1996: 326-344 for details).

are at the basis of any kind of human cognition. The present approach thus follows what Lakoff (1990: 40) has called the 'cognitive commitment', i.e. "a commitment to make one's account of human language accord with what is generally known about the mind and brain, from other disciplines". That is, "language and linguistic organization should reflect general cognitive principles rather than cognitive principles that are specific to language" (Evans and Green 2006: 41). In its restriction to a fairly small set of basic cognitive mechanisms, the present model is similar to a number of other accounts in the cognitive framework. Tomasello (2003a: 3-4), for instance, claims that only two sets of skills are needed to explain language-acquisition processes, namely skills related to 'intention-reading' and skills related to 'pattern-finding'. Similarly, Langacker (2000b: 3-5) in a discussion of dynamic usage-based models identifies a small number of "basic and very general psychological phenomena that are essential to language but not limited to it". These are 'abstraction', "the emergence of structure through reinforcement of the commonality inherent in multiple experiences", 'association', "in which one kind of experience is able to evoke another", 'entrenchment', the assumption that "[t]he occurrence of psychological events leaves some kind of trace that facilitates their re-occurrence", and 'comparison' "the ability to compare two structures and detect any discrepancy between them", and". The present model makes use of similar mechanisms.

The first mechanism is that of 'categorization' on the basis of similarities and dissimilarities between events (see section 3.1)[35]. Word forms, for instance, can be similar or dissimilar with regard to semantic, formal, distributional or situational criteria, which may lead to the formation of classes of words. Classes usually only exist in contradistinction to other classes (a well-known structuralist position). For instance, the semantic class described by the feature [+female] is only established due to the fact that there are elements described by the feature [-female]. This mechanisms groups together what Langacker (2000b) above refers to as 'abstraction' and 'comparison'.

The second mechanism employed in the present framework is that of 'associating' an event A with an event B[36]. This mechanism follows the assumption

35 Also see Gasser and Smith (1998: 272-273) for the fundamental role of "similarity-based associative learning" and Taylor's (2008: 60) claim that "[t]he very structure of language itself is a matter of categorization."

36 'Event', here, is used in a very general way: it can refer to non-linguistic aspects like movements, actions, sensations, etc., to aspects related to language, such as words, sounds, mean-

that "any two things that consistently occur together are likely to become associated" (Lamb 1998: 271). As in the case of categorization, association is also tied to the notion of distinction: association is based on distinctively frequent co-occurrence, not just frequent co-occurrence. For instance, although all birds breathe, breathing is not associated (in the sense it is used here) with birds, since breathing co-occurs equally frequently with a large number of other species. In contrast, the feature of wings is associated with birds.

Recall from section 2.2.2.10 that a distinction was drawn between 'direct association' and 'indirect association'. The first related to the actual co-occurrence of events, such as the predicative use of a negated form (*un-*) of and adjective. This would lead to the co-activation of the two respective nodes in the network and the creation of a direct connection between the two: the two events have become associated. Nodes can also be indirectly associated. For instance, the predicative use and the attributive use of an adjective form rule each other out, which means that the respective nodes are never co-activated at the same time. As a consequence, there is no direct (excitatory) connection between the two. Yet still, they are connected indirectly through the nodes that represent individual adjectives and the category node |*ADJECTIVE*| (see figure 3.5 in section 3.1).

The role of 'entrenchment' is different from that of the other two mechanisms. It is at the same time more and less basic than categorization and association; more basic, since categorization and association depend on frequency (the experiential correlate of entrenchment) to come into being; less basic, since categorization and association are the general structure-building mechanisms, while entrenchment influences the accessibility of such structures during processing.

4.2.1 The formation and representation of classes

In section 3.1 it was shown how the progression from data to description is essentially based on a two-step process of reiterated abstractions. Abstraction away from irrelevant aspects leads to the formation of classes, which then can serve to describe data from a new angle, thus leading to yet other classes of elements. The formation of classes leads to a twofold reduction of complexity of

ing, and also to events in the brain, such as the activation of particular neurons in the brain. In the present approach, 'event' will mostly refer to the activation of nodes in the network.

primary data. Firstly, it abstracts away from irrelevant aspects of primary data. For instance, the human brain does not have to keep track of all the different kinds of birds, but instead can create one large class *BIRD* which is homogeneous enough to allow generalizations that are true for all or most members of that class. For instance, the human brain does not have to store the feature 'lays eggs' for each individual kind of bird but only has to store this once for the whole class. Related to this is the second kind of reduction of complexity. This is based on Rosch's (1978) psychological principle 'perceived world structure', which makes reference to the basically associative and correlational structure of the world around us. According to this principle, classes are formed whenever patterns of co-occurrence of features are witnessed on a regular basis. The formation of a class or category is the outcome of an association of these features. The existence of one feature of a particular class makes the occurrence of other features of the same class highly probable. It is here that the reduction of complexity lies. If in the jungle I meet an animal with a more or less orange and white fur with black stripes, four feet and a tail, I can be sure that this animal also has sharp teeth and claws and is a predator without a need to check whether these features are actually given. In a similar vein categorization allows an organism to predict relevant features on the basis of incomplete data. It seems reasonable to assume that linguistic categorization makes use of the same advantage. According to Taylor (2008: 59-60), "language does not present itself to us as an unstructured set of equiprobable elements. Words tend to select their context, constructions tend to select their lexical content, and semantic structures tend to select their syntactic and lexical realizations." For instance, if at the beginning of a sentence I encounter the definite article, I can be certain that this definite article introduces an NP (see Kimball's 1973: 29 parsing principle 'New Nodes'), which, most likely, will serve as the subject of the clause. I will also know that this NP makes reference either to an entity encountered before or to some aspect of my world knowledge. All these bits of knowledge depend on the category 'NP' that is part of the language system and on the fact that this category is based on what Rosch (1978b) refers to as the "correlational structure" of the world, in this case: the language world.

From a very basic point of view, categorization is the result of perceiving similarities and dissimilarities of given units. These similarities can be of many different kinds ranging, as pointed out above, from semantic, formal, and distributional to situational criteria or a mixture of these.

As another example let us consider again the category of adjectives that has to some extent been discussed in section 2.2.2.10 with regard to how learning happens in the network model, namely the association of features relating to the adjective HAPPY. Other adjectives (e.g. FRIENDLY) will contribute to the association of these features. As a consequence, the five nodes representing adjective features will be more strongly connected to each other than they will be to the individual adjective nodes. That is, the association of the feature nodes is not the result of the co-occurrence of adjective features in the use of one individual adjective like HAPPY but it emerges from the experience of usage patterns of many adjectives (see section 3.1). This is an important point because it is here that the notion of abstraction comes in: to each of the individual adjectives a number of other nodes are connected in the network, e.g. important collocations or the individual word forms. However, these are not co-activated frequently enough together with the five feature nodes to become part of the 'sub-network' of features related to adjectives. That is, the five adjective features, in Rosch's words, are part of the correlational structure of the (linguistic) world, whereas other features of individual adjectives are not part of these correlations. The network, in creating the category *ADJECTIVE* (by associating and linking the five feature nodes), abstracts away from these features, i.e. in Langacker's (2000a: 93) words: the "abstractive process 'filters out' those facets of the individual experiences which do not recur." Above it was said that categorization is the result of perceiving similarities. This is exactly what happens in the network: 'perceiving similarities' means that different stimuli or events trigger the activation of identical portions of the network. These identical parts become deeply entrenched and their individual nodes become connected very strongly. Other nodes that are connected to individual adjective nodes will not be part of this closely connected substructure. As was shown in section 3.1, this process of abstraction is not in any way a 'conscious' decision of some 'authority' somewhere hidden in the network. Abstraction and categorization simply emerge as a result of the nature of the network and the processes that go on in the network. Figure 4.5 below shows the category *ADJECTIVE* in the network.

What figure 4.5 still lacks is a link between |HAPPY| and |*ADJECTIVE*|. This connection will be established over time because any time *happy* is used in one of the five ways represented by the feature nodes, the nodes |HAPPY| and |*ADJECTIVE*| will be co-activated. The use of the form *unhappy*, for instance, will activate the node |prefix *un-*| and the node |HAPPY|. From the node |prefix *un-*| activation will spread to the node |*ADJECTIVE*|, resulting in a co-activation of |HAPPY| and |*ADJECTIVE*|. Repeated co-activation will result in a link between the two nodes: the organism has learned that HAPPY is an adjective. In the same way the network will learn that FRIENDLY is an adjective.

The connection of a given adjective to the adjective node also explains the 'creative' use of an adjective, i.e. the use of an adjective in a way in which it has

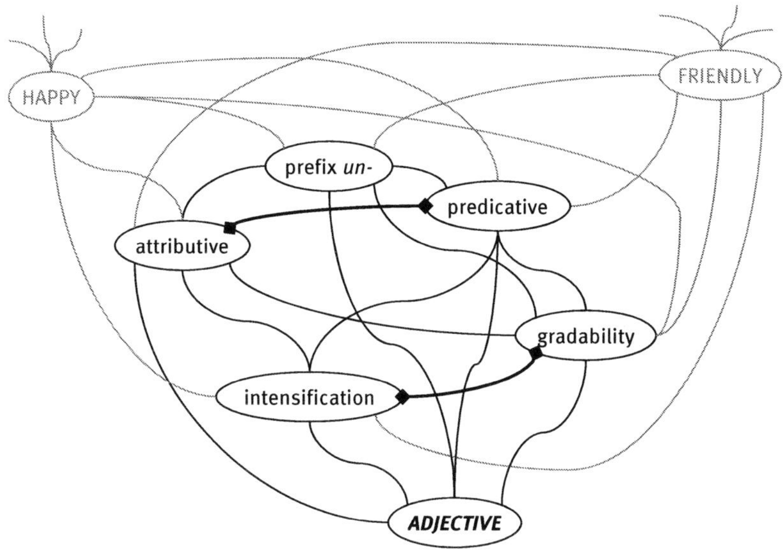

Figure 4.5: Features and instantiations of the class *ADJECTIVE*. (= Figure 3.5, repeated here for reasons of convenience)

not been heard or read before. Let us assume the organism has repeatedly encountered forms of the adjective HEALTHY in predicative and attributive use, in graded form and with intensification by *very*. These experiences will lead to the creation of a connection between the node |*ADJECTIVE*| and the node |HEALTHY|. Once this connection has been established, the formation of the form *unhealthy* is licensed since it is part of the organism's knowledge about the way adjectives are used. From now on, the organism may produce the form *unhealthy*, even though this form has never been encountered before.

To conclude this section let us take a look at the question of classes and their subclasses. In section 3.1 the notion of 'instantiation' was claimed to be the most fundamental relation in linguistic description. It is related to Halliday's (1961) scale of delicacy, which captures 'degrees of detail' in description. In section 2.1.6 I showed how the ability of a system to apply different degrees of detail will enhance processing in the system. At some points the processor may be in need of very detailed information. At other points only general information may be needed while more detailed information would be useless and only burden the processor. Therefore the concepts 'instantiation' and 'degrees of detail' should be implemented in the present network model. Usually this takes the shape of hierarchies of some kind or another. Examples are Collins and Quillian (1969) and Hudson (2007a) whose networks make use of hierarchical assemblies of nodes connected through ISA (= is a(n instance of)) relations (e.g. the oak ISA a tree). Such hierarchies, in my view, entail a number of problems.

The first problem is to decide on the ranking of subclasses. Taking pronouns as an example, for some questions and for some accounts it might be useful to distinguish on a first level between demonstrative, relative, etc. pronouns. For each of these subclasses further subclasses can then be created on the basis of the distinction between singular and plural pronouns. For other questions and other accounts, however, a different arrangement might be more useful, starting off with a first distinction of the two subclasses *SINGULAR* and *PLURAL PRONOUNS*, which are then further distinguished. As discussed in section 3.1, there is no intrinsic way of describing and categorising data. Groups or categories can be formed on the basis of any feature or set of features found in the data, as Harris (1954: 146) makes clear: "language can be structured in respect to various independent features", leading to different ways of categorising the same data. A similar intuition is captured by Quirk et al.'s (1985: 90) notion of 'multiple analysis': "[t]here are occasions [...] when [...] alternative analyses seem to be needed, on the grounds that some of the generalizations that have to be made require one analysis, and some require another." This 'multiple analysis' is inherent in the present model; it follows as a consequence from the nature of the processes that are involved in the evolution and the functioning of the network. The present network model is flexible enough to allow different ways of categorization to coexist alongside each other, as will be shown presently.

Another problem discussed in the previous chapter was the question of generalization: at what point do we decide not to come up with a further rule to describe a phenomenon or with a class or category to capture similarities between entities. As Quirk et al. (1985: 15) state, such decisions are often arbitrary, but a strictly hierarchical model has to make those decisions.

Finally, in hierarchical models it is not clear where the information of subordinate categories is stored. Goldberg (1995: 74) distinguishes between 'virtual copying' (information is inferred from superordinate categories) and 'real copying' models (information is stored in all categories; see section 2.2.2.8). I follow a different approach where hierarchies and sub-categories are created online, as it were. In this way, we can solve the above problems.

The instantiation relation can be understood in two ways which relate to the notions of extensional and intensional definition of sets. The first refers to definition by listing the elements in a set (or the members of a class). From this

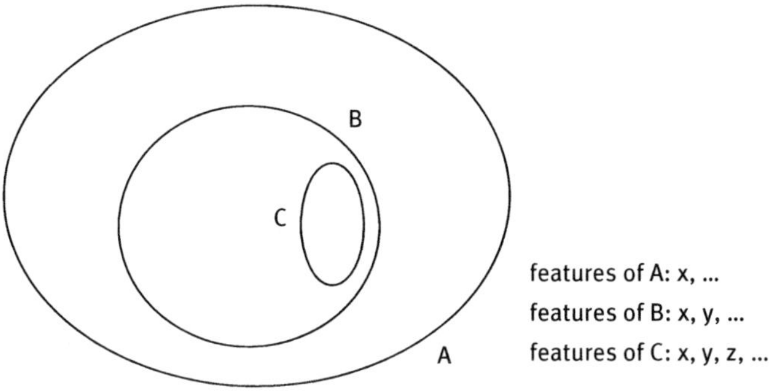

Figure 4.6: 'Instantiation' from an extensional and an intensional perspective.

perspective, instantiations are seen as subsets of a larger set, as shown on the left-hand side of figure 4.6. The second, intension, refers to definition by listing defining features. From this perspective, the instantiations of a particular class all share one or more criterial features but may have other irrelevant features. Subsets (or subclasses), i.e. instantiations of instantiations, are defined by adding further features which must be given. The extensional and the intensional definition are inversely related (cf. Lipka 2002: 65). Large sets have many members but few defining features, small sets have few members but many defining features, as shown in figure 4.6.

In figure 4.6 all elements in C are instantiations of B, which are instantiations of A. That is, the set C is a proper subset of set B, which is a proper subset of set A. From the intensional perspective, we find that all elements in C are defined by three necessary features, namely x, y, and z. All of the elements in C are also elements in B: they fulfil the criterion for membership in B, since they all show the features x and y. The set B also has elements which do not have the feature z, which is why B is a superset to set C. All the elements of B are also members of the set A, since all of them share the one defining feature x.

The network model advocated here follows the intensional definition of sets. At the same time, as described in section 2.2.2.6, the present model is partly distributed, i.e. major categories are represented by a specific node, while smaller subcategories do not necessarily have their own node but are created online through the co-activation of several feature nodes together with a superordinate category node. Let us consider the class of pronouns as illustration. This class includes a (fairly large) number of word forms, such as *I, you, this, mine, that, yours, who,* etc. In the present network model this is expressed

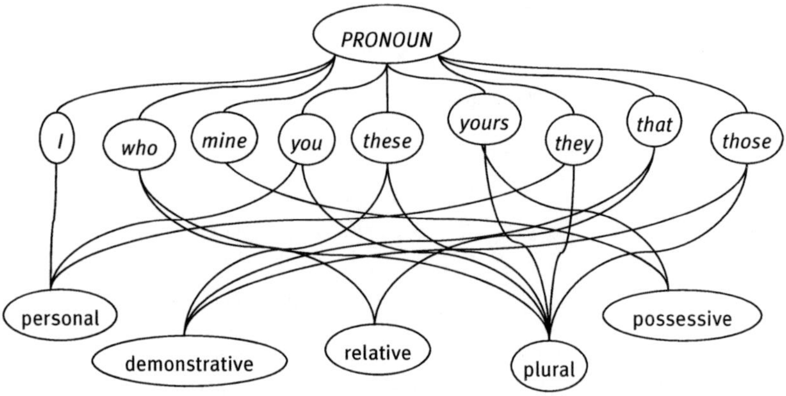

Figure 4.7: Pronouns and their subclasses in the network (some pronouns and features have been omitted for reasons of presentational clarity).

through a link between the node |*PRONOUN*| and all of the word forms which belong to that word class. Now there are a number of features that are relevant for pronouns, such as 'demonstrative', 'possessive', 'relative', 'personal', 'plural', and so on. Each of these features is also linked to every word form that exhibits this feature. Figure 4.7 represents this situation.

As stated above, the information about classes in this network lies in the (co-)activation of nodes at a particular point in time. The class of pronouns, for instance, is represented by an active node |*PRONOUN*|. This activation spreads to the individual word forms and activates all of these to the same extent. The class of demonstrative pronouns is defined by another activation pattern, namely the co-activation of |*PRONOUN*| and |demonstrative|. Again, the activation of the |*PRONOUN*| node spreads to all the word forms that are connected to this node. Further activation spreads from the |demonstrative| node. Within the set of word forms that is activated at this point in time, some are activated more strongly, since they receive activation from two nodes. These most strongly activated nodes (henceforth: nodes with a relative activation maximum) are the demonstrative pronouns. In a similar fashion, we represent relative pronouns or distinguish plural from singular pronouns. The more feature nodes are added, the smaller the classes, i.e. the number of nodes with a relative activation maximum, become. The class of plural demonstrative pronouns is defined by the co-activation of |*PRONOUN*|, |demonstrative| and |plural| which results in relative maximal activation for the nodes representing |*these*| and |*those*|.

The strength of this way of representation is that we do not have to make a decision as to the relative importance of the individual defining criteria. We also do not have to decide how the class of pronouns is best segmented: is the distinction between singular and plural primary or that between personal, interrogative, demonstrative, and so on? Furthermore, with this approach we do not have to distinguish between 'virtual copying' and 'real copying'. For instance, the nodes representing the characteristics of pronouns are immediately connected to the node |*PRONOUN*|. No matter whether the general concept 'pronoun' or the more specific concept 'demonstrative plural pronoun' is active, the information connected to the node |*PRONOUN*| is accessed equally fast in both cases. This is not the case in a fully local network representation, e.g. in the style of Collins and Quillian (1969). In a network of this kind, activation would have to spread all the way up to the top of the hierarchy to get access to the information that is stored for pronouns in general. Processing is forced to proceed in a serial fashion. The present network is much more efficient in this respect, since it allows the parallel accessing of the individual bits of information. It, therefore, appears to be more in line with Lamb's (1998: 95) claim that a model of the language system "must represent a competence to perform."

Most importantly, this way of representing classes and subclasses enables us to implement into the network model the notion of 'degrees of detail' in a very elegant fashion. For instance, if a clause starts with the pronoun *they*, this will activate the |plural| node. It is this bit of information that is relevant for the processing of the rest of the clause, i.e. subject-verb concord: the activation of the |plural| node will also spread to all plural verb forms. Thus the possible verb forms in the clause have already been reduced by 50% without even having seen or heard the verb that actually occurs in the clause. Maybe the advantage becomes most obvious in speech, where the distinction of plural or singular might be difficult to detect in the form of the verb alone. If the auditive input activates both the singular and plural form of a verb, the spreading activation of the feature 'plural' will add to the overall activation of the plural form of the verb. Note that the same will happen if the clause starts with *these* or *those*. In both cases, the additional information, i.e. 'personal' with *they* and 'demonstrative' with the latter two, is irrelevant for the form of the verb and does not impede the spreading of this piece of information. Also, the distinction between 'near' and 'far' encoded in *these* and *those*, respectively is irrelevant as far as the verb is concerned.

4.2.2 Gradience in the network model

In section 4.1 three kinds of gradience were distinguished: degrees of representativity, fuzzy boundaries and multiple or indeterminate membership. Consider figure 4.8 below.

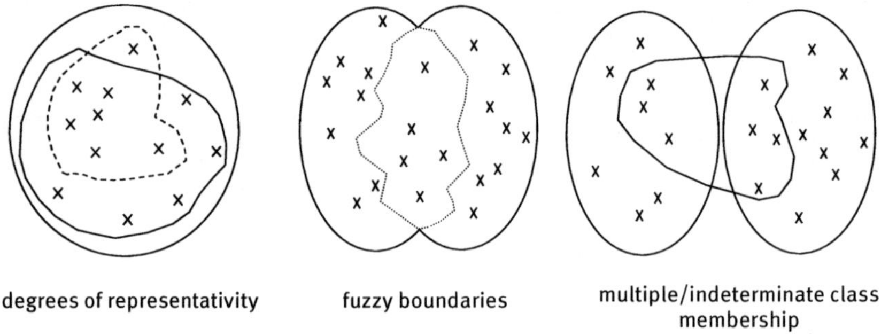

Figure 4.8: Gradience in linguistics: more and less representative members, fuzzy category boundaries and multiple membership. (= Figure 4.3, repeated here for convenience)

The first type of gradience is what Aarts (2007) calls 'subsective gradience'. He writes:

> Subsective Gradience [...] is the phenomenon whereby a particular set of elements displays a categorical shading in prototypicality from a central core to a more peripheral boundary. (Aarts 2007: 97)

'Categorial shading in prototypicality' is best understood with regard to two aspects. The first relates to the features that define a category, the second to the degree to which members of the category exhibit these features[37]. The central concept regarding the first aspect is that of 'cue validity', i.e. the extent to which a particular feature is indicative of the whole category. The feature 'has feathers', for instance, is more indicative of the category *BIRD* than the feature 'can fly', because only birds have feathers but it is not only birds that can fly. A model of the language system should be able to accommodate such insights into the definitorial structure of categories. As we have seen in the previous section, the category *ADJECTIVE* can be defined with regard to five central properties name-

37 The pairs 'element'/'set', 'member'/'class' or 'member'/'category' can be used interchangeably.

ly attributive and predicative position, intensification, gradability and prefixation with *un-*. It can be expected that these features are not equally typical of the category at issue. A look at corpus data is thus useful in this respect. Let us consider the five major word classes of English, i.e. adjectives, nouns, verbs, adverbs and prepositions. To what extent do these show the five properties central to adjectives? The following examples are all taken from ICE-GB; some examples have been modified slightly.

(2) *predicative*
(2a) I was **lucky** (S1A-001_090)
I find it **fascinating** (S1A-002_035)
(2b) Oh yes this is a really good **idea** (S1A-002_132)
Oh she's called **Jennifer** (S1A-006_122)
(2c) He's away **all** next week (S1A-005_132)
It annoys me to see it **there**. (S1A-007_068)
(2d) He's **on** the toaster (S1A-032_050)
What did you see as missing **from** other activities (S1A-001_001)

(3) *attributive*
(3a) But that's a **natural** part of art (S1A-001_081)
(3b) one or two **eighteenth-century** books (S1A-013_019)
(3c) **Very** Normandy yes (S1A-009_134)

(4) *intensification by very*
(4a) A **very narrow** field (S1A-0012_037)
(4b) **Very Los Angeles** (S1A-041_056)
(4c) **Very nicely** done (S1A-009_194)
(4d) It's **very near** Astor College (S1A-014_227)
(4e) I was **very impressed** (S1B-047_139)[38]

(5) *prefix un-*[39]
(5a) Well I think it's a bit **unreasonable** (S1A-006_323)

---

38 In cases like these, the annotators of ICE-GB are not consistent. In some cases, for instance, *very impressed* is parsed as an adjective premodified by an adverb in other cases it is parsed as a verb that is premodified by an adverb.

39 I am aware of the fact that the aspect of prefixation involves a couple of theoretical issues concerning the internal morphological structure of complex word forms and the productivity of the prefix *un-* with different word classes.

(5b) There was a mood of numbness and **unreality** (W2C-013_002))
(5c) there is a sort of community centre that hovers **uneasily** in a disused church (S1A-056_122))
(5d) **Unlike** the Mascot 3 design language (W2a-038_135)
(5e) so we **unpacked** our stuff and trooped in (S1A-036_149)

(6) *gradability*
(6a) the question is **bigger** than that (S1A-001_054)[40]
(6b) But she obviously hasn't the **faintest** idea (S1A-006_132)
(6c) that closeness makes a **more interesting** choreography (S1A-002_046)[41]
(6d) Not the **most romantic** reason in the world (S1A-050_198)
(6e) The **most general-purpose** of pencils is HB (W2D-016_022)
(6f) But it's much **more Norse**[42]
(6g) you can book it up a week **later** or something (S1A-025_247)[43]
(6h) **worst** affected is likely to be the yellow-bellied sea-snake (W2B-029_104)
(6i) dBase four is **more widely** available actually (S1A-029_341)[44]
(6j) The fovea's the **most densely** innervated part (S1B-015_170)
(6k) **more on** the left than on the right (W2D-019_054)
(6l) The soft and acid water areas are **most at risk** from lead (W2D-012_023)[45]
(6m) Those who stay at home are often **more tempted** by revenge (W2E-007_036)[46]
(6n) Goldman is **most perturbed** by what happened to Mrs Lennox(W2F-016_074)

40 The search also included nominal adjectives (NADJ). Comparative and superlative together are 2,655 cases.
41 The FTF searched for *more/most* as intensifying adverbs which did not have to precede the Adj immediately. This way cases that contained intervening materials was also included, e.g. *more sort of translucent* (S1A-085:148) (8 cases). The total of cases was 1,108; this included 55 cases of nominal adjective, e.g. *There are weeks when bitty things are the most productive* (S1B_012:010).
42 Cases of doubt like the following were left in, since I wanted to follow the ICE-GB scheme as much as possible.
43 *More* and *most* as comparative and superlative adverbs were not counted → 919 (with them: 2,711)
44 The string is basically the same as in the case of adjective and nouns. Results for graded adverbs: 251.
45 Since the adverbial premodifier did not have to immediately precede the preposition, cases like *more or less at this point here* (S2A-032:012) were also included.
46 Since the adverbial premodifier did not have to immediately precede the verb, cases like *more or less forgotten* (S1A-057:087) were also included.

Table 4.1: Absolute and relative frequencies of major word classes exhibiting features related to adjectives.
*The numbers marked by a bar, ', are rounded on the basis of a sample of approximately 100 tokens of words beginning in *un-* in ICE-GB that were analysed manually to weed out forms like *unitary*.

	attributive	predicative	intens. *very*	gradability	prefix *un-**
Adjective	42,582/95.6%	14,968/42.7%	1,712[47]/78.3%	3,798/55.8%	1,063'[48]/68.5%
Noun	204/0.5%	9,950/28.4%	6/0.3%	2[49]/0.0%	193'/12.4%
Verb	0/0.00%	0/0.00	3/0.1%	16/0.2%	69'/4.5%
Adverb	1,748/3.9%	1,662/4.7%	458/20.9%	2,955/43.4%	191'/12.3%
Preposition	0/0.00%	5,750/16.4%	8[50]/0.4%	39[51]/0.6%	36/2.3%
Others		2,695 / 7.7%			
Total	**44,534**	**35,025**	**2,187**	**6,810**	**1,552**

Table 4.1 shows the frequencies with which the five major word classes exhibit properties that are thought of as being central to the category 'adjective'; figure 4.9 shows the representation of these facts in the network. The table makes clear that all of the five features are more or less typical of adjectives, although we see a fair amount of variation with relative frequencies ranging from 42.7% to 95.6%. These numbers, then, allow us to rank the five features under scrutiny with regard to their indicativeness of the category 'adjective', i.e. with regard to their cue validity. The attributive use is most indicative of the category 'adjective', followed by the features intensification by *very* and *un*-prefixation. Only

47 This number also includes 16 instances of nominal adjectives, e.g. *the very earliest*.
48 This number includes 25 instances of nominal adjectives prefixed by *un-*.
49 ICE-CUP produced a total of 8 hits, 6 of which were not worth including like *the more experience you get* (W1B-021:084).
50 The question is, of course, that it is not really clear whether we should regard *very* as modifying the preposition or the whole prepositional phrase (see also Quirk et al. 1985: 449). Given the huge difference between grading in adjectives and adverbs as opposed to prepositions, this problem does not have a lot of relevance for the present discussion.
51 In these 39 cases it is, of course, not really clear whether we should regard *more* and *most* as modifying the preposition or the whole prepositional phrase (see also Quirk et al. 1985: 449). Given the huge difference between grading in adjectives and adverbs as opposed to prepositions, this problem does not have a lot of relevance for the present discussion.

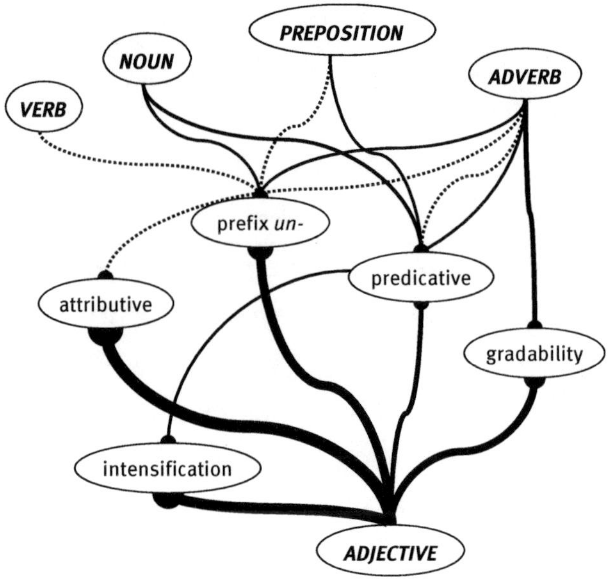

Figure 4.9: The representation of cue validity in the network (Relative frequencies below 1% have been ignored for reasons of presentational clarity).

slightly more than 50% of all graded word forms from the major word classes are adjectives and less than 50% of subject or object complements (i.e. predicative use) are actually realised by adjectives. Moreover, the feature gradability is almost as indicative of the category 'adverb' as of the category 'adjective', and nouns are responsible for almost one third of all predicative uses of the parts of speech in question. These last two features have a low cue validity, not only because the relative percentage of adjectives among the tokens are only around 50%, but also because the relative percentages of tokens from other word classes are also fairly high. Figure 4.9 shows how this situation is represented in the network model.

It is important to note that the connections between the features and the categories are uni-directional, i.e. they only tell us to what extent a particular use of a form leads us to expect a particular word-class category. In the same way that feathers are highly indicative of birds, an attributive use of a form is highly indicative of adjectives. In contrast to that, just like the ability to fly may hint at birds, insects or planes, predicative use may betray an adjective but also a noun and in very rare cases a preposition or an adverb.

Of course, the network also contains information on categories as such, i.e. it tells us which of the possible features related to a category are usually realised. This knowledge is similar to the knowledge that humans exploit when asked to list features that are typical of birds, e.g. having feathers, having a beak, the ability to fly and so on. ICE-GB contains 59,997 adjectives. Table 4.2 shows the absolute and relative frequencies of the realizations of the five features under scrutiny.

Table 4.2: Absolute and relative frequencies of realizations of features related to adjectives (N = 64,123[52]).
* The numbers marked by a bar, ', are rounded on the basis of a sample of approximately 100 tokens of words beginning in *un-* in ICE-GB that was analysed manually to weed out forms like *under* or *understand.*

	Attributive	Predicative	intens. *very*	gradability	prefix *un-*[53]
Adjective	42,582 / 66.4%	14,968 / 23.3%	1,712 / 2.7%	3,798 / 5.9%	1,063' / 1.7%

The frequencies in table 4.2 can be implemented into the present network model without any problems, as is shown in figure 4.10: the most frequently realised feature with adjectives is the attributive use, followed by predicative use. The three remaining features are not instantiated that often, as represented by the thin lines leading form the category node to the feature nodes.

It has repeatedly been stated in this study that a model of the language system "must represent a competence to perform" (Lamb 2000: 95). How can information like that shown in figure 4.10 contribute to performance? The advantage of this kind of information lies in the fact that once we have identified an entity as a member of a category, we know that features of that category are also likely to be relevant for the entity at issue. This knowledge is exploited during online processing. For instance, ICE-GB tells us that of those noun phrases that have a determiner, 91,088 have no kind of premodification, whereas 25,119 are premodified. That is, as soon as the processor encounters a deter-

52 The total of realizations of the five features in adjectives is higher than the number of adjectives in ICE-GB (59,997) because a given adjective may show more than one feature.

53 The numbers marked by asterisk are rounded on the basis of a sample of approximately 100 tokens of words beginning in *un-* in GBoP that was analysed manually to weed out forms like *under* or *understand*.

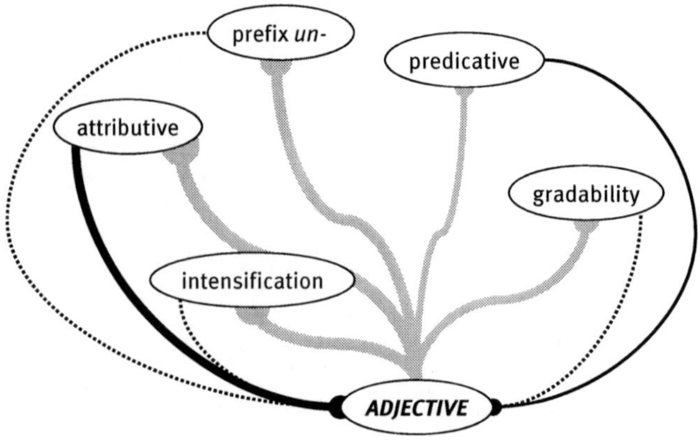

Figure 4.10: The category *ADJECTIVE* and its features.

miner (which will lead the processor to expect a noun phrase) different sets of noun phrase structures will start to become activated, with a strong bias towards non-premodified structures. Let us now assume that the word following the determiner is the intensifier *very*. This will lead to an activation of the node |intensification| in the above figure, which will spread to the node |*ADJECTIVE*| and activate that node. The node |*ADJECTIVE*| will, then, spread activation through the feature nodes to which it is connected. More specifically, activation will travel very fast to the node |attributive|, which will then pass on its activation to structures that are associated with this feature (these links are not shown in figure 4.10), i.e. premodified noun phrase structures. This aspect will be discussed in more detail in section 6.3.

So far we have focused on the first aspect of prototypicality, namely the degree to which features of a category are indicative of that category. The second aspect mentioned above concerns the representativity of the individual members of a category. This is usually defined with regard to the number of features that members of a class share. Those that share all features are at the centre of the given class, while those that share only some are at the periphery. Examples abound in the literature. In section 4.1 we have discussed Ross' (1973 [2004]) 'nouniness squish', which shows that syntactic constructions are 'nouny' to a stronger or a lesser extent, i.e. they exhibit more or less features typically associated with nouns. Let us here consider, once more, the syntactic category *ADJECTIVE*, as discussed in Aarts (2007; see Taylor 1998: 182-3 for a similar discussion). He explores the different degrees of adjective-hood of the adjectives *happy*, *thin*, *alive*, and *utter* by analysing them with regard to the five central properties of adjectives discussed above, i.e. attributive and predicative position, intensification, gradability and prefixation with *un-*. The four adjectives instantiate these features to varying degrees: While *happy* exhibits all of these criteria, *thin*, *alive*, and *utter* cannot be subjected to prefixation with *un-*. In addition, *alive* does not occur in attributive position (**an alive hamster*[54]), is difficult to grade (?*alive* - *more alive* - *most alive*), and the form *unalive* is not attested. *Utter* occurs in attributive position but fails to satisfy any of the other criteria. The association of a word form with the category adjective evolves by frequent co-activation of a feature of the category *ADJECTIVE* together with the word form node. Table 4.3 shows how often the 153 instantiations of HAPPY and the one instantiation of UTTER exhibit these features in ICE-GB.

Table 4.3: Absolute of realizations of adjective-features in HAPPY and UTTER.

	attributive	predicative	intens. *very*	gradability	prefix *un-*
HAPPY (n=153)	25	114	9	17	23
UTTER (n=1)	1	0	0	0	0

From table 4.3 it becomes clear that a given adjective does not exhibit adjectival features with equal likelihood. The connection between the feature node |predicative| and the node |HAPPY|, therefore, is a lot stronger than the connection between the node |HAPPY| and the other feature nodes. The connection between the node |UTTER| and the feature node |attributive| is weaker still.

From an active feature node activation will spread to the |*ADJECTIVE*| node which will lead to a co-activation of the |*ADJECTIVE*| node and the word form node and, eventually, to a connection between the word form node and the category node |*ADJECTIVE*| itself (as shown in section 3.2); the network has learned that the word form is an adjective. Since not all members of the category *ADJECTIVE* exhibit all of the features, a network representation needs to provide a mechanism to implement the override of features that are not inherited; these are realised by inhibitory connections in the present model (see section 2.2.2.9).

54 Note, however, that Aarts (2007: 107) provides one attested example of *alive* in attributive position: "Snow, who lives in Kentish Town, has an *alive* presence [...]."

By way of example, figure 4.11 shows how the adjectives UTTER and HAPPY are represented.

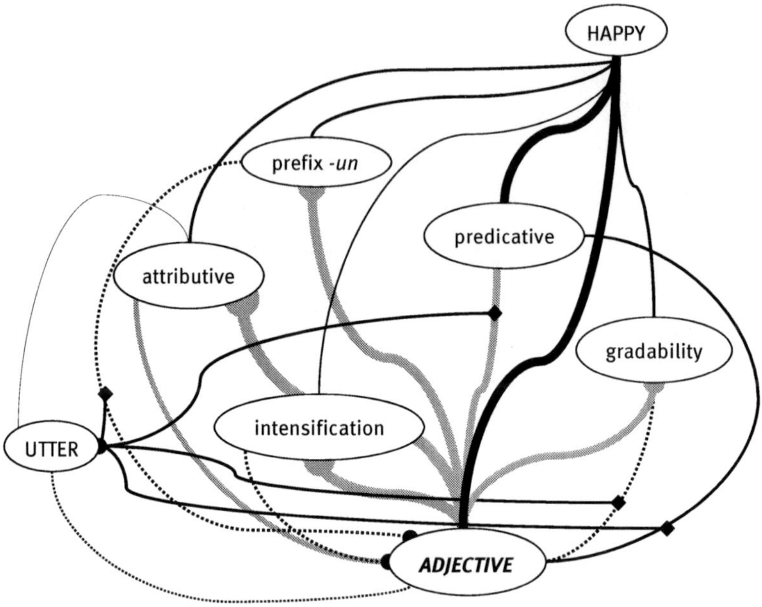

Figure 4.11: The representation of the adjectives UTTER and HAPPY.

As can be seen in the figure 4.11, the node |HAPPY| is strongly connected to the category node, whereas |UTTER| is only connected very weakly. The figure also represents the differences in frequencies with which the two adjectives exhibit the five features in a representative corpus. The adjective *utter* does not have any connections to feature nodes apart from the node |attributive|. In addition to that, there are also inhibitory connections extending from the node |UTTER|. These are important because without them the activation of the node |UTTER| would spread through the |*ADJECTIVE*| node to all the feature nodes of adjectives, which would mean, for instance, that *utter* could be used predicatively and that it could be intensified by *very*, and so on.

Why is UTTER not categorised as a noun? After all, the attributive function is also a function of nouns. The network model provides a natural explanation through the feature of competition (see section 2.2.2.5): The feature 'attributive' is more strongly connected to adjectives than to nouns (see table 4.1 above), which means that the connection between the feature node and the word-class node is stronger for the first than the second. This leads to a faster spreading of activation from the node |attributive| to the node |*ADJECTIVE*| than from the same node to the node |*NOUN*|. The adjective node, as soon as it is activated, will block the activation of competing nodes, in this case the node noun, with the help of inhibitory connections, so that the only co-activation pattern is that of the nodes |UTTER| and |*ADJECTIVE*| and not |UTTER| and |*NOUN*|. Hence, UTTER is seen as an adjective rather than as a noun.

In this context a problem that has been raised by Croft (2001: 34-44) and is discussed in Aarts (2007) deserves mention:

> If we say that a word like *utter* is an adjective by virtue of the fact that it can occur prenominally, although not in other adjective positions [...], then we also need to call *boy* in *boy actor* an adjective, as its distributional pattern is exactly the same as that of *utter* [...].. (Aarts 2007: 130)

This is, of course, only true if we focus on this single occurrence of *boy* in *boy actor*. Any corpus will yield a large number of instances where *boy* is used in typical noun functions. Because of this the node |BOY| will have a much stronger connection to the node |*NOUN*| than the node |*ADJECTIVE*|, and the word will always be treated as a noun even though it occurs in a typical adjective position. *Utter*, in contrast, is only found in attributive position, which is most strongly connected to adjectives, and hence leads to an association of utter with the word class adjective.

The present representation of a category and its members, then, implements various aspects that are part of our knowledge of categories: firstly, it tells us which features define a category. Secondly, it shows to what extent the different features are indicative of that category. Thirdly, it provides information as to what extent the category as a whole exhibits the defining features. Fourthly, it represents to what extent the individual members exhibit the defining features. Fifthly, the present kind of representation reveals to what extent an individual member can be regarded as a prototypical exemplar of the category: a member is prototypical with regard to the mere frequency with which it is used as a member of that category, as is shown in the different strengths of the connections between the node |*ADJECTIVE*| and the nodes |UTTER| and |HAPPY|, respectively. In addition, and more in line with the usual understanding of prototypicality (i.e. in Aarts' (2007) sense of 'subsective gradience'), an adjective is prototypical in the sense that it shows all of the adjective-related features. That is, it is represented by a node that does not have any inhibitory links to the connections between the category adjective and its features, e.g. the adjective HAPPY. A peripheral adjective like UTTER, in contrast, has inhibitory links to a large portion of the category-feature connections. This is in line with Hudson (2007a: 24), who writes: "good members inherit all the default properties, worse members override some of them, and borderline members override so many that it is debatable whether they are members at all [...]."

While the concept 'degrees of representativity' (or 'subsective gradience') concerns the members within one class, the second kind of gradience, 'fuzzy boundaries', makes reference to the classes themselves; more specifically, to the fact that class boundaries are not clearly demarcated and that classes may shade into one another. A case in point is the distinction between adjectives and nouns. As we have seen in table 4.1 above there is no feature of adjectives that is not shown by members of the class noun. What we do find, though, is a large difference in the frequency with which most of these features are instantiated by nouns. With regard to absolute frequencies, only the number for predicative use of nouns and adjectives, are of a similar magnitude, i.e. 9,950 and 14,968, respectively. In case of the prefix *un-*, the number of adjective tokens is more than five times higher than the number of nouns that show this prefix. With all of the other features, adjectives outnumber nouns by a factor of more than 100. To some extent, then, there is an overlap of the two classes with regard to their defining features. On the other hand, nouns show features that are not shown by adjectives[55], namely the genitive *'s* or *'* and the plural marker *-s*. These are instantiated with frequencies of 3,233 and 42,821, respectively. Since these morphological markers are restricted to nouns they have a maximum cue validity for that category. The feature 'predicative' has a medium to low cue validity which is shown by the fact that 28.4% of all subject or object complements are realised by noun phrases headed by a noun. The other three adjective-related features are of a low or very low cue validity, ranging from 12.4% to 0.0% (see table 4.4).

(7) **genitive *'s***
(7a) do you remember the ones you took of **Napoleon's** bedroom (S1a-009_009)
(7b) a police officer had caught the **accused's** son. (W2B-020_020)

(8) **plural –*s***
(8a) So stir **yourselves** tonight. (W2E-003_078)

55 Or only in the peripheral case of nominal adjectives.

(8b) there were two **strands.** (S1A- 001_033)
(8c) there were **hundreds** of cabins (S1A-021_070)

(9) **subject**
(9a) that **language** was being channelled into a very narrow field (S1A-001_037)
(9b) Uhm **strong** is all right (S1A-046_270)

(10) **object (direct & indirect)**
(10a) this is a dance group which does not exclude **people** (S1A-001_030)
(10b) we need to give the restaurant **a ring** (S1A-071_342)
(10c) How else can one hope **to differentiate abnormal from normal** (W1A-007_087)
(10d) he had told unemployed **"if it isn't hurting it's not working"**. (W2C-018_064)

Table 4.4: Realization frequencies of adjective- and noun-related features

	attrib.	predic.	intens. *very*	grad.	prefix *un-**	gen. *'s*	plural *-s*	subj.	obj. (dir. & ind.)
Adj.	42,582	14,968	1,712[56]	3,798	1,063'[57]	5	0	223[58]	138
	95.6%	42.7%	78.3%	55.8%	68.5%	0.1%	0.0%	0.2%	0.2%
Noun	204	9,950	6	2[59]	193'	3,233	42,821[60]	39,081	32,628
	0.5%	28.4%	0.3%	0.0%	12.4%	96.5%	97.8%	36%	57.2%

Both adjectives and nouns can occur in attributive position, premodifying the head of a noun phrase, and predicatively, instantiating the complement slot in an SVC or SVOC clause. This kind of gradience, too, can be represented without any problems in the network model advocated here. Figure 4.12 shows the cate-

56 This number also includes 16 instances of nominal adjectives, e.g. *the very earliest*.
57 This number includes 25 instances of nominal adjectives prefixed by *un-*.
58 This number includes nominal adjectives. Other adjective do not occur in that function.
59 ICE-CUP produced a total of 8 hits, 6 of which were not worth including like *the more experience you get* (W1B-021:084).
60 This is an estimate on a sample of 90 plural nouns ending in –s. This sample was subjected to a manual analysis to exclude cases of plural nouns that ended in –s, with the *s* not being a plural marker. No instance was found.

gory 'adjective' with the five features discussed above and the category 'noun' which shares two of these features but also exhibits properties not shared by adjectives, namely plural and genitive marking[61] and the use of subject and direct or indirect object.

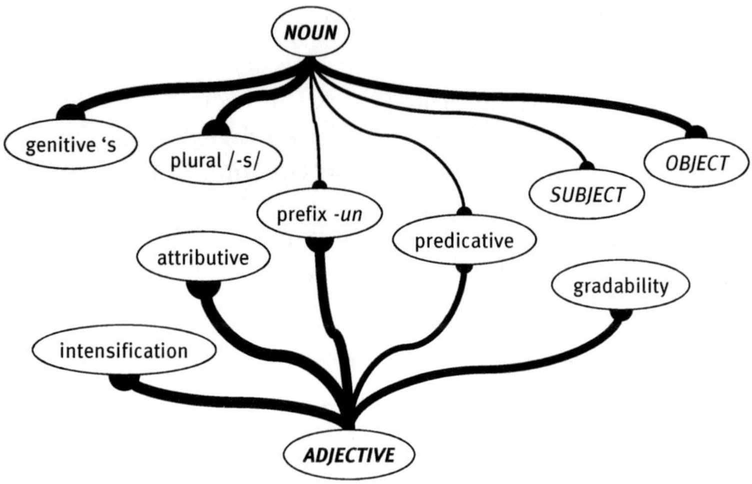

Figure 4.12: The fuzzy boundaries between adjectives and nouns in the network.

Finally, the third type of gradience, 'multiple membership', does not concern classes but individual items. While usually one item can be unambiguously assigned to one class, some items show features of two distinct and non-overlapping classes. This kind of gradience is what Aarts (2007) calls intersective gradience, which he defines as follows:

> IG [intersective gradience] involves two categories α and β, and obtains where there exists a set γ of elements characterized by a subset of α-like properties and a subset of β-like properties. (Aarts 2007: 79)

---

61 The feature 'plural *–s*' is realized as follows: The phoneme /s/ is indicative of nouns if it occurs at the end of the word (= activation of |END|) and node |plural| is activated. In that case, the connection of |/s/| to |*NOUN*| receives a very strong boost. If either |END| or |plural| is not activated, the activation of |/s/| will not lead to an activation of the node |*NOUN*|. 'genitive –s' is realized similarly.

The example given in section 4.1 was *off*, which shares properties both of the category *PREPOSITION* and *ADVERB*. Here, we will discuss the phenomenon of multiple membership with regard to nouns and verbs and the category *GERUND*, "one of the most troublesome areas of English grammar" (Hudson 2007a: 184; see Aarts 2008 for a critical overview of different approaches to the gerund). The problem, obviously, is that gerunds show features of both nouns and verbs. Let us consider Quirk et al.'s (1985: 1290-1291) examples of the form *painting* and their discussion thereof (also see Aarts 2007: 143-145 for a discussion and Hudson 2007a: ch. 4 for a discussion of gerunds in his network). Among the features typical of nouns we find the use of the definite article or a possessive determiner, premodification by an adjective and postmodification by a prepositional phrase. Typical verb-related features are the modification of the verb by an adverb and the use of the verb together with a direct object. From top to bottom, we see that this form *painting* shows clear noun-like behaviour at the top of the scale starting with example (11) below and clear verb-like behaviour (i.e. heading a clause) at the bottom of the scale, the instances in the middle exhibit properties of both nouns and verbs.

(11) The painting of Brown is as skilful as that of Gainsborough.
(12) Brown's deft painting of his daughter is a delight to watch.
(13) I dislike Brown's painting his daughter.[62]
(14) Brown's deftly painting his daughter is a delight to watch.
(15) I dislike Brown painting his daughter.
(16) I watched Brown painting his daughter.
(17) Brown deftly painting his daughter is a delight to watch.
(18) Painting his daughter, Brown noticed his hand was shaking.
(19) Brown painting his daughter that day, I decided to go for a walk.
(20) The man painting the girl is Brown.
(21) The silently painting man is Brown.
(22) Brown is painting his daughter.

Arguably the least clear cases (and those usually referred to as 'gerunds'; Quirk et al. 1985: 1291-92) are examples (13) and (14). The main reason for treating the form *painting* as verbal in these cases is the fact that all of them take an NP

62 Note that in Quirk et al. (1985) example (14) is listed before (13). This is counterintuitive as Aarts (2007: 143) points out: "in [... (14)] the adverb *deftly* modifies *painting*, thus making it more verbal than *painting* in [... (13)], which lacks this modifier."

complementation. The adverb *deftly* in (14) is another indicator of the verb status of *painting*. At the same time, the specifying genitive NP *Brown's* clearly points at the nounhood of *painting* in (13) and (14). Leaving further criteria aside for the moment, we can see that *painting* as exemplified in (13) to (14) exhibits characteristics both of nouns and verbs, a clear case of multiple or indeterminate class membership.

How should cases like these best be accommodated in a model of grammar? Three general possibilities can be thought of. 1) Gerunds are verbs that show some properties of nouns, 2) gerunds are nouns that show some properties of verbs, and 3) gerunds are both, nouns and verbs at the same time. Hudson (2007a: ch. 4; 2003) espouses the third option and suggests to treat gerunds as they have often been treated, i.e. as "single words which are both verbs and nouns" (2007a: 210). This analysis rests on the assumption that verbal and nominal characteristics are "always orthogonal: nominal features are exclusively concerned with relations external to the gerund phrase, and verbal features with its internal patterns" (210). Since a gerund ISA both a verb and a noun at the same time, it inherits features from both verbs and nouns; gerunds are conceptualised as a case of multiple default inheritance. A problem for this analysis, as Hudson himself admits, is the fact that gerunds may be preceded by possessive determiners and noun phrases in genitive case or the determiners *no* or *any*.

(23) We were talking about John's/his having a sabbatical.
(24) No playing loud music!
(25) There isn't any telling what they will do. (Hudson 2007a: 185-186)

The distribution of determiners is an internal characteristic of noun phrases, i.e. the nominal features of gerunds are not only external. Hudson explains such cases as "debris of history" (202), being due to "the development of modern gerunds from ordinary nominalizations" (205), and treats them as exceptions to the general rule described above.

Aarts (2008) dismisses an explanation in terms of multiple default inheritance as unsatisfactory:

> Given the unexplained data concerning the prenominal dependents of gerunds and their erratic behaviour (some gerunds extrapose, while others do not; some of them behave like NPs, while others do not), their treatment in terms of MDI [= multiple default inheritance] is called into question. (Aarts 2008: 22)

In addition, he draws attention to the fact that other structures exist "for which we cannot maintain a complementary distribution of external and internal features" (22). A case in point are deverbal adjectives like MOVED, CRUSHED or UNOCCUPIED. These do show adjectival features, namely their ability to occupy the attributive position in an NP and to be prefixed by *un*-, but cannot be intensified or graded. At the same time, their morphology (the suffx *–ed*) shows them to be verbal, as does the fact that they can be preceded by adverbal premodifiers. So, deverbal adjectives show features of both, verbs and adjectives but these "don't distribute neatly into a phrase-external set and a phrase-internal set" (22).

In sight of such principled problems, Aarts argues against an analysis of gerunds that "assume[s] that they belong to two classes at the same time" (28). Instead, he suggests treating gerunds in terms of intersective gradience. More specifically, he follows the first and the second option mentioned above, i.e. treating gerunds as verbs that show some properties of nouns and as nouns that show some properties of verbs. Consider the following three examples.

(26) We were talking about **John having a sabbatical.** [Aarts' (2008) (1)]
(27) We were talking about **John's/his having a sabbatical.** [Aarts' (2008) (11)]
(28) We were talking about **John's competent teaching of his students.** [Aarts' (2008) (33)]

While all of the examples (potentially) show nominal as well as verbal properties, they differ significantly with regard to the relative proportion of the two kinds of properties. In (26) one nominal property stands against nine verbal properties, e.g. possible preceding manner adverb, possible voice modifications (see Aarts 2008: 25 for a detailed discussion). In (27) the number of verbal properties remains the same but we have an additional nominal property. (28), in contrast, shows a predominance of nominal properties. Aarts, therefore, argues to treat (26) and (27) as 'nominal verbs', whereas *teaching* in (28) is analysed as a 'verbal noun'. It is important to note that in Aarts' account these labels "do not add to the inventory of existing categories" (Aarts 2008: 28); we still only have two categories, namely 'noun' and 'verb'. Intersective gradience does not dispense with clearly demarcated categories, these remain "strictly bounded, and there is no overlapping" (Aarts 2008: 26). Two categories only can 'converge' if an element shows features of both categories. So, example (26) shows a slight convergence of the category 'verb' to the category 'noun', whereas in (27) this convergence is stronger. In (28) the directionality of convergence is reversed.

The present network model is basically in line with Aarts' suggestion, although it advocates some modifications, as we will see later. The similarity to Aarts lies in the fact that the 'decision' whether to analyse a gerund as a verb or a noun depends on the outcome of a competition between the two nodes |*VERB*| and |*NOUN*|. Whichever of the two gets fully activated sooner 'wins the race'. Due to the general competitiveness in the network, the fully active |*VERB*| node will inhibit possible other candidates and vice versa. In the present approach, therefore, a solution like that suggested by Hudson (2007a) and others (see Aarts 2008 for a discussion) is not an option. The network, in the state depicted above, will force a decision between categorization as noun or as verb: any occurrence of an *–ing* form, eventually, will result in the activation of either the node |*VERB*| or the node |*NOUN*|. However, since some feature nodes relating to the 'loser' are also active, the resulting pattern of activation either interprets an *–ing* form as a verb with some additional nominal properties or a noun with some additional verbal properties.

Nevertheless, in contrast to Aarts, the present model does not base the decision about the noun- or the verb status of an *–ing* form on possible or potential noun- or verb-like features, but on actual features. The activation of nodes representing possible features presupposes the activation of the node representing the category that is defined by these features. That is, to claim that *having* in example (26) shows nine verb-related features would only be possible if the node |*VERB*| had already been activated, which would mean that a decision about the nature of this word form has already been made. What is relevant in the present model are features nodes that are activated because the respective features are exhibited in a given set of data. In example (26), then, the balance in favour of a verb interpretation of *having* is not as strong in the present model, since the form shows one noun-like feature, i.e. heading a phrase that usually is occupied by an NP, and three verb-like features, i.e. a non-genitival subject, an object complement and the ending *–ing*. In Example (27) the balance, then, is 2 to 3 in favour of a verb interpretation. In (28) the form *teaching* only shows one verbal feature but four noun features. Figure 4.13 shows the activation pattern in the case of examples (26) and (28).

The above discussion illustrates how the nature of the network model and its model-internal restrictions can provide clues as to the plausibility of different approaches to linguistic phenomena. In the present model with its implementation of spreading activation and competition, an approach that endorses multiple word classes for a single word form is not possible. That is, the nature of the present model advocates a treatment of gerunds along the lines of Aarts (2007 and 2008).

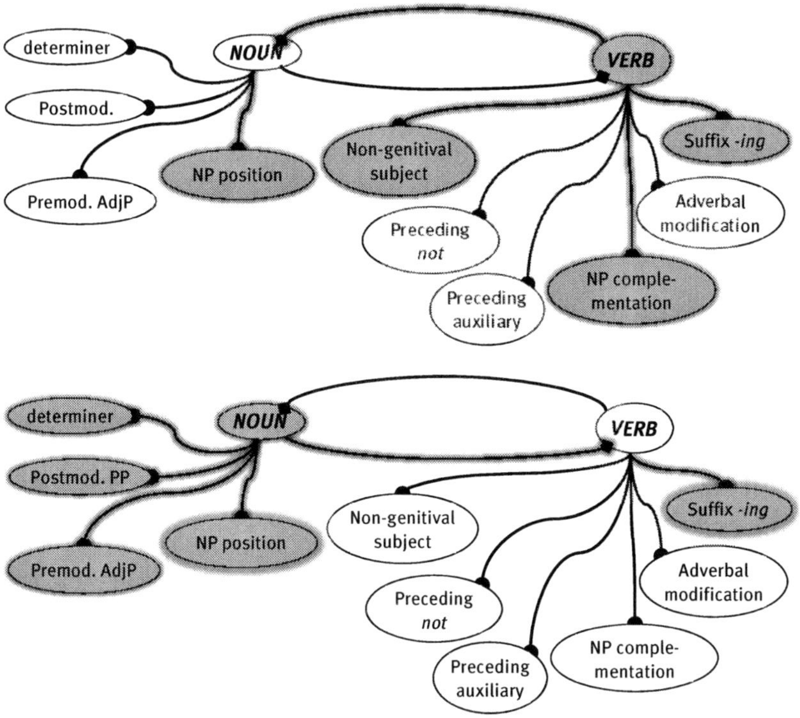

Figure 4.13: Activation patterns with *We were talking about **John having a sabbatical*** (*having* is a nominal verb) and *We were talking about **John's competent teaching of his students*** (*teaching* is a verbal noun). Note that not all relevant features are portrayed.

Yet, at the same time, the nature of the network model suggests an important modification of Aarts' analysis. While it recommends following Aarts in "that there is no need to assume that they [gerunds] belong to two classes at the same time" (2008: 28), the present model does also suggest a general openness for a possible mixed category that combines verbal and nominal features, which Aarts denies:

> Classes α and β are said to 'converge' by virtue of the fact that there exist elements which display properties of both categories. **Importantly, though, I will argue that α and β themselves are strictly bounded, and do not overlap**. (Aarts 2007: 79; my emphasis)
> These labels [i.e. nominal verb and verbal noun] do not add to the inventory of existing categories" (Aarts 2008: 28)

If 'overlap of classes' merely refers to the fact that a given (linguistic) item (Aarts' 'element') cannot be a member of two classes at once, I agree with Aarts. But I would not agree if this ruled out (as it seems to do) the possibility of classes sharing a number of features, i.e. the existence of fuzzy classes. In the present model, the formation of such fuzzy classes is a natural consequence of the occurrence of intersective gradience. If the co-activation of a set of nominal and a set of verbal features co-occurs frequently enough these features will become associated and they will form their own category. So, to rule out the existence of a mixed category *GERUND* (or whatever its name) does not seem plausible to me. To assume the existence of such a category does not pose any problems for the present model. Many category nodes can compete for full activation in parallel; as soon as one has reached a relative activation maximum all the competitors will be inhibited. Since competition is a parallel and not a serial phenomenon, fuzzy categories do not have any influence on processing or production; there is no downside to it. On the other hand, the possibility of fuzzy categories has to be given in any linguistic model that wants to allow for the emergence of new categories and take seriously the "view of language as a complex adaptive system" (Bybee 2010: 2).

4.2.3 Ambiguity, vagueness and polysemy

The concepts 'vagueness', 'polysemy', 'ambiguity' and the study of their interrelations have spawned a large number of cognitively oriented research in the last one or two decades (see, for instance, Cuyckens and Zawada (eds.) (2001) or Nehrlich et al. (eds.) (2003) and the contributions therein). According to Geeraerts (1993 [2006]: 104), vagueness is characterised by the fact that "a particular piece of semantic information is [not] part of the underlying semantic structure of the item [...]". Examples are the lexical units TEACHER or STUDENT. These items do not specify the sex of the person referred to and this piece of information is usually not relevant in the contexts in which the terms are used; for instance, the respective social roles associated with the two concepts are independent of the sex. This is what distinguishes vagueness from polysemy, where two related concepts that share the same written and spoken form differ in a piece of semantic information that is part of the underlying semantic structure. An example would be the lexical unit TREE, which can refer to a biological object or to a diagram that portrays hierarchical relations. In contrast to the examples TEACHER or STUDENT where information on the sex is irrelevant, the semantic aspects of biological object or diagram are usually relevant and it is part of our conceptualization of these items. Ambiguous items, in contrast to polysemous ones, are thought of as not being related in their semantic content, such as the two meanings of BANK, i.e. as riverside or financial institution.

Attempts to draw a clear distinction between the three notions go back as far as Aristotle and involve definitional tests (Aristotle), logical tests (Quine 1960) and linguistic tests (Lakoff 1970) (cf. Tuggy 1993 [2006]: 167 and Geeraerts 1993 [2006]: 106). However, as Geeraerts shows, the three kinds of tests may yield conflicting results and, in some cases, their outcome is heavily dependent on the context. Particularly troublesome is the notion of 'polysemy'. Geeraerts attributes these problems partly to the fact that it is not yet clear what a distinct meaning actually is: "any search for polysemy criteria will be hampered by the fact that we do not know precisely what it is we want a criterion for" (136). As a consequence, he argues for a change of "our metaphorical, pre-theoretical image of what meanings are", in particular the idea that "meanings are things, prepackaged chunks of information that are contained in and carried about by words bags" (137). Instead he suggests to conceive of words as "searchlights that highlight, upon each application, a particular subfield of their domain of application" (137). The number of domains that can be highlighted is not necessarily fixed and restricted; a searchlight has a considerable amount of freedom in highlighting different domains (although within certain limits). That is, on each use of a word, different semantic aspects are activated and focused on. Which areas and which aspects are highlighted depends on the context: "meaning is radically context-dependent" (138). This, in turn, suggests that meanings are made or construed rather than found: "Rather than a single unique meaning, there would only be the interpretations that we impose on the material" (139). The present network model does justice to this fundamentally interpretative nature of meaning.

In contrast to schematic network models that are presented in Langacker (1988b) or Tuggy (1993 [2006], 2005, or 2007), the present network model is more in line with what Geeraerts (1995: 25) calls the 'overlapping set model'. In the present approach, word meanings are conceived of as sets, with the sets being defined intensionally, i.e. with regard to the semantic features that the referents of a given word exhibit. This brings the present model close to the basic understanding of categories as sets of co-occuring attributes as described in Rosch's writings (see section 4.2.1) and is in line with Geeraerts' (1989 [2006]: 4) observation that "there can be no semantic description without some sort of decompositional analysis." Let us take Brugman and Lakoff's (1988 [2006]; see also Brugman 1981 [1988] and Lakoff 1987) discussion of OVER[63] as a starting point.

Brugman and Lakoff discuss the word as an instance of a 'radial network', a structure

> [...] with a central member and a network of links to other members. Each noncentral member of the category is a variant of the central member or is a variant on variant[.] (Brugman & Lakoff 1988 [2006]: 109)

The central sense of OVER, according to Brugman and Lakoff, is the above-and-across sense, as in *the plane flew over*. This sense merely indicates that something (in Langacker's (1987) terms: the trajector) moves over something (the landmark). The only information that this sense of OVER contains is the fact that the trajector moves "all the way *across* the landmark from the boundary on one side to the boundary on the other" (Brugman & Lakoff 1988 [2006]: 109). OVER in this sense, for instance, is not specific with regard to contact or non-contact between the trajector and the landmark. This is captured in specific subsenses of OVER, which are all treated as 'instances' of the more general sense. Two such instances would be:

(29) Sam climbed over the wall
(30) The bird flew over the wall

In both cases, the trajector moves across the landmark, but it is only in (29) that the trajector is in contact with the landmark. Another relevant feature is 'vertical':

(31) Sam drove over the bridge
(32) Sam walked over the hill

Both senses of OVER entail the 'contact' feature, but only in (32) is the landmark, the hill, extended vertically; the landmark in (31), the bridge, is not. Another feature is that of 'extension', i.e. "the landmark extends over a distance or area" (114). This distinction is exemplified in (30) as opposed to (33) below:

---

63 Other studies on OVER spawned by Brugman's seminal work include Deane (1993), Kreitzer (1997), Tyler and Evans (2001 [2007]) and Geeraerts (1992 [2006]) for Dutch OVER. See Rudzka-Ostyn (1989) for a similar network for the related meanings of the verb ASK. See Gries (2006) for criticism of such models.

(33) The plane flew over the hill

In both cases, the landmark has a vertical dimension and does not have contact with the trajector. The only distinction is that between an extended and non-extended landmark, i.e. the hill as opposed to the wall.

A closer look at the six examples above reveals that a special kind of relation exists between some but not others. For instance, the three senses of OVER exemplified in (29), (31) and (32) are similar, since they share the 'contact' attribute. Similarly, (30) and (33) are related, as they have the features 'no contact' and 'vertical' in common. Relations of this kind is what Brugman and Lakoff call 'similarity links'. Such a link does not obtain between (32) and (34): while the former shows the attributes 'contact', 'extension' and 'vertical' the latter does not. So they are not similar in any respect.

(34) The bird flew over the line

Senses may also be linked through metaphorical extensions[64]. Consider the following example:

(35) Harry still hasn't gotten over his divorce

Brugman and Lakoff (1988 [2006]: 132) claim that the sense of OVER shown here is related to the sense instantiated in sentences like (32) above, *Sam walked over the hill*. This relation is based on two metaphors: the first understands obstacles as vertical landmarks, and the second understands one's life as a journey: "[...] the divorce in [*sic!* is] an obstacle (metaphorically, a vertical extended landmark) on the path defined by life's journey" (132).

In the following, I will show how the non-metaphorical senses of OVER are represented and realised in the network. Contrary to Brugman and Lakoff, who considered the 'above and across' sense of OVER to be basic, I take 'above' to be the basic meaning of OVER. In the present network model, this would be represented by a semantic feature node ||[+above]|| which would be activated any time the word form *over* is encountered. More specific meanings involve additional information regarding the nature of the landmark, i.e. extended or not, and vertically elevated or not, and the question whether there is contact between

64 The authors also propose a fourth kind of linking, namely the transformational link, which is related to the similarity link. See pages 119-120 for details.

landmark and trajector or not. This is represented through the nodes ||[+extended]||, ||[+vertical elevation]||, and ||[+contact]||, respectively. If the node ||[+extended]|| was activated together with the nodes ||[+above]|| and ||[+across]||, this would result in the sense as exemplified in *The bird flew over the yard*. If the node ||[+contact]|| was also activated, the sense would be that of *over* in *The car drove over the bridge*, and so on. The question, then, is where this activation comes from. I think it makes sense to assume that the activation of the ||[+above]|| node depends on the occurrence of the word form *over*. All the other nodes are activated on the basis of contextual information. The node ||[+across]||, for instance, can only be activated if there is movement involved, i.e. the verb form *hover* does not activate this node, whereas forms like *run* or *fly* do. The kind of action involved also influences the activation of the ||[+contact]|| node: An action like running or driving assumes contact to a surface, whereas hovering and flying do not. The nature of the landmark, naturally, will lead to (non-)activation of the nodes ||[+extended]|| as well as ||[+vertical elevation]||. That is, any occurrence of the word form *over* would lead to an interpretation of its meaning on the basis of the context in which it occurs (an assumption that is also in line with Hawkins' principle of 'Minimize Forms' discussed in section 6.3).

In the present network model, the different meanings of OVER would, thus, not be part of the network, but created online during processing on the basis of the semantic features associated with the verbs and nouns that co-occur with the preposition. This is shown in figure 4.14.

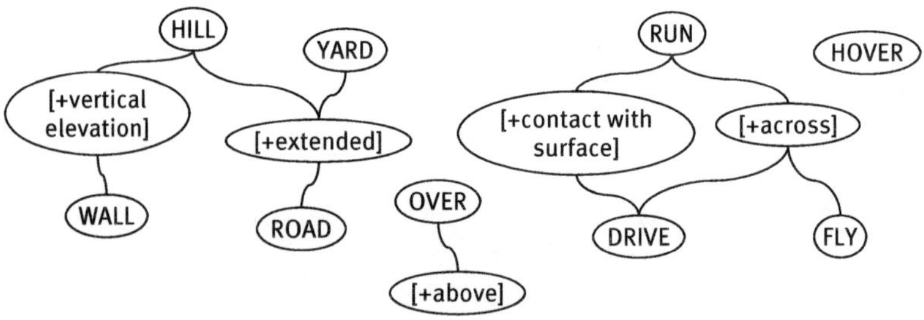

Figure 4.14: Meaning aspects of OVER and co-occurring verbs and nouns.

In figure 4.14, the node |OVER| is connected to the meaning node ||[+above]|| only, since this meaning is activated any time the word form is encountered. Therefore, each encounter of the word form *over* will lead to a full activation of this node. The more specific meanings arise from the more specific facets like 'vertical elevation' or 'contact' which, in the present model, reside in the surrounding context (apart from *hover* which is unspecified in this respect). The activation of the |DRIVE| or the |RUN| node spreads to the meaning node ||[+contact with surface]||, and the activation of the |WALL| or the |HILL| node activates the node ||[+vertical elevation]||. It follows from this that these aspects do not need to be encoded in the preposition itself[65]. This also makes sense if we take into consideration that we cannot know which exact meaning of *over* is meant if we do not have any context, a fact that is not surprising considering that "[l]anguage users encounter meaning primarily as a property of utterances, not of decontextualized words" (Taylor et al. 2003: 6). As a consequence, it is difficult to tell the exact number of possible meanings of the lexical unit. Rather, "[t]he number of meanings that one recognises will depend on the schematicity, or, alternatively, the delicacy of one's analysis" (Taylor 1995: 18). In the present network, the number of meanings is limited by the number of possible situations in which *over* is used to express the element of 'over-ness' that the situation contains. A possible counter-argument might be that this leads to a proliferation of senses. After all, given a high enough degree of delicacy, each situation is unique. A plane, for instance, can fly over a yard at an altitude of 100 meters, 400 meters, 1000 meters. What prevents the network from establishing a semantic-feature node for each of these altitudes? The answer lies in the fact that only repeated exposure to a particular stimulus leads to the creation of a node in the network. Even if the observer was able to identify a range of different altitudes, it is fairly unlikely that similar altitudes are experienced with a high enough frequency to become entrenched in the system. The fact that a plane does not have contact to the landmark when flying, in contrast, can be experienced in any situation in which a plane flies and, accordingly, will be represented in the network. This is in line with Taylor's (1992: 156) view that meanings are stored on a basic-level degree of abstraction "where a person can form maximally schematic mental images of objects and activities." In the present network model, the preference for storage at this level is a result of the mere influence of frequency on entrenchment. It is, therefore, a natural consequence of the basic features of the network model.

---

65 Note that a similar argument is put forward in construction grammar. Instead of multiplying the meaning of verbs, construction grammar argues that verbs have a fairly general meaning and additional meaning aspects are provided by the constructions themselves.

The present model, then, conceptualises OVER as a case of vagueness. However, the network model is highly flexible with regard to vagueness, polysemy or ambiguity. For instance, if two situations, say, driving over a hill and flying over a yard, were to be encountered very often by a language user, the semantic features associated with the respective situations would become connected in the network since they are co-activated frequently. As a consequence, the lexical-unit node |OVER| would then be related to two sets of semantic-feature nodes (||[+above]||, ||[+across]||, ||[+contact]||, ||[+vertical elevation]||, and ||[+above]||, ||[+across]||, ||[+extended]||, respectively) which overlap in the nodes ||[+above]|| and ||[+across]||, since these semantic elements are shared in both situations. The lexical unit OVER would then have moved from vagueness to polysemy. This shows that the network is flexible enough to accommodate changes in the way the human mind conceptualises a particular meaning.

On a more general note, the question of vagueness, polysemy and ambiguity is directly related to the number and entrenchment of connections between a word-form node and semantic-feature nodes, and between the semantic-feature nodes themselves. In the case of vagueness, as above, a word-form node will only be strongly connected to one or two feature nodes, which accounts for the more general and schematic meaning of a vague lexical unit. These nodes represent meaning aspects which are highlighted any time the searchlight is in operation. Nodes representing the more specific meaning aspects do not have a strong link to the word-form node. As a consequence, an activation of the word-form node would not automatically lead to a full activation of these specific nodes. This accounts for the fact that we find it difficult to talk about the meaning of OVER if we do not have a particular situation in mind. A prototypical polysemous item will have a strong connection to most of the semantic features with which it is associated. That is, the respective nodes will all have a strong connection to the word-form node and the semantic-feature nodes will also be connected to each other, since they are often co-activated. Any occurrence of a polysemous word form will activate this set of strongly associated feature nodes, which accounts for the impression of relatedness in polysemous meanings, e.g. for TREE. This set of strongly related feature nodes serves as a highly salient unifying schema (Taylor 2003: 470). The distinctiveness of polysemous items stems from a (usually small) number of additional semantic feature nodes that are activated depending on the context, e.g. ||[+biological]|| or ||[+diagram]|| in the case of TREE. Since these are part of the conceptualization of the meaning of the lexical unit, they are more strongly linked to the word-form node than the context-dependent features in the case of vagueness. This expresses that we are basically aware of the two meanings of TREE, even though we still need contextual information to tell us which meaning is intended in a given utterance. Finally, an ambiguous word form would have strong connections to two sets of semantic-feature nodes. Nodes within these sets are strongly connected, since they are frequently co-activated but there will usually not be any connections of feature nodes between these two sets. In an idealised form, the distinction between vagueness, polysemy and ambiguity is represented as shown in figure 4.15 in the present network model.

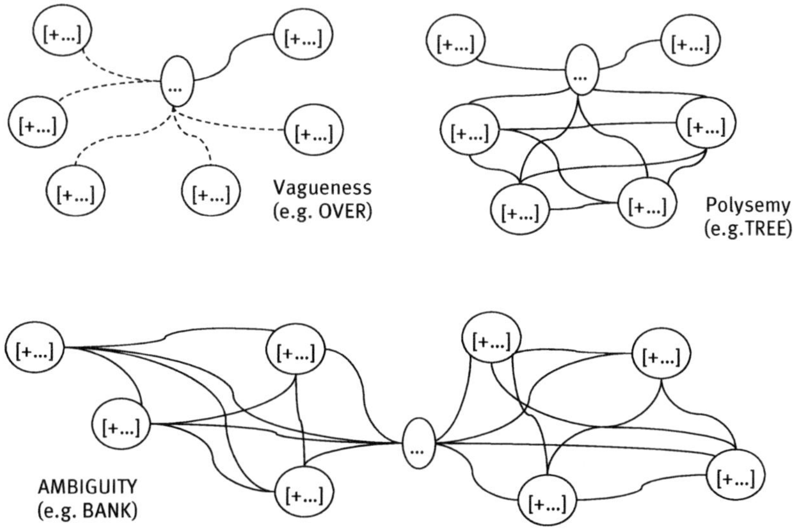

Figure 4.15: Vagueness, polysemy and ambiguity in the present network model.

The situation depicted in figure 4.15 is in line with Langacker's (1987: 126) representation of vagueness and ambiguity (see figure 4.16). The first is represented by the fact that a fairly entrenched schematic meaning is given, while the more specific senses are not strongly entrenched. In figure 4.15 this is depicted by the fact that the central node (in the network portion representing vagueness) is strongly linked only to one meaning node, whereas the links to other semantic features are weak. In the case of ambiguity, the word form node in the middle is strongly linked to two separated network portions. Since these do not overlap, there is no network portion that could represent a more schematic sense shared by both meanings of the word form. The same situation is shown in Langacker's representation (figure 4.16).

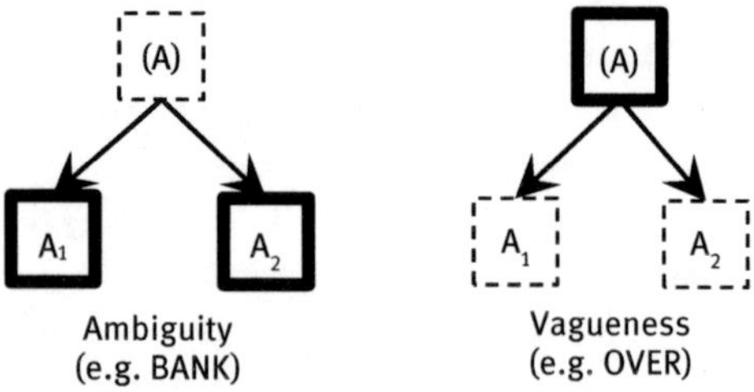

Figure 4.16: Ambiguity and vagueness in Langacker (2000a: 126) (with kind permission of de Gruyter Mouton).

On the whole, the present network model is in line with Geeraerts' searchlight metaphor of meaning. It accounts for the fact that in many cases, meaning is not fixed but construed on the basis of contextual information. At the same time, the network allows for more or less fixed meanings. These have achieved their status through frequent exposure to highly similar contexts, which leads to frequent co-activation of semantic-feature nodes, which, in turn, results in strong connections between these individual nodes. The present model, then, allows for 'sense-storage' as well as 'sense-generation' (Taylor 2003: 642-644).

4.2.4 The formation and representation of sequences and structures

The basics of representation of sequences have been discussed in section 2.2.2.9. We will now apply these basics to explore how the network model advocated in this study captures the structure of phonological word forms. This will make necessary the introduction of a few additional mechanisms.

Let us take as examples the word forms *hunt*, *cut* and *nun*. The same two problems that were discussed in section 2.2.2.9 also apply to these three words, and the solution is the same. *Nun* poses an additional problem, namely the fact that the same phoneme occurs twice in the word. A possible solution might be to have two phoneme nodes |/n/$_1$| and |/n/$_2$|. Yet, this solution does not seem very elegant and might lead to a proliferation of nodes where it is not necessary. A more elegant solution would be one which lead to a second activation of the node |/n/| after the node |/ʌ/|. This can be achieved by including an additional link leading from |/ʌ/| to |/n/|. As soon as the former is activated, it will spread its activation to the latter, i.e. the activation sequence |/n/|, |/ʌ/|, |/n/| has been realised. The obvious problem, here, is that any activation of the node |/ʌ/| will now lead to the activation of the node |/n/|. To make sure that this only happens

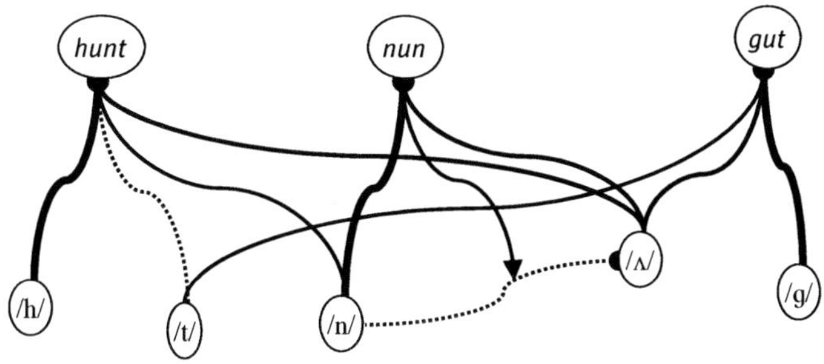

Figure 4.17: |/ʌ/| activates |/n/| with the word form *nun* but not with other word forms

with the word form *nun* we can make use of a node-link connection, as is shown in figure 4.17.

The connection between the two phoneme nodes is very thin. This represents the fact that this connection is too weak for the activation to spread from the source to the target node quickly enough. It is only because of the 'boost' coming from the word form node |*nun*| that the phoneme node |/ʌ/| can activate the node |/n/|. If this boost is missing, for instance in the case of *cut*, the phoneme node |/ʌ/| will not be able to activate the node |/n/|.

A final addition to the above network is the implementation of beginning-of-word and end-of-word nodes, |START| and |END|, respectively. As it is well known, these pieces of knowledge have to be learnt by children and this has to be located somewhere in a plausible model of language. We will also need the end node in discussion in section 4.2.5 when we explore the formation of the three regular past tense allomorphs. The knowledge about beginnings and ends of words can be added to the network in a very simple way: all possible phonemes that can start a word are very weakly linked to a node |START| in the network, and similarly for all phonemes that can end a word. Of course, we have to ensure that each word gets only one beginning and one end. As in the figure above, this is done by the help of node-to-link links: the node |*hunt*|, for instance, is connected to the link that connects the nodes |START| and |/h/|. As soon as the word-form node is activated it will spread this activation to the link between the two nodes which will result in a pattern of co-activation of the three nodes, representing the fact that the phoneme /h/ is the beginning of the word form *hunt*. Consider figure 4.18 which illustrates how the knowledge about the beginning of words is represented in the network. The knowledge about

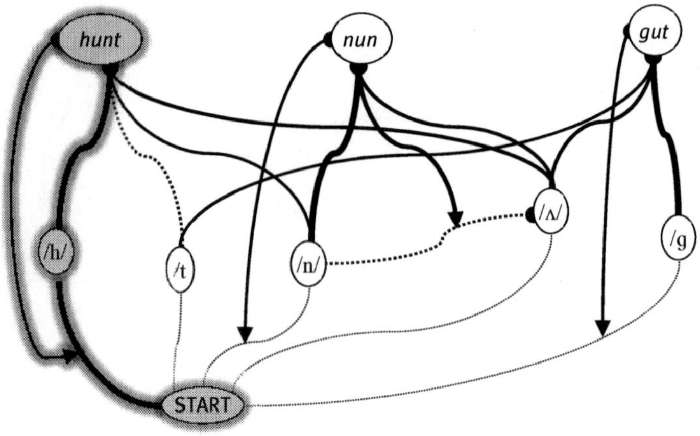

Figure 4.18: The word form *hunt* begins in /h/.

how words end is represented in the same way. This will become relevant in the next section.

The discussion above has described the production side of words. Given an activated word form node, activation will spread in such a way to the constituent phoneme nodes that each of them will be fully activated in the correct order. To account for the reception of phonological words we only need to apply the mechanisms described in section 2.2.2.9 above. A particular problem discussed in that context was that of two sequences that consist of the same elements. As an example we will briefly discuss the forms *tug* and *gut*. A solution to the problem of activating the correct form is to make the degree of spreading of activation of a phoneme node to a given word-form node dependent on whether the phoneme node representing the immediately preceding sound has been activated. For instance, let us assume the node |/ʌ/| has been activated, i.e. the sound has been recognised by the organism. If the sound occurs in the context of *tug*, the activated node should spread its activation more strongly to the word form node |*tug*| than to the node |*gut*|. That is, we have to implement in the network some kind of influence of the node |/t/| on the spreading of activation of the node |/ʌ/| to the node |*tug*|.

In figure 4.19, the links from the phoneme nodes to the respective word form nodes are fairly weak, they have to be boosted. If the organism hears the word *tug*, the node |START| and the node |/t/| will be activated, since /t/is the first sound of that word. A fully activated |/t/| node spreads activation to both |*tug*| and |*gut*|, but only the link to |*tug*| is boosted by the node |START|, i.e. |*tug*|

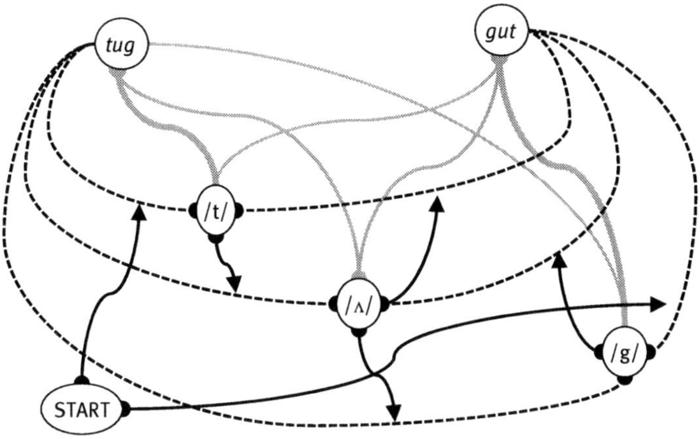

Figure 4.19: *gut* and *tug* as they are represented in the network.

will become significantly more activated. At the same time, the fully active |/t/| node also boosts the link from |/ʌ/| to the node |*tug*| so that the activation traveling from this phoneme node (as soon as the sound has been heard) to the word-form node |*tug*| is boosted as well. Again, activation traveling from there to the node |*gut*| is not boosted, and |*tug*| will be more strongly activated than |*gut*|. Finally, on hearing the sound /g/ the node |/ʌ/| will be activated and will spread activation both to |*tug*| and |*gut*|. Again, the activation traveling to |*tug*| will be boosted by the node |/ʌ/| and then fully activated. If the receiver hears the word *tug*, the sequence of phonemes will activate the node |*tug*|, i.e. sequence can be accounted for in the present network model.

The solution suggested here can also explain findings of experiments relating to the cohort model of word recognition. The cohort model (Marslen Wilson 1987) of lexical retrieval tries to account for the speed of word recognition by "assuming a distributed, parallel processing system" (78) in which many possible word candidates are accessed and assessed at the same time. The basic idea is that recognition starts early in the word ("when the first 100-150 ms have been heard"; 78) and does not wait till the end of the word has been reached. On the basis of the input available after this short period of time the organism already activates all the candidates that match the input data. As more data become available the number of possible canditates shrinks until, eventually only one candidate is left. One prediction this model makes is that a number of of different concepts is activated until the final candidates has been singled out.

This prediction has been borne out by experimental data from cross-modal priming tasks, e.g. the 'captain-captive experiment'. This experiment tries "to tap the activation of different semantic codes early in the recognition process" (88). The two words *captain* and *captive* share the first four phonemes, i.e. in the model suggested both words and semantic concepts related to them should be active up to the point where the fifth phoneme is recognised. In the experiment subjects were presented with probe words that were semantically related either to *captain* or to *captive*, for instance *boat* and *guard*, respectively. The two probe words were visually presented at different points in time: either just before the separation-point or at the end of the word. The dependent variable was the time

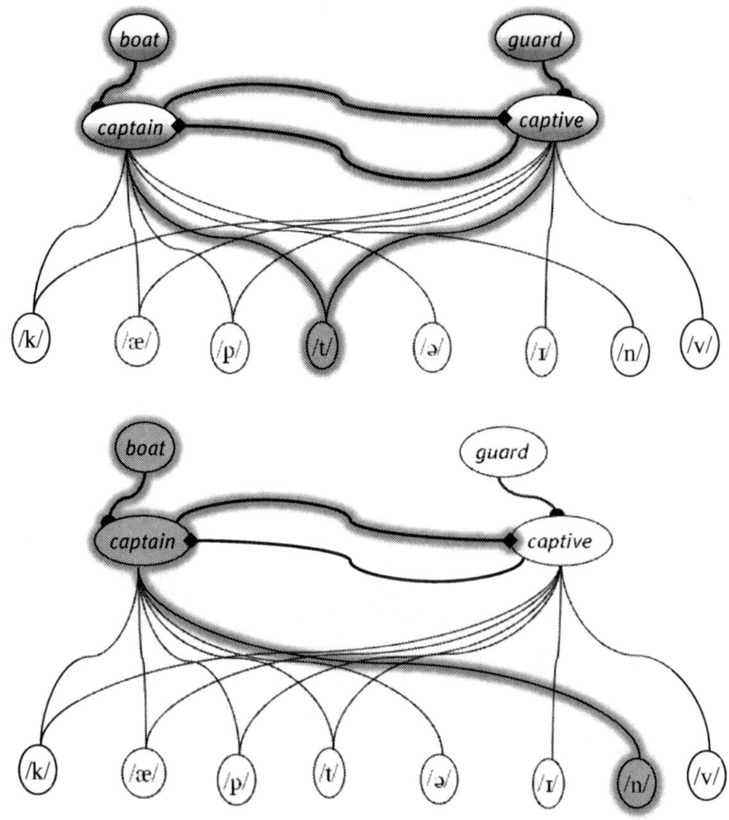

Figure 4.20: The network representation of the intermodal priming experiment under conditions 1 (top) and 2 (bottom) (note that some details have been omitted). (=Figures 2.18,19, repeated here for convenience)

it took subjects to decide whether the probe words were words or not. The results showed that under the first condition both *boat* and *guard* were primed by the sequence of the four phonemes. Under the second condition only that probe word was primed which was semantically related to the auditorily presented word, e.g. *captain* primes *boat* but not *guard*.

The illustrations in figure 4.20 (repeated from section 2.2.2.5 for convenience) show these two situations. In the first case, even though neither of the word form nodes is fully activated, both are activated to some extent and spread some activation to the semantically related nodes. These are, therefore, partly activated as well, which explains the priming effect. In the second case, the node |*captain*| has received considerably more activation than the node |*captive*|, which eventually leads to the complete inhibition of the latter node; the priming effects still shows for *boat* but not for *guard*.

The explanation of sentence structure, more specifically the production of sentence structures, is trickier. The problem, here, is that a thought, i.e. a proposition or a set of propositions, is a simultaneous affair (see section 2.2.2.5 for details), while the production of a sentence that represents that thought is a linear process. Let us consider the proposition HIT(*john*, *paul*). In the network this would be represented by a co-activation pattern in which a node |*John*| activates the agent node, a node |*hit*| activates the verb node and the node |*Paul*| activates the patient node[66]. All of these nodes and the respective links between them are activated at the same time. How can we account for the correct order of the individual constituents?

In the present model this is achieved through the nodes that represent the clause elements, i.e. subject, object_1, object_2, complement, adverbial and verb. Clause structure is implemented with the help of differences in the activation thresholds of the individual nodes and with additional connections between the nodes. For instance, to guarantee that the clause elements subject, object_1, and verb are realised in the correct order we will assume that the node |*SUBJECT*| has the lowest activation threshold, followed by the node |$\mathit{VERB}_{\text{cl}}$|, followed by the node |OBJECT_1|. Moreover, the node |$\mathit{VERB}_{\text{cl}}$| has such a high threshold that it can only become activated with the help of additional activation coming from the node |*SUBJECT*|. That is, only if |*SUBJECT*| is activated fully (which will lead to the production of the respective string of words that realises the subject) will the node |$\mathit{VERB}_{\text{cl}}$| be able to become fully active: other things being equal, subjects will always be realised before verbs. Similarly, the node |OBJECT_1| needs

66 This is only a rough approximation. A more detailed account is given in section 2.2.5.

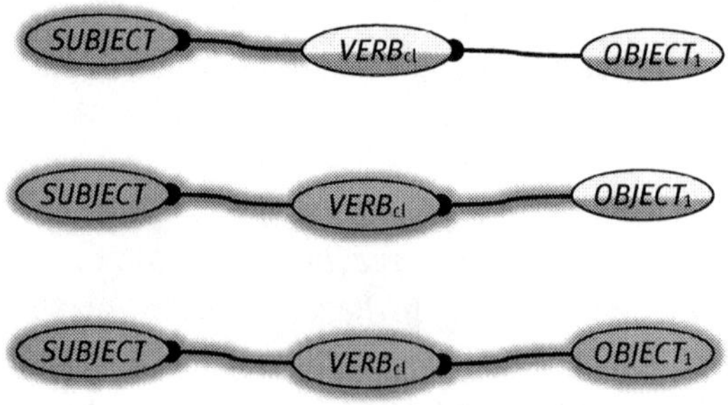

Figure 4.21: The network part that is responsible for the sequence of clause elements at three successive points in time. Note that all three nodes receive activation from other nodes not shown in the figure, but only for the node subject this activation is sufficient to activate the node fully. The other nodes depend on additional activation from the node immediately to the left.

activation which it can only get from the node |*VERB*$_{cl}$|, i.e. the monotransitive object will always follow the verb. This sequence of activation is shown in figure 4.21.

The realization of the clause elements by (strings of) words is mediated through nodes that represent participant roles and a node |Verb$_{sem}$| (not as clause element but as semantic unit). The node |Agent| is connected to the node |*SUBJECT*|, since agents are usually realised as the subject of a clause. The |Patient| node is linked to the node |*OBJECT*$_1$|, and the two verb nodes are linked. As was described above, the node |John| is linked via an active connection to the node |Agent|. The meaning node itself, of course, is linked to the word form node |*John*|. All in all, we have an activation pattern that links the

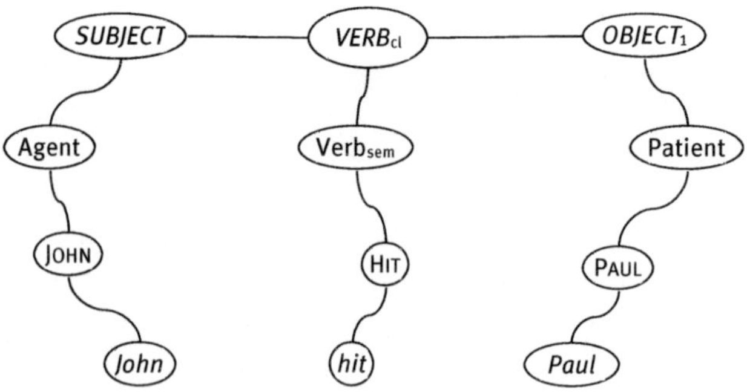

Figure 4.22: Clause structure and meaning in the network model.

word form node to the subject node. In this way the present network model represents the fact that the word form *John* realises the subject of the whole clause. The same holds for the rest of the clause as can be seen in figure 4.22

In the present network model the order in which elements become realised depends on the order in which the clause-element nodes become fully activated. This allows us to introduce word order variation in a very elegant way by manipulating the amounts of activation that spread to these nodes. A fronted clause, for instance, would be realised by making sure that the node |$OBJECT_1$| becomes fully activated before |*SUBJECT*|, which needs to be fully activated before |$VERB_{cl}$|. As is shown in figure 4.23, a node |fronting| is added to the network which has a fairly strong connection to the node |$OBJECT_1$|. At the same time |fronting| inhibits the node |*SUBJECT* | (recall that the full activation of |$VERB_{cl}$| depends on additional activation coming from |*SUBJECT*|). It is only when the node |$OBJECT_1$| is fully active that the node |*SUBJECT*| and |$VERB_{cl}$| can become activated because the node |$OBJECT_1$| inhibits the inhibitory connection that originates in the node |fronting|. Once |*SUBJECT*| is active it will support the activation of |$VERB_{cl}$|. As can be seen, the activation of the node |fronting| leads to the activation sequence that we are aiming for: |$OBJECT_1$| - |*SUBJECT*| - |$VERB_c$|.

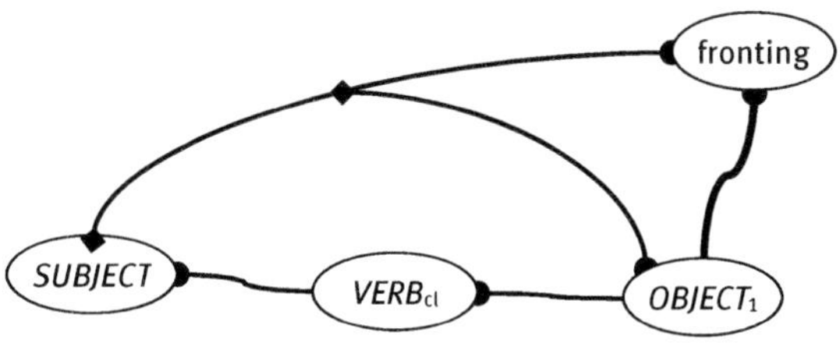

Figure 4.23: Fronting in the present network model.

Another word order phenomenon is that of inversion, i.e. the sequence complement – verb – subject. Again, the node |inversion| will lead to the activation of |*COMPLEMENT*|, while suppressing the node |*SUBJECT*|. When the node |*COMPLEMENT*| is fully active (and, as a consequence, the relevant word forms are realised) it will provide activation for |$VERB_{cl}$| through a link that is boosted by the node |inversion|. The node |$VERB_{cl}$| inhibits the inhibitory link from |inversion| to |*SUBJECT*|. As soon as |$VERB_{cl}$| is activated the node |*SUBJECT*| can

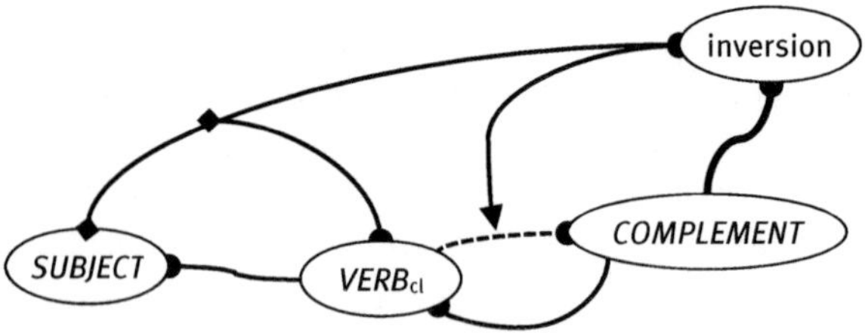

Figure 4.24: Inversion in the present network model.

become activated as well, resulting in the activation sequence |*COMPLEMENT*| – |*VERB*$_{cl}$| – |*SUBJECT*| (see figure 4.24).

Before we move on to more complex structures, a comment is in order here concerning the interaction of elements in a given structure. By way of example let us consider the phenomenon of subject-verb concord. To account for this we need to make sure that the agent's (or the subject's) values for the category 'person' and 'number' influence the choice of the inflected verb form. With the example *John reads books*, for instance, it is the features 'third person' and 'singular' (related to *John*) that have to be transferred to the verb and not the features 'third person' and 'plural' (related to *books*). This problem can be solved, if we assume feature nodes that are attached to the node |*SUBJECT*|. Depending on which of these subject-feature nodes are active, different forms of the inflected verb are realised.

The major problem, here, is that many nodes compete for agenthood and, as a consequence, for being realised as the subject. This situation has been discussed in detail in section (2.2.2.5). Both, *John* and *books* are generally possible subjects and, accordingly, both, as soon as they are active, will spread activation to their relevant number and person nodes. In the present example, this means that three nodes are activated, namely |3rd|, |sing.| and |pl.|. Obviously, only the activation of the first two should be passed on to the equivalent nodes connected to |*SUBJECT*|, from where the activation is passed on to activate the correct verb-form node, in this case |*reads*|. That is, only that conceptual node which is connected to |Agent| should pass on information about number and person, but not those conceptual nodes that are connected to other semantic roles. What is needed is the *if-then* pattern discussed in section 2.2.2.4. If *John* is the agent, then the information about the number and person of *John* should be passed on to the subject of the clause, or, conversely, those features that are not in congruence with *John* should be blocked. Figure 4.25 shows how this is implemented in the network.

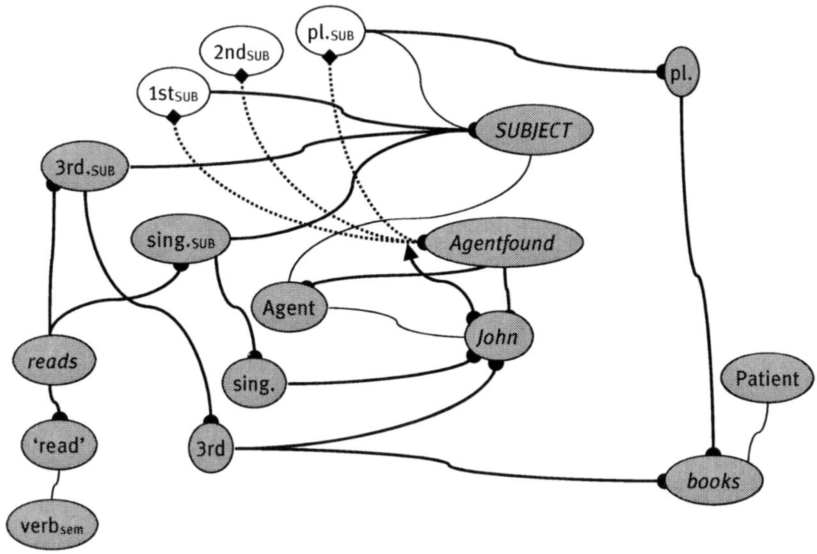

Figure 4.25: Choosing the right verb form if the agent *John* is the subject of the clause *John reads books*. (details omitted)

As described in section 2.2.2.5, '*if John is agent then block 1st and 2nd person and plural number*' is realised through inhibitory links that originate in the node |*AGENTfound*|. These links lead from |*AGENTfound*| to all possible person and number nodes related to the subject (only the three relevant ones are shown in figure 4.25). These links are very weak, so that they depend on supplementary activation from other nodes. If John is the agent, the node |*John*| boosts these three inhibitory links which means that the nodes that are not in congruence with the number and person of *John* cannot become activated even though they may receive activation from other nodes. At the same time, the nodes that are in congruence with *John*, i.e. |sing.SUB| and |3^{rd}SUB|, are not inhibited and can pass their activation on to the verb-form node that is in concord with these features - |*reads*|. Of all the forms of the verb *read*, this is the one that is most strongly activated and, therefore, will be realised. The features of the agent/subject have been successfully transferred to the finite verb form. In a similar fashion, the nodes |1^{st}SUB| and |pl.SUB| would be the only ones that were not inhibited, if the agent was *we* and these features would be transferred to the verb form.

To a certain extent, words, i.e. sequences of sounds or letters, or clauses are fairly simple sequences and structures. To illustrate that the network is also able to accommodate more complex structures, the following explains how the complex verb phrase, e.g. 'Modal + *have* + *been* + *being* + –*ed* participle' is realised in the network model.

One problem for a structure like the one above is that it cannot be derived as a schema from a large number of instantiations of this particular pattern; usually it does not occur at all in authentic language data. Instead, we can only assume that the language user over the years has encountered a large number of less complex verb phrases. In what follows I will show how on the basis of these smaller structures highly complex structures can evolve in the network, even though they are usually not instantiated in language use. Consequently, this section will have to show that the network model is also able to implement what Langacker (2000b: 4-5) refers to as 'compositionality'.

In the following I make use of what I will call here 'basic complex verb phrases'. This somewhat contradictory term refers to verb phrases which instantiate exactly one of the grammatical categories expressed in the complex verb phrase. They are complex in that they consist of two verb forms, and they are basic in that the category that they express is not decomposable. The English language has four of such basic complex verb phrases:

1) modality: modal auxiliary + infinitive[67]
2) perfective aspect: HAVE + -*ed* participle
3) progressive aspect: BE + -*ing* participle
4) passive voice: BE + -*ed* participle[68]

All of these are highly frequent and we can assume that they are deeply entrenched in the cognitive system of the language user. More specifically, the category 'modality' will be associated with the co-occurrence of a modal auxiliary and an infinitive verb form, passive voice will be associated with a form of BE and past participle verb forms, and so on. In the network model, these associations

---

67 The question is, if here we should rather talk of 'unmarked verb form' instead of 'infinitive'. From a network perspective, this would not pose any problem, since the distinction between the many 'unmarked verb forms' of English, i.e. as infinitive or 1st, 2nd, etc. person present tense, is only based on the context. This contextual information translates into patterns of activation in the network, such as |modal aux| or |*we*| together with the node representing an 'unmarked verb form' node, e.g. |*go*|. How the unmarked verb form has to be interpreted would thus not be linked to the word form node itself but would be given by other nodes that are activated (almost) at the same time. However, I will stick here to the traditional terminology to avoid confusion.

68 We will ignore tense here, since this is not realized by structure but by form in the first verbal element.

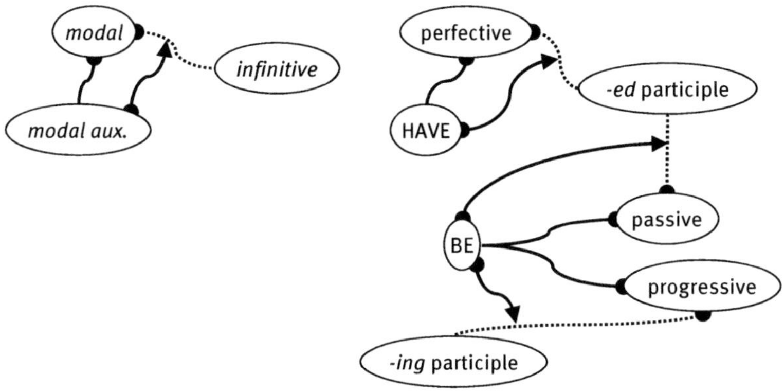

Figure 4.26: Basic complex verb phrases in the network model.

are represented as shown in figure 4.26 below. The basic underlying mechanism is that of the *if-then* pattern in the network, e.g. 'if the modal-auxiliary part of the modal meaning has been activated then activate the infinitive part'.

Each of the basic complex verb phrases consists of a node that represents the grammatical category, e.g. |modal|, and two other nodes that represent the constituents, e.g. |modal aux.| and |infinitive|. To guarantee that the two constituents are produced in the correct order, the link from the grammatical category node to the second constituent node is very weak and, thus, needs amplification, which it receives as soon as the node that represents the first constituent is activated. As a consequence the first constituent will always be realised before the second one. For instance, the activation of the node |modal| will spread to the nodes |modal aux.| and |infinitive|. The former will be activated first and it is only when this node sends activation to the link between |modal| and |infinitive| that the activation from the node |modal| can spread to |infinitive| in sufficient quantity. That is, the node |modal aux.| will activate a word form node representing a modal verb, e.g. |*will*| or |*might*|, before the node |infinitive| can start to activate one of the nodes representing infinitives, e.g. |*run*| or |*read*|. Because of this the network will only produce correct strings like *will run* or *might read*, but never **run will* or **read might*.

It seems reasonable to assume that the processor has information about the sequence of grammatical categories expressed in the complex VP. This is due to the fact that any occurrence of a complex VP will instantiate parts of the sequence 'modal + perfective + progressive + passive'. From these parts the whole sequence can be abstracted. The rationale is as follows: If I know the sequences

'A+B', 'A+C', and 'B+C', I also know that a sequence that contains all three elements will have the order 'A+B+C'. With regard to the complex verb phrase, the occurrence of sequences like 'has been playing', for instance, will establish the order 'perfective + progressive'; the occurrence of strings like *should be playing* and *should have played* leads to the sequence 'modal + progressive' and 'modal + perfective', respectively. From this we can abstract the sequence 'modal + perfective + progressive'.[69] Let us now turn to the emergence and representation of complex VP structures in the network.

What happens if the system wants to produce a complex VP which realizes the grammatical categories 'modal' and 'perfective' and the meaning 'play'[70]? The activation of |modal| will spread to the node |modal aux.| and from there to a modal auxiliary, e.g. *will.* Activation will also spread from |modal aux.| to the node |infinitive|, which is boosted by the nodes spreading from |modal aux.|. Similarly, the activation of the node |perfective| will spread to |HAVE| and |-*ed* participle|. Both the node |infinitive| and the node |HAVE| share one element, namely the form *have.* Of all the many infinitives that get activation through the |infinitive| node there is one node that will reach a relative activation maximum, namely the infinitive form *have,* since this form is also activated by the node |HAVE|. Similarly, of all the –*ed* participle forms that receive activation from the node |-*ed* participle|, one is singled out since it also receives activation from the meaning node |M(play)|. This activation pattern will lead to the grammatical string '*will have played*', as portrayed in figure 4.27.

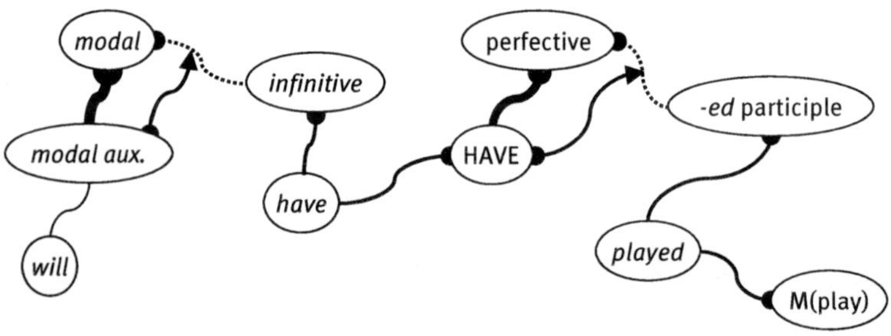

Figure 4.27: The activation pattern for 'modal + perfective' with the lexical verb PLAY.

69 See also Lamb's (1998: 272) concept 'transition pairs' and the discussion of their relevance for learning sequence.

70 For the sake of simplicity we will not specify any particular modal meaning.

A problem that has not been discussed so far is how we arrive at the order 'modal + perfective'. It does not seem reasonable to assume that the 'thought' or 'conceptualization' of PLAY together with modal and perfective aspect has an intrinsic order – the thought does not appear to be arrangeable in a linear sequence. In the present model this means that the nodes |modal|, |perfective|, and |M(play)| all become activated at the same time. Without a mechanism that accounts for the sequence 'modal + perfective', a possible result of the activation spreading might be *will play had*. How does the model 'know' that the infinitive following the modal auxiliary must be *have* and not *play* (note that the node |*play*| (not shown in Figure 4.27) also receives activation from two nodes, namely |M(play) | and |infinitive|)? The answer, as in the case of word forms and the phonemes that realise them, lies in the strength of the connections between the nodes |modal|, |perfective| and |M(play)| and the nodes which they activate. This is expressed by the different strengths of the connections leading from the node |modal| to |modal aux.|, |perfective| and |HAVE|, as well as |M(play)| and |*played*|. Even if we assume that the three source nodes are fully activated at the same time, the realization of the modal part of the string will be started before the realization of the perfective part, which will be started before the lexical verb part. The individual parts of the complex verb phrase are realised in the correct order. The same mechanism is also at work with the following examples (it will, however, not be discussed at any great length).

Let us next consider the pattern 'perfective + progressive + M(play)' (figure 4.28). As before, the node |perfective| will activate |HAVE| and |-*ed* participle|. The node |progressive| spreads its activation to the nodes |BE| and |-*ing* participle|. Note, however, that as above the figure below shows different strengths of connections. Because of these, the perfective part of the complex verb phrase will be realised first. More specifically, the first form to be realised is a form of HAVE (which one exactly is irrelevant here). The activation of the node |HAVE| supports the spreading of activation from |perfective| to |-*ed* participle|. Once this node is active it will start to activate all past participle nodes in the network. In the meantime the activation has spread from |progressive| to |BE| and from there on to all the forms of |BE|. Among these, the node |*been*| which already receives activation from the node |-*ed* participle| and hence is the most active node of all past participle nodes and will, accordingly, be realised. Eventually, the activation spreading from |progressive| to |-*ing* participle| has, since it is boosted by |BE|, activated the node |-*ing* participle| which will partly activate all –*ing* forms. One of these, namely *playing*, receives additional activation from the node |M(play)| and will be realised.

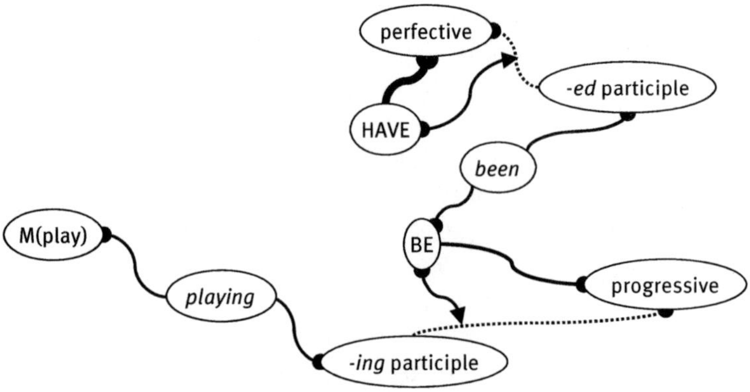

Figure 4.28: The activation pattern for 'perfective + progressive' with the lexical verb PLAY.

Again, it becomes apparent how important 'timing' through different connection strengths is. First of all, it guarantees that all of the elements occur in the right order. Secondly, it prevents 'clashes' of different word forms of the same lexeme. In the present case the network model would not know which form of BE to choose, if all nodes were allowed to spread the activation with the same speed. In that case, the two nodes |*been*| and |*being*| would both become equally activated because both receive activation from two nodes, namely |BE| and |-*ed* participle| or |-*ing* participle|, respectively. Because of the different connection strengths leading away from the two nodes |perfective| and |progressive|, the node |-*ing* participle| is not yet active while |-*ed* participle| is. So, of all the forms of BE, *been* is the one that gets singled out.

A similar problem occurs with the sequence 'progressive + passive + M(play)', since both the progressive and the passive involve a form of BE. This problem is solved by the same mechanism, which leads to such an order of activation that the node |-*ing* participle| is activated together with the node |BE|, whereas the node |-*ed* participle| is still more or less dormant at that point in time (see figure 4.29).

In the above, I have shown how the structures 'modal + perfective', 'perfective + progressive', and 'progressive + passive' are represented in the network. From this it should be clear how other, more complex, structures, can be arrived at. The most complex VP structure, i.e. 'modal + perfective + progressive + passive', can be represented by joining together the structures depicted in figures 4.27-29. The complete network constellation for the fully expanded verb phrase is given in figure 4.30 below.

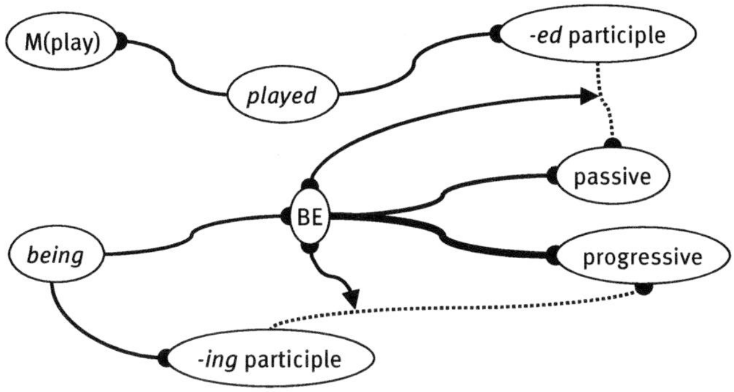

Figure 4.29: The activation pattern for 'progressive + passive' with the lexical verb PLAY.

To sum up what has been said about the complex verb phrase structure, figure 4.30 illustrates how the verb phrase (*will*) *have been being played* is captured in the present network model. The starting point for the activation is the five nodes in grey. The co-activation of these five nodes represents the 'thought' that precedes the articulation of the string. Above it was said that each meaning element and each grammatical category is active simultaneously, that is, all of them are activated at the same time. If all five nodes spread their activation with the same speed and if all neighbouring nodes were fully active at the same time, it would be impossible in the network to guarantee the correct sequence of elements. To make sure that elements occur in the right order, the links that con-

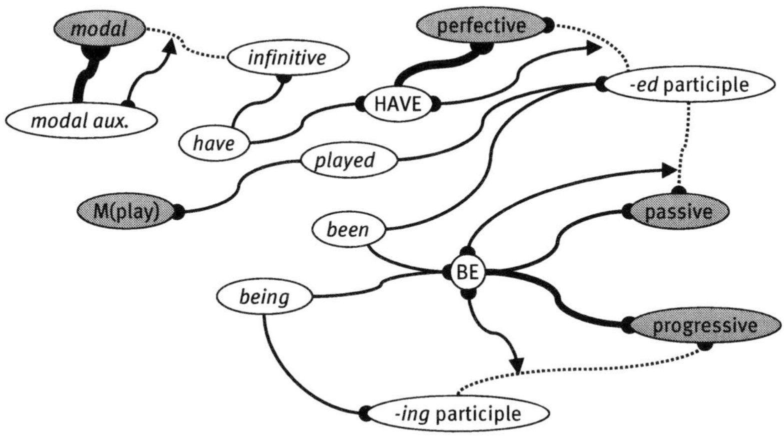

Figure 4.30: The complex VP *(will) have been being played* in the network model.

nect the five nodes in grey to their neighbouring nodes pass on the activation with different speeds: while activation spreads very quickly from the node |modal| (which is responsible for the first element in the complex verb phrase), it spreads fairly slowly from the lexical verb nodes (which are responsible for the last element). These differences in strength are such that the node relevant for the realization of the second part of modality (infinitive) is activated at the same time as the node relevant for the realization of the first part of perfective aspect (i.e. |HAVE|). This guarantees the correct form of the auxiliary, namely *have*. The perfective portion of the network 'overlaps' in a similar way with the progressive portion (resulting in *been*) and so on.

In a similar fashion, other structures, such as those of other phrases or of clauses, can be implemented in the current network model. One fundamental mechanism at work in the implementation of sequence is the *if-then* pattern. It makes sure that nodes are activated and that relevant word forms are realised in the correct order. It was shown how this mechanism leads to the formation of more or less simple structural representations in the network. Most importantly, it was shown that, on the basis of these simple structures alone, the network is able to produce highly complex structures even though these may never have been encountered before. The network model advocated here thus does not have any problems to account for aspects of productivity. This will also be seen in the following section, where the representation of rules in the network model is discussed.

4.2.5 The representation of rules

The appropriate description and representation of patterns in language data is one aim of the linguistic enterprise. Another aim is, of course, to create, generate or predict language strings that have not been encountered before. That is, the network has to show that it is able to implement grammatical rules.

As a first example of rules let us consider the formation of the regular past tense in English. The problem for us will be to explain how, on the basis of a number of known regular past tense forms, the general rule for past tense formation can be extracted from or induced in the data. Note that here I do not aim at developing a model of the acquisition of the regular past tense allomorphs by a human infant. The focus at present lies in showing that the envisaged network model, in principle, is able to learn by establishing nodes and connections and that the model can accommodate grammatical rules merely by establishing such nodes and links. Nevertheless, the 'learning' described in the following might, with the necessary refinements, serve as a basis for the description of language acquisition, since in this model I will only make use of very basic cognitive mechanisms, that also the infant has at its disposal, as described in section 4.2.

In the following we will make a number of simplifying assumptions about the state of the network at which the 'learning' takes place. These simplifications will make it easier to present and understand the basic processes that are going on, but they do not in any way invalidate the claims about the potential of the network model. In particular, the following assumptions are made: 1) In this example we will only be concerned with the spoken word forms, since these are more interesting in regard to the formation of the regular past tense. 2) The network is able to draw a distinction between homophonous forms, i.e. the network already has distinguished past tense forms from homophonous past participle forms (see section 6.3 for word-sense disambiguation). 3) The network has already learned or knows a number of past tense word forms together with their meanings, such as *loved* and 'M(love) + in the past' or *went* and 'M(go) + in the past'[71] (see figure 4.31). 4) All of these forms are understood and processed as holistic units, i.e. the network has not yet learned the general rule that underlies the formations of the past tense forms. The following will show how this rule can be established with the help of the two basic cognitive mechanisms described in section 4.2.

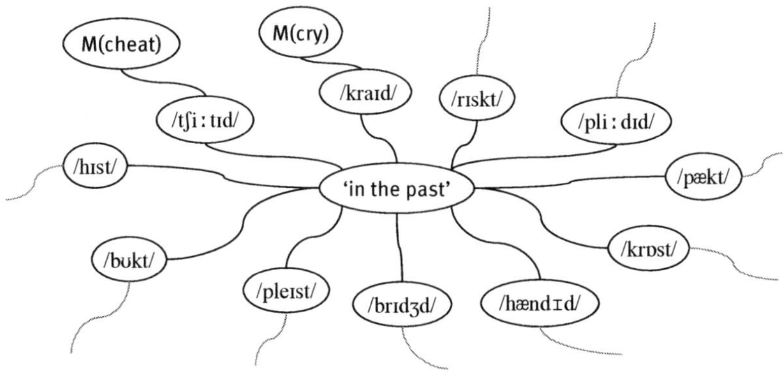

Figure 4.31: Past tense forms and their meanings in a holistic model. (note that the meaning nodes are not made explicit for all of the past tense forms)

71 Recall that M(___) denotes the meaning of the word form in brackets (see section 2.2.3).

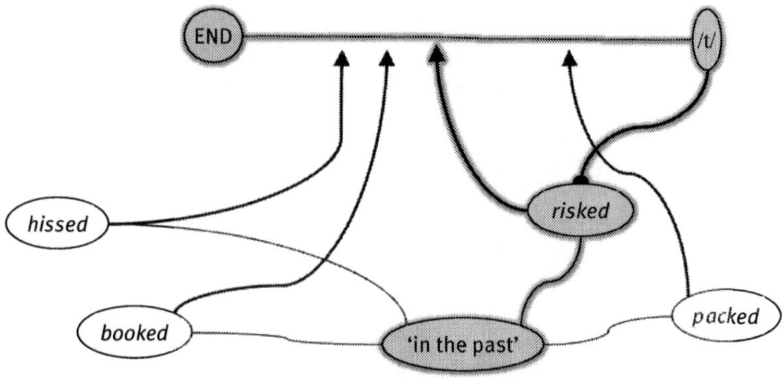

Figure 4.32: The co-activation of nodes relevant for the formation of the past tense allomorph /t/ (some details have been omitted).

The beginning state of our network is a collection of pairings of past tense forms and their respective meanings. At this stage the word forms are perceived and processed as holistic units, as figure 4.31 shows. The term 'holistic', here, refers to the fact that the word forms are not analysed in their component parts: the word form [tʃiːtɪd], for instance, will be connected to the meaning nodes |M(cheat)| and |'in the past'| without decomposing it into [tʃiːt] and [-ɪd] and their respective meanings.

The next step in learning the past tense allomorphs (among the lines of Bybee 1985 or 1988) is to associate particular endings of words with the meaning 'in the past'. How is this achieved? In the previous section the |START| node was introduced and it was said that the |END| node worked just the same. Let us consider the situation for a number of words ending in /-t/. Any time a past tense form is activated the meaning node 'in the past' will be co-activated; this is also true for any past tense form ending in /-t/. For each of these forms, in addition, the final /-t/ will be linked to and co-activated together with the |END| node. This situation is depicted for the past tense form *risked* in figure 4.32.

The organism repeatedly encounters the same situation with different word forms, i.e. there is a frequent co-activation of the three nodes |'in the past'|, |END| and |/t/|. This co-activation will lead to the association of the three nodes through additional links: the past tense allomorph /-t/ has been 'discovered', as shown in figure 4.33.

Note again that the abstraction involved in the discovery of the past tense allomorph is a consequence of the nature of network and the processes going on in it. The nodes that represent the allomorph become associated only because

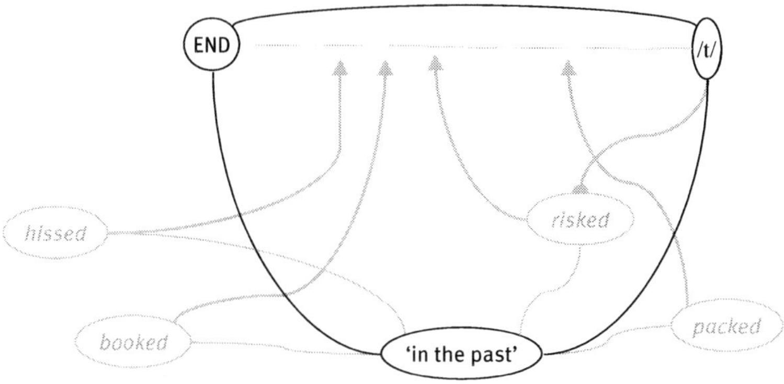

Figure 4.33: The past tense allomorph /-t/ in the network.

they are co-activated any time a past tense form ending in /-t/ is encountered. Again, additional features (i.e. nodes) related to the individual word forms will be abstracted away from, simply because they do not co-occur frequently enough.

A slight modification to figure 4.33 above has to be made, if we want to make sure that the phoneme /-t/ only triggers the meaning 'in the past', if it occurs in word-final position. This can be implemented without any problems, if the link between the phoneme node and the meaning node is a very weak one, which is boosted by a link originating in the node |END|. The occurrence of the sound [t] will only be indicative of past tense, if it occurs at the end of the word.

The allomorph /-d/ is represented in the same fashion and the argument is exactly the same. Slightly different is the allomorph /-ɪd/, because in this case two phonemes are involved. It was said in section 2.1.3 that the frequent occurrence of a string of elements will lead to the formation of a 'unit' that represents this experience. This is the same with the string /-ɪd/: as it occurs very often, a node will be established in the network that represents this sequence. If we assume the existence of such a node, the argument for how the /-ɪd/ allomorph is learnt is the same as for the other two allomorphs.

So far the network model merely contains the information that a particular group of endings, i.e. /-ɪd/, /-d/, and /-t/, can be used to express past tense meaning. The network so far manages to represent and describe patterns that show in language data, but it does not yet provide us with the possibility to make predictions about future. We have not yet managed to implement the rule of past tense formation, i.e. the network does not yet show which ending is used when. Again, the implementation of the rule of past tense formation is based on very fundamental and simple mechanisms of association and spreading activation.

Let us consider the production of past tense forms first. As an example we will take the past tense on /-t/. The node |/t/|, as argued above, is not only connected to the meaning node |'in the past'|, but is also strongly connected to a number of other phoneme nodes (all those that represent unvoiced sounds apart from /t/) because these phoneme nodes tend to co-occur with /t/ fairly frequently. More specifically, the phoneme nodes are likely to pre-activate the node |/t/|. In a similar fashion, the other two allomorphs are associated with the phonemes that precede them. The following figure depicts this situation and includes the verb *kiss* in the network to show how a regular past tense in /-t/ is formed.

The formation of the past tense form of *kiss* (figure 4.34) starts with an activation of the two meaning nodes |'in the past'| and |M(kiss)|. From the first node, activation will travel to the three phonemes nodes that realise the past

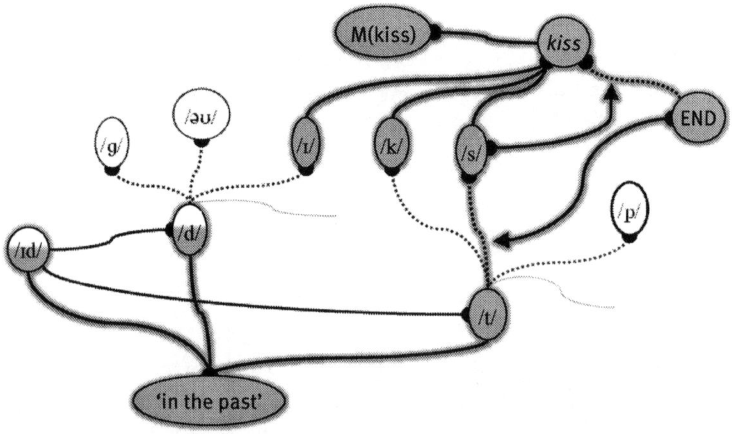

Figure 4.34: Composing the past tense of *kiss*. Activation starts from the two meaning nodes[72].

72 A slightly different version would not only include the individual phonemes but articulatory features like /+plosive/, /-plosive/, /+voice/, /-voice/ etc. The past tense allomorph nodes would then not necessarily have to be associated with the individual phonemes but with those features nodes, e.g. |/+plosive/| and |/+alveolar/| would prime the node |/-ɪd/|.

tense allomorphs. These nodes will be activated to some extent. The decision which node to activate fully depends on the base form at hand. In the present case (*kiss*) the node |M(kiss)| will spread activation to |*kiss*| which will then, one after the other, activate the three relevant phoneme nodes.

All of these are, of course, linked to one of the three allomorph nodes, which might lead to problems: a fully activated node |/ɪ/|, for instance, will start spreading activation to the node |/d/|, because it is associated with that node. To prevent that from occurring, a node-to-link connection is implemented in the network. As above, the links from the individual phonemes to the allomorph phonemes are fairly weak (indicated by a dotted line), i.e. activation spreading from one to the other takes a lot of time. The links from the phoneme nodes to their respective past tense allomorph node receive supplementary activation, if the phoneme is the last phoneme in the word. With *kiss*, for example, the node |/s/| represents the end of the word. As soon as the phoneme node is activated, it will boost the link from |*kiss*| to |END|, which will result in the full activation of the latter node. This node, in turn, will spread activation to the weak link between |/s/| and the node |/t/|, which is the matching realization of the past tense in that case. Again, we see the usefulness of the *if-then* structure discussed in section 2.2.2.4. The part of the network just discussed implements the following: if the word ends in –*s*, then boost the activation that the node |/s/| sends to the node |/-t/|. That is, activation spreading from |/s/| to |/t/| is amplified, which will contribute significantly to the overall activation of the node |/t/|, which eventually will then be realised as the past tense allomorph.[73] The resulting sequence of realised phonemes is thus: /k/, /ɪ/, /s/, /t/ – the correct form.

The analysis (i.e. the de-composition) of past tense forms is less complicated than their production or composition. The activation of the first three phoneme nodes will lead to a full activation of the word form node |*kiss*|, which will activate the associated meaning node. The remaining phoneme /t/ will activate the respective node which will pass this activation on to |'in the past'|. The co-activation of the two nodes |M(kiss)| and |'in the past'| is how the network captures the decomposition of the complex form *kissed* (figure 4.35).

So far, we have shown that grammatical rules, in particular the rule for regular past tense formation, can be implemented in the network merely by estab-

73 Note that we are not concerned with the actual articulation of past tense form here. The focus at this stage lies in showing how the appropriate past tense ending is chosen on the basis of the meaning that should be expressed.

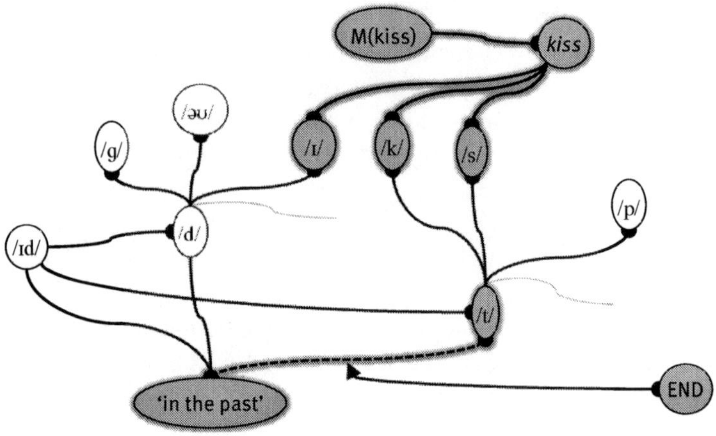

Figure 4.35: Decomposing *kissed*. Activation starts from the phoneme nodes.

lishing nodes and connections of varying strengths between individual nodes. The rule for regular past tenses, thus, is not formulated as an algorithm, but is distributed in the nodes and connections in the network. It was shown that the network presentation is able to account for the regularities that are found in language data, since both the composition/production and de-composition/analysis of isolated past tense forms can be accounted for by merely following the routes that activation takes through this network. Note again that the 'learning' that has been sketched out in this network is the result of two basic cognitive mechanisms, which come into play at different stages of learning; these are summarized in figure 4.36 below.

Since learning can take place in the model presented here, it is in general also applicable to the description of language acquisition. Acquiring a language, in the present model, can be represented by establishing nodes and connections between nodes and by specifying the degree of entrenchment of individual nodes and the strength of connections between them. In the following, I will show how a well-known phenomenon of language acquisition, namely over-generalization of the rule for regular past tense forms[74], can be accounted for by changes in the network representation of the language system.

Let us consider the example of the past tense form *went*, i.e. [went]. This form is one among the many holistic past tense forms which characterize the

74 See Cazden (1968), or Kuczaj (1977 and 1978) for details.

cognitive mechanism	**status of the network**
	holistic form-meaning pairings
perception of similarities & categorization	↓
	category: past tense forms
perception of similarities & categorization	↓
	categories: past tenses ending in /-ɪd/,/-d/, and /-t/
association of isolated events (and nodes)	↓
	past tense allomorphs: association of meaning and form
perception of similarities & categorization	↓
	categories: present tense forms ending in /-d/, /-t/, etc. related to endings ➔ 'rule' for regular past tense composition and de-composition.

Figure 4.36: Mechanisms in the development of the regular past tense rule.

initial state of our network. Like all other forms at this stage, the form [went] will be treated as a holistic unit paired with the meaning units 'M(go)' and 'in the past', i.e. there will be a strong connection between the three nodes |/went/|, |M(go) | and | 'in the past'|. It follows that at this stage, the young child will provide the correct past tense of go any time it is produced, since all past tense forms are stored as fixed form-meaning pairs. In contrast to most of the other past tense forms, the past tense [went] will not be associated with any of the three regular allomorph classes, i.e. there will be no connection between the node |/went/| and the nodes |/ɪd/|, |/d/|, and |/t/|. As a consequence, the form [went] will remain represented in the network as an unanalysable unit with a fixed meaning connected to it. At the same time the non-past form [gəʊ] also is part of the network (represented by the node |go|) and, just like the regular non-past forms [rəʊ] or [fləʊ], connected to that portion of the network where the formation of regular past tenses is implemented. The search for the correct form to the meaning 'M(go) in the past' thus leads to a race between the composition of the past tense based on the meaning components 'M(go)'and 'in the past'[75] and the retrieval of the form *went*. This competition either leads to the correct form [went] or to the composed but incorrect form [gəʊd], as shown in figure 4.37.

---

75 For a discussion of 'parallel dual-route models' see Baayen et al. (1997) and Baayen & Schreuder (1999).

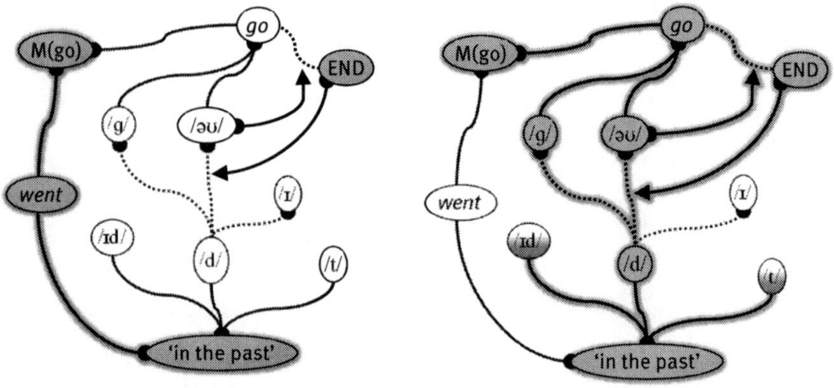

Figure 4.37: The whole-word route and the composition route of the past tense of *go*.

Which route wins depends on the extent to which the different processes have been trained and are more deeply entrenched in the cognitive system. Once the past tense allomorphs have been 'discovered', their representation in the cognitive system will be very strong, since the frequency of regular past tense forms is a lot higher than that of the irregular form *went*. The other network portion relevant for the formation of regular past tenses is that part which relates word endings to the allomorph nodes, in the present case the link from |/əʊ/| to |/d/| and those parts relating to the representation of the fact that the word *go* ends in [əʊ]. Note that the boosting of the link from |/əʊ/| to |/d/| is not restricted to the word form *go* but relates to any word form that ends in this diphthong (regardless of regular or irregular past tense), e.g. *row*, *know*, *grow*, *flow*, *swallow* or *follow*. As a consequence, the connection of the word ending node |/əʊ/| and the past tense allomorph node |/d/| and any portions involved in the boosting of that connection are also well-trained. The composition route will win out over the whole-word route, thus leading to the well-known overgeneralization in this and similar cases.

Such cases of overgeneralization are, as we all know, only temporal. At some point in language acquisition the child will re-learn the correct past tense form. This can also be explained through changes in connection strengths between nodes in the network. Any time the infant utters the wrong past tense form, it will most probably be corrected by one of its interlocutors, so that from now on the connection relevant for the whole-word route will be strengthened any time the she or he produces the wrong past tense form. In the long run, the connection between the nodes representing the holistic meaning and the form will be stronger and faster than the incorrect composite route. It is important to note, though, that the incorrect composition still is 'dormant' in the network, but it is always slower than the whole-word route. If the whole-word route is not exercised for a long period of time, the connection might lose its strength over time and the composition route might be faster again. This way, the present network is able to explain why "morphological irregularity is always centered in the high frequency items of a language" (Bybee & Thompson 1997: 380).

This discussion has shown how important aspects of language acquisition can be accounted for in the present network model. A major advantage of this model is that we do not have to make a decision between those elements that are analysed or composed on the basis of grammatical rules and those that are stored as holistic units and retrieved from memory as wholes. This is due to the fact that the present model is a competition model (see section 2.2.2.5). As soon as a node in the network becomes activated, this activation spreads along connections to neighbouring nodes. As was described above, this leads to a race of activations in which the faster, i.e. the better trained, path wins. This results in a strengthening of this path and thus leads to faster spreading of activation through this path the next time. At the same time, activation will also spread along other paths, but the fastest path wins. Nevertheless, the slower path usually remains implemented in the network. In this way we can account for the fact that, in a number of cases, regular composite forms are stored in the language system, although the grammatical rule that generates these forms is already fully implemented. This aspect of the network model is explored in the following.

4.2.6 Rules and their instantiations: redundancy and related issues

In section 2.1.2 it was argued that it is necessary for the present model of the language system to store redundant information, such as regular word forms of a lexeme, even though they could in principle be composed and decomposed on the basis of a grammatical rule, which needs to be part of the model anyway. The present section will discuss the ideas glanced at in 2.1.2 in more detail.

The importance of frequency in the shaping of the language system has been underlined by many researchers over the last one or two decades. According to some, frequency effects are all-pervasive and can be found in any area of language processing and production. A case in point is Ellis (2002), who claims that "frequency effects in the processing of phonology, phonotactics, reading, spelling, lexis, morphosyntax, formulaic language, language comprehension, grammaticality, sentence production, and syntax" (143)[76].

Even though some researchers in the field doubt this special role of frequency (see, for instance, Eubank & Gregg 2002 or Bley-Vroman 2002), and others point to limits of purely frequency-based accounts (e.g. Garret 2001, Gass & Mackey 2002, Gibson et al. 1996, and Larsen-Freeman 2002) or regard frequency as only one factor among others (e.g. Tarone 2002)[77], there is a large number of studies that suggest that frequency is a major determinant in many areas of linguistics: for instance, research report on frequency effects in sound change within and across words (e.g. Phillips 2001 or Pierrehumbert 2001, and Bush 2001, respectively), in ambiguity resolution (e.g. MacDonald 1994, or Hare et al. 2001; but see Gibson & Schütze 1999 and Pickering et al. 2000 for dissenting views), processing (e.g. Verhoeven et al. 2004) or grammaticalization (e.g. Hoffmann 2005 and Krug 2001) to name but a few.

A particularly useful and widely discussed notion in the area of frequency effects in language is that of 'entrenchment', already mentioned occasionally in the previous sections. Entrenchment, introduced by Ronald Langacker (e.g. 1987 and 2000b), is regarded as one of a "number of basic and very general psychological phenomena that are essential to language" (2000b: 3). The basic idea is that very frequent "psychological events leave some kind of trace that facilitates their re-occurrence" (3). Such traces have been verified in a number of psychological experiments. The influence of word frequency, for instance, is described as "one of the most robust findings in both speech production [...] and language comprehension" by Bertram, Baayen and Schreuder (2000a: 390; see also references therein), i.e. highly frequent words are processed faster and more accurately than those with low frequencies. It is important to note, though, that this observation does not only hold for monomorphemic words but also for morphologically complex ones. For Dutch regular plurals in *–en*, for instance, Baayen et al. (1997) report on correlations of response latencies (i.e.

76 See, for instance, the edited volume by Bybee and Hopper (2001), which documents frequency effects on many levels of linguistic description.

77 Not surprisingly, Ellis (2002) also does not regard frequency as the sole *explanans* in linguistic theory. With regard to language acquisition he writes: "Of course, frequency is not a sufficient explanation [...]. There are many other determinants of acquisition. Semantic basicness, salience, communicative intent, and relevance are major determining factors in the acquisition process [...]" (174). Still, he argues that "there is now ample justification for its reinstatement as an all-pervasive causal factor" (179).

reaction times) in lexical decision tasks and frequencies of occurrence[78]. In one experiment, subjects had to decide whether a letter string that was presented was a Dutch word or not. It was found that latencies were smaller for highly frequent plurals than for less frequent ones. The authors claim that their experimental results suggest an explanation in terms of processing effort:

> Many mental activities require forms of computation. Some computations must be carried out so many times that it becomes advantageous to store the results, so that the outcome can be immediately retrieved from memory. (Baayen el al. 1997: 94)

A similar view is expressed by Langacker (2000b: 3), when he writes that "[t]hrough repetition, even a highly complex event can coalesce into a well-rehearsed routine that is easily elicited and reliably executed". This view has far-reaching consequences for a model of the language system. More specifically, the idea of coalescence of complex (and hence decomposable) units into one unit that is accessed as a whole undermines one of the major tenets of more traditional approaches in linguistics and grammar; namely, the idea of a syntactic component that takes care of anything that is regular in language, and a lexicon which serves as the "the dumping ground of irregularity" (Du Bois 2003: 48). This traditional view (see, for instance, Pinker and Prince 1994 or Clahsen 1999, among others), is driven by what Croft and Cruse (2004: 278) term 'storage parsimony', a principle that advocates the non-redundant storage of information (see also Baayen's 2003: 243 related notion of 'greedy' as opposed to 'lazy' learning). That is, any language phenomenon that is regular and can thus be computed by the application of a set of rules is not stored in the mental grammar but computed online during production and processing. This assumption has been called into question by Lamb (2000: 93) among many others. He emphasizes "[t]he fact that it is possible to construct a theory of linguistic extension [i.e. language data] in this way is neither justification nor evidence for assuming that somehow the mind of the ordinary speaker performs such mental acrobatics". Grammar models driven by storage parsimony, according to Langacker (1987: 28), are a consequence of what he calls the 'exclusionary fallacy', an assumption which wrongly suggests "that one analysis, motivation, categorization, cause, function, or explanation for a linguistic phenomenon necessarily precludes another." A special instance of the exclusionary fallacy is the 'rule/list fallacy', i.e.:

78 See Bien et al. (2005) for a discussion of frequency effects in the production of compounds; see Ellis (2002) for an overview of frequency effects in different areas of language.

> the assumption, on grounds of simplicity, that particular statements (i.e. lists) must be excised from the grammar of a language if general statements (i.e. rules) that subsume them can be established. Given the general N + -s noun-pluralizing rule of English, for instance, specific plural forms following that rule (*beads, shoes, toes, walls*) would not be listed in an optimal grammar. (Langacker 1987: 29)

Such a view on the language system seems to lack psychological plausibility. Dabrowska (2004: 27) points to the fact that "[h]uman brains are relatively slow processors, but have enormous storage capacity. From a psychological point of view, therefore, retrieval from memory is the preferred strategy". Langacker integrates storage as well as rules in the following "viable alternative" to the 'rule vs. list' approach, namely

> to include in the grammar both rules and instantiating expressions. This option allows any valid generalizations to be captured (by means of rules), and while the descriptions it affords may not be maximally economical, they have to be preferred on grounds of psychological accuracy to the extent that specific expressions do in fact become established as well-rehearsed units. Such units are cognitive entities in their own right whose existence is not reducible to that of the general patterns they instantiate. (Langacker, 2000b: 2)

This view also seems plausible considering recent theories of language acquisition. In a number of papers, Tomasello and his collaborators argue that complex constructions are learned the same way as lexical items. Tomasello and Abott-Smith (2002) write:

> Children acquire the more regular and rule-based construction of a language in the same way they acquire the more arbitrary and idiosyncratic constructions: they learn them. And, as in the learning of all complex cognitive activities, their initial learning is of concrete things – particular words (e.g. cat), complex expressions (e.g. I-wanna-do-it), or mixed constructions such as Where's-the ___ (which are partially concrete and partially abstract) – which is then followed at some point by the construction of abstract categories and schemas out of these concrete pieces of language [...] (Tomasello & Abott-Smith 2002: 207-208)

For instance, with regard to the acquisition of the transitive construction, Dodson and Tomasello (1998: 618) conclude that "children below approximately 2;10 [2 years and 10 months] do not have a verb-general transitive construction, but rather they have a collection of relatively independent verb island constructions". That is, young children have not acquired the use of transitive verbs as soon as they produce their first transitive construction. Rather, in the early months of language acquisition, complex constructions seem to be related to a number of specific instantiations of these constructions, in this case constructions centering around verbs, and the more general transitive construction is only abstracted later. In a more recent study Childers and Tomasello (2001) mitigate the importance of the verb in the acquisition of the transitive construction and suggest that pronoun configurations in language input might be of prime importance. This, however, does not invalidate the general claim that regular and rule-based constructions are acquired on the basis of a set of specific exemplars that have been rote-learned by the child. Experiments on the acquisition of the German *Perfekt* show similar results (see Wittek & Tomasello 2002 for details). On the whole, Tomasello and his co-workers find that

> children's early linguistic representations are very likely based in specific item-based constructions (with some abstract slots), and it is only in the late preschool period that their utterance-level constructions take on adultlike abstractness. (Tomasello 2006: 285; see also Abbot-Smith & Tomasello 2006)

It is important to note, though, that "as children create more general constructions, they do not throw away their more item-based and local constructions" (Tomasello 2003b: 11). In this way, rules or abstract constructions and concrete instantiations are supposed to co-exist, at least in the mental grammar of the child during language acquisition[79].

To what extent and for how long rules and instantiating items co-exist is a question that has not yet been answered fully.[80] Evidence suggests that at least highly frequent instantiations of regular phenomena are stored in addition to the rule that 'generates' them. An analysis of regular and irregular verb forms by Stemberger and MacWhinney (1988: 112) shows that "high-frequency regularly inflected forms [... are] stored in the lexicon and [...] that low-frequency regularly inflected forms are not stored in the lexicon" (see also Baayen et al. 1997 or Gordon & Alegre 1999 for similar evidence). For instance, the number of errors in producing regular past tense verb forms is higher for low-frequency than for

---

79 See Dabrowska (2006) for similar conclusions concerning the acquisition of diminutives in Polish.

80 Note that some approaches (e.g. connectionist models) dispense with rules altogether, a view which is partly supported by experimental data. Kroot et al. (2001: 53) claim that "at least in the domain of morphological processing, there are no rules that are formed on the basis of initially stored examples of complex words, with the initial exemplars fading from memory. Instead, we assume that many fully regular complex words, both inflected and derived, remain available in the mental lexicon [...] and serve as exemplars for the analogical formation of novel forms. In other words, we hypothesize that rules are essentially analogical in nature [...]." See also Bybee (2006 or 2010) and her exemplar model.

high-frequency verbs in naturally occurring as well as experimental data, a frequency effect that clearly implies storage for highly frequent regular forms[81]. As Bybee and Thompson (1997) remark:

> [t]he effects of frequency have important implications for our notions of mental representation. There is not necessarily just one representation per construction; rather, a specific instance of a construction, with specific lexical items in it, can have its own representation in memory if it is of high frequency. (Bybee & Thompson 1997: 386).

In the following, I will show how the redundant storage of complex forms emerges as a consequence of the nature of the network model advocated here.

Let us again consider the analysis of the regular past tense form *kissed*. This word form will be decomposed according to the formation of past tenses, which will lead to an activation of the respective meaning nodes, as shown in figure 4.35 above. Since the two meanings are co-activated they will lead to the formation of a complex meaning, namely 'M(kiss)' + 'in the past'. Note that both

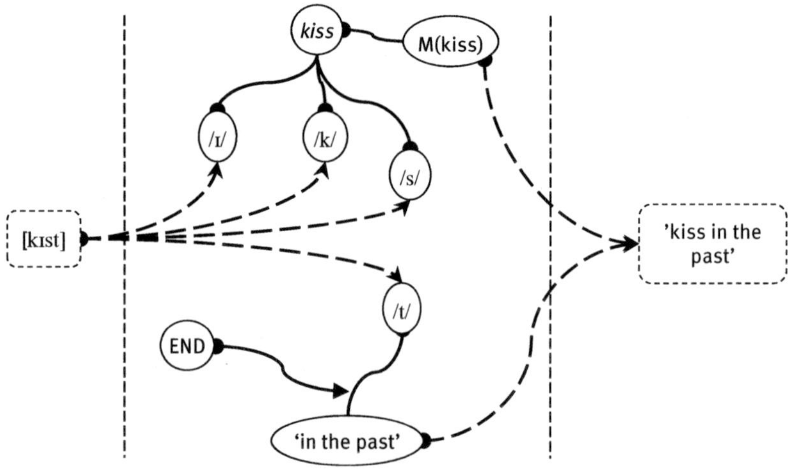

Figure 4.38: Decomposing [kɪst].

---

81 See Hay (2001: 1060) for a slightly different view. She claims that the compositionality of complex forms does not depend on the absolute but on the relative frequency of the complex form, i.e. "the frequency of the derived form relative to its base". Note also that frequency is not the only factor that influences storing or parsing/computation in morphology (see Bertram, Schreuder and Baayen 2000).

the past tense form and its meaning are not yet established in the network; rather, let us assume that the past tense form is encountered the first time and analysed in the way described above. This is depicted in figure 4.38, where the dotted boxes and broken lines do not refer to connections in the network but to an incoming stimulus and an outgoing response; the portions of the network that are involved in the processing are in solid lines and enclosed within the vertical lines.

In line with the concept of entrenchment, i.e. the view that "the occurrence of psychological events leaves some kind of trace that facilitates their reoccurrence" (Langacker 2000b: 3), the frequent occurrence of the form [kɪst] will lead to the establishment of a node that represents this form in the network model. Similarly, the complex meaning will become represented as a node in the network, and so will the connections leading from the node |/kɪst/| and those leading to the complex meaning node. The complex form and the complex meaning have become part of the network, as in figure 4.39.

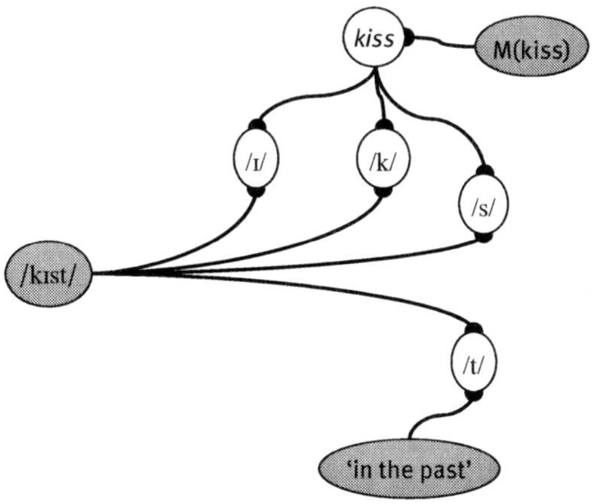

Figure 4.39: /kɪst/ and its meaning as part of the network.

Each analysis of the word form [kɪst] will lead to a strengthening of the connections in the network (in the direction from left to right), which will result in an increase in the speed of analysis of the word form. That is, the decomposition of the word form [kɪst] will be faster every time it is exercised (assuming, of course, that the intervals between successive decompositions are not too large). If we further assume that the activation of a node does not end abruptly but recedes gradually (see section 2.2.2.3), we find that, while the activation of |/kɪst/|

spreads through the network, the node itself will retain some of its original activation, dependent on the time that has passed since the node was activated. If the decomposition of [kɪst] is not yet 'trained', the respective node will have lost most of its activation by the time the result of the decomposition is arrived at. Through successive decomposition the speed of analysis will increase, and the node |/kɪst/| will have retained some of its activation when the nodes that represent the meaning of the form becomes activated, i.e. the three nodes are co-activated to some extent. The faster the analysis along the decomposition route, the higher the degree of co-activation of the three nodes. This will eventually lead to a direct connection between the node |/kɪst/| and its meaning nodes, which from that point onwards competes with the decomposition route and eventually might be faster than decomposition. The 'storage' of frequently used regular complex forms is, thus, a by-product of the general nature of the processes going on in the network, since networks "readily, in fact automatically, perform parallel processing" (Lamb 1998: 166). Therefore, it is in the nature of the present network model to realize what Langacker (2000b: 2) suggests as a 'viable alternative' to the traditional 'rule-list approach', namely "to include in the grammar both rules and instantiating expressions." Figure 4.40 below portrays this kind of co-existence in the present network model:

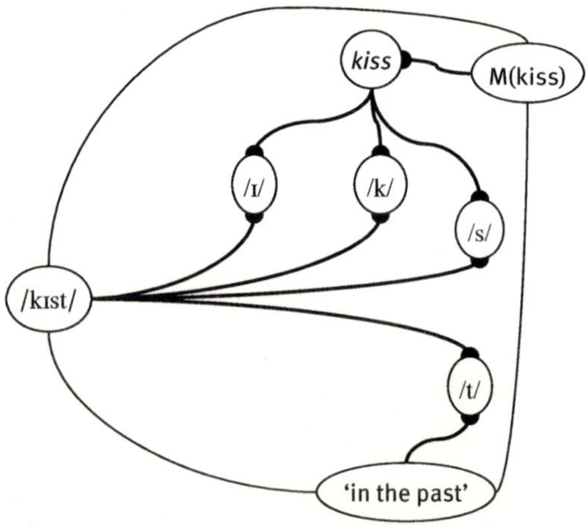

Figure 4.40: (De-)composition and whole-word route in the network.

The same argument holds for the composition of the past tense form and as such does not need to be explained in detail. The important aspect, again, is the fact that both rule and instantiation may co-exist in the network. This co-existence does not in any way invalidate the network model. On the contrary, the same mechanisms that are at work in the development of the network and in the learning that takes place in the network are also responsible for the development of holistic processing of decomposable units. This follows as a consequence of the nature of the network.

In the same way that entrenchment leads to redundant lexical storage of regular decomposable items it also keeps highly frequent items from changing their overt form. As Bybee (1985: 120; see also 2010: 25) shows, highly frequent irregular verb forms tend to remain irregular, while less frequent ones tend to become regular[82]. For instance, the frequently used verbs DRIVE, RIDE, KNOW and BUY have remained irregular, whereas rare verbs like BIDE, WEEP, SOW have been regularized. A verb like DREAM shows both forms; "morphological irregularity is always centered in the high frequency items of a language" (Bybee & Thompson 1997: 380). This effect is most strongly seen in the richness of forms of the lexeme BE. Being the most frequent verb in English, it shows a greater variety of forms than any other Modern English verb. Obviously, the frequency of occurrence and use in this case has influenced "the strength of representation in memory" (380).

The present network model is in line with these claims. The process of regular past tense formation can be regarded as extremely well entrenched in the cognitive system. The links from the meaning node |'in the past'| to the three allomorph nodes are very strong and activation will pass extremely quickly from the meaning node to these three nodes. These three allomorph nodes need additional activation from the node that represents the final phoneme of the base form. In the network, this mechanism, as was shown in section 4.2.5 is implemented by an *if-then* structure: if the word ends in a particular phoneme, say /m/, amplify the link that leads from this sound to the respective realization of past tense, in this case /-d/. Figure 4.41 illustrates this pattern with the example of the regular past tense formation of the verb DREAM. The activation of the node |/m/| will amplify the activation spreading from |*dream*| to |END|, thus leading to a full activation of the latter. This, in turn, will boost the activation leading from |/m/| to |/d/|, which would lead to the realization of [-d] as past tense morpheme. The important point is that the second part contributing to the realization of the regular past tense is also very deeply entrenched. For in-

---

82 See Corbett et al. (2001) for similar findings for irregularity in Russian. See Viereck (1989) for a more critical view of the explanatory power of frequency.

Table 4.5: Regular and irregular realizations of past tense for *buy* and *dream* in the BNC.

	Regular	Irregular
BUY	3 (*buyed*)	4280 (*bought*)
DREAM	314 (*dreamed*)	152 (*dreamt*)

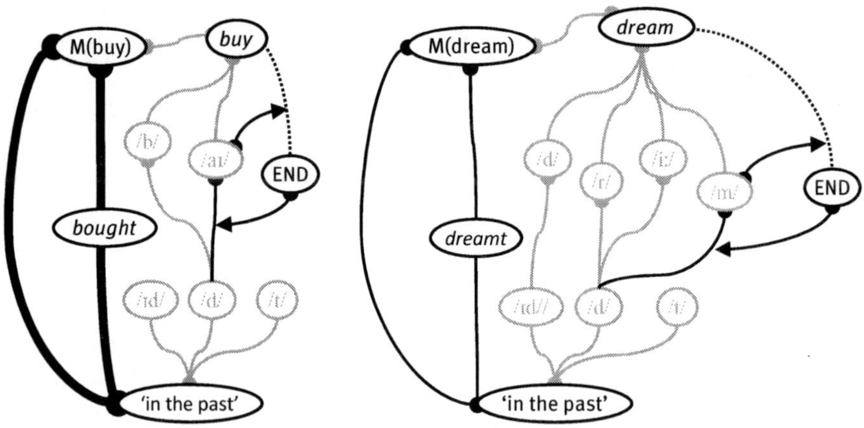

Figure 4.41: Two degrees of potential for regularization of irregular past tense forms in the network.

stance, a look at the BNC shows that the frequency of past tense forms ending in /md/ is similar to the frequency of those ending in /aɪd/ (somewhere in the vicinity of 50,000 and 40,000, respectively). It, thus, makes sense to assume that the process of regular past tense formation is more or less equally well entrenched for all possible base-final phonemes. Whether a past tense form will be formed regularly or not, then, depends on the entrenchment of those parts of the network that represent the irregular formation.

The network accounts for different degrees of entrenchment by the strengths of nodes and connections between nodes. Let us take a look at how the base forms *dream* and *buy* and their past tense form are realised in the network. Table 4.5 shows the frequencies of regular and irregular past tenses of these two words. The numbers are taken from the British National Corpus

(BNC). Figure 4.41 'translates' these numbers into strengths of connections in the network model. The parts that are relevant for the present discussion are in black print.

As can be seen in figure 4.41, the parts of the network responsible for regular past tense are similar with regard to the degree of entrenchment that they represent. The critical feature is the entrenchment of those portions of the network that represent the irregular past tense forms. With regard to *buy* there is a huge difference between the degree of entrenchment of the irregular and the regular network portion; with *dream* the two parts show a similar degree of entrenchment. While with *buy* it is unlikely, *dream* is likely to become regularized. This way, the present model manages implements findings on analogical leveling, as for instance described by Bybee:

> Since high-frequency exemplars have stronger representations than low-frequency ones [...] they are much more accessible than low-frequency exemplars. Their greater accessibility makes it much less likely that speakers would create alternate forms [...] that could eventually replace the irregular form. (Bybee 2010: 66-67)

4.2.7 A network view on morphological productivity

The discussion so far has placed an emphasis on token frequency, for instance, the frequency with which one particular word form, e.g. *kissed*, occurs in language use. As has been argued in above, this form is an instantiation of a particular process in English which could be glossed as 'add /t/ to a verb ending in /s/, /k/, etc. and you get the verb in the past'. This process is realized by different verb stems, such as *kiss* or *pack*. Each of the different verb stems are referred to as types. Accordingly, the type frequency of the process described above was the number of different verb stems that pertain to this process, i.e. the number of different instantiations of an identical process.

With regard to the regular past tense allomorph {-t}, we would speak of a high type frequency, which arguably leads to a deep entrenchment of this process (i.e. verb + {-t} = 'M(verb) in the past') into the mental grammar of the speaker. Note that type frequency depends on different instantiations of an identical process. If, for instance, a speaker would encounter many cases (e.g. 1,000) of, say, *kissed* but no other instances of regular past tense forms, the token frequency would be 1,000, the type frequency would be 1. A general 'rule' or category cannot be formed this way. Instead, let us assume that the speaker encounters a high number of different types of past tense forms (e.g. 100) which occur ten times each, the token frequency would still be 1,000, but the type frequency would be 100. In this case, the speaker would be able to abstract the rule for regular past tense formation from the individual cases:

> The more lexical items that are heard in a certain position in a construction, the less likely it is that the construction will be associated with a particular lexical item and the more likely it is that a general category will be formed over the items that occur in that position. [...] Furthermore, high type frequency ensures that a construction will be used frequently, which will strengthen its representational schema, making it more accessible for further use, possibly with new items. (Bybee & Thompson 1997: 384)

Like token frequency, the influence of type frequency has been documented in many studies. Schreuder and Baayen (1997), for instance, investigate the influence of what they call the morphological family size of a stem on word recognition (among other things). The term 'morphological family' refers to "the set of words derived from a given stem by means of either compounding (*tablespoon, timetable*) or derivation (*tablet, tabular*)" (121). While above we have been talking about the process of regular plural formation, the process under scrutiny now is derivation on the basis of *table*. The morphological family, thus, refers to all word-form types derived from this base. The size of this morphological family refers to the number of word-form types that can be formed with this particular base (excluding the base word itself). The influence of morphological family size was tested by lexical decision task experiments, i.e. subjects were presented with a string of letters and had to decide as quickly and accurately as possible, if the string was a word or not. It was found that simplex singular nouns were recognized faster, if the size of their morphological family was larger, i.e. the word-form-type frequency of the derivations of a simplex singular noun influences the processing speed of the noun itself. A similar experiment revealed that large morphological family sizes also lead to a quicker recognition of morphologically complex word forms (Bertram, Baayen and Schreuder 2000).

Type frequency can be connected to productivity and interacts with token frequency in interesting ways. Let us consider the case of regular past tense forms again. If, as we have seen, regular past tense forms are stored in the lexicon, does that have any influence on the productivity of the past tense morpheme? To put the question another way: what would happen, if a language user encountered many different instantiations of regular past tense forms, all of which were extremely frequent, maybe *kissed* or *packed*? Would high type frequency still guarantee productivity, if all types had a very high token frequency?

According to one family of models, namely competition models, morphologically complex words are accessed in two different ways, namely on the whole-word route and the compositional route, as we have seen above. In the first case, the word is not decomposed but the meaning of the regularly inflected form (which is stored in the lexicon) is accessed directly without an 'analyzing detour'. On the compositional route, the form is decomposed, each part accessed individually and then the meaning components are put together. It is important to note that

> [t]hese two routes are said to work in parallel and in competition. The whole-word access route is faster unless the item frequency of the complex word is very low. In that case, the compositional route wins out and the whole-word representation is not accessed. (Gordon & Alegre 1999: 213)

Frequent past tense forms like *kissed* are supposed to be stored as holistic units (see above) and they are accessed as a complete unit. That is, frequent regular forms will not be decomposed into their component parts and the decomposition route will not be exercised anymore. If all instantiations of the regular past tense occurred with high frequency (and, accordingly, none of the forms would be decomposed), the regular past tense formation would eventually 'get lost', since it is not exercised anymore (see Baayen & Renouf 1996 for a similar argument with regard to morphological productivity and measures thereof). As this thought experiment makes clear, high type frequency alone does not guarantee productivity. There must also be a (as yet unspecified) number of types with low token frequency for a pattern to become productive.

A case in point are the two morphemes {-ful$_1$} and {-ful$_2$}, relating to 'measure', e.g. *spoonful*, and 'property', e.g. *useful*, respectively. As Plag (2003: 57; see also Plag et al. 1999) shows, both morphemes have a similar type frequency in the written part of the BNC (i.e. c. 90 million words), namely 136 to 154. If type frequency alone was decisive for productivity, both derivational morphemes should be almost equally productive. However, the two show huge differences in the total number of tokens and in the number of very rare tokens, i.e. *hapax legomena*. As to the first, {-ful$_1$} occurs only 2,615 times in the corpus while {-ful$_2$} occurs 77,316 times. Also, many of the word forms instantiating the second type are extremely frequent, ranging from 10,366 for the most frequent to 4,202 for the sixth-most frequent type. These six types make up over half of the tokens of {-ful$_2$}. With regard to rare tokens, we find that the second type shows only 22 *hapax legomena*, i.e. types that are realized only once in the corpus, while the first is instantiated by 60 *hapax legomena*.

These differences are relevant for productivity as Baayen and Renouf (1996) make clear:

> [...] unproductive morphological categories will be characterized by a preponderance of high-frequency types, by low numbers of low-frequency types, and by very few, if any, hapax legomena, especially as the size of the sample (corpus or text) increases. Conversely, the availability of a productive word-formation rule for a given affix in the mental lexicon guarantees that even the lowest-frequency complex words with that affix can be produced or understood. Thus large numbers of hapax legomena are a sure sign that an affix is productive. (Baayen and Renouf 1996: 74)

Accordingly, {-ful$_2$} is a rather unproductive morpheme, while {-ful$_1$} is highly productive. With regard to the present network model, it is important to emphasize that both productive and unproductive morphemes show highly characteristic patterns of connectivity. In the first case, the lines leading away from the morpheme node to the nodes that represent its instantiating tokens would generally be rather thin, indicating a low token frequency of each of the instantiating types. In contrast, unproductive morphemes would be connected to their instantiating tokens by rather thick lines, indicating high frequency. The situation that Plag (2003) describes for the morphemes {-ful$_1$} and {-ful$_2$} would be represented in the present network model as shown in figure 4.42 below. Each line leading away from the two nodes represents a different type, i.e. a different lexical unit derived with the help of the morpheme within the node. Both nodes have the same number of lines, i.e. the type frequency is identical for both morphemes. But the individual lines show different degrees of thickness. Token frequencies are generally lower for the types related to {-ful$_1$} than for those related to {-ful$_2$}. In this way, the present network model manages to capture degrees of morphological productivity.

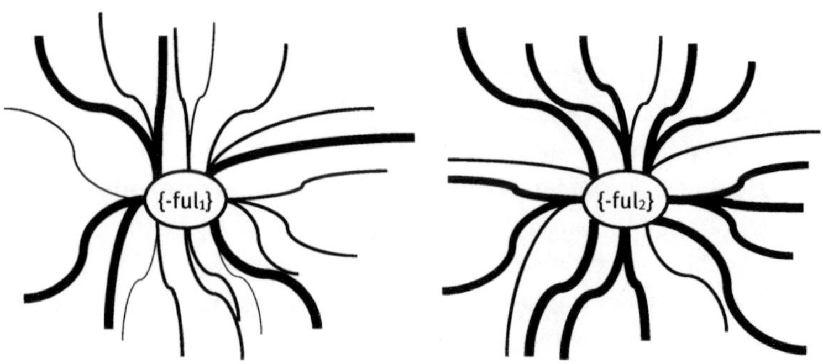

Figure 4.42: Degrees of morphological productivity in the network.

5 Cognitive schemas

Whereas the previous chapter focused on traditional descriptive concepts, categories and rules, the present chapter discusses a number of concepts that could be subsumed under the umbrella term 'cognitive schema'. This chapter begins with a description of schemas[83] from a psychological perspective and then discusses how this notion has found its way into linguistics, in particular in the area of construction grammar and pattern grammar. In addition, we will also look at what I would like to call 'recurrent item strings'. This term subsumes basic corpus linguistic notions such as 'collocation', 'colligation', POS-gram, etc. All of these also qualify as cognitive schemas, since they are based on language use and do away with the traditional separation of lexis and grammar. The chapter concludes with a description of how the network model advocated here accounts for such schemas.

5.1 Schemas in psychology and linguistics

Language schemas as described in cognitive linguistics can be related back to fairly old and time-tested concepts in cognitive psychology[84], where the idea that human memory is organised in terms of "interacting knowledge structures" (Rumelhart & Ortony 1977: 100) has been discussed and elaborated under various terms and guises. The most 'traditional' of these, 'schema', was introduced into modern psychology as early as 1932 in the writings of Bartlett (cf. Rumelhart & Ortony 1977: 100), and has been used ever since by researchers in the field. Other, sometimes narrower but essentially similar, terms from the field of Artificial Intelligence are 'frame' (Minsky 1975) and 'script' (Schank 1975 and Schank & Abelson 1977), and even the more linguistic notion of 'superstructure' (van Dijk 1977 and 1980) can be regarded as a schema in the above sense.

83 Both 'schemas' and 'schemata' are used as plurals for 'schema'. The first alternative seems to be more frequently used, which is why I will use 'schemas' in the following.
84 But see Kazdin (2000: 160), who writes that in psychology "[s]chemas have been criticized as absurdly constructionalist, theoretically imprecise, [and] operationally not falsifiable [...]".

Linguistic schemas qualify as one instance of schemas in general and they show the same characteristics. Like Rumelhart and Ortony (1977: 101) for general schemas, Langacker (2000b) emphasizes the importance of different levels of abstraction with linguistic schemas. In his view, schemas and schematization are closely linked to what he calls 'granularity' or 'resolution':

> schematization [...] involve[s] our capacity to operate at varying levels of 'granularity' (or 'resolution'). Structures that appear very different when examined in fine-grained details may nonetheless be quite comparable in a coarse-grained view. A schema is the commonality that emerges from distinct structures when one abstracts away from their points of difference by portraying them with lesser precision and specificity. (Langacker 2000b: 4)

The notion of schematization, thus, comes very close to the idea of delicacy, which Halliday (1961: 272) defines as "the scale of differentiation, or depth in detail." Recall that with regard to delicacy, in section 3.1 the relationship of instantiation was understood as being fundamental. In cognitive linguistics different degrees of abstraction are also regarded as relevant and the instantiation relation is understood to hold between schemas on different levels of abstraction as well (see, for instance, Taylor 2002: 23).

Both, traditional descriptive rules and schemas of cognitive linguistics are based on "actual instances of language use" (Barlow & Kemmer 1994: 25), but, in contrast to traditional descriptive grammars, schemas, to some extent, seem to be still closer to actual instances. This becomes apparent when we take into consideration that traditional descriptive grammars usually stick to the rank distinctions as, for instance, they are laid out in Halliday (1961; see section 3.1). Structures of one rank are understood as being composed of (classes of) units of the next lower rank and therefore only describable with regard to the next lower level. Clause structure, for instance, is mostly described on the basis of classes of phrases, phrases are described in terms of classes of words, and so on. Cognitive schemas are not restricted in this respect. They show a high degree of what could be called 'rank-permeability', i.e. units of different ranks may interact freely in the description of a schema. In addition, the kind of information represented by schemas is rather unrestricted. For instance, schemas may encode information on sequence they may combine grammatical categories with lexical items, they may include information on constituency, etc. (see Barlow and Kemmer 1994: 27). Consider the examples below.

(1) ${}_{\text{S}}$[NP VP]
(2) ${}_{\text{S}}$[a stitch in time saves nine]
(3) ${}_{\text{N}}$[stitch]

(4) VP[lose REFL]
(5) NP[N or no N]
(6) VP[lose [POSS way]]

Schemas are "simply a distillation of patterns found in a language" and thus may "crosscut lexical and phrasal levels" (28) if a particular pattern is tied to one particular lexical item or phrase. In this sense, we can say that schemas are less 'theory-based' or 'theory-restrained' than the descriptions found in traditional grammars.

In line with these observations and the claim that psychological schemas have variables (Rumelhart and Ortony 1977) is Barlow and Kemmer's (1994: 25) understanding of schemas as templates: "[...] a particular utterance may be modelled on a schema, and yet deviate from it in some manner that is not predictable." In this way, and in line with the variable nature of cognitive schemas, variation and deviation are regarded as central to the language system, and cognitive schemas, therefore, dispense with the distinction of "a well-behaved (rule-governed) core and a potentially deviant periphery to be accounted for in terms of stylistic rules, idioms, lexical exceptions, etc." (25) Grammar is regarded as an essentially gradient system where "constructions are to be seen as [...] more or less analytic, more or less fixed, and more or less idiomatic" (19).

Constructions, in the technical sense of construction grammar, qualify as an example of schemas. According to Taylor (1998), the rise of construction grammar can be seen to some extent in the attempts to account for the idiomatic expressions of a language, which were impossible to capture in more traditional approaches (apart from merely listing them). However, at closer scrutiny, it was found that a clear-cut distinction between the idiomatic and the fully regular in language is not drawn easily, since non-regular or not completely regular tokens in language and language use are far more pervasive than recognized hitherto.

To give but one example: Tomasello (2003a: 102) draws attention to the problematic class of "mixed constructions, which have some components based on more regular rule-like patterns and some components based on more idiosyncratic conventions including particular words and/or morphemes". That is, we are dealing with strings that combine abstract slots and fixed lexical items or morphemes. A case in point is Kay and Fillmore's (1999) WXDY (*What's X doing Y?*) construction[85], exemplified in sentences like *what's the dog doing eating my*

85 See Fillmore, Kay and O'Connor's (1988) *let-alone* construction for another example.

sausages, what was the man doing all untidy and dirty, or *what are the dirty plates doing on my table*. All of these examples are fixed to some degree, as the obligatory lexical items *what* and *doing* make clear. The construction also contains variable parts. These are variable to different extents: while the slot after *what* has to be filled by a form of BE, the next slot can be filled by any noun phrase and the final slot by different kinds of phrases. The construction thus merges rather general and rule-based strings and units with fixed lexical items. At the same time, this example illustrates another feature that is usually regarded as critical for constructions, namely the fact that the meaning of the whole is more than the meaning of the sum of its parts. In this case, the additional meaning is that of 'incongruity'.

With what began as an attempt to account for the idiomatic and the irregular, it was soon found that the same descriptive apparatus can be applied to the more regular aspects of language, as Taylor (1998: 187) emphasizes:

> [...] once we have in place the descriptive apparatus to account for construction idioms, we can easily extend it to the grammatical core of a language. [...] The only difference between idiomatic and core constructions is that the former are subject to many more idiosyncratic conditions than the latter – this, essentially, is what makes them idiomatic. But in terms of their status as constructions, core sentence types do not differ in any fundamental way from 'construction idioms'.

Consider the following examples.

(7) He gave Peter the book.
(8) Mary sold him the chair.
(9) I handed her a pen.
(10) I bought Mary the rights to the film.

In all of these instances, a transfer (either concrete or abstract) is taking place, which gives rise to a possible new construction. Tomasello (2003a: 99) writes: "the pattern X VERB*ed* Y *the* Z is a construction of English that signifies some kind of transfer of possession (either literal or metaphorical)". Goldberg describes this ditransitive construction as shown in figure 5.1: The basic meaning of the ditransitive construction is 'the agent causes the recipient to receive the patient', as shown on the top of figure 5.1. The syntactic pattern associated with that construction is shown on the bottom: the agent is mapped onto the subject, the recipient on the first object and the patient on the second object. The middle part of the figure is reserved for specific instances of verbs that operate in this construction. The verb *to hand*, for instance, contributes its participant roles of

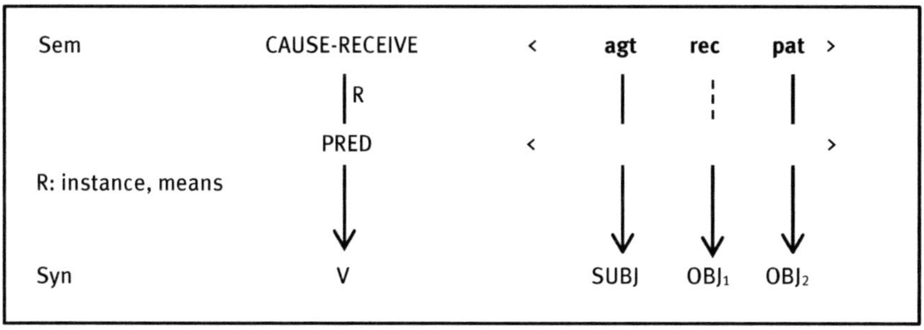

Figure 5.1: The ditransitive construction after Goldberg (1995: 50); slightly adapted.

'hander', 'handed' and 'handee', which are fused with the respective argument roles and syntactic slots. The next section will show how this construction is captured in the present network model.

Many researchers in construction grammar claim that constructions are organised as nodes in a network, which can be conceived of as being related through instantiation relations.

(11) [Verb Phrase]
|
[Verb Obj]
|
[*kick* Obj]
|
[*kick* [*the bucket*]] (Croft & Cruse 2004: 263)

Each of the expressions in angular brackets represents one construction. Recall that all constructions are considered as pairings of form and meaning. Roughly, the meaning of the top level construction could be glossed with 'action' or 'doing something', whereas the construction on the second level specifies that something is done to somebody, i.e. part of its meaning is the existence of a patient. The next construction [*kick* Obj] is warranted by the fact that it provides information on the argument structure of the verb KICK and, finally, the last construction is idiomatic, i.e. its meaning cannot be derived from any other construction.

Also, example (11) makes clear the rise in schematicity from the lowest to the highest level, and shows the instantiation relation that obtains between a construction and its parents and grandparents. [*kick* [*the bucket*]] is an instance of each of the more schematic constructions to which it is linked.

Many of the aspects discussed with regard to constructions can also be found in patterns (in the technical sense used in Hunston and Francis' Pattern Grammar approach). Patterns are regarded as an attempt to describe "the interaction between the particular lexical items in [... a corpus] and the grammatical patterns that they form a part of" (Hunston & Francis 2000: 1). The identification of patterns is essentially lexically based and starts off from a particular lexical item and the words and phrases that usually co-occur together with it. Accordingly, patterns are defined as "all the words and structures which are regularly associated with the word and which contribute to its meaning." (37) Patterns of the verb *divide*, for example, include the following:

(12) '***divide*** n *between/among* pl-n'
Drain the noodles and **<u>divide</u> them among the individual serving bowls**.
(cf. Francis, Huston & Manning 1996: 361)

(13) '*be* ***divide***-ed *between/among* pl-n'
The tips **<u>are divided up</u>** equally **between the staff**, and then added on to their wage packet. (cf. Francis, Huston & Manning 1996: 361)

(14) '***divide*** n adv/prep'
Such a system **<u>would divide</u> the country on tribal lines**.
(cf. Francis, Huston & Manning 1996: 324)

These three patterns are schematic descriptions of the occurrences of *divide* in authentic data and thus can also be understood as distillations of patterns found in language data. The further study of such patterns reveals that many other verbs share the same pattern:

(15) Election coverage on radio and television **<u>will be split</u> between the party in power and the opposition parties.**

(16) The programme aims to **<u>forge</u> links between higher education and small businesses.**

(17) The liquid crystal **<u>is sandwiched</u> between two glass plates**, each of which carries a polarising filter.

(18) He **<u>numbered</u> several Americans among his friends**.
(cf. Francis, Huston & Manning 1996: 361 - 362)

From a more schematic point of view, we thus can posit a fairly abstract pattern, namely 'V n *between/among* pl-n', which is instantiated by less schematic patterns where the V slot is instantiated by individual verbs. Intermediate between these two levels, Hunston and Francis (2000: 83) identify a level where "particular patterns will tend to be associated with lexical items that have particular meanings". More precisely, a slot in a particular pattern attracts items that can be assigned to a fairly restricted number of meaning groups. Examples (15) to (18) exemplify four such groups, namely the 'divide', the 'forge', the 'sandwich' and the 'number' group. The 'divide' group, for instance, in addition to *divide* and *split*, contains the verbs *distribute*, *split up*, and *share out*. All of these verbs, according to Francis, Hunston and Manning (1996: 361) share the fact that they are "concerned with dividing something up between two or more people or groups." To give another example, the 'sandwich' group, containing *sandwich*, *interpose* and *intersperse*, encompasses verbs that are "concerned with putting something between two or more things, either physically or metaphorically" (361).

With regard to what was said above, we can at least make out three levels of schematicity, all of which can be (although the authors do not explicitly do this) related through an 'instantiation' relation[86]:

(19) 'V n *between/among* pl-n'

'V_{divide} n *between/among* pl-n' ...

'*divide* n *between/among* pl-n' 'split n between/among pl-n' ...

Similarly to constructions, patterns can be regarded as linguistic schemas. Both concepts are variable with regard to rank, i.e. combine elements of different ranks in one sequence, they show different degrees of specificity and schematization, and are organised in taxonomic networks according to these degrees. The present network can account for all of these characteristics.

86 Patterns may become even more schematic. The complementation potential of adjectives, for instance, is described with the help of four highly abstract patterns, namely 'ADJ *–ing*', 'ADJ *to*-inf', 'ADJ *that*-clause', and 'ADJ prep' (cf. Hunston and Francis 2000: 58).

5.2 Cognitive schemas in the network model

5.2.1 Regular clausal constructions

Above it was shown that clausal constructions in construction grammar, and in contradistinction to traditional approaches, have a meaning on their own which exists independently of the lexical items that appear in the construction. What is more, the meaning of a construction cannot be calculated as the sum of its parts. Therefore, a plausible model of grammar should incorporate this (or a similar) concept and the present model will indeed do so. Another reason for the incorporation of this concept lies in the fact that, say, the ditransitive construction, as exemplified in the clause *I handed Peter the book*, can be understood as a schema (in the sense of "a distillation of patterns found in a language"; Barlow and Kemmer 1994: 28) just as any collocational or other pattern that is implemented in the network.

Any construction consists of a meaning and a form side. As an example, let us consider the ditransitive construction, which was glanced at above. The semantics, according to Goldberg (1995: 49), can be described as 'X causes Y to receive Z'. As can be seen, this meaning is related to particular roles in the construction, namely X, Y and Z, which Goldberg calls argument roles. In the case of the ditransitive construction, X would be described as 'agent', Y as 'patient' and Z as 'recipient'. The semantics of the construction, thus, can be paraphrased as 'A causes R to receive P'. Other aspects of meaning depend on the semantics of the verb that occurs in the construction. Following Fillmore (e.g. 1977 and 1985), Goldberg (1995) suggests that each verb evokes specific partici-

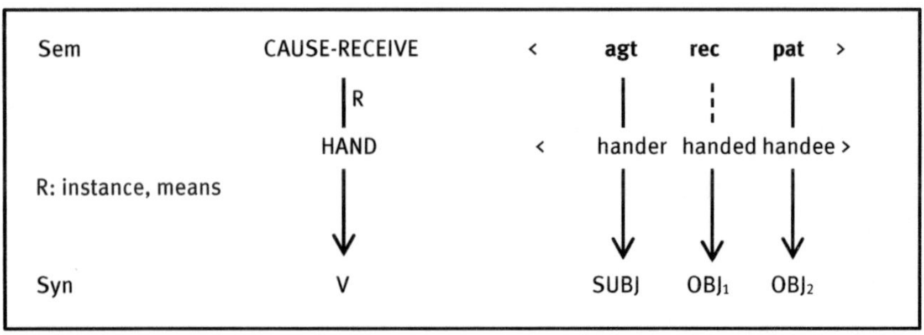

Figure 5.2: The fusion of argument and participant roles after Goldberg (1995: 51); slightly adapted.

pant roles. The verb HAND, thus, is claimed to evoke the roles of 'hander', 'handed' and 'handee' (see above). These participant roles are mapped onto the argument roles in a canonical way, i.e. the hander as agent, the handed as patient and the handee as recipient (Goldberg 1995: 51). Figure 5.1 above can therefore be supplemented as shown in figure 5.2.

In a similar way, other participant roles are connected to the three arguments roles, for instance 'giver', 'given' and 'givee' for the verb GIVE. Figure 5.3 shows the network representation of the ditransitive construction together with its relation to the verb *hand*:

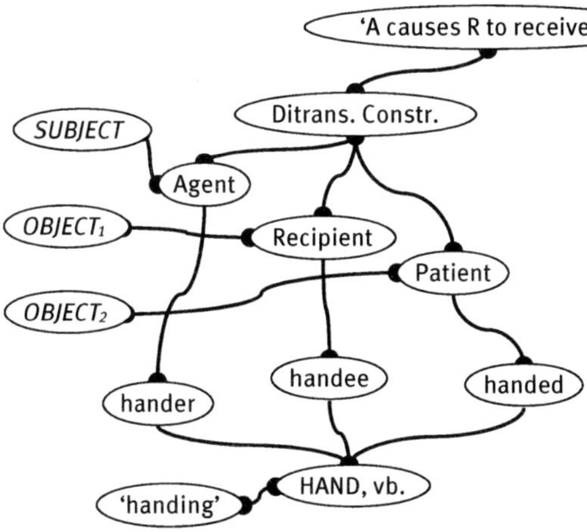

Figure 5.3: The ditransitive construction and its connection to the participant roles of the verb HAND in the network.

The top half of figure 5.3 contains the language users knowledge of the ditransitive construction as described in Goldberg's schema. The lower half represents the participant roles of the verb *hand*. The vertical lines between the two parts show the way these are mapped onto the argument roles of the construction.

The present way of representation is very much in line with the cognitive-linguistics spirit of schemas as distillations of patterns in language use. A similar idea can be found in Hudson (2007a: 154), where he presents a "frighteningly complicated WG network" of the same situation. However, he substitutes the more template-like model with a "much simpler" version that is based on inheritance (see figure 5.4):

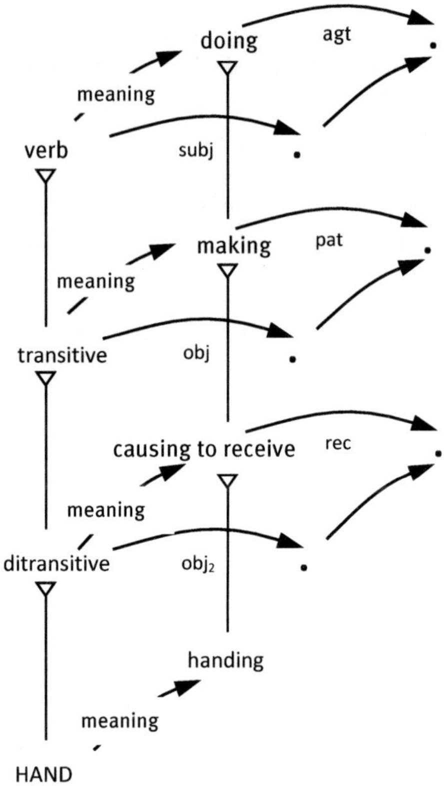

Figure 5.4: Hudson's (2007a: 155) "improved WG analysis of ditransitive HAND" (with kind permission of Richard Hudson).

> As soon as we classify HAND as an example of a ditransitive verb, all its syntactic and semantic dependencies may be inherited. Moreover, ditransitive verbs inherit the default mapping between subject and agent from the entry for Verbs; and if we classify Ditransitive as a subclass of Transitive, it inherits objects and their default mapping to patients. [...] the ditransitive construction has been analysed into three different constructions, each consisting of one verb class and one dependency. There is no single 'frame' which holds them all together into a single construction because there is no need for one. What holds the three parts together is inheritance [...]. Hudson (2007a: 154-155)

The disadvantage of inheritance in that particular case, as I see it, is that it increases the amount of processing the language user has to do to arrive at all the relevant pieces of information. Note that the complete information on this construction is gathered bit by bit in a serial fashion, i.e. from 'HAND' over 'ditransitive' and 'transitive' to 'verb'. Because of that it will take 'a long time' for the user to activate the knowledge that HAND needs a subject, which realises the agent of the action described in the verb. In the model suggested in this study all relevant bits of knowledge are accessed simultaneously and in parallel. This would also be the case in the first "frighteningly complicated WG network" of ditransitive HAND. The step to the "improved WG analysis" that we see above is a step away from cognitive considerations. The present network model tries to do justice to these cognitive claims.

Another point of criticism concerns the fact that, if I understand Hudson correctly, he generally attributes the causing-to-receive meaning to the ditransitivity of the verb. This is plausible with a verb like HAND or GIVE but the point that construction grammar makes is that apart from the ditransitivity meaning residing in the verb, the meaning 'X causes R to receive P' resides in the construction. This is an important point and has been discussed at length in Goldberg (1995). Verbs like PAINT and BAKE are not generally considered ditransitive. The ditransitive meaning in sentences like *he painted her a picture* or *they baked her a cake* is contributed by the construction in which the verb appears. Otherwise, we would either have to assume that as part of their basic meaning PAINT or BAKE have "a sense which involves something like 'X intends to cause Y to have Z'" (Goldberg 1995: 9), or we would have to assume that there are different meanings of the verbs at issue, one of them involving a causing-to-receive meaning[87] (a solution that seems to be favoured by Langacker 2008: 248). Neither of the two solutions seems plausible. The first because such a sense just is not part of the basic meaning, the second because it would lead to a proliferation of senses (see Goldberg 1995: 11). Instead, the meaning is considered to be part of the construction involved, as in the present model.

If the meaning is part of the construction, we are faced with the problem of a mismatch between the number of argument roles (related to the construction involved) and a number of participant roles (related to the verb involved). In the case of HAND discussed above mapping participants onto arguments is no problem, since there are three of each. How does the present network model explain a sentence like *they baked her a cake*, where the verb only has two participant

87 This solution seems to be favoured by Langacker (2008: 247-248) when he writes "we can reasonably say that the verb has taken on an extended meaning – one that incorporates the notion of transfer, as well as its basic content of creation [...]. To be sure, it assumes this meaning only in the context of the [ditransitive construction]."

roles, namely 'baker' and 'baked'. In those cases the construction itself contributes a third participant role, i.e. a 'bakee', which is fused with the recipient role (this is expressed by the dotted line leading from 'Recipient' to the relevant participant-role slot in figure 5.2). How does the network solve this problem?

The solution to that problem is very simple. Basically, the network solves the problem 'on its own'. It might seem that the solution shown in figure 5.5 is 'too simple to be true'. However, firstly, this network represents what we know about the ditransitive construction. Secondly, it represents what we know about the verb BAKE; thinking about the act of baking, we think of somebody who bakes and something that is being baked, and nothing else. It just does not make any sense to assume some kind of hidden node |bakee|. This would be the same as providing a large number of different senses of the verb, which, eventually, would lead to the proliferation of senses that we wanted to avoid. Even though the recipient role is not connected to a relevant participant role, it is no problem to interpret a sentence like *he baked her a cake*. The correct interpretation, in my view, depends on the correct mapping of the relevant words or strings of words to the relevant argument roles. That is, *he* as agent, *her* as recipient and *a cake* as patient. As soon as the respective nodes and connections are active, the network represents the meaning 'he, a baker, causes the recipient to receive something he has baked, namely a cake' (but see Hudson 2008: 292-295 for a sketch of best-fit binding as an alternative explanation).

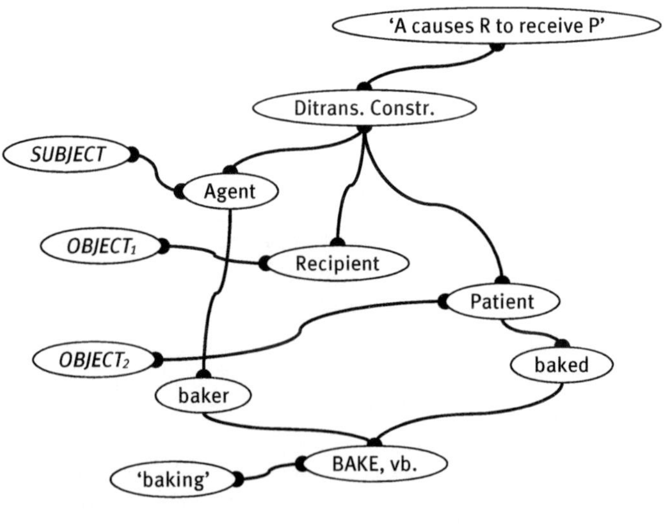

Figure 5.5: The two-participants verb BAKE and the three-arguments ditransitive construction.

Why, then, bother implementing participant roles at all? They have a facilitating effect on processing. Participants are related to particular argument roles, e.g. a baker is an agent, something baked is a patient, and so on. The network represents this knowledge with the help of a uni-directional link that leads from the participant-role node to the argument-role node. The link does not go both ways, since it does not make much sense to assume that the node |Agent|, for instance, has outgoing connections to all possible participants that may be mapped onto the agent role. This would require claiming that it is possible for a language user to list all possible agents of a language, which seems implausible. Of course, this can be done, but it seems reasonable to assume that this is achieved in an indirect way: we think about events (which will lead to the activation of a verb node), and we check which of the participant roles would usually be related to the agent role. To look in more detail at how the knowledge of participant roles comes in handy during processing, let us consider the example *I handed Peter the book.*

Understanding the clause *I handed Peter the book* in the present model means assigning the argument roles to the respective NPs of the clause, i.e. *I* as the agent, *Peter* as the recipient and *the book* as the patient. The node |*hand*| will spread activation to the three participant-role nodes, which are connected to their respective argument-role node. The clause is understood when the following pattern of activation is given.

The problem now is to explain how the individual word forms become connected to the argument roles of agent, patient and recipient. In this respect, the

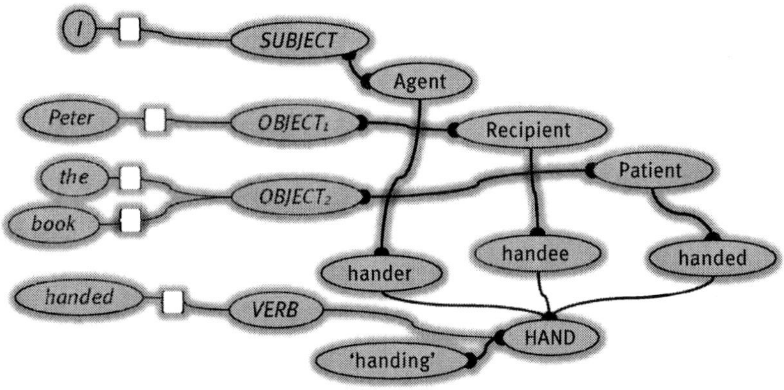

Figure 5.6: Having understood the clause *I handed Peter the book*. (The curly brackets on the left represent details that have been omitted)

concept of rank-permeability (see section 2.1.7) is of extreme importance. The recognition of a word form, for instance, will activate the relevant node in the network and this node will spread its activation across the network regardless of the rank of the neighbouring nodes. Activation will thus spread to other word forms, if they are in a collocational relation to the first node. Activation will also spread to the word class node of which the first node is a member. In addition, activation will spread to structures connected to the given word form: either, because the word form itself stands in some colligational relation to a specific structure or because the word class to which it belongs occurs in a particular structure. It follows that rank-permeability is a natural consequence of the design of the network, more specifically the connectivity within the network. This feature is highly relevant for processing: The analysis of structures does not proceed orderly from one rank to the other. Rather, the network model makes clear that, at any point in time, the processor will make use of any piece of information that is available (see also the discussion of cue validity in section 6.1). 'Information', here, refers to the information that lies in the nodes and in the connectivity of the network. Each word form in a string will activate particular portions of the network and will, eventually, result in an activation pattern that mirrors the correct analysis of the string. The question for now is how do the individual connections between the network nodes contribute to this analysis.

Let us discuss the clause *I handed Peter the book*. As will be shown, several pieces of information come into play to relate the word forms to their correct argument role. It will also be seen how in the process of analysing this clause a large number of alternative analyses are pursued in parallel until, eventually, only one possible analysis remains (see the discussion of competition in the network in section 2.2.2.5). Note that the parallel processing of alternatives is a natural consequence of the structure of the network: as soon as one word-form node in the network becomes activated, this activation will spread through the network in all possible directions. The subsequent activation of a further word-form node will also spread through the network. Some portions of the network activated by the first node will be singled out, since they also receive activation from the second node. In this way, the number of possible analyses will be reduced, since the correct analysis will be represented in those nodes that receive a relative activation maximum. The number of possible analyses will be reduced with further input until, eventually, we are left with only one possible analysis. According to this rationale, the activation of the node |*I*| in the network will trigger a number of argument-roles nodes in the network, such as |Agent|, |Cause| or |Theme| (here I stick to the framework advocated in Goldberg 1995), which again are related to a number of clausal constructions, the respective

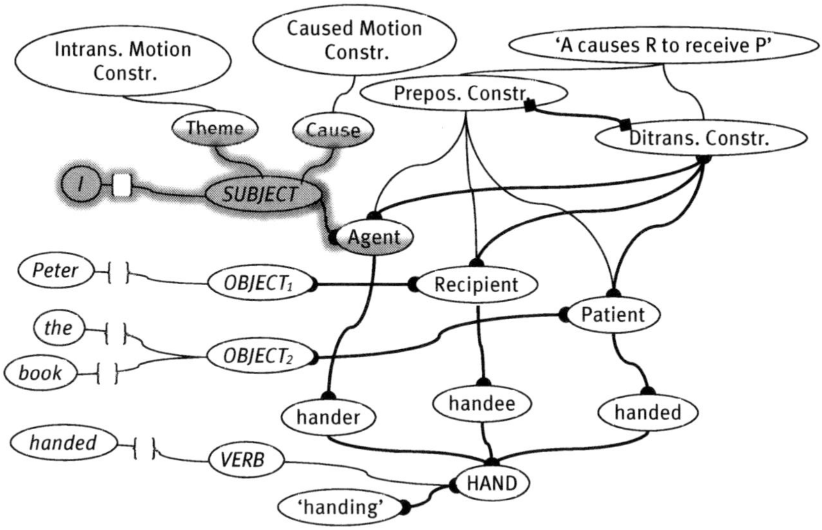

Figure 5.7: Activation spreading from |*I*|.

nodes of which and the semantics of which will be activated in the network; see figure 5.7.

In first approximation, we can assume that the activation of the node |*handed*|, as shown in figure 5.8 below, will spread to the participant roles associated with the verb, which in turn will spread their activation to the argument-role nodes to which they are connected. The latter are not yet fully activated as will become clear below. At this stage the number of possible analyses will already have been reduced enormously: |*I*| will be associated with the agent role, since this node receives activation from both the |*I*| node (mediated through |SUBJECT|) and the |*handed*| node. The |Agent| node thus is already fully activated while the competing nodes |Cause| and |Theme| are not. Also, the number of possible clausal constructions has been reduced drastically, due to the activation of the node |Agent|: The nodes |Intrans. Motion Constr. | and |Caused Motion Construction| receive no further activation, since it has become clear that *I* is neither theme nor cause. In addition, the node |'A causes R to receive P'| is fully activated since this meaning is connected to the word form node |*handed*|. This mirrors the intuition that we know that the verb HAND encodes the 'giving event' even if we are not sure about the construction in which this

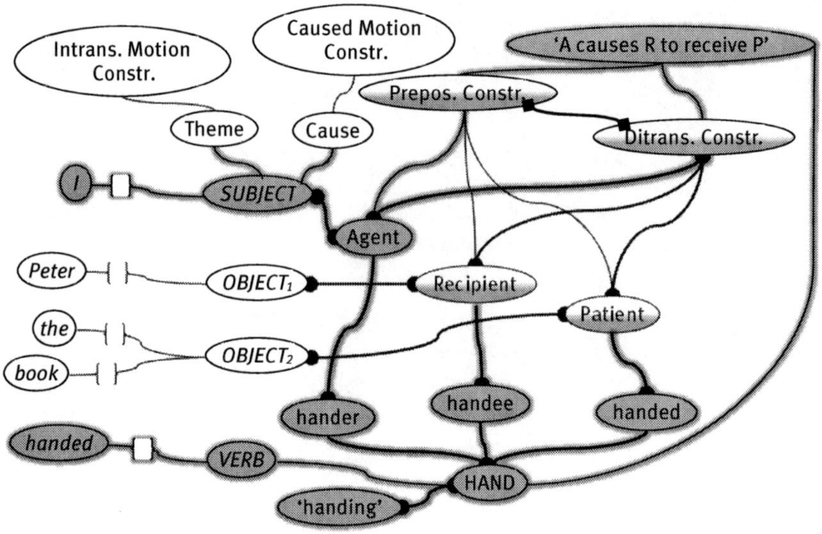

Figure 5.8: Activation spreading from |*I*| and |*handed*|.

event is encoded. That is why neither of the nodes |Ditrans. Constr.| and |Prepos. Constr.| are yet fully active.

Before we can discuss the consequences of the activation of the node |*Peter*|, we need to introduce a small refinement into the model, which can be seen in figure 5.9. This refinement concerns the connections that the node |*OBJECT*$_1$| has in the network. The problem, more specifically, is that even though a given NP is the first object in a clause this does not mean that it necessarily instantiates the recipient, since it might also be the patient of a prepositional construction, as for instance in *I handed Peter over to the police*. To account for this, the node |*OBJECT*$_1$| is connected to both the nodes |Recipient| and |Patient|. The node |*OBJECT*$_2$| is connected to the node |Patient| but also has an inhibitory link to the connection of |*OBJECT*$_1$| and |Patient|. In addition, this node has an excitatory link to the connection of |*OBJECT*$_1$| and |Recipient|. That is, if there is a second object in the clause, the second object will be given patient status and the first object will be the recipient.

The final step of the analysis will be reached at the point when the string *the book* is processed. A second NP which is not subordinate or coordinate to the first NP will qualify as the second object and, accordingly, activate the node

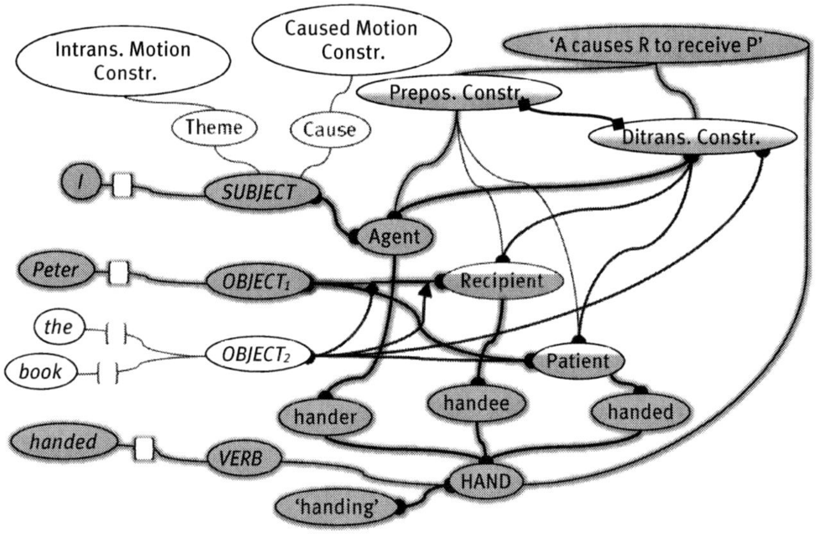

Figure 5.9: Activation spreading from |*I*|, |*handed*| and |*Peter*|.

|*OBJECT₂*|. This activation will lead to a complete inhibition of the connection |*OBJECT₁*| and |Patient| but will eventually fully activate the |Patient| node through its own connection to this node. In addition, the activation of |*OBJECT₂*| will amplify the activation travelling from |*OBJECT₁*| to |Recipient|, which eventually will lead to a full activation of the latter node. Note also that the activation of |*OBJECT₂*| leads to the full activation of |Ditrans. Constr. |, which will lead to the inhibition of the node |Prepos. Constr.|. Processing is completed.

So far, the network manages to account for the comprehension of ditransitive constructions. The verb HAND, like other ditransitive verbs, can also occur in a prepositional construction and the network needs to be able to account for that as well. Hudson (2008: 280) suggests "distinguish[ing] two sub-lexemes of give, each of which isa GIVE: $\text{GIVE}_{\text{ditransitive}}$ and $\text{GIVE}_{\text{prepositional}}$" and goes on: "sub-lexemes are an important part of any WG analysis, and no doubt give has many other sub-lexemes, such as the one for mono-transitive uses as in *He gave a pound*." In this Hudson departs significantly from the analysis along the lines of Goldbergian Construction Grammar that is favoured in the present model. While the latter tries to avoid sense-proliferation, Hudson seems to advocate it. If the node |$\text{GIVE}_{\text{ditransitive}}$| is activated, the recipient will be realised as an indirect object and, if the node |$\text{GIVE}_{\text{prepositional}}$| is activated, the recipient is realised as a prepositional object.

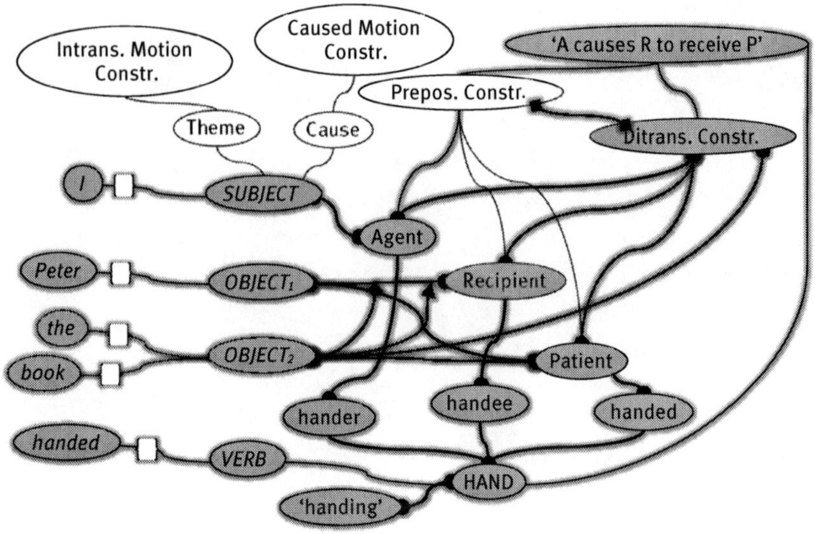

Figure 5.10: Complete processing of the clause *I handed Peter the book*.

Are there processing arguments for one or the other position with regard to the present network? As far as I can see, the introduction of new sub-lexeme nodes into the network shown in figure 5.10 does not provide any advantages either for comprehension or production. In the case of comprehension, the hearer will not be able to decide which of the sub-lexemes is meant until he or she encounters the prepositional object. From the perspective of the producer, additional sub-lexeme nodes do not seem to make sense, since all the information about the structure (in the present model) is captured in the node |Prepos. Construct. |. Instead of a large number of sub-lexeme nodes, the present model, thus, favours basic verb meanings that are enriched by the constructions in which they occur.

Still, we have to account for the choice between the two constructions. This is done by an additional node |*ADVERBIAL*|, which is connected to the node |Recipient| and has an inhibitory link to the connection of |$OBJECT_1$| and |Recipient|. As soon as an adverbial is identified, this will be given the status of the recipient and the object (either preceding or following) will be the patient. Note also that the node |*ADVERBIAL*| is linked to the node |Prepos. Constr.|. As soon as a recipient adverbial has been identified, we know that we are dealing with a prepositional construction. Similarly, the node |$OBJECT_2$| is connected to the node |Ditrans. Constr.|, since the occurrence of a second object identifies this construction. The relevant network portion is shown in figure 5.11.

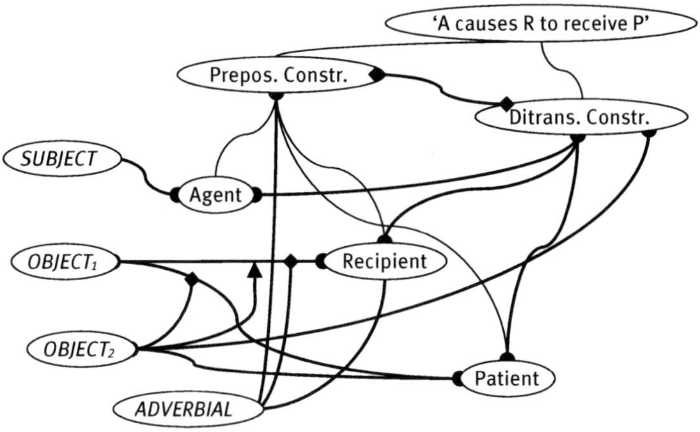

Figure 5.11: Prepositional construction and ditransitive construction in the network.

5.2.2 Idiosyncratic constructions and patterns

As was described above, construction grammar started as an attempt to account for the idiosyncratic in language. In what follows I will give an account of the WXDY construction (e.g. *what's the dog doing eating my sausages*) and its representation in the present network model. Constructions of this kind are highly interesting since they combine fixed lexical elements with more abstract elements, like lexemes and phrases. They merge general and rather rule-based strings with fixed lexical elements. In addition, the WXDY construction illustrates that the meaning of the whole is more than the sum of the meaning of its parts.

Here, we will focus on the production of this construction. This can be explained easily and elegantly by separating the construction into two major meaning components: a basic or unmarked proposition, e.g. HAND (*I, Peter, the book*), and an additional meaning component that might be called 'incongruity'. Instead of merely stating that *I handed Peter the book*, the WXDY version of that sentence *What was I doing handing Peter the book* stresses the incongruity of the event. The WXDY construction, therefore, is accounted for by adequately explaining how the first sentence is transformed into the second sentence, if the meaning facet of incongruity is added. In a description of a transformational kind, the construction at issue might be described as follows:

(20) $S\ V_{tense}\ O_1\ O_2 \rightarrow$ *What* BE_{tense} S *doing* $V_{ing}\ O_1\ O_2$

Everything that is needed for the above manipulation has been described in previous chapters of this study. The network model is able to explain the insertion of lexical elements, i.e. *what* and *doing*, and it is able to account for the transfer of features (see section 4.2.4), in this case the tense marking of the finite verb in the original version of the sentence.

As can be seen from figure 5.12, the WXDY construction depends on an additional node |'incongruity'|. This node is responsible for the insertion of additional elements into the existing clause structure of the underlying unmarked clause. If we assume that |'incongruity'| reaches its full level of activation first, we see that it will prevent the other clause elements from being realised. In section 4.2.4 it was described how the clause will only be produced when the subject node is fully active. In the model described above, however, the node 'incongruity' inhibits |*SUBJECT*|, i.e. the unmarked form of the clause cannot be realised. Instead, the first element to be realised is the word form *what*. The second element is a form of BE. Which form of BE is realised depends on the subject-related features (as described in section 4.2.4) and on the meaning node |'in the past'| (the activation of which is part of the overall meaning of *I handed Peter the book*); in the present case it is the form *was*, since it is that node that is most strongly activated. The activation of the node |BE| paves the way for the activation of |*SUBJECT*|, since |BE| inhibits the inhibitory connection that suppresses the node |*SUBJECT*|. Once this node is active, it leads to the realization of the relevant noun phrase, in that case *I*. In addition, the node |*SUBJECT*| also amplifies the activation that the node |'incongruity'| sends towards the node |*doing*|, which, as a consequence, becomes fully activated and the word form is realised. In addition, the activation of the node inhibits the inhibitory link that suppresses the activation of the node |*VERB*|. Once this node is active, the rest of the clause will be produced in its unmarked form, i.e. verb – $object_1$ – $object_2$. On the whole, the activation of the node |'incongruity'| turns the unmarked clause *I handed Peter the book* into the WXDY version *What was I doing handing Peter the book.*

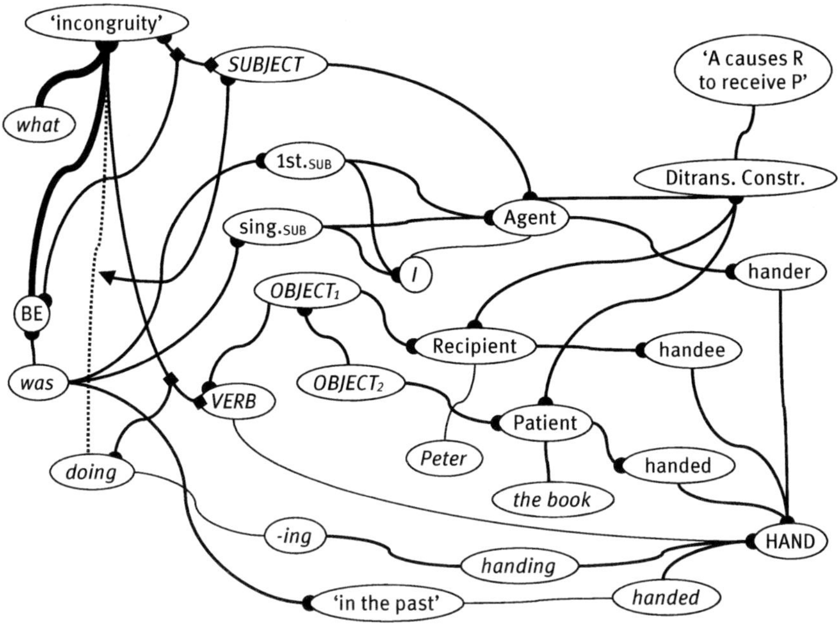

Figure 5.12: The WXDY construction in the network.

Most of the patterns discussed by Hunston and Francis are similar to constructions like WXDY in that they combine fixed lexical items with larger, more abstract elements like lexemes or phrases. In addition, patterns are useful to illustrate the different levels of schematicity that are held as important for and characteristic of cognitive schemas. The pattern '***divide*** n *between/among* pl-n' (as exemplified in *drain the noodles and* ***divide them among the individual serving bowls***; cf. Francis, Huston & Manning 1996: 361) is illustrative in both respects.

In section 5.1 above it was said that the same pattern is also found with other verbs, as the following examples (repeated from above) show:

(21) Election coverage on radio and television **will be split between the party in power and the opposition parties.**
(22) The programme aims to **forge links between higher education and small businesses.**
(23) The liquid crystal **is sandwiched between two glass plates**, each of which carries a polarising filter.

(24) He **<u>numbered</u> several Americans among his friends.**
(cf. Francis, Huston & Manning 1996: 361 - 362)

These examples hint at the more abstract pattern 'V n *between/among* pl-n'. In between this abstract pattern and the concrete patterns where the element V is realised by individual words, patterns on a semi-schematic level have also been identified, namely those where the V element is realised by verbs that are similar in meanings, such as *divide, split, distribute, split up*, and *share out*, all of which are ways of expressing the concept of dividing. In section 5.1 this hierarchical relationship was represented as repeated below.

(25) 'V n *between/among* pl-n'

'V_{divide} n *between/among* pl-n' ...

'*divide* n *between/among* pl-n' 'split n between/among pl-n' ...

In what follows I will show that the present network model not only is able to implement patterns of different levels of schematicity, but also is able to represent hierarchical relationships between patterns of the kind above.

We start with the concrete pattern '*divide* n *between/among* pl-n', a sequence of elements that can be implemented in the network through the mech-

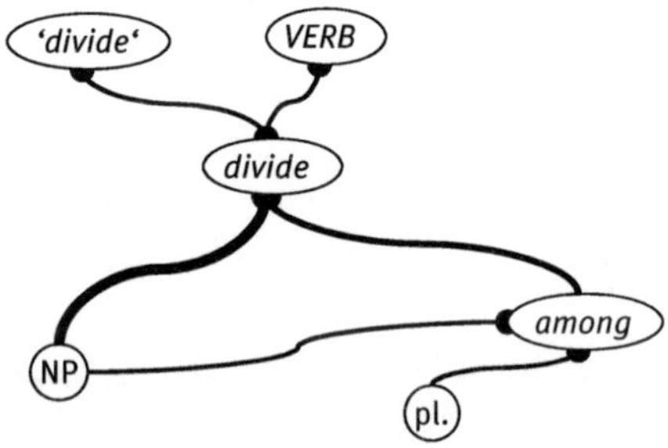

Figure 5.13: The network representation of the pattern '*divide* n *between/among* pl-n'. (The node |*between*| has been left out for reasons of presentational clarity. The node would be integrated into the network in the same fashion as |*among*|. In addition, the two nodes would be connected by inhibitory links to ensure that only one of the two is realised.)

anisms described in section 2.2.2. The pattern hinges on the verb *divide*, which triggers the activation of the other elements of the pattern. The activation of |*divide*| will spread to the nodes |NP| and |*among*|. Since the connection to the former is stronger than the connection to the latter, the node |NP| will be activated first. The following activation of |*among*| will lead to a second activation of the node |NP| together with the node |pl.|. This particular co-activation pattern makes sure that only plural NPs become realised. The nodes representing the elements of the pattern '*divide* n *between/among* pl-n' are activated in the correct order (see figure 5.13).

With any activation of this pattern, the nodes |*VERB*| and |'divide'| will also become activated, since the verb *divide* is connected to both nodes. Other verbs, e.g. *split* or *distribute*, will also activate the same nodes, since they are closely connected in meaning to the verb *divide*. Eventually, this will result in the creation of additional links of |'divide'| and |*VERB*| to the pattern itself, since these nodes become associated with the pattern. The more schematic patterns have also become a part of the network.

Note that the line connecting |'divide'| and the elements of the pattern is very thin and is boosted by activation coming from the node |*VERB*|. This is necessary because the meaning aspect 'divide' is also activated with word forms

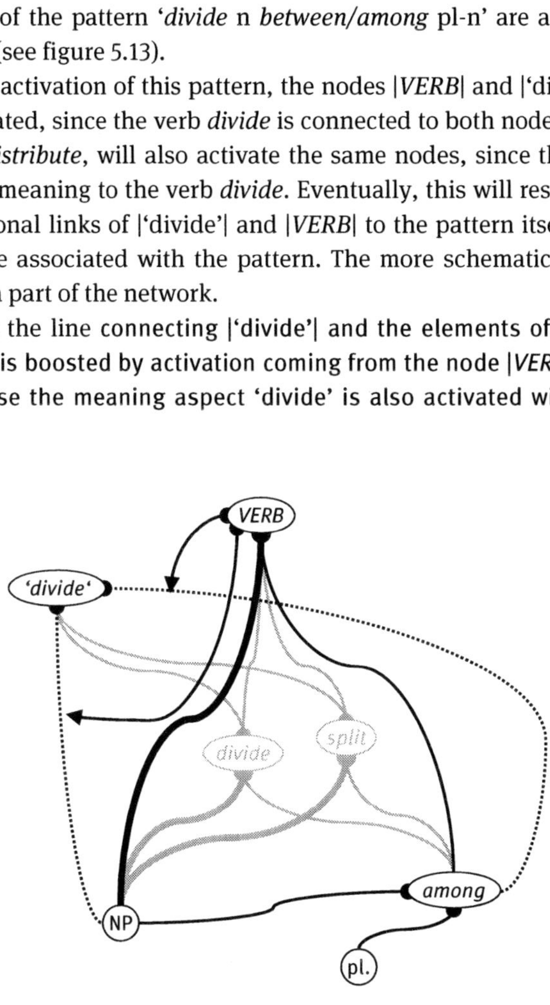

Figure 5.14: The network representation of the patterns 'V_{divide} n *between/among* pl-n' and 'V n *between/among* pl-n'. The node |*between*| has been left out for reasons of presentational clarity.

other than verbs, e.g. in *divided* or *division*. The boosting connections make sure that the pattern is only activated with verbs that show this meaning aspect.

Verbs with slightly different meanings also enter the same pattern, e.g. verbs of the 'sandwich' meaning family (*The liquid crystal is sandwiched between two glass plates).* These will further contribute to the most schematic pattern, since they activate the node |*VERB*| every time such a pattern is instantiated, and they will lead to the creation of a new pattern of intermediate schematicity, namely '$V_{sandwich}$ n *between/among* pl-n'. The complete network representation of the patterns discussed is shown in figure 5.15. Instead of the hierarchical (and local) representation shown in (25), the present model favours a distributed representation of the different degrees of schematicity. The pattern '*divide* n *among* pl-n' is not primarily understood as an instantiation of the more general patterns 'V_{divide} n *among* n-pl' and 'V n *among* n-pl', i.e. the three patterns are not related through ISA-relations; the speaker's knowledge of the patterns "is not something that [... he] *has*" (Langacker 1987: 382). The interrelations between the patterns only become available through spreading of activation. The activation of the node |*divide*| will spread to the nodes |'divide'| and |*VERB*|. It is because of this spreading of activation and of a particular resulting pattern of activation in the network that the relations between the three kinds of patterns become apparent, i.e. the speaker's knowledge is in "what he *does*" (Langacker 1987: 382).

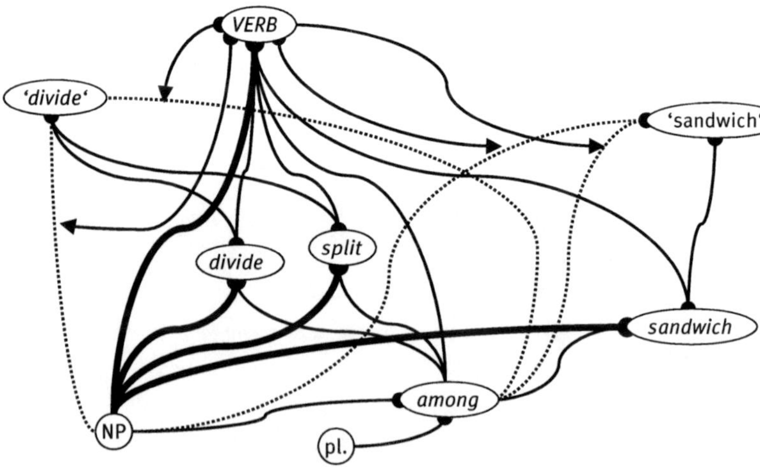

Figure 5.15: The network representation of patterns of the 'n *between/among* pl-n'-type, showing three different levels of schematicity.

On the whole, it has been shown how the network is able to implement concepts that are currently discussed and explored in the context of cognitive linguistics, i.e. schemas as distillations of patterns of language use that combine abstract and highly variable elements with concrete elements like word forms. In addition, it has been shown that the network is able to accommodate hierarchical relations that are assumed to exist between patterns of different degrees of schematicity. The next section discusses concepts explored in corpus-linguistic circles. These concepts are similar to the ones discussed above in that they are based on language use and in that they dispense with the strict distinction between lexis and grammar and, accordingly, combine elements of different rank.

5.3 Recurrent item strings

The present section discusses a number of concepts that make reference to patterns of co-occurrence that occur in natural language data. Some of these are very close to the actual strings of word forms that occur in texts; other concepts make use of more abstract linguistic categories, such as lexical units, parts of speech or syntactic constructions. Since the number of concepts is extremely large and terminology far from uniform (see, among others, Wray 2002a: 8-10, or Moon 1998a: 2-5), I will use the term 'recurrent item string' as an umbrella term for all notions that have been discussed with regard to such patterns of co-occurrence. 'Item' refers to different kinds of linguistic units, 'string' refers to the fact that the individual items are somehow related to one another syntagmatically, although they need not be continuous. Finally, 'recurrent' in this context means that these strings of items (note that *recurrent* does not premodify *item* but *item strings*) for the most part occur with at least a particular threshold frequency in a given corpus (although not all researchers are explicit about that) or that the co-occurrence of the items involved is more frequent than would be the case on the basis of mere chance.

The study of such recurrent item strings, under the headings 'phraseology', 'collocation', 'prefabs', 'formulaic language', etc., has been a constant area of discussion over the last few decades and more recently has gained renewed interest, due to technological advances and due to the increasing interest in corpus linguistics, the influence of such strings in language teaching (see, for instance, Granger 1998, Howarth 1996, 1998a and 1998b, Bardovi-Harlig 2002, Nesselhauf 2003 and 2005, or Wray 2000c) and their relevance to models of language description, such as Systemic Functional Grammar (see, among others, Hunston 2006 and Tucker 2006) or construction grammar (see, for instance, Stefanowitsch & Gries 2003 and 2005, Gries & Stefanowitsch 2004a and 2004b, and Gries et al. 2005). This section provides an overview of some of the concepts that have been discussed in the last fifty years (see Nesselhauf 2004 and Bartsch 2004 for a treatment of further concepts).

For the purposes of the present study a detailed discussion of the large variety of concepts that have been explored in this field of research is unnecessary. What seems more useful is to take a look at the dimensions along which recurrent item strings can vary. With regard to the present network model, it is then sufficient to show that it can accommodate the most 'extreme' phenomena in relation to these dimensions. Anything less extreme can then be accounted for as well.

At least the following five parameters can be distinguished (see Bartsch 2004, or Fillmore et al. 1988 for examples of other descriptive frameworks and Gries 2008 for a similar list):

1. Grammatical status of items
2. Continuity/discontinuity and range of discontinuous strings
3. Variability of the strings
4. The frequency of occurrence/statistical significance of co-occurrence
5. Grammatical status of recurrent item strings

Each of the five dimensions will be discussed in turn. With regard to the grammatical status of the items that occur in the string, a lot of variation can be witnessed. At issue here is the rank of the elements that enter into recurrent item strings. Some phenomena only refer to word forms. Sinclair, for instance, describes 'collocation' as "a frequent co-occurrence of words" (Sinclair 1996: 80) or as "the occurrence of two or more words within a short space of each other in the text" (Sinclair 1991: 170). A number of other concepts similarly focus on lexical items. Stubbs (2007: 90) describes his 'n-grams' as "a recurrent string of uninterrupted word forms". Almost identical concepts are Biber et al.'s 'lexical bundles', which are "the most frequent recurring lexical sequences in a register" (Biber et al. 2004: 376, see also Biber et al. 1999)[88], and Altenberg's (1993: 227) "recurrent word combinations, i.e. continuous strings of words occurring more than once in identical form" (see also Altenberg and Eeg-Olofsson 1990,

88 Other terms are also found frequently include 'lexical phrases', 'routine formulas', '(semi)fixed expressions' or 'prefabs'.

and Eeg-Olofsson and Altenberg 1996). Examples of the above concepts are *in and out of the*, *part of the*, and *it seemed to him that*. Other researchers do not restrict themselves to word forms but extend their concepts to relationships that obtain between lexical units and their derivations. Altenberg and Eeg-Olofsson's (1990), for instance, talk of 'collocation in the stricter sense', which

> goes beyond [... the] notion of textual co-occurrence and emphasizes the relationship *between lexical items in language* [...and] cuts across word classes (cf. *drink heavily, heavy drinker, heavy drinking*), applies to discontinuous items (*he drinks pretty heavily*), and presupposes lemmatization (*drink/drinks/drank/drinking heavily*). (Altenberg and Eeg-Olofsson 1990: 3-4)

The same opinion is reflected in Lipka (2002: 182), when he claims that the sentence "*A bullfighter fights bulls at a bullfight* [...] contains three instances of collocation of *fight* and *bull*"[89]. More abstract still are concepts that include highly abstract elements such as parts of speech or syntactic constructions. A case in point is the concept of 'colligation'. The term was coined by John Rupert Firth, who writes:

> The statement of meaning at the grammatical level is in terms of word and sentence classes or of similar categories and of the interrelation of those categories in *colligations*. (Firth 1957 [1968]: 181)

Colligation should be interpreted as a statement about the interrelation and mutual expectancy of grammatical categories, which abstracts away from the level of given word forms:

> Grammatical relations should not be regarded as relations between words as such – between *watched* and *him* in 'I watched him' – but between a personal pronoun, first person singular nominative, the past tense of a transitive verb and the third person pronoun singular in the oblique or objective form. (Firth 1957 [1968]: 181)

This understanding of the term 'colligation' is captured (to some degree) and operationalised in Stubbs' (2007) concept of Part-of-Speech grams, or POS-grams[90]. The term refers to recurrent strings of word class categories, such as

---

89 What Lipka most probably has in mind when he talks about collocations are 'lexical units', i.e. the union of a set of word forms and a single sense, and their derivations. *Bull* in the example above makes reference to 'male cows' only and not to the male of a larger animal species (elephants, whales, etc.) or to official statements from the Pope.

90 The notion of POS-grams is more restricted than that of colligation, even if the latter is restricted to interrelations among word classes, since POS-grams are essentially continuous.

'PRP ATO NN1 PRF ATO'[91] which stands for the sequence 'preposition other than *of* + article + singular common noun + preposition *of* + article' (e.g. *at the end of the*).

The increase in the degree of abstraction that can be witnessed in the move from word form over lexical item and its derivations to part of speech arguably reaches an endpoint in Sinclair's 'semantic preference' and 'semantic prosody'[92]. In the discussion of the phrase *naked eye*, Sinclar (1996) finds that, in addition to collocations (in 95% of all tokens *naked eye* is preceded by the definite article *the*) and colligations (90% of the cases of *naked eye* have a preposition as the second left-collocate), words that occur at the third slot to the left usually have a particular meaning component:

> Whatever the word class, whatever the collocation, almost all of the instances with a preposition at N-2 have a word or phrase to do with visibility either at N-3 or nearby. (Sinclair 1996: 86)

It is interesting to note that semantic preferences cut across word-classes (Esser 1999: 158). The semantic preference of visibility may thus be expressed either by verbs (*detect*, *spot*, or *perceived*) or by adjectives (*apparent*, *evident*, or *obvious*). In this vein, the phrase *naked eye* shows a preference at N-3 for words that contain a particular semantic feature, namely a semantic preference for words that contain the feature 'having to do with visibility'.

Sinclair (1996) also notes that the pattern described above has:

> a semantic prosody of 'difficulty', which is evident in 85% of the instances. It may be shown by a word such as *small, faint, weak, difficult* with *see* [...] and *barely, rarely, just* with *visible* [...] or by a negative with 'visibility' or *invisible* itself; or it may just be hinted at by a modal verb such as *can* or *could*. (Sinclair 1996: 87)

The difference between semantic preference and semantic prosody lies in the fact that the former includes any kind of semantic feature, whereas the latter is restricted to evaluative (in the broadest sense) features.

Important colligational relations between word classes, such as the relation between a determiner and its head, in contrast, can also be discontinuous.

91 Obviously, these types of recurrent strings are always tied to a particular kind of annotation in a particular corpus, as also Stubbs (2004) points out. In the above case the symbols refer to the headers used for the British National Corpus.

92 See also Hoey (2005 and 2006) for a discussion of a similar concept, namely 'semantic association'.

In addition to the degree of abstraction of the elements that enter into relationships of co-occurrence, different concepts also vary with regard to whether they allow intervening elements or not. A large number of concepts are continuous in the sense that all 'slots' within the string are restricted in some way and in the sense that no other material may intervene. This is the case with n-grams, lexical bundles or POS-grams, which have already been mentioned. Other examples are idioms (see Skandera 2004), polywords or institutionalised expressions. The last two are discussed in the context of *lexical phrases*, a concept developed by Nattinger and DeCarrico (1992) (see also Nattinger 1980, 1988, DeCarrico/Nattinger 1988, and Nattinger/DeCarrico 1989). Lexical phrases are defined as

> 'chunks' of language of varying length, phrases like *as it were, on the other hand, as X would have us believe*, and so on. As such, they are multi-word lexical phenomena [...], conventionalized form/function composites that occur more frequently and have more idiomatically determined meaning than language that is put together each time. These phrases include short relatively fixed phrases [...] or longer phrases or clauses [...], each with a fixed, basic frame, with slots for various fillers [...]. Each is associated with a particular discourse function. (Nattinger/DeCarrico (1992: 1)

Examples of polywords are *for the most part, in a nutshell*, and *by and large*. They operate on word level. Institutionalised expressions, in contrast, are sentence level units, such as *a watched pot never boils*, *give me a break*, or *long time no see*.

Other constructs are inherently discontinuous in that they allow for one (or two) slots that are variable. But at the same time, they can be regarded as being continuous, since the filled instantiations occur as a whole and are not interrupted by further intervening material. The intervening material could thus be described as 'structurally licensed'. Among this class are collocational frameworks or p-frames. The former are described by Renouf and Sinclair (1991: 128) as consisting of "a discontinuous sequence of two words, positioned at one word remove from each other", i.e. collocational frameworks have one variable slot between two fixed components. Examples of such frameworks are '*a* + ? + *of*' or '*too* + ? + *to*', instantiated by recurrent units such as *a lot of*, or *too weak to*, respectively. These collocational frameworks can, to some extent at least, be regarded as abstractions from collocations in the sense of n-grams or lexical bundles or recurrent word combinations. The first pattern above, for instance, is instantiated by a large number of different tokens, such as *a <u>kind</u> of, a <u>number</u> of, a <u>couple</u> of, a <u>series</u> of, a <u>piece</u> of*, and so on. Stubbs (2007: 90-91, see also 2004) presents a similar idea, namely that of 'phrase-frames' or 'p-frames', "an n-gram with one variable slot", such as '*plays a ? role in*'. Obviously, collocational frameworks "are one special case of phrase-frames".

In contrast to this group of concepts, where the intervening material is structurally licensed, there are a number of concepts which also allow distant dependencies between their individual items. This is true for the usual understanding of 'collocation' and also for semantic preferences and semantic prosodies.

The third aspect, the flexibility or variability of the recurrent item string relates to the other two in that a string of adjacent word forms like an n-gram is by definition less flexible than strings of items where the items are of a more abstract kind, like parts of speech or semantic features, and may be separated by intervening material. So, the most rigidly fixed strings are n-grams, lexical bundles, recurrent word combinations, polywords and institutionalized expressions, as they do not allow any variation of the items themselves or their position in the string. Next in line would be idioms, since these are mostly fixed and usually do not allow much variation as regards word order. Collocations in Sinclair's sense are also fixed regarding the items, but more flexible concerning the position of the items, which shows in the fact that items need not be adjacent. Still more flexible are collocations as understood by Altenberg and Eeg-Olofsson (1990) or by Lipka (2002), since they concern not word forms but lexical units and their derivations, while at the same time allowing for intervening material between items. Collocational frameworks and p-frames show an increase in flexibility as they allow one slot that is completely free (or two in the latter case). While with the last two concepts there is usually just one vacant slot, POS-grams consist of nothing but variable slots and thus are more flexible, although this variability is constrained by word class categories. Most variable among all of the approaches are relations of semantic preference and prosody. These notions are expressed through semantic features which in turn can be realized in many structurally different ways and also in various positions (although there are positional preferences, too).

With regard to the criterion of statistical significance of the respective strings, we find that most of the concepts take this aspect into account, although usually there is no definite threshold above which a recurrent string is frequent enough to be considered relevant. With those strings that combine abstract elements or leave slots completely variable, frequency is especially interesting, since the individual instantiations of the abstract string often are not particularly frequent. A case in point are collocational frameworks. Renouf and Sinclair (1991: 129) report that the collocational framework '*many + ? + of*', for instance, is instantiated 402 times in their 10-million-word corpus and has

159 different fillers. Of these, only 5, namely *thousands*, *years*, *kinds*, *parts*, and *millions* occur with absolute frequencies above 10. The vast majority of all fillers, i.e. 112 out of 159 instances, are recorded only once in the above framework. That is, the individual tokens would not be noted as significantly frequent. The more abstract type, however, is instantiated very frequently.

The last aspect to be discussed in this section is the question as to whether the instantiations of the recurrent item strings are linguistically relevant units, i.e. units of a grammatical, semantic or pragmatic kind. It is very rare that the recurrent item string qualifies as a grammatical unit. Polywords, by definition, have grammatical status, since they are understood as a lexical item that consists of more than one word form; idioms usually have phrase or clause status and institutionalised expressions usually are clauses as well. Some authors regard grammatical-unit status as prerequisite (e.g. Kjellmer's (1990, 1991) conception of 'collocation'). But in general, recurrent item strings may create grammatical units, but they may also fail to do so. This group encompasses collocations, n-grams, lexical bundles, collocational frameworks, p-frames, POS-grams, and semantic preferences and prosodies. Representative in that respect is Biber et al. (1999, 2003, and 2004) and their treatment of lexical bundles:

> most lexical bundles do not represent a complete structural unit. For example, only 15 per cent of the lexical bundles in conversation can be regarded as complete phrases or clauses, while less than 5 per cent of the lexical bundles in academic prose represent complete structural units [...]. (Biber et al. 2004: 377)

Similarly, most recurrent item strings neither form a semantic or pragmatic unit. One exception are idioms. Their special status is licensed by the fact that they are more than the sum of their parts, their opacity in meaning. A concept that shows a specific pragmatic function is that of lexicalized sentence stems. It was put forward by Pawley and Syder in their influential 1983 article, which defines 'lexicalized sentence stems' as "a unit of clause length or longer whose grammatical form and lexical content is wholly or largely fixed" (191). A sentence stem consists of

> either a complete sentence, or, more commonly, an expression which is something less than a complete sentence. In the latter case, the sentence structure is fully specified along with the nucleus of lexical and grammatical morphemes which normally include the verb and certain of its arguments; however, one or more structural elements is a class, represented by a category symbol such as TENSE, NP or PRO. (210)

Examples of sentence stems and their realizations are the following (Pawley and Syder 1983: 210-211):

(26) NP be-TENSE sorry to keep-TENSE you waiting
I'm sorry to keep you waiting.
I'm so sorry to have kept you waiting.
Mr X is sorry to keep you waiting all this time.

(27) Who (the EXPLET) do-PRES NP$_i$ think PRO$_i$ be-PRES!
Who the hell do you think you are.
Who does that woman think she is.

Lexicalized sentence stems differ from idioms in that the former are usually literal expressions. But they may "have conversational uses (implicatures, speech act functions, etc.) in addition to their literal senses, and these additional uses may also be conventionalized and to some extent arbitrary [...]" (211). This is illustrated in examples like *Who does that woman think she is* (see (27) above), which expresses indignation on the part of the speaker, although this is not conveyed by the literal meaning of the expression.

On the whole, there is a large number of concepts developed in corpus linguistic research that form a highly heterogeneous set. The next section will show that the present network model is able to do justice to this variability.

5.4 Recurrent item strings in the network model

On the basis of the previous discussion it seems reasonable to first focus on two of the variables mentioned above. The first, the degree of abstraction of elements that create the string, touches on the question as to what the elements in the string actually represent. This aspect encompasses the distinctions between word forms, lexemes, word classes, semantic features, etc. The second, continuity or discontinuity of the string, refers to the degree to which unspecified material may or may not intervene between the elements specified. The emphasis here is on unspecified material. For instance, collocational frameworks, such as 'a + ? + *of*', could be regarded as a string of recurrent items, namely *a* and *of* which are not adjacent. On the other hand, the whole string together with the open slot forms one fixed structural unit. It therefore makes more sense to treat the open slot as a highly abstract filler, which is only restricted by the fact that it must be a word form that enters in the string. In contrast, the collocates in collocations in Halliday's sense, i.e. lexemes and their derivations, are not tied to a

Table 5.1: Recurrent item strings with regard to the variables degree of abstraction and continuity.

	No intervening material	Intervening material
filler concrete (word forms)	e.g. idioms n-grams lexical bundles recurrent word combinations polywords institutionalized expressions	e.g. collocations (Sinclair) discontinuous recurrent word combinations
fillers abstract (lexemes, semantic features, ...)	e.g. p-frames collocational frameworks POS-grams Patterns lexicalized sentence stems	e.g. collocations (Halliday) semantic preferences semantic prosodies

particular structure: collocates may occur in different orders and there may be intervening material which is irrelevant to the description of the recurrent item string. On the basis of these remarks we can distinguish four essentially different types of recurrent item strings, as shown in table 5.1. The following sections will discuss the influence of each of the two variables.

5.4.1 Concrete fillers with no intervening material

We will start off with recurrent item strings that consist of concrete word forms and allow no intervening material. As an example we discuss the string *naked eye* (see Sinclair 1996). Although this string is very short. it serves to represent all the features that are relevant for any of the recurrent item strings which can be categorised by the upper left corner of table 5.1. All the considerations that apply to *naked eye* will also apply to any of the other concepts.

In the network model advocated here, the basic mechanism at work in the formation of recurrent item strings is that frequent co-activation of nodes leads to association between these nodes (see section 2.2.2.10). This mechanism can also be applied to the string *naked eye*. Each time this string occurs in language use, the nodes that represent the individual word forms will become activated one after the other. Since a node will retain its activation for some time, the node representing *naked* will still be activated to some degree when the node representing *eye* is activated. That is, they are co-activated for a certain amount of time. If this co-activation patterns recurs fairly frequently, this will lead to strong associations between the two word forms in the network. Note that the operative mechanism here is the same as the one that explains the co-existence of rules and (some of) their instantiations in the network.

Frequency in and of itself does not guarantee status as a phraseological unit. The string *naked eye* is far less frequent than many other strings. It occurs only 149 times in the BNC, and strings like *my father* (n=3501) or *my mother* (n=3336) are more frequent by far. Still, our intuition would rather grant a special status to *naked eye* and not to the other strings. The reason for this becomes clear, if we consider a fact that is already expressed in one of the earliest claims on the nature of collocations; Firth writes:

> The habitual collocations in which words under study appear are quite simply the mere word accompaniment, the other word-material in which they are most commonly or most characteristically embedded. (Firth 1957 [1968]: 180)

This quote shows that the nature of collocation can be viewed from two angles (although Firth seems to regard these angles as essentially identical). One has to do with the mere frequency of the co-occurrence and is expressed in the term 'most commonly', whereas the other concerns expectations or statistical significance and is expressed by 'most characteristically'. The former aspect touches on the notion of relative connection strength discussed in section 2.2.2.2 and on the notion of predictability. *My* very commonly co-occurs with *father* or *mother*, but also with a large number of other word forms. As a consequence, none of these co-occurrences are especially characteristic, i.e. the relative strength is similar for a large number of connections. In contrast, *naked* does not co-occur as frequently with *eye*, but the co-occurrence is highly characteristic of *naked*. This intuition is captured by metrics of collocational strength like the log-likelihood value. The log-likelihood values for the strongest right-collocates of *my* (span=1) in a random sample of 1,906[93] occurrences of *my* in the BNC, range from 397 for *father*, 309 for *own*, 259 for *mother*, and so on. In contrast, for *naked* the strongest collocate, *eye*, shows a log-likelihood value of 1,761, the second strongest, *body*, a value of 428, and the value for the third strongest collocate, *except for*, is 296. This comparison makes clear that, while *my* occurs very com-

---

93 The number of tokens is due to the fact that *naked* occurs only 1,906 times in the BNC.

monly with forms like *father*, *own*, or *mother*, it does not occur characteristically with any of these forms. The reverse holds true for *naked*: The co-occurrence of *naked* and *eye* is not nearly as common as that of *my* and *father*, but it is far more characteristic than the occurrence of *naked* together with any other word form. In the present network model this characteristic co-occurrence can be captured by the thickness of the connections between nodes (see section 2.2.2.3), as shown in figure 5.16 below. Note that the thickness of the links do not represent the mere frequency of occurrences of *my* and *naked* together with the word forms to which the links lead. Instead, the thicker the connection, the more characteristic is the co-occurrence of the two word forms that are connected. The lines thus mirror probabilities that the word form represented by the source node is associated with that in the target node. These probabilities are low for *mother*, *own*, or *father*, since *my* co-occurs very frequently with a large number of words, without occurring characteristically with any of them. In contrast, *naked* is by far not as often followed by *eye* as *my* is followed by *own*, but the probability for *eye* to occur given the occurrence of *naked* is much higher. This is mirrored by the thickness of the connection between |*naked*| and |*eye*|.

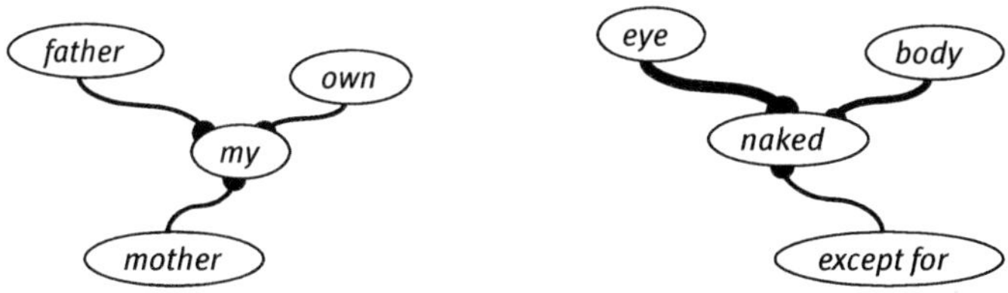

Figure 5.16: The difference between common co-occurrences and characteristic co-occurrences.

The present network, then, does not capture collocation in the sense of "a frequent co-occurrence of words" (Sinclair 1996: 80), but 'collocation' in the sense of "habitual associations of a word with other items" (Partington 1998: 16) or as "significant collocations" (Sinclair & Jones 1974: 19).

An aspect which has not been discussed so far is that of idiomatic meaning that may be found with collocations. The string *naked eye*, for instance, is not fully transparent, since *naked* in this case does not mean 'undressed' but rather 'not fitted with/supported by instruments or tools'. Hence, the string *naked eye* is best paraphrased by 'an eye not fitted with/supported by instruments or tools'. How can this be represented in the present network model? Following

Lakoff (1987), we might assume that the original meaning of *naked* in this case has undergone a metaphorical extension from 'undressed' to 'not fitted with/supported by instruments or machinery'. Leaving aside for the moment the question of how this new meaning has arisen, we can represent the two meanings of *naked* by two individual meaning nodes in the network. Of the two possible meanings the 'undressed' meaning is the more frequently used one. Accordingly, it is more strongly connected to *naked* and will be more strongly activated than the second meaning. However, the link leading from the node *naked* to the second meaning node will be amplified in the context of *eye*. The occurrence of *eye* thus boosts the activation that leads to this meaning node[94], and the overall activation of the second meaning of *naked* is stronger than the meaning 'undressed'. The meaning of the whole phrase *naked eye* can consequently be composed of the individual meanings of its constituents. The same would account for Lakoff's (1987) example *spill the beans*, meaning 'divulge (secret) information'.

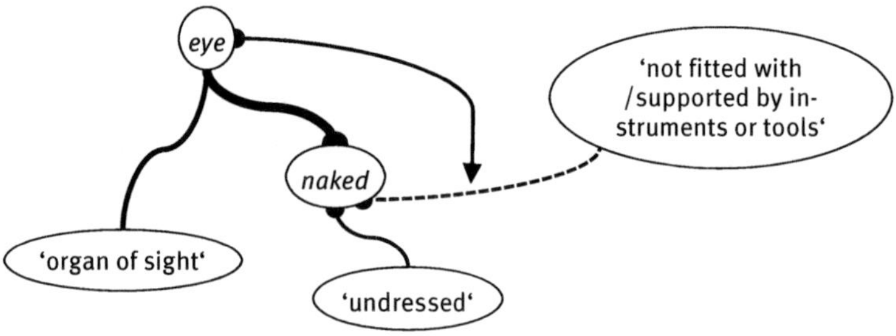

Figure 5.17: The compositionality of the meaning *naked eye*.

Of course, given a high enough frequency of co-occurrence, the two word forms may be regarded as one complex lexical unit with one meaning. This process would be identical to the one described in section 4.2.6 with regard to the co-existence of rules and instantiations and the question of decomposition or whole-word route. In this case, the idiomatic meaning of *naked* would be part of the meaning of the whole phrase *naked eye*.

94 This idea may appear strange at first sight, but note that in the BNC *naked* is the fifth-strongest left-collocate (span=1) of *eye*. It therefore seems reasonable to assume that the form *eye* and this particular meaning of *naked* are associated to a certain degree.

For the condition that idioms are truly opaque, the situation is even less complicated. Idioms like *kick the bucket* have to be learned by rote like any other lexical item. That is, they have unit-status and thus are represented by their own (complex) node which is connected to the respective meaning.

5.4.2 Abstract fillers in continuous strings

As an example of this case, let us first consider Stubbs' (2007: 90-91) concept of p-frame. A p-frame was defined as "an n-gram with one variable slot", such as '*a + ? + of*' exemplified in strings like *a number of* or *a lot of.* Looking at the first, '*a* + ? + *of*', in more detail we find that it is instantiated 253,150 times in the 100 million words BNC[95]. We further find that the number of possible different instantiations, i.e. the number of different types or variants, is 3,322. Among these are *a number of, a couple of, a lot of, a series of, a threat of, a ridge of,* ranging in frequencies from 15,126 for the first example down to 15 for the last one.

In the network model advocated here, the notion of p-frame is represented as follows. As was described above, the present model is essentially based on actually occurring word forms. The starting point for the formation of a p-frame like '*a* + ? + *of*', thus, are the many instantiations in which it is realized. Again, the responsible mechanism is that of (frequent) co-activation of nodes which will lead to strong associations between individual lexical items. This is represented by the thickness of the connecting lines between the nodes representing the word forms that occur in the instantiations of this p-frame[96]. This way we see that highly frequent realizations of the p-frames are likely to be conceived of as one single unit (e.g. *a number of*), whereas less frequent ones like *a ridge of* are not perceived as such. Starting off from the individual realizations the more abstract p-frame evolves, if we take into consideration that each of the fillers of the frame will spread its activation to neighbouring nodes in the network. One such node is the node |*NOUN*|, since all of the fillers are nouns. This is also depicted in figure 5.18. Each time an instantiation of the p-frame occurs, the abstract node |*NOUN*| is activated together with the nodes representing *a* and *of.* That is, the three nodes will be co-activated in the network and thus be strongly activated which will result in the more abstract string ('*a* + NOUN + *of*'). The highest degree of abstraction, i.e. 'a + ? + *of*', could be represented through the

95 The data are drawn from "Phrases in English" ('http://phrasesinenglish.org').
96 In this case, again, we make us of sequential connections as p-frames have a fixed order.

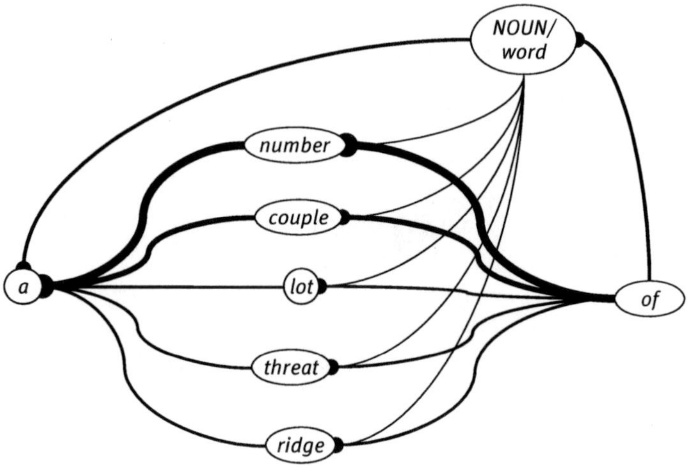

Figure 5.18: The p-frame '*a* + *?* + *of*' and some of its instantiations.

fact that any word form also instantiates a highly abstract node |word|. That is we might assume that the node |word| also becomes co-activated with each instantiation of this particular p-frame. In this manner we have arrived at the representation of the p-frame in the present network model. In figure 5.18 the two nodes |*NOUN*| and |word| are represented by one box for convenience.

The discussion already indicates how more abstract recurrent item strings evolve in the network model. As an example we will discuss Stubbs' concept of POS-grams. Recall that POS-grams are sequences of parts of speech, for instance 'AT0 AJ0 NN1' or 'PRP AT0 NN1', i.e. the sequence of article, general positive adjective and singular common noun or the sequence of preposition (excluding *of*), article and singular common noun, respectively. As before, POS-grams are abstracted away from strings of actually occurring word forms, as we will show with regard to the POS-gram 'AT0 AJ0 NN1'. In the BNC, this POS-gram is realized by 87,233 types (i.e. there are 87,233 different strings of word forms that instantiate this POS-gram), each of which is realized at least 3 times in the whole corpus. Possible types are *a long time* (n=3,607), *a wide range* (n=2,324), *the local authority* (n=1,386), or *the whole thing* (n=1,067). Depending on their frequencies, the individual word forms that occur within the strings show stronger or weaker associations. These will not interest us at the moment. More relevant for the present discussion is that for each of these strings the occurrence of the first word form will also activate the |*ARTICLE*| node, the second

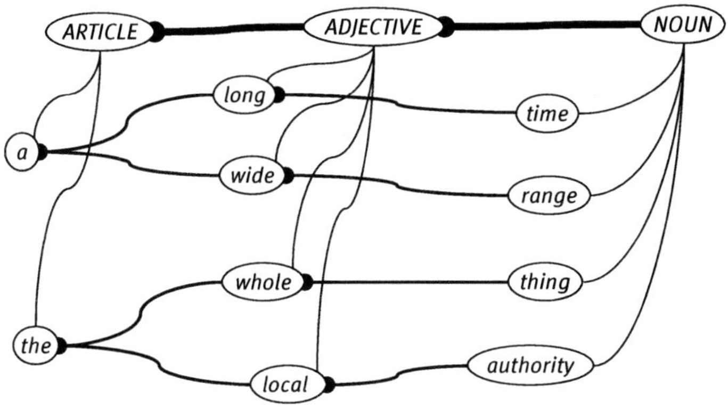

Figure 5.19: POS-grams in the network model.

word form will activate the |*ADJECTIVE*| node, and the third will activate the |*NOUN*| node. That is, any time one of the 87,233 types is instantiated in language use the respective part-of-speech nodes will also be activated in the system. Again, co-activation will lead to association of the three word-class nodes, as depicted in figure 5.19.

This way of representation makes explicit how associations between more abstract 'units' may be established despite none of the concrete instantiations in themselves being frequent enough to lead to a strong association between them. Even if *a wide range* or *the local authority* are not very frequent in actual language and, accordingly, the two strings are not strongly associated in the network, each of their occurrences will contribute to the association between the abstract nodes |*ARTICLE*|, |*ADJECTIVE*| and |*NOUN*|. It follows from this that even if sets of individual word forms are not strongly associated in the network, the abstract units to which they are related may still become strongly associated on the basis of the rather infrequent co-occurrences of individual strings.

5.4.3 Concrete and abstract fillers with intervening material

As far as the present network model is concerned, there is no real difference between recurrent item strings that allow intervening material and those that do not. The relevant question is that of sufficiently frequent co-activation of nodes which over time will lead to a strong association between individual nodes. The problem in this respect is the question as to the degree to which two nodes are co-activated, if the triggering word forms are not adjacent. It was said above that nodes do not lose their activation abruptly but that it recedes gradually. Even if two nodes are not activated simultaneously, we can assume that the node that was activated first still retains a lot of activation when the second node is fully activated not too much later. As a result both nodes will be activated quite strongly at the same point in time. Consider figure 2.42, repeated here as figure 5.20.

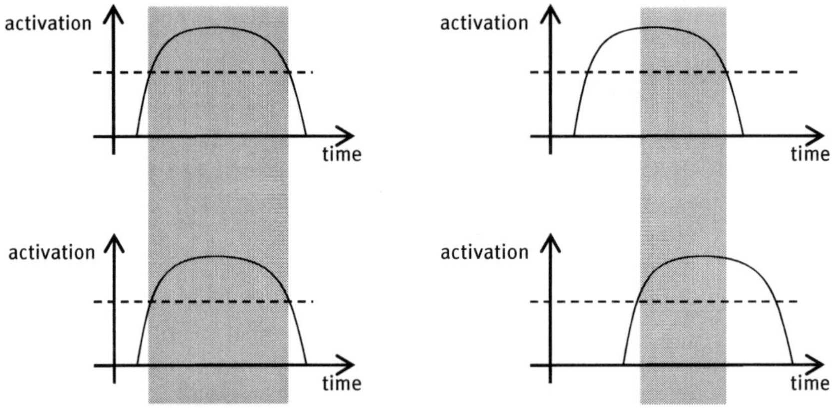

Figure 5.20: Different extents of co-activation. (= figure 2.42, here repeated for convenience)

If this successive activation occurs frequently, the nodes will become associated in the network. But if the first node has lost most or all of its activation when the second node becomes activated, there will be no association between the two nodes. The question, thus, is as to how long a node remains active once it has been triggered. This is a question which cannot be answered satisfactorily in this context. Nevertheless, the psychological concept of working memory and its capacity may be able to shed some light. Estimations as to working memory capacity are divergent, but they generally seem to be somewhere in the vicinity of Miller's (1956) "magic number seven", i.e. as Miller has already suggested 7 +/- 2 chunks (e.g. sounds/ letters, morphemes or words), with the capacity for word storage rather at the lower end of this interval.[97] Without going into detail

97 See Baddeley et al. (1975), Hulme et al. (1995) and Cowan (2001 & 2005) for a more detailed treatment of working memory capacity.

here, we may assume that if the co-occurrence of two word forms is within the limits of working memory, the respective nodes will be co-activated in the network. Note that the same intuition is captured by the fact that all concepts in the area of recurrent item strings either assume that the elements that make up the string are adjacent or that these elements co-occur within a particular span of words. We may assume that even with discontinuous recurrent item strings the nodes that are of relevance are sufficiently activated, even if irrelevant language material is intervening.

Still, what role does the intervening material play? The simple answer is: none. To give but one example, in section 5.4 it was shown that Halliday's (1966) concept of collocation is not based on the co-occurrence of actual word forms. He considers collocational relations to obtain between lexical units and their derivations: *a strong argument*, *he argued strongly*, *the strength of his argument* and *his argument was strengthened* are all considered as instantiations of one collocational relation, namely that between the lexical units STRONG and ARGUE and their respective derivations (151). In the present network model (see figure 5.21), those units that are similar with regard to one or more aspects are considered as being strongly associated. This comes into play at this point with regard to the association of lexical units and their instantiating word forms. Any occurrence of one of the strings named above will lead to the activation of the respective word form nodes. From there the activation will spread into the network until eventually the lexical-unit nodes |STRONG| and |ARGUE|

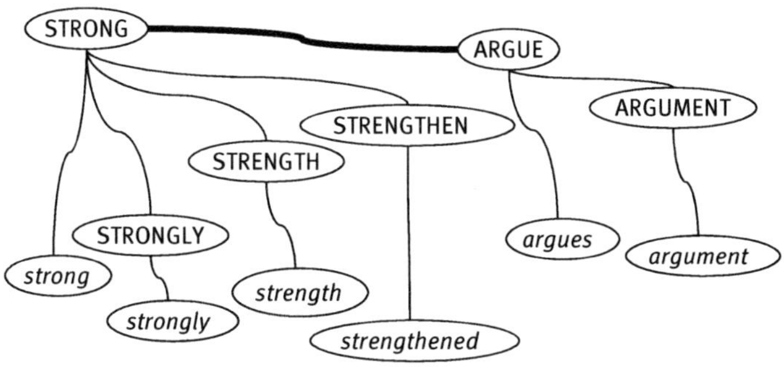

Figure 5.21: Halliday's (1966) notion of collocation as a relationship between lexical units and their derivations in the network mode. Note that the lines in this figure represent (unspecified) associations. Such associations can be of different kinds, such as that between a lexical unit and its derivations, a lexical unit and its instantiating word forms, or collocational relations between lexical units. The figure does not make any distinctions in this respect.

will become activated. As in the other cases discussed before, this co-activation, if frequent enough, will lead to a strong association between the two lexemes. This again is represented by the thick line that connects the two lexical-unit nodes. This is the same mechanism that was discussed in the previous section.

Returning to our original question, the role of intervening language material, we can note that there may be a large number of other nodes that may be co-activated together with the two nodes at issue here. Yet, while the nodes |STRONG| and |ARGUE| are activated every time this collocation is instantiated, nodes referring to intervening material are not co-activated frequently enough to be associated with the two nodes that are central for the collocation. As long as the intervening material does not co-occur on a sufficiently regular basis, and as long as it does not separate the word forms relating to the central nodes so significantly that they are beyond the capacity of working memory, intervening language material does not play a role in discontinuous recurrent item strings.

This section has shown how the different concepts discussed under the umbrella term 'recurrent item string' can be accommodated in the network model advocated in this study. The next section will try to shed some light on the relation of the use of pre-fabricated chunks as opposed to the general productivity of language.

5.4.4 The interaction of idiomaticity and productivity

Traditionally, there has always been a sharp line drawn between those aspects of language that can be captured by the productive exploitation of grammatical rules and the prefabricated aspects of language use, which usually do not make full use of the potential that grammatical rules allow and often are idiomatic in nature. As a consequence, idiomatic expressions have usually been relegated to the lexicon, where they are stored as holistic units that defy grammatical analysis, mostly due to the fact that the idiomatic whole is more than the sum of its parts. A similar view is expressed in Sinclair's (1991) distinction between idiom and open-choice principle. The former refers to the assumption that

> a language user has available to him or her a large number of semi-preconstructed phrases that constitute single choices, even though they might appear to be analysable into segments. (Sinclair 1991: 110)

What Sinclair calls the 'open-choice principle', in contrast, makes reference to the productivity aspect of language, i.e. the notion of rules of grammar that provide a string of slots that then can be filled by any kind of lexical item that fulfils the syntactic and semantic requirements. Recent corpus-linguistic research suggests that these two ways of producing and analysing text are not mutually exclusive; the language user does not switch between these two modes. Rather, "the two modes of interpretation coexist and compete with one another inside one and the same stretch of text" (Sánchez 2006: 74). This becomes obvious as soon as we take the comprehension of idioms into account, as Nooteboom et al. (2002) make clear with the example *Bill took Janet to task* ('Bill strongly criticized Janet for something she had done'). In this case "we do not know in advance whether we are dealing with an idiom, so we have to follow the route of compositional construction in this case until the very end" (6). From the production point of view we also find that often some kind of computation (and productivity) is given with idioms. A case in point is Barlow's (2000) discussion of the idiom *make hay while the sun shines*, meaning 'take advantage of favourable conditions'. Among the instantiations that Barlow (2000: 337-338) lists we find *made hay while their quarterback shined*, *make political hay*, or *cannot make hay in such political sunshine*. Such variations, according to Barlow, show that

> there must be some kind of internal analysis of the set expression. An X-bar analysis or labelling of some sort must be applied to the idiomatic string in order to modify the canonical form to fit the current circumstances. (Barlow 2000: 336)

In this, Barlow emphasizes a point that is not focal in Sinclair's writing: although idioms or prefabs may constitute single choices, the features associated with their constituent parts also come into play. In a similar vein, Bybee (2010: 25) claims that "[w]hile an idiom such as *pull strings* has its own metaphorical meaning, it is nevertheless associated with the words *pull* and *strings* as independent words." In addition, "[j]ust because a multi-word expression is stored and processed as a chunk does not mean that it does not have internal structure" (36). This understanding of the processing of idioms is in line with the general nature of the present network model, as will be shown presently.

The idiom under scrutiny can be understood as a pairing of a meaning node with a number of nodes that represent the individual elements in the idiom. These elements are of two kinds, namely word forms, i.e. *hay*, *while*, *the*, and *sun*, as well as lexical units, i.e. MAKE and SHINE. Since these elements occur in a fixed order, the network representation of this idiom is similar to the representation of word forms as sequences of phonemes (see section 2.2.2.9): the

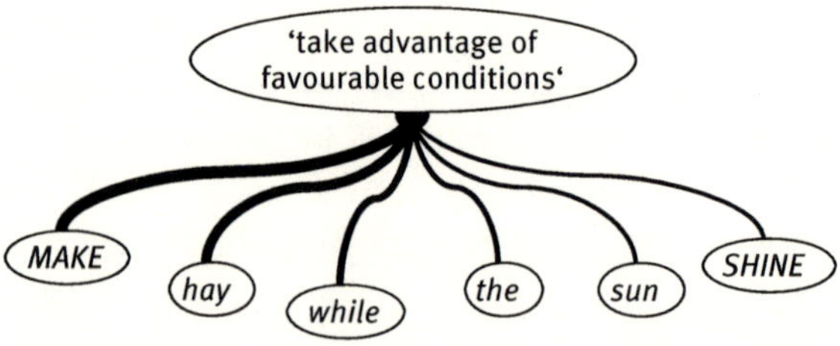

Figure 5.22: The idiom 'make hay while the sun shines' as a single choice in the network.

strength of connection between the meaning node and the individual elements decreases the further towards the end an element occurs (figure 5.22).

The word form and lexical unit nodes are not isolated in the network, but are connected to other nodes. Even in the case of idioms, where a set of word forms is activated simultaneously, this activation will still spread to neighbouring nodes, which represent information on the word class of the word forms, their respective syntactic functions, and so on. Each use of an idiom will thus automatically activate those bits of grammatical knowledge attached to the elements within the idiom. This makes clear that in the present network model the idiomatic and the productive aspects of language use cannot be separated from each other; both aspects are always present in the production of idioms. This is obvious with inflectional variations.

The idiom, as represented in the present model, contains the lexical unit nodes |MAKE| and |SHINE|. These are associated with possible instantiating word forms. Which of these become realised depends on the activation of additional meaning nodes, e.g. |'past'| or |'progressive'|. Figure 5.23 shows how the network represents the fact that the act of taking advantage of favourable conditions occurred in the past: the meaning node |'past'| will be activated together with the node |'take advantage of favourable conditions'|. The |'past'| node will also activate the word form nodes |*made*| and |*shone*|, since these are past tense forms. These already receive some activation from the lexical-unit nodes. On the whole, the past tense forms are more strongly activated than the present tense ones, since each of the former receives activation from two nodes. This shows how the idiomatic and the regular or productive interact in the production of idioms. In the same way, all kinds of inflectional variability in idioms or fixed expressions could be explained.

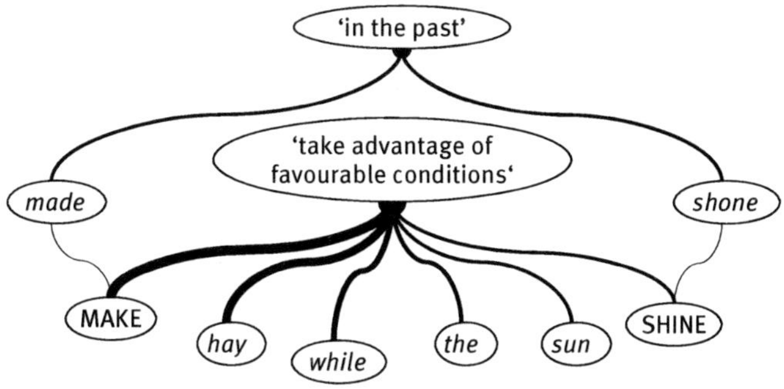

Figure 5.23: Inflectional variability of the idiom 'make hay while the sun shines' in the network.

The more substantial semantic variability of idioms can be explained in the same fashion; let us consider the variant *make political hay while the sun shines*. First, it is important to note that the meaning 'take advantage of favourable conditions', although it can be related to the idioms as a whole, can still be decomposed into meaning components relating to the traditional distinction of verb and object. These, in turn, are related to substrings in the idiom. Instead of figure 5.23, we thus have a slightly more complicated picture of the situation, depicted in figure 5.24 below.

The variant *make political hay while the sun shines* provides additional information as to the nature of the advantage that can be taken, i.e. political advantage. On the left-hand side of the meaning components in figure 5.24 we thus have an additional meaning which could be captured loosely by the phrase 'related to politics'. How do we get from here to the insertion of the premodify-

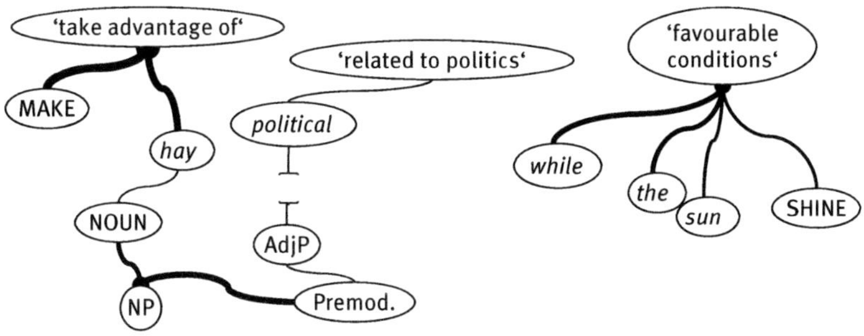

Figure 5.24: Semantic variability of the idiom 'make hay while the sun shines' in the network.

ing adjective *political*? In the usual idiom, the meaning of 'take advantage of' is mapped onto the clause *make hay*, i.e. the respective word form nodes are activated in the network. Again, the activation spreads through the network. In particular, the activation of the node |*hay*| will spread through the node |*NOUN*| (since *hay* is a noun) to the node |NP| (since nouns serve as heads in NPs). This node, in turn, is connected to a number of nodes that may form part of the structure of the NP (heavily simplified). Among them, the node |premodifying adjective|. The meaning node |'related to politics'| in turn is connected to a number of (strings of) word forms that may be used to express this meaning, among them the adjective |*political*|, which, being an adjective, will also be connected to the node |AdjP|. Again, we see how the idiomatic and the productive work hand in hand in the present network model.

On the whole, it has been shown how the many different kinds of recurrent item strings can be implemented in the present network approach to the language system. It has also been shown how the idiomatic meaning often associated with recurrent item strings can be accommodated. Finally, this section has made clear how, in the present network model, the idiomatic and the productive side of language always co-exist in the comprehension and production of idioms.

5.5 Frequency and other causes for entrenchment in the present network model

The network model advocated here has granted the aspect of frequency a basic role in the formation of network structures, since it is responsible for entrenchment of units and strength of associations between nodes. This may give rise to the impression that frequency was the only way in which strings of word forms may become entrenched and achieve unit status in the network. However, there are also other factors that enhance entrenchment[98]. Some of these will be discussed in the following.

As already stated in the previous section, frequency alone will not guarantee unit status in the present network model, since frequency only makes claims about what commonly co-occurs. More important than this aspect, as we have seen, is that of characteristic co-occurrence, which in turn is close to the notion

98 Also see the discussion of Ellis (2002) in section 4.2.6 and Schmid's (2007) discussion of 'salience'.

of 'predictability', a term central to the interpretation of 'association' employed in the present study. In summary, frequency is usually relevant if and only if it is conspicuous, i.e. a particular pattern of co-occurrence must stand out in comparison to other actual patterns.

Other causes of unit status need to be taken into consideration as well. One, as has already been stated above, is the idiomaticity of some patterns of co-occurrence. If the meaning of a string of word forms is different from the sum of its parts, i.e. if the string is opaque to some extent, this will automatically result in unit status for the string under scrutiny: "[w]e have more direct evidence of unit status when an expression consistently displays some idiosyncrasy that does not follow from any regular pattern" (Langacker 2008: 238). This is the same intuition that is captured in Goldberg's (1995) definition of construction:

> a construction is posited in the grammar if it can be shown that its meaning and/or its form is not compositionally derived from other constructions existing in the language [...]. (Goldberg 1995: 4)

This line of thought, in my view, can be extended in two directions. Firstly, a string of word forms will also gain unit status, if it has a special pragmatic function. This would explain the special status of sentence builders (see section 5.3), such as '*I think that* X' or '*The thing is* X', which are used to fulfil an important pragmatic function, in this case the introduction of one's own point of view. Unit status, thus, can also be achieved through the 'usefulness' of a particular string of words.

The second kind of extension of Goldberg's definition touches on the status of a string of items as grammatical unit. It stands to reason that recurrent item strings that are grammatical units become more deeply entrenched in the cognitive system: First, they can be connected to an already existing node in the network and are thus stored as one member of an already given class, and second, they may facilitate processing by representing one particularly frequently used possible instantiation of a particular element. It is for this reason that a POS-gram like 'article + adjective + noun' is more likely to have unit status than a POS-gram like 'adjective + noun + preposition'.

6 Beyond grammar: language use and the network

While the previous chapters has been concerned with units and rules in language and linguistics, i.e. with the language system, the present chapter will look at the use and exploitation of the language system. It is concerned with an overview of different regularities and principles that are found in linguistics, and encompasses those aspects that are, in a sense, pre-grammatical, i.e. it will be concerned with phenomena that are not confined to a particular grammatical model but are of a more general relevance. The focus will be on those regularities and principles that in some way or other can be related to processing issues. It will be shown that all the aspects to be discussed can be subsumed under two basic necessities, namely the need for using an efficient code and the need for guaranteeing efficient and accurate decoding.

6.1 The nature of categories and its relevance for processing

As discussed previously, the present model adheres to the view expressed by Lamb (2000: 95), namely that a model of language "must represent a competence to perform". That is, the linguistic categories are geared towards fast and efficient processing and production. In this, linguistic categories are no different from other categories in human cognition. Important contributions in this area of research have been made by Eleanor Rosch and her colleagues (see, among others, Rosch 1973a and b, 1978a and b, and Rosch & Mervis 1975). There is no need here to give a comprehensive review of her work[99] but it seems reasonable to discuss some of the key points, namely 'cognitive economy', 'perceived world structure', 'basic-level category' and 'cue validity', and see how these are implemented in the present network model.

Fundamental to Rosch's prototype theory (1978b) is the assumption that human categorization is not arbitrary but the "result of psychological principles

99 For fuller treatments, the reader is referred to Mangasser-Wahl (2000), Mervis and Rosch (1981), Taylor (1989), and Schmid (1993) and (2000). Also, the account given here is rather uncritical. Critical appraisals may be found in Geeraerts (1989 [2006]), Kleiber (^{2}1998), Posner (1986), Schmid (1993), or Wierzbicka (1985 and 1990).

in categorization, which are subject to investigation" (27). She suggests two such principles, namely 'cognitive economy' and 'perceived world structure'.

The first principle, cognitive economy, can be understood as the outcome of a struggle for least effort and involves a trade-off between the number of different categories and the information that a category provides. If an organism divides its environment into a few categories only, cognitive effort on mental storage of categories will be low; yet, at the same time, the information value of category labels will be low, too. Maximum information through category labels could be obtained, if categories would discriminate as finely as possible between entities in the environment. A consequence would be an extremely large number of categories, thus increasing the mental effort that is used to organize the categories beyond a reasonable limit (cf. Tversky 1986: 64). In this vein, cognitive economy can be seen as balancing the two opposing tendencies of maximizing information provided by category labels, while simultaneously minimizing the number of categories needed to describe the world.

The second principle, perceived world structure, is informed by the fact that

> the perceived world is not an unstructured total set of equiprobable co-occurring attributes. Rather, the material objects of the world are perceived to possess [...] high correlational structure. That is, given a knower who perceives the complex attributes of feathers, fur, and wings, it is an empirical fact provided by the perceived world that wings co-occur with feathers more than with fur. [...] combinations of what we perceive as the attributes of real objects do not occur uniformly. (Rosch 1978b: 29; see also Mervis & Rosch 1981: 91-92)

It follows that the occurrence of a particular attribute increases the probability of occurrence of some other attributes, while at the same time decreasing the probability of others. For instance, the occurrence of wings, as in the example given by Rosch, will make feathers highly probable and fins impossible.

According to Rosch, these two principles influence human categorization on two dimensions, a vertical and a horizontal one. The first "concerns the level of inclusiveness of the category" (1978b: 30), i.e. the distinction of, say, *ANIMAL*, *DOG*, and *GERMAN SHEPHERD*. Here, the principles of economy and perceived world structure imply "that not all possible levels of categorization are equally good and useful" (30). It is at one level, the basic level, where both principles are optimally met, as will be shown below (also see Tversky 1986 for a discussion of the basic level). The second dimension, the horizontal one, "concerns the segmentation of categories at the same level of inclusiveness" (30), i.e. *DOG* vs. *CAT* vs. *BIRD*, etc. With regard to this dimension the two principles of categorization seem to imply that categories are defined in terms of prototypes which "contain the attributes most representative of items inside and least representative of items outside the category" (30). Since the concept of prototype has already been discussed in the context of gradience (see section 4.2.2), the following will focus on the idea of basic-level categories and the fundamental role of cue validity.

The basic level of categorization is claimed to be the one level that instantiates the two principles of categorization to the highest degree, since basic-level categories "are those which carry the most information [...] and are [...] most differentiated from one another" (Rosch et al. 1976: 382). Relevant to this context is the concept of 'cue validity'[100]. Cue validity is the property of a given feature to be indicative of a particular category. For instance, the feature 'is feathered' is more indicative of the category *BIRD* than the feature 'biped', i.e. the former is a better cue to the category *BIRD* than the latter and thus has higher cue validity. Categories, too, have cue validity. The cue validity of a category is defined as "the summation of the cue validities for that category of each of the attributes of the category" (Rosch 1978b: 30-31). If then a category has a high overall cue validity, this implies that many of the attributes in this category are (almost) unique to this category, which shows that the category is highly differentiated from other categories. Basic-level categories, according to Rosch, are "at the most inclusive level of abstraction at which there are attributes common to all or most members of the category" (31). One such category would be that of *BIRD*. Many of its members share a large number of attributes. With the next higher category, *ANIMAL*, the number of common attributes is much lower. It follows from this that the overall cue validity of such a superordinate category is fairly low, since the number of common attributes is low. With categories lower than the basic level, the number of common features is very high, despite many of these common features also being shared by many other categories. Canaries, for instance, have a large number of features that are also shared by sparrows. On the other hand, the number of features restricted to canaries or sparrows is fairly small. It follows that most of the features of the respective categories have a low cue validity and the number of features with high cue validity is very small, which again, leads to a fairly low cue validity for each of the subordinate categories.

These theoretical implications have been corroborated by a number of experiments (Rosch et al. 1976). For instance, subjects were asked to name attrib-

---

100 In this context, see Taylor's (2008: 44-46) discussion of "categories as sets of weighted attributes" (44).

utes associated with category labels, such as *FURNITURE*, CHAIR, and KITCHEN CHAIR. The results show that the number of common attributes for the superordinate categories was very low, while those listed for basic and subordinate levels were both high. In addition, "the number of attributes added at the subordinate level [... were] significantly fewer than the number added at the basic level" (391). On the whole, we see that superordinate categories are informationally weak, since they do not provide much information due to the category members not sharing many features. Subordinate categories are informationally rich, but not much richer than the basic-level categories. It follows that the increase in mental effort that results from the necessity to handle a large number of subordinate categories is not justified by the informational gain that is provided by the more delicate categorization. On the whole, "it seems to be cognitively advantageous to divide reality into categories at the basic level, and this is why basic-level categories [...] are considered the most deeply entrenched categories at our disposal" (Schmid 2007: 124)[101].

In the present model the relevance of basic-level categories and cue validity follows as a consequence from the nature of the network, and it will automatically be exploited in language processing. Consider the example of noun phrases. For this category, definite or indefinite articles are features of high cue validity. In the model advocated here this is represented by the fact that the nodes for definite and indefinite article are directly linked to the node |NP| and to no other nodes. The activation of the nodes representing the definite or the indefinite article will automatically spread to the |NP| node, which will pass its activation on to other nodes to which it is connected, such as the quantifier or the adjective node as possible kinds of premodification. Note that at this point also the notion of basic-level category comes into play. In section 4.2.1 it was shown that the present model does not contain categories of all degrees of delicacy. For instance, the model does not provide a specific node for a category like *PLURAL PRONOUN*. Rather, this category is created online through the fact that two nodes, namely |plural| and |*PRONOUN*|, are activated simultaneously in the network. In a similar way, the network only provides nodes for rather abstract phrasal categories, such as *VP*, *PP* or *NP*. More delicate distinctions, such as 'premodified NP' or 'NP postmodified by a PP' can only be drawn on the basis of the activation of further nodes in the network.

---

101 In this respect, see Geeraerts et al. (1994), who report on deeper entrenchment for subordinate categories than for basic-level categories with some clothing items, and Schmid's (1996 and 2007) discussion of their findings.

This feature of the present network model mirrors Rosch's concepts of superordinate vs. basic-level vs. subordinate categories and the idea of cognitive economy behind these concepts. Imagine the network model contained only highly specific categories, such as *PREMODIFIED NP* or *POSTMODIFIED NP*. The processor would not be able to identify any of these on the basis of the definite or indefinite article alone. As a consequence the informativity that is contained in the mere occurrence of an article could not be exploited for further processing. If, on the other hand, the network only contained highly general categories like *PHRASE* (as opposed to *CLAUSE* and *WORD FORM*), this category would be activated through the occurrence of an article (since that is one possible way to start a phrase). Yet, since this category is so general, the respective node would be connected to an extremely large number of nodes in the network. It is true that all of these would receive some activation but the contribution to the overall activation would be so small that it can be neglected.

This also makes clear why the highly abstract categories developed in X'-Theory (see section 4.1) do not play a major role in the current model. A category like *XP*, which subsumes phrases and clauses of all types, would not provide any processing advantages. A system which is geared towards efficiency could not make use of such a category. Accordingly, such extremely abstract categories are not necessary in a model which aims for psychological and cognitive plausibility.

Another example of the importance of such basic-level categories concerns the semantic and syntactic analysis of clauses with regard to their argument roles and how these are realized. Consider the ditransitive construction with its associated roles agent, recipient and patient (see also section 5.2.1). Mukherjee (2005: 99) reports that this construction occurs in eighteen different patterns for the verb GIVE and in 21 patterns for the verb TELL. It is not necessary to discuss these in detail here (see section 6.3 for details). Let it suffice to say that not all of these patterns are identifiable early in the clause. But the occurrence of a verb form like *give* or *tells* already makes clear that the construction under analysis is of the ditransitive kind. Without being certain about the exact type of ditransitive construction, the processor already has at its disposal some information that will help the processing of the whole construction, such as the argument roles of the construction itself, how these will be related to the participant roles of the verb and how these are most likely to be realized formally (see section 6.3 for details). All these bits of information will facilitate processing. The kind of verb is a feature with high cue validity in regard to the kind of construction involved, and supports the efficient processing of linguistic structures.

6.2 The exploitation of expectation

Underlying the notion of cue validity is the idea that the occurrence of a particular feature leads us to expect a particular category. Such expectations, generally, are the result of the nature of linguistic (and other) categories itself and, therefore, are of a more fundamental or basic kind. The expectations that will be explored in this section could be likened to a 'fine-tuning' of the existing system on the basis of the experience that the organism has made. The human mind makes use of past experience to interpret and process present experience. Past experience can be of different kinds. It entails world knowledge that is represented in schemas, frames or scripts, knowledge about the correlative structure of the surrounding world and knowledge about the correlative or associative structure of language, as documented in statistical regularities in usage data. All of these aspects are easily accounted for in the present network model.

The influence of world knowledge is represented in a way similar to the influence of frequency distributions and collocations. It is commonly assumed that the activation of one particular concept activates related concepts to a certain degree. For instance, the mention of *flower* would activate kinds of flowers, such as 'tulip', 'rose', and 'dandelion', and it would also activate concepts like 'blossom', 'leaf', 'stem', etc. The impact of such relations has been discussed in a large number of studies on information status and the related notions of 'givenenss' and 'newness', and the role of world knowledge in the processing of linguistic structures. Prince (1981) and Birner (1994, 1996), for instance, speak of 'inferrable' entities, i.e. items that are linked to one another by "logical – or, more commonly, plausible – reasoning" (Prince 1981: 236). A similar intuition is captured by Lambrecht's (1994) term 'inferentially accessible'. Allerton (1978: 140) talks about 'implicit mention' as exemplified by the associations of "*handbrake*, *drive*, *Ford* with *car* [...]", and approaches in artificial intelligence speak of 'frames' Minsky (1975) and 'scripts' (Schank & Abelson 1977).[102] Maybe most similar to the view entertained here is Chafe (e.g. 1974, 1976, 1980, and 1994), who understands 'givenness' in terms of 'consciousness' and 'activation'. He claims that consciousness has a focus: Only one concept can be fully active at a particular point in time. But this active information is "surrounded by a periphery of *semiactive* information that provides a context for it" (1994: 29). That is, an active concept will to some extent activate all the concepts that are related to it, or, in Chafe's words 'provide a context for it'.

102 See Hellman (1996) for a general discussion of the concept of 'inference'.

In the present network model such relations will be represented similarly to the collocational relations described above. The only difference being that the links between the individual nodes are not of a unidirectional kind, but are bidirectional. Let us illustrate this point with an example of spoken text discussed in Chafe (1987).

(1) I can recall a big undergraduate class that I had, where everybody loved the instructor, and he was a real old world Swiss guy, this was a biology course, and he left all of the - sort of – real contact with students up to his assistants. And he would come into his class at precisely one minute after the hour or something like that, and he would immediately open his notes up in the front of the room and every lecture after the first started the same way. (Chafe 1987: 23; note that paralinguistic information has been removed from the original example)

According to Chafe (30), the string *a big undergraduate class* evokes the 'class' schema which at least includes the following participants and events[103]: Students, an instructor, teaching assistants, the instructor's notes, a classroom, a lecture. In the present network model, such a schema would be represented by a network of meaning nodes, where each node is connected to each other node (see figure 6.1).

The activation of, say, the node |UNDERGRADUATE CLASS| will lead to a partial activation of all the meaning nodes to which it is connected, and so will the nodes representing the other concepts. As a consequence, all related concepts will be activated to some extent even though they may not have been mentioned before. Inferential or schema relations of this kind will facilitate language processing. As soon as the concept UNDERGRADUATE CLASS is activated, the 'class' schema becomes activated leading to a certain expectation as to concepts that are likely to become activated in the near future. The network correlate of these expectations is meaning nodes that are activated to some extent.

It stands to reason that knowledge of genres and text types has a similar (although maybe weaker) influence on processing. It is reasonable to assume that one part of the competent native speaker's cognitive system is knowledge about basic genres and text types. In the present network model, these would be represented by a node representing the genre (e.g. |'narrative'|) which is related to word forms and even syntactic structures that are common within a particu-

103 The specific elements included in this schema differ from person to person.

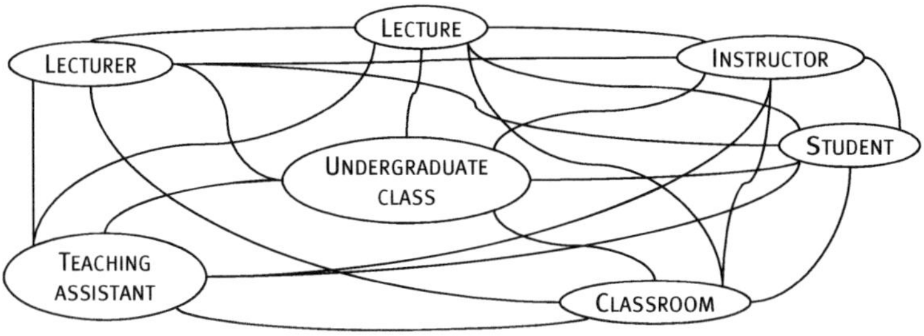

Figure 6.1: The 'class' schema

lar genre. By way of illustration, consider narrative discourse and its high frequency of third person pronouns and past tense forms. As soon as the speaker has realized that the text he or she is reading is a narrative (for instance through the well-known phrase *Once upon a time* or by *I can recall* in example (1) above), the respective node in the network would be activated and then spread its activation to those nodes that represent third person pronouns and past tense. In this way the retrieval of third person pronoun forms and the processing of past tense forms would be facilitated.

Similarly, being engaged in a face-to-face conversation with a friend, first and second person pronouns and present tense forms would receive a slight amount of activation due to the fact that these are frequent in this genre and that it can be assumed that the language user is aware of these facts.

As a last example, consider Hoey's (2005) discussion of contextually limited collocations:

> [...] the collocation of *recent* and *research* [...] is largely limited to academic writing and news reports of research. [...] *research* is primed in the minds of academic language users to occur with *recent* in such contexts and no others. The words are not primed to occur in recipes, legal documentation or casual conversation [...]. (Hoey 2005: 10)

In the present network model, this phenomenon is captured by links that lead from one particular node to an inter-nodal link in the network (cf. the discussion of node-connection links in section 2.2.3). The inter-nodal link, as has been laid out above, represents the collocational relation between two word forms. Following Hoey (2005: 10), it is reasonable to assume that this collocational relation is not static but may be altered by contextual factors. With regard to the quote from Hoey, the genre node |academic| will have a connection to each of the word form nodes (|*recent*| and |*research*|), since both are more frequent in academic discourse than is, say, crime or science fiction genres, and a third

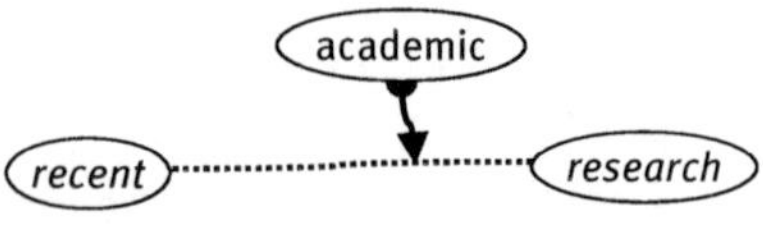

Figure 6.2: The influence of the genre 'academic' on collocational strength. (= figure 2.50, repeated here for convenience)

connection to the link between these two word forms. The activation of the genre node |academic| will thus also spread its activation to the link between |*recent*| and |*research*|. In this way, the network model accounts for strengthening of this particular collocation in the genre 'academic writing'[104], see figure 6.2.

Finally, expectations can also be based on statistical regularities that show up in language use. The interest in statistical regularities in language dates back more than half a century, as the publication of George Kinsley Zipf's (1949) seminal work *Human Behavior and the Principle of Least Effort. An Introduction to Human Ecology*[105] and Gustav Herdan's (1956) *Language as Choice and Chance* make evident. But also fairly recent studies (e.g. Mindt 2002) show that frequency-related aspects of language use still remain a topic worthy of investigation.

Many of the findings provided in this line of research are fascinating. For instance, Zipf (1949: 63) finds that there is a fundamental relation of word frequency and word length: the higher the frequency the shorter the word. According to Zipf, this relationship is attested for different corpora and different languages and also valid for the morphemes of languages (97).

Another example is provided by Herdan's (1956: 176-181) analyses of the number of syllables per word in English, German and Russian text samples. For most of the over 20 texts analysed (exceptions being two samples by Pushkin and Tolstoy), the largest proportion of words consists of only one syllable with frequencies declining rapidly from two to seven syllables in most cases. For instance, with four samples of different Carlyle texts, the relative frequency of monosyllabic words is 69.6%, followed by two-syllable words with 18.2% and

---

104 In a similar fashion, the network model would account for other influences of genre. For instance, the genre node |face-to-face conversation| could strengthen the connection between the node |subject| and the node |*I*|, since this is the typical realization of the subject in this genre. In this way, the network model could also account for the context-dependence of prototypicality (see section 6.1).

105 See also Zipf's (1935 [1965]) *The Psycho-Biology of Language*, where some of the aspects discussed in detail in Zipf (1949) are already hinted at.

three-syllable words with 8%; these frequencies follow an exponential function of decay.

Similar regularities are reported by Mindt (2002), who, in search of the nature of grammatical rules, finds that the "ideal type of grammatical rule" (199) (i.e. the rule without exception) is very rare. Much more frequent is what Mindt terms the "standard result" (199). This kind of grammatical rule shows a regular behaviour from a statistical point of view, in exhibiting a particular distribution of frequency, namely:

> 1. Of the many possible realisations, only three make up the core of an individual grammatical phenomenon.
> 2. The core realisations of a grammatical phenomenon are not distributed evenly. They follow a declining pattern which resembles a mathematical function (i.e. the exponential function of decay). This function corresponds to a natural process.
> 3. The core makes up c. 95 % or more of all cases [...]. There is a remainder which makes up c. 5 % of all occurrences or less. (Mindt 2002: 210)

Interestingly, these regular tendencies are attested for quite distinct levels of linguistic description, such as syntax or semantics. For instance, Mindt shows that the frequency of verb phrases depends on the length of the verb phrase: the most frequent kind of verb phrase (one element only) occurs in 69% of all cases, followed by two-element and three-element verb phrases with 25% and 5%, respectively. These three elements constitute the core, which makes up 99% of all instances (201).

A similar distribution is found with regard to a phenomenon that sits on the "borderline between lexis and grammar" (205), i.e. the number of words that can occur between a modal verb and the following infinitive. In an analysis of a one million fictional-text sub-corpus of the BNC, Mindt finds between 0 and 8 inserts, with relative frequencies decreasing from 68.6% for zero inserts to 28.1% for one and 3% for two inserts (205-207). Again, the first three form a core with a cumulative frequency of almost 100%.

As an example from the realm of semantics consider the modal meanings of WILL, of which Mindt identifies the following five: 'certainty'/'prediction', 'volition'/'intention', 'possibility'/'high probability', 'inference'/'deduction' and 'habit'. As in the previous cases, the first three of these constitute a core with the respective relative frequencies of 71%, 16% and 10%, which amount to a relative frequency of 97% (203).

What do statistical regularities like the ones described above tell us; what is their significance, if there is any at all? First of all, one has to be aware of the fact that, although statistical regularities are often very impressive, they can be found in any set of data. If the researcher is open for any kind of regularity in a given data set, he or she is bound to find, sometimes quite astonishing, regular patterns.[106] They are not of particular interest *per se*. Such findings do become relevant, however, when they are related to other statistical regularities or if the analyst is able to provide underlying motivations. As to the comparison of statistical regularities of different realms of a particular language, Herdan (1956) finds that the distributions of linguistic phenomena are usually quite stable. This leads him to formulate a "statistical view of Saussure's distinction" (79):

> [...] what 'la langue' comprises are not only engrams as lexical forms, *but these engrams plus their respective probabilities of occurrence*. [...] language is the collective term for linguistic engrams (phonemes, word-engrams, metric form engrams) together with their particular probabilities of occurrence. The engram concept is thus inseparably connected with that of frequency of occurrence, and if by linguistic normative laws we understand something which regulates the relative frequency of linguistic forms belonging to a certain class, then our statistical conception of 'la langue' implies such normative laws, as whose realisation we must regard the empirically determined frequency of 'la parole'. (Herdan 1956: 79-80)

This statement almost seems prophetic if we consider the fact that a number of modern approaches to linguistics are of a probabilistic kind or at least grant frequency and frequency effects an important role in their models (see the discussion of recurrent item strings in sections 5.3 and 5.4 above).

The present study follows Bod et al. (2003: 3), who claim that "[f]requency affects language processes, and so it must be represented somewhere. The language-processing system tracks, records, and exploits frequencies of various kinds of events." The notion of frequencies in language use has its psychological correlate in the notion of entrenchment, i.e. the assumption that "psychological events leaves some kind of trace that facilitates their reoccurrence" (Langacker 2000b: 3). Different strengths of such traces can be found with the degree to which instantiations or members of one particular class are prominent in the cognitive system. Consider, for instance, Mindt's (2002: 203) findings

106 An illustrative non-linguistic example is given by Jager (1992), who found that amazing relations hold between different measurements of his bicycle. In particular, he found that fairly simple mathematical formulae that combine the values of the diameter of the lamp, the front tyre and other parts of his bicycle yield the values of a number of physical and cosmic constants such as the speed of light and the gravitational constant. These results are merely due to the fact that the possible number of 'simple combinations' of the measurements of his bicycle is actually quite large, namely 83,521. Accordingly, the probability to find some particular constant in these values is very high.

about the distribution of the five modal meanings of WILL. He finds that in 71 % of all cases, WILL expresses 'certainty' or 'prediction', in 16 % of all cases the meaning is that of 'volition' or 'intention' and in 10 % 'possibility' or 'high probability'. The other two meanings, 'inference'/'deduction' and 'habit' are only instantiated in 3 % of all cases. In our network model this situation would be represented as in figure 6.3 below.

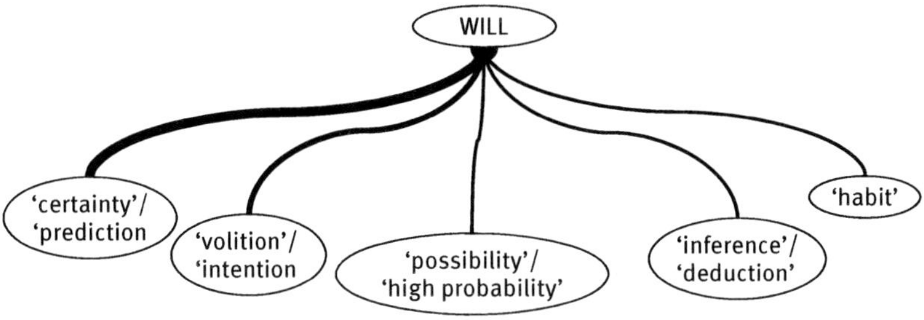

Figure 6.3: Degrees of entrenchment of the meanings of WILL.

Any occurrence of a form of the lexeme WILL will spread to all of its potential meanings. Some of these will receive more activation in a shorter period of time due to the fact that they are more deeply entrenched (as is symbolized by the thickness of the connections). Consequently, the node |'certainty'/'prediction'| will be more strongly activated than the node |'habit'| in a fixed amount of time. This does not mean that any occurrence of a form of WILL will automatically be interpreted as expressing 'certainty' or 'prediction'. However, this way the most likely meaning is already activated to a fairly high extent, which will lead to a very fast full activation, if further evidence contained in the clause corroborates this interpretation (see the discussion of 'summation of activation' in section 2.2.2.3). We can thus regard the interpretation of WILL as expressing 'certainty' or 'prediction' as the default case. If the rest of the clause indicates that the form of WILL is to be interpreted in its 'habit' meaning, the full activation of this node is reached later, since the amount of activation from the occurrence of the form of WILL alone will not have led to a strong activation of this meaning node. Different degrees of entrenchment can thus be related to the degree with which particular nodes in the network can be expected to become activated, if a connected node is activated.

In a similar way, the present network model would account for frequency variations among constructions that are in systematic correspondence. Wasow and Arnold (2003: 132) claim that "[v]erbs allowing variation in ordering among their following constituents often exhibit biases towards one ordering rather than the other." A case in point is the dative alternation, i.e. the variation in ditransitive constructions between both objects encoded in NPs or in an NP plus a PP (*He gave Peter the book* as opposed to *He gave the book to Peter*). The authors find that GIVE and HAND prefer the first variant, whereas the second is far more frequent with SEND and SELL. They "provisionally conclude that speakers' mental lexicons include information about the tendency of particular verbs to appear more or less frequently in various syntactic contexts" (133). The question is where to locate this information in the network.

A first, and maybe obvious, solution seems to be to have links that connect nodes of individual verbs to the constructions that they prefer. In figure 6.4, then, the node |HAND| would have a link to the node |Ditrans. Constr.|, and the node |SELL| would be linked to |Prepos. Constr.|. This would suffice to explain the language user's preference for one construction with one verb and the other construction with the other verb in production. However, this solution would not be able to explain facilitative effects that the knowledge of the verb might have. These effects are due to the fact that verbs like SELL or HAND give us a fairly good idea in which way argument roles are realised. In the first case the

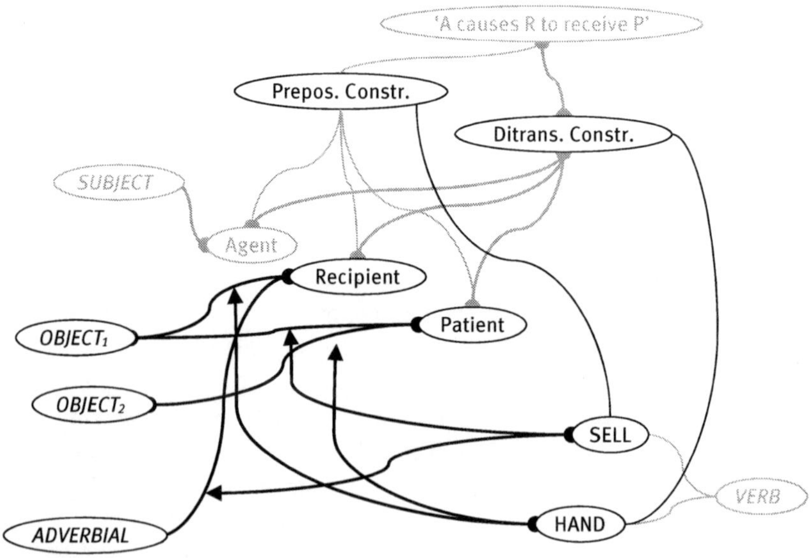

Figure 6.4: Verbal preferences for constructions.

patient is likely to be realised as the first object in the clause, the recipient as an adverbial. In the second case, the first object realises the recipient, and the patient is usually realised by the second object. It is this knowledge that the user makes use of during processing ditransitive verbs. In figure 6.4 this knowledge is implemented by links that boost the connections between the clause element nodes and the argument role nodes. For instance, the node |SELL| leads to a temporary strengthening of the links between |*ADVERBIAL*| and |Recipient|, and |$OBJECT_1$| and |Patient|. This way, the verb SELL prepares the processing of a prepositional construction, which we would expect given the language user's experience that this verb is usually used in that construction.

In the same way that experience with frequencies influences the choice of meanings in polysemous words and the processing of syntactic constructions, it also guides the processing of word forms when these have been experienced as co-occurring frequently. Jurafsky (2003) writes:

> the probability of a word given the previous or following word plays a role in comprehension and production. Words with a high joint or conditional probability given preceding or following words have shorter durations in production. In comprehension, any ambiguous words in a high-frequency word-pair are likely to be disambiguated consistently with the category of the word-pair itself. (Jurafsky 2003: 53)

Examples of such joint probabilities abound in language. Sinclair (1996) discusses the patterned behaviour of the string *naked eye*, instantiations of which (all taken from the BNC) are shown below.

(2) The mite is just visible to the **naked eye** and feeds on honey bees and their grubs by sucking their body fluids. (AJB 111)
(3) We'd been prepared to buy houses with flaws invisible to the **naked eye**, but now we'd fallen for one with all its flaws only too obviously visible. (AM5 1182)
(4) And their small size enables tiny arthropods, some almost too small to see with the **naked eye [...]. (**AMM 934)
(5) But many kinds of bacteria in nature form elaborate colonies, often quite visible to the **naked eye**, in which different individuals perform different functions, so that the whole colony functions as if it were a single organism. (AMS 263)
(6) Because they are so faint, not a single one is visible to the **naked eye**. (ANX 2515)
(7) Quite often, olivine and pyroxene begin to crystallize out early on, so they may be present in the final rock as quite large crystals, up to a centimetre

across, many times larger than the crystals surrounding them, and easily visible with the **naked eye**. (ASR 1039)

(8) He showed some incredible coloured slides giving close-up detail of petal formation and patterns not often seen by the **naked eye**. (B03 1863)

(9) The bone shows very fine splitting along the lines of orientation of the collagen fibres (Fig. 1.4A) and slight erosion of the pits and canals, but these are only visible under high magnification and cannot be seen by the **naked eye**. (B2C 255)

Sinclair has argued that the string *naked eye* is typically preceded by a combination of a lexical item related to visibility, a preposition and the definite article:

> "visibility + preposition + the + naked + eye" (Sinclair 1996: 87; see section 5.3)[107]

In contrast to Sinclair, who discusses the left-collocates of the phrase *naked eye*, we are at present interested only in right-collocates of a particular linguistic item, since these are more relevant for language processing. That is, it is relevant for the present model to know that *naked* is often followed by *eye*, but not that *eye* is often preceded by *naked*. With regard to Sinclair's observation above, we would thus need to find out if verbs or adjectives relating to visibility are often followed by prepositions, the definite article, and *naked* and *eye*. This seems to be the case for the adjectives *visible* and *invisible*, as will be demonstrated with the example *(in)visible to the naked eye*. Table 6.1 shows how the log-likelihood values for the positions to the right change for the strings *(in)visible*, *(in)visible to* and *(in)visible to the* in the BNC.

We see that on encountering the word *visible* there is no particularly strong expectation for the preposition *to*. It occurs at rank 20 and its log-likelihood value is approximately one eighth of the value of the word form on rank 1. Even though, at this point, there already is a strong expectation for the second word to the right to be *the*, the third word to the right to be *naked* and the fourth word to the right to be *eye*. For each of these positions the respective words are the top collocate, with the log-likelihood values at least double as high as the values for the second collocate from the top. These expectancies rise when the processor encounters the second word of the string, *to*. This rise does not show in a rise of log-likelihood values, but instead shows in a rise of the ratio of log-

107 Note that the semantic prosody that Sinclair describes with regard to this example is left out, since it is often based on intuition and since there is apparently not a strong predictive power of such prosodies.

Table 6.1: The development of log-likelihood values during the processing of the string *(in)visible to the naked eye*. The numbers before the semicolon refer to the rank of the lexical item with regard to its log-likelihood value and to the log-likelihood value itself (in brackets). The pair after the semicolon provides the same information either for the highest-ranking collocate (when the word form at issue is not number 1) or the second highest collocate (when the word form at issue is number 1).

	to	*the*	*naked*	*eye*
visible	20 (51), 1 (385)	1 (591), 2(284)	1 (500), 2 (58)	1 (405), 2(59)
visible to	-	1 (173), 2 (50)	1(291), 2(8)	1(285), 2(14)
visible to the	-	-	1(323); 2 (-)	1(319); 2(8)
invisible	6 (57); 1(253)	3(29), 1(89)	1(134); 2(40)	1(140); 2(14)
invisible to	-	1 (116); 2(36)	1(198); 2(71)	1(226), 2(14)
invisible to the	-	-	1(217); 2(80)	1(251); 2(5)

likelihood values of the collocates at rank 1 and rank 2. This development of expectancies is similar for *invisible* (although less pronounced). Figure 6.5 shows how *visible to the naked eye* is represented in the network.

Apart from |*to*|, all other word form nodes are linked via a fairly strong excitatory connection from the node |*visible*|. This expresses the fact that the word forms *the*, *naked* and *eye* are strongly primed by the word *visible*. We also have a number of further excitatory links. |*to*| is linked to the node |*the*|, which represents the fact that *the* is a strong right-collocate of *to*. In addition, |*to*| has three links that boost the connections coming from the node |*visible*|. This way, conditional probabilities are implemented. The occurrence of *to* primes the occurrence of *the*, since the latter is a right collocate of the former. However, if the

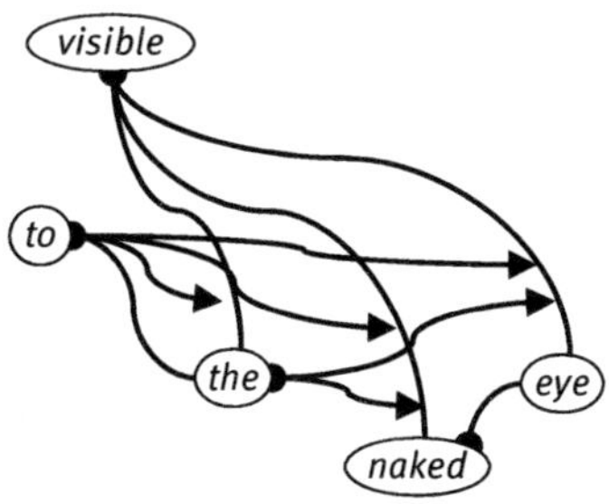

Figure 6.5: The string *visible to the naked eye* in the network.

form *visible* has been encountered, the priming effect will be even stronger. The notion of conditional probabilities becomes particularly clear with the example of *the* and *naked*. The latter is not a collocate of the former, which is why there is no direct connection between the two. However, if the word form *visible* has been encountered, the occurrence of *the* increases the expectation of the occurrence of *naked*, represented by the boosting link that leads from |*the*| and ends in the connection between |*visible*| and |*naked*|. While processing the string *visible to the naked eye* the connections of the network result in a very strong accumulative preparatory activation of the nodes |*naked*| and |*eye*|. This represents phenomena like being able to complete a sentence while a person utters it. For most of us it would not be difficult to guess that a string like *the cell is just visible to the* ... ends in *naked eye* and most of us would be very certain that *the cell is just visible to the naked* ... will be concluded by *eye*. These phenomena are accounted for in the present model.

The activation of |*visible*|, as shown in figure 6.6, will lead to a slight activation of the three word-form nodes |*the*|, |*naked*| and |*eye*|. As soon as the processor encounters the word form *to*, the respective node will be activated resulting in yet further activation of |*the*|, |*naked*| and |*eye*|, since |*to*| boosts the activation

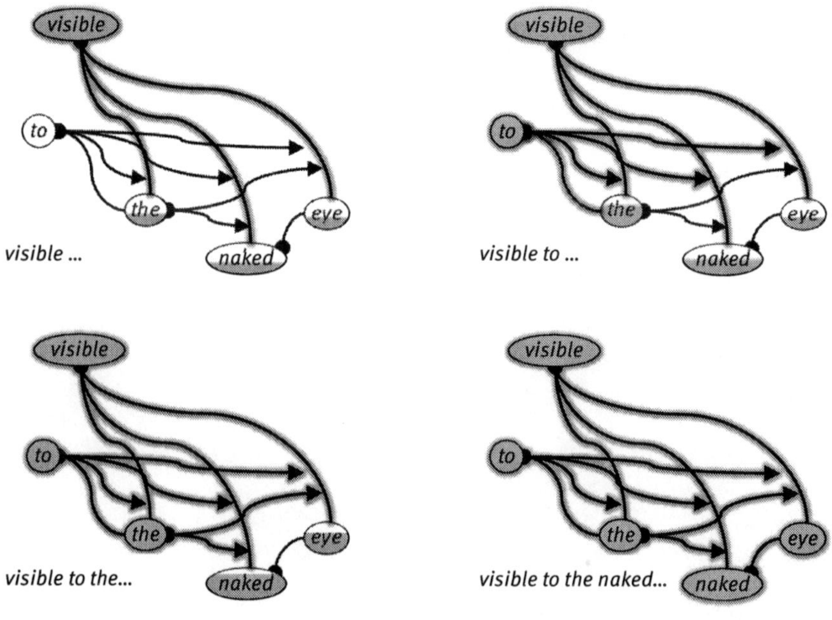

Figure 6.6: Different stages of processing *visible to the naked (eye)*.

coming from |*visible*|. In addition, |*to*| also contributes to the activation of |*the*| since the two are collocates. The activation of |*the*| will result in a further increase of the activation of |*naked*| and |*eye*|, since it amplifies the activation coming from |*visible*|. Finally, the activation of |*naked*| will contribute to the activation of |*eye*|. It is very likely, that the node |*eye*| will now become fully activated. The processor will be able to complete the string *visible to the naked* ... even though the last word has not yet been uttered.

It should have become clear from the above, that entrenchment (here: its influence on the strength of collocational relations) is of extreme importance for the processing of strings of word forms. In the above example, such relations came into play (to varying degrees) in the processing of four word forms. It stands to reason that the facilitating effect of entrenchment will contribute strongly to the processing of lexical strings.

6.3 Processing principles

A discussion of language use needs to explore the large number of processing principles that have been documented in numerous studies. 'Processing', here, is understood as 'syntactic processing' and refers to the interpretation of a sentence in isolation and not as part of a larger stretch of discourse. That is, concepts like the 'given-new contract' (e.g. Clark & Clark 1977, Clark & Haviland 1977 and Haviland & Clark 1974), Firbas' (1992) notion of 'communicative dynamism'[108], or Leech's (1983) textual rhetoric (with the exception of end-weight)) will not be discussed here. They are concerned with the efficient processing of text and are, therefore, only marginally relevant for the present network model. Also irrelevant for the present purposes are those principles that Leech (1983) subsumes under interpersonal rhetoric, e.g. Grice's (1975) Co-operative Principle or his own Politeness Principle, Irony Principle and some

---

108 While the general idea of a progression from given or known to new or unknown elements in a clause is fairly undisputed, there are many different attempts to describe and determine information states: These range from Henry Weil's ([1844] 1978) study on word order, Gabelentz's (1901: 365-373) notions of 'psychological subject' and 'psychological predicate', and the Prague-School concept of 'Functional Sentence Perspective' (see, for instance, Mathesius (1961 [1975]) or Daneš 1974) to more modern approaches, such as Prince (1981, 1992), Chafe (1974, 1976, 1996, among others), Lambrecht (1994), and Kreyer (2006) to name just a few (see Kreyer 2006 for a detailed discussion of the different approaches).

other principles of lesser order. They are not relevant to the present discussion, because they are not so much concerned with the manipulation and processing of structure but rather with the manipulation and processing of propositional content.

The present section will start with a discussion of processing principles that have been explored by John Hawkins in a number of publications (see, for instance, Hawkins 1990, 1993, 1998, 1999a, b, 2001a, b, 2002a, b and 2004, and Lohse and Hawkins 2004). Over the last decade, his theories have been subject to some revisions and same major extensions. Therefore, it seems suitable to begin the following description with a discussion of his earlier monograph (1994) and conclude with a description of the more recent view of his theories. According to Hawkins (1994: xi), "even highly abstract and fundamental properties of syntax can be derived from simple principles of processing that are needed anyway, in order to explain how language is used." The major principle of this kind is the principle of Early Immediate Constituents (EIC). It has its predecessors in Behaghel's (1932: 6) *Gesetz der Wachsenden Glieder,* Leech's (1983) Maxim of End-weight or Dik's (1989) Principle of Increasing Complexity, all of which claim that 'light' constituents have a tendency to precede 'heavy' ones. Hawkins' theory provides a very succinct formulation of this insight and thereby fills a conspicuous gap that Leech (1983: 65) draws attention to: "[...] the exact formulation of and motivation for this [i.e. the end-weight] maxim are not clear, but that it exists in some form or other for English and other SVO (subject-verb-object) languages is hardly to be doubted". The principle of Early Immediate Constituents states that

> words and constituents occur in the orders they do so that syntactic groupings and their immediate constituents (ICs) can be recognized (and produced) as rapidly and efficiently as possible in language performance. Different orderings of elements result in more or less rapid IC recognition. (Hawkins 1994: 57)

The following example of Heavy-NP shift (1993: 234-5, see also 1994: 57) illustrates this basic idea:

(10a) I $_{VP}$[gave $_{NP}$[the valuable book that was extremely difficult to find] $_{PP}$[to Mary]]

(10b) I $_{VP}$[gave $_{PP}$[to Mary] $_{NP}$[the valuable book that was extremely difficult to find]]

The immediate constituents of the VPs in examples (10a) and (10b) are the verb itself and the following NP and PP. During parsing, these constituents are constructed as soon as possible. That is, the article *the* uniquely constructs the NP, whereas the preposition *to* uniquely constructs the PP (see Hawkins' (1993: 235) principle 'Mother Node Construction'; see also Kimball's (1973) seven principles of parsing). Due to the position of the lengthy NP in (10a), the last of the immediate constituents *to Mary* is only recognized after eleven words have been processed. If the NP is deferred to the final position, the immediate constituents are recognized much sooner, i.e. after four words have been processed. In the examples above, then, (10b) would be processed with less effort than (10a) due to the order of the constituents within the sentence.[109]

Hawkins (1994) claims that the Principle of Early Immediate Constituents makes predictions for word order preferences in performance data. More specifically, of all those grammatical constructions within a set of data, those will be preferred that follow EIC, i.e. that guarantee the most rapid recognition of immediate constituents. Orders that result in a less rapid recognition "will be a distinct minority, and [...] the quantity of these non-optimal cases relative to their optimal counterparts will decline" (84) in direct relation to the extent to which they follow EIC.

Hawkins' (2004) newer formulation of his theory depends on a more general idea of complexity, which encompasses syntactic as well as semantic aspects:

> Complexity increases with the number of conventionally associated (syntactic and semantic) properties that are assigned to them when constructing syntactic and semantic representations for sentences. That is, it increases with more forms, and with more conventionally associated properties. It also increases with larger formal domains for the assignment of these properties. (Hawkins 2004: 9)

Maximal efficiency is achieved if two general guidelines are followed, namely 'Express the most with the least' and 'Express it earliest'. The first is governed by the two principles 'Minimize Forms' and 'Minimize Domains', the second by the principle 'Maximize On-line Processing'. We will discuss each of the three principles in turn.

Minimize Forms (MiF) follows the slogan 'Express the most with the least'. While MiD is concerned with the properties and relations that are associated with terminal nodes, MiF is concerned with the terminal nodes themselves: a reduction of the linguistic form of terminal symbols will also lead to an increase

---

109 Note that, here, we are discussing the analysis of sentences in isolation. In some contexts, of course, the order in (10a) may be preferred, for instance, for pragmatic reasons.

in efficiency. This is what has already been shown by Zipf (1949) and his inverse relationship between frequency and length of words that he reports on (cf. Hawkins 2004: 27). Other cases in point are the use of abbreviations or acronyms or the use of anaphoric pronouns instead of full NPs, or other cohesive devices like substitution and ellipsis[110].

Another facet of MiF, and more relevant for the present discussion, concerns the amount of linguistic properties that are related to a linguistic form. Hawkins asks: "why not reduce their [the linguistic forms'] associated linguistic properties to the minimum point at which communicative goals can be met?" (27). The underlying intuition, in his view, is

> that it is preferable to reduce the number of distinct form-property pairs in a language as much as possible, as long as the intended contextually appropriate meaning can be recovered from reduced linguistic forms with more general meaning. (28)

The intended more specific meaning will usually be made clear from the context and real-world knowledge. This second aspect of MiF, according to Hawkins, is instantiated by cases of lexical or structural ambiguity where more than one property is assigned to only one form, as in the phrase *the shooting of the hunters*. With such ambiguities, but also through vagueness and zero specification, efficiency is increased as "the total number of forms that are needed in a language" (40) is reduced. This corresponds to what Zipf (1949) has called *speaker's economy*. According to Zipf this aspect of economy is balanced by the *auditor's economy*, which implies that a large number of unique form-property pairs is efficient from the addressee's point of view, since they do not have to resolve ambiguities or underspecification (21). Hawkins (2004: 41), in contrast, does not seem to regard such a balancing force as necessary. In his view, reduction of the number of forms does not increase the processing load for the addressee, "[s]ince the knowledge sources and inferences that lead to enrichment [i.e. assigning the intended property to a given form] are already accessible and active in language use [...]". It is obvious though (and I assume that Hawkins would agree) that the ancillary nature of context also has its limitations; context cannot always provide all the information needed and, consequently, the influence

110 Compare Leech's (1983: 67) Economy Principle: "If one can shorten the text while keeping the message unimpaired, this reduces the amount of time and effort involved both in encoding and in decoding."

of MiF, although probably far-reaching, must be checked in some way or another (see also Leech's (1983) Clarity Principle).

Still, it has been shown in the discussion of the meaning of OVER in section 4.2.3 that vagueness and/or underspecification of meaning are not a problem for the present network model. Meaning evolves from the co-activation of meaning nodes in the network. Whether these meaning nodes are activated because they are immediately linked to one specific lexical item or whether they receive activation from sources other than this one lexical item is irrelevant for understanding in the present model. Accordingly, the meaning of the preposition OVER is vague or underspecified in the present model, as figure 4.14 shows (here repeated as figure 6.7). This is possible because "the knowledge sources and inferences that lead to enrichment are already accessible and active in language use [...]" (Hawkins 2004: 41), namely through the activation that the relevant meaning nodes receive from other (co-textual) lexical items.

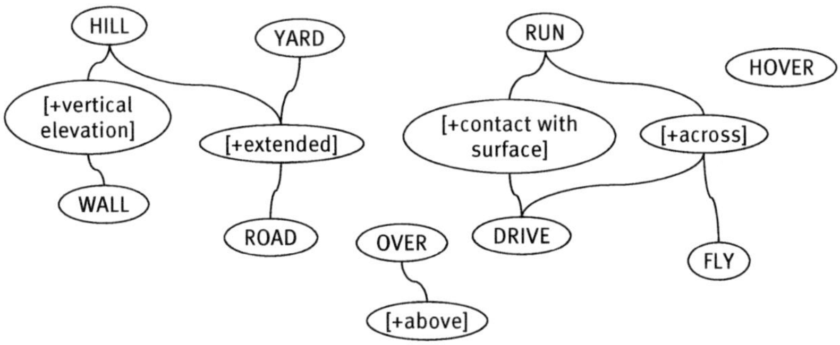

Figure 6.7: Meaning aspects of OVER and co-occurring verbs and nouns. (= figure 4.14., repeated here for convenience)

Another case in point is the vagueness or underspecification of verbs with regard to the number of participant roles. As we have seen in section 5.2.1, the present model follows the view of construction grammar in attributing a possible ditransitive meaning of a verb like BAKE to the construction in which the verb occurs. In contrast to Hudson (2008), who suggests having sub-lexemes for any possible meaning, the model advocated here is more in line with MiF.

In addition to vagueness, ambiguity can also lead to the reduction of the number of unique form-meaning pairs. A case in point is conversion. Consider the form *break*, which is ambiguous with regard to one grammatical feature, namely its word class. Such cases of homonymy are only problematic if word forms are considered in isolation. As soon as context is taken into account, the respective word forms can be assigned an unambiguous meaning, as can be seen if we look at any corpus.

(11) Apple buds began to **break** soon after Christmas. (BNC: A0G_2144)
(12) Their choristers' voices will **break.** (BNC: B71_1834)
(13) Before you **break** your neck. (BNC: KB8_1400)
(14) Come on, let's take a **break.** (BNC: FYY_1007)
(15) Wonderful place for a short **break.** (BNC: A0R_76)

Usually the noun or verb status of *break* is already clear before the word form itself is encountered. In many cases, the word form is immediately preceded by the form *to*, for instance as part of a catenative structure such as *begin to V* or *want to V*; this makes obvious the verb status of the form. Frequently, *break* is immediately preceded by an auxiliary, again indicating the verb status of the form in question. Also, *break* often follows a pronoun in nominative case and, thus, unambiguously can be classified as a verb. *Break* as noun is often indicated by a preceding article or other determiner, either immediately or after a preceding adjective. It is obvious from these examples that homonymy is only problematic in isolation. As shown above, in the vast majority of all cases, the surrounding word forms and the grammatical information contained in the clause lead to disambiguation quickly (note that world knowledge and information conveyed in the preceding clauses have not been taken into consideration here). This is also captured in our network model of language. The ambiguity of *break* is reflected by the fact that the word form is part of two generally unrelated network areas, i.e. that relating to nouns and that relating to verbs. While the occurrence of the form in isolation would leave the network undecided as to which understanding of the form is favoured, the surrounding context will already have activated either the noun- or the verb-related portion of the network to some extent, so that on encountering *break* the additional activation coming from the word-form node will lead to full activation of either of the two – the potential ambiguity has been resolved even before it has actually occurred. Figure 6.8 shows the bits of the network involved in that process. The figure is rather sketchy with some details left out, but it should nevertheless serve to portray the general idea.

Examples (11) to (13) above will activate one or more nodes on the top right of figure 6.8. These activate nodes will spread their activation to other nodes, including the node |*VERB*|. On the occurrence of the word form *break* the rele-

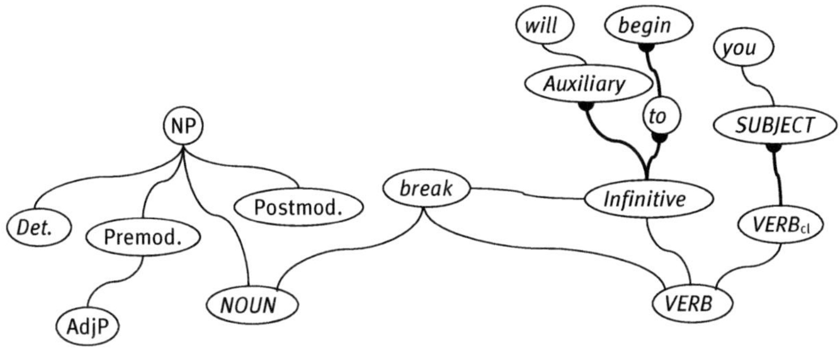

Figure 6.8: The ambiguous word form *break* and its connectivity in the network.

vant node will become fully activated and spread activation to both the nodes |*VERB*| and |*NOUN*|. Since the first is already partially activated, the word form will be interpreted as a verb. Conversely, the preceding words in examples (14) and (15) will have the node |*NOUN*| activated to a certain extent, since the determiner unambiguously introduces an NP. Once the node |NP| is activated, it spreads its activation to all nodes that represents elements of an NP, most importantly of all, the node |*NOUN*|. The occurrence of the word form *break* further contributes to the activation of this node, so that *break* is now interpreted as a noun and not as a verb. Ambiguity, similarly to vagueness and underspecification, is usually not a problem, and this is also shown in the network model. The present model, thus, is in line with Hawkins' 'Minimize Form'.

Like 'Minimize Forms' the second principle, 'Minimize Domains' (MiD), in Hawkins' (2004) view, can be regarded as "a simple principle of least effort" (27):

> [...] when some property is assigned within a combinatorial or dependency domain, the size of that domain should be as small as possible. In other words, parse the fewest possible forms and their associated properties in order to assign the property in question. (26-27)

It is easy to see that MiD is a reformulation of the earlier principle of EIC (cf. 32). Consider examples (2) again, here repeated as (16) for convenience:

(16a) I $_{VP}$[gave $_{NP}$[the valuable book that was extremely difficult to find] $_{PP}$[to Mary]]

(16b) I $_{VP}$[gave $_{PP}$[to Mary] $_{NP}$[the valuable book that was extremely difficult to find]]

A combinatorial or dependency domain is defined by Hawkins as:

> the smallest connected sequence of terminal elements and their associated syntactic and semantic properties that must be processed for the production and/or recognition of the combinatorial or dependency relation in question. (32)

EIC merely focuses on the syntactic properties, i.e. constituency relations within a parse string. The relations between a constituent and its immediate constituents, therefore, is only a special case of the combinatorial and dependency relations that are captured in MiD. In examples (16) above, the relations under scrutiny (from an EIC point of view) are the relations between the mother node VP and the children nodes V, NP and PP. The last three nodes have to be constructed to assign the property 'VP' to the respective node. In (16a) the parser needs to process 11 terminal symbols and their associated syntactic structures to construct the VP as 'V + NP + PP' (if we assume that the recognition of the preposition *to* uniquely constructs a PP-node). In (16b) parsing effort is reduced considerably, since the fourth word of the VP, *the*, uniquely construes the still missing NP-node, which yields the complete structure for the VP, i.e. 'V + PP + NP'. EIC, then, is captured by MiD, since constituency relations are just one kind of combinatorial and dependency relations.

This shows that "MiD is a much more general principle than EIC" (Hawkins 2004: 33). EIC does not predict any differences in parsing effort between the two VPs in example (17), since it is only concerned with the recognition of the ICs of the VP, i.e. V, PP_1, and PP_2. Since both PPs are of equal length and since the prepositions *on* and *in* uniquely identify the respective PP, the structure of the VP is recognized after five words in each case.

(17a) counted on my son in these years
(17b) counted in these years on my son

In contrast to EIC, the more general MiD also takes lexico-semantic dependencies into consideration. In the above case, one such dependency is given between the lexical verb form *counted* and its complement *on my son*. This dependency is resolved earlier in (17a) since the verb and its complement are adjacent; the dependency domain is minimal in (17a) but not in (17b). While both variants are equivalent with regard to the parsing of the syntactic structure (in terms of, say, phrase marker), the semantic structure is processed more efficiently in (17a).[111, 112]

Obviously, dependencies on the syntactic and semantic level can pull in different directions: if the first PP in (17a) was very long, e.g. *on my son who was living in Hamburg as a student*, the advantage of being able to construct the semantic dependencies quite early in the clause might be overridden by the disadvantage in constructing the complete VP node.

While MiD and MiF follow the slogan 'Express the most with the least', the third principle 'Maximize On-line Processing' (MaOP) is a consequence of the need to express what needs to be expressed as early as possible, i.e. 'Express it earliest'. In essence, the principle claims that of two given alternatives that alternative is preferred which allows the higher number of assignments of ultimate properties as each terminal symbol is processed. Consider the example below (Hawkins 2004: 51):

(18a) I $_{VP}$[realize $_{S2}$[the boy knows the answer]]
(18b) I $_{VP}$[realize $_{S2}$[that the boy knows the answer]]

One of the ultimate properties that have to be assigned in processing the sentences above is that the subordinate clause functions as a complement to the main verb *realize*. In (18a) this property can only be assigned after the fifth word (*knows*), since the NP *the boy* does not uniquely construct the sentential complement node; only in conjunction with the finite verb form is the clause recognized, which thus constructs the necessary node. In the more explicit counterpart (18b) the property at issue, according to Hawkins, can already be assigned after the third word (*that*), since the complementizer uniquely constructs this

111 Of course, argument or complement structure to a certain degree can also be understood as syntactic structure.

112 In this respect also consider Behaghel's (1932: 4) First Law: "Das oberste Gesetz ist dieses, daß das geistig eng Zusammengehörige auch eng zusammengestellt wird." My translation into English: 'The most fundamental law is that things which are adjacent conceptually should be adjacent in the utterance.' Similarly, Givón (1995: 179) states in his 'adjacency principle' that "[s]patio-temporal distance in the stream of speech tends to reflect conceptual distance". See also Thompson (1995) and her application of this aspect of iconicity to the phenomenon of dative shift.

node[113]. Properties that cannot be assigned until very late in the parse string consequently increase the work load on the parser.

The work load may also be increased by properties that are wrongly assigned to a particular string, i.e. in the case of garden-path sentences:

(19a) I $_{VP}$[believe $_{S2}$[the boy knows the answer]]
(19b) I $_{VP}$[believe $_{S2}$[that the boy knows the answer]]

In examples (19), the main verb allows two kinds of arguments, namely an NP and a clausal object. The NP *the boy* fits the subcategorization frame of *believe* as 'accusative object of the verb', and the parser misassigns this property to the NP. Thereby, the total of assigned on-line properties is increased, which also increases the work load for the parser, since the 'correct' property, i.e. nominal subject of the verb *knows* of the complement clause, will also have to be assigned. This additional instance of (wrong) property assignment does not occur in the more explicit counterpart in (19b).

From the discussion so far it becomes clear the MiD and MaOP are closely related. The first has to do with one property that is assigned to the string, and it is best, if this property is assignable within as small of a range of terminal symbols (i.e. word forms) as possible. MaOP, in contrast makes claims about the full set of properties that need to be assigned to a string of word forms and it predicts that that order is preferred which allows the earliest assignment of the largest number of ultimate properties. It stands to reason that property assignment will usually be early if domains are minimal. We are thus fairly safe in treating MaOP as a 'global' version of MiD, although earliness and minimization may compete (see Hakwins 2004: 28).

As an illustration of how MaOP is reflected in the present network model let us take a look at the instance of Heavy-NP shift discussed above:

(20a) I gave the valuable book that was extremely expensive to Mary.
(20b) I gave to Mary the valuable book that was extremely expensive.

---

113 Actually, this is not quite correct, since *that* may also be a pronoun and thus realize an NP. This ambiguity is only resolved at the definite article. It follows that the complement clause node can only be assigned after the fourth not the third word.

What are the syntactic and semantic properties of the two strings above, and how does the present network model explain why the second variant is easier to process?[114]

Along the lines of section 5.2.1 discussed above, we claim that among the ultimate properties that have to be assigned to the strings above are the construction, which they instantiate, i.e. the prepositional construction, its meaning and its argument roles, and the participant roles of the verb. The predictions that Hawkins describes for the ordering of elements and the speed with which properties can be assigned to a string of word forms, arise naturally, if we take the connectivity in the network into account and the fact that a node will start to spread its activation as soon as it is activated. The relevant processes in the network have been described in section 5.2.1 and do not need to be repeated here in detail. The argument can be made by taking a closer look at figure 5.11, repeated here as figure 6.9. Two things become apparent. On processing sentences like the ones above (i.e. with a ditransitive verb), two nodes compete for activation, namely |Prepos. Constr.| and |Ditrans. Constr.|. Which of the two it will be depends on whether the input leads to the activation of the node |*OBJECT*$_2$| or the node |*ADVERBIAL*|. In the above example sentences this question is resolved after only three words in (20b). At this point, the node |Prepos.

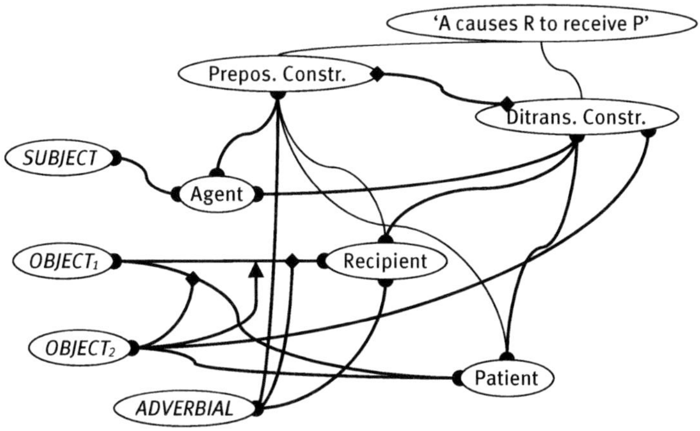

Figure 6.9: The prepositional construction and the ditransitive construction in the network. (= figure 5.11, repeated here for convenience)

114 Note that we are focusing on the syntactic and semantic analysis of the isolated sentence.

Constr.| is already fully activated. As a consequence, the two argument roles |Recipient| and |Patient| become fully active (the node |Agent| has already been activated before). In addition, the connection between the node |*ADVERBIAL*| and the node |Recipient| is active, which represents the fact that the recipient is mapped onto the adverbial. The full activation of the node |*ADVERBIAL*| also blocks the link between |Recipient| and |$OBJECT_1$|. Finally, the fully active node |Patient| sends activation to the node |$OBJECT_1$|. Both activation patterns prepare for the mapping of |Patient| and |$OBJECT_1$|. In contrast to that, after having processed three words of sentence (20a) only one node has been fully activated, namely the node |$OBJECT_1$|, since the definite article introduces an NP which qualifies as an object of the construction. Neither of the other nodes discussed above can be fully activated at that point already and none of the mappings can be concluded. The idea of 'earliest assignment of ultimate properties' translates into earliest realization of the final activation pattern in the network. Obviously, with (20b) a much larger portion of the final activation pattern is already active after three words than in (20a).

The processing advantage of *I counted on my son in these years* as opposed *to I counted in these years on my son* can be explained in a similar fashion, which is why I refrain from a detailed discussion here.

More interesting is the problem of garden path effects which occurs in the first but not in the second example of the pair *I believe **---/that** the boy knows the answer.* This draws attention to another aspect of processing: while the principles discussed so far focus on the speed of processing, the example above shows that alongside speed we also need to consider the accuracy of processing. The so-called 'complexity principle' takes this into account. The complexity principle was developed by Rohdenburg in a number of papers (1995a, b, 1996, 1998a, b, 1999, 2000, 2002, 2003, 2006, and 2007 among others). He writes:

> The complexity principle states that in the case of more or less explicit constructional alternatives [...], the more explicit option(s) will tend to be preferred in cognitively more complex environments. (2003: 205; see also 2006: 51)[115]

Cognitive complexity, in Rohdenburg's understanding, is related to processing of linguistic structures and encompasses phenomena like discontinuity of items, heaviness of items, or large numbers of syntactic or semantic features

115 See also Givón's (1985 and 1991b) 'code quantity principle'.

that have to be processed[116]. With regard to variation in predicative expressions (e.g. *he became useless*), for instance, he writes:

> [A]ny factors complicating the processing of the structural relationships involved will tend to favour a more explicit rendering of the relevant predicative expression. (Rohdenburg 1998b: 223)

One of the many examples given by Rohdenburg is the variable occurrence of *to be* in copulative constructions with *become* in 17th century English prose, a contrast exemplified in the examples below.

(21) Dr. Sanderson's model for reformation became then useless. (Rohdenburg 1998b: 205)
(22) ...; but earnest persuasion of friends became at last to be so powerful, as to ... (Rohdenburg 1998b: 206)
(23) ... he becomes from a samlet not so big as a gudgeon, to be a salmon ... (Rohdenburg, 1998b: 205)

In his analysis of a number of such copulative constructions with *become*, Rohdenburg finds that the more explicit variant, i.e. *become to be ...*, is more frequently used if the verb and the predicative are separated by intervening material. More specifically, of all the 83 cases where verb and predicative are adjacent, *to be* occurs only once. Conversely, in the 10 cases where the two are separated, *to be* occurs six times, i.e. in 60% of all instances. Also, he finds a correlation between the likelihood of occurrence of *to be* and the complexity of the intervening material; that is, the larger the number of words between the verb and the predicative, the more likely the occurrence of *to be*. His explanation is that the discontinuity resulting from the intervening material leads to an increase in processing effort (i.e. cognitive complexity), which then is reduced by making use of a more explicit variant of the construction in question.

Another piece of evidence is more or less explicit linking of subordinated interrogative clauses to their governing verbs. The 19th and 20th century use of the verb CONSULT allows several possibilities, namely an inexplicit variant, i.e.

---

116 See Rohdenburg (2006: 65) for a list of complexity factors. See also Givón (1991a and 1995) for a detailed discussion of cognitive complexity and its possible sources, many of which are also analysed by Rohdenburg in the context of the complexity principle.

zero, and several more explicit variants, i.e. a preposition, a *to*-infinitive or the string *and see* (Rohdenburg 2003: 218). Consider the examples below[117]:

(24) I never consult other men **Ø** how they would have acted. (Rohdenburg 2003: 218)
(25) When the time approached for him to leave prison, his mother and father consulted **as to** what course they should adopt. (Rohdenburg 2003: 218)
(26) Mrs. Margery Mumbleby ... consulting sporting records **to see** whether foxes were in the habit of doing such things ... (Rohdenburg 2003: 218)

Rohdenburg's data, drawn from historical corpora of British and American English, show that intransitive uses of the verb (as in example (25)) only show explicit links in 18.9% of all cases, whereas the transitive uses (examples (24) and (26)) show a proportion of 63.3% of explicit links. This is in line with his argument, since he regards transitive verbs as cognitively more complex than intransitive ones.

As a final example let us consider the dependency of explicitness of interrogative clause linking on noun phrase complexity with prepositional objects. Here, Rohdenburg distinguishes the zero case from the more explicit variants of linking by *as to* and by a number of marked infinitives like *to decide*:

(27) It is up to them/the people concerned ***(to decide)*** how they want to go about it. (Rohdenburg 2003: 222)

According to the theory, the more complex environment, in this case the full NP *the people*, would favour the more explicit link through the infinitive *to decide*. This is what is borne out by Rohdenburg's data: if the prepositional object is realized by a personal pronoun, only 25% of all instances use the more explicit variant, whereas with full NPs the explicit link occurs in 73.2% (222).

As these examples show, Rohdenburg's notion of cognitive complexity is in line with Hawkins' thoughts about processing effort. Higher cognitive complexity obtains where constituents are separated by intervening constituents (see Hawkins' 'Minimize Domains'), or where more syntactic and semantic properties have to be assigned to a string of words, as in the case of intransitive versus transitive verbs and full NP versus pronoun. This view can also be found in Hawkins (2004: 9), when he claims that "[c]omplexity increases with the num-

117 Rohdenburg does not give an example of the '*and see*' variant.

ber of conventionally associated (syntactic and semantic) properties that are assigned to them [i.e. terminal items] when constructing syntactic and semantic representations for sentences."

In some respects Rohdenburg's complexity principle seems to come to conclusions different from Hawkins' theory. While Hawkins' principle 'Minimize Forms' aims at the general reduction of terminal strings, Rohdenburg's complexity principle makes opposite predictions, since more explicitness often also means more formal coding, as the examples discussed above show. Hawkins (2001) also seems to be aware of such cases, since he concedes that there are "competing motivations in performance and grammar" (366). More specifically:

> Property transfers across large (and non-adjacent) processing domains are dispreferred, plausibly because these domains are already complex and involve much simultaneous processing. These domains prefer explicit formal marking, which makes the dependent category more self-sufficient and processible independently of the category upon which it depends. Explicit formal marking is required in large domains in both performance and grammar [...]. Hawkins (2001: 367-368; see also Hawkins 2003)

It follows that processing effort is not merely a function of the amount of terminal symbols or of syntactico-semantic features to be processed. On the contrary, greater explicitness, i.e. a larger amount of syntactic structure, can also enhance processing. This is also mirrored in language change: Rohdenburg (2003) presents data which show that "more explicit novel constructions are established earlier and faster in more complex environments [... and] more explicit recessive constructions tend to be preserved better and longer in the same types of context" (243; see also 2000: 25). It seems as if two variables seem to be of relevance here, namely speed of processing as well as accuracy of processing[118]. In some situations an increase in accuracy is bought at the expense of an increase in processing effort.

Let us take to following example to see what the network model has to say about the complexity principle.

---

118 Accuracy also seems to be of relevance with the principle of *horror aequi*, which describes "the widespread (and presumably universal) tendency to avoid the use of formally (near-) identical and (near-) adjacent (non-coordinate) grammatical elements or structures" (Rohdenburg 2003: 236). For further studies on this principle see Vosberg (2003 and 2006) and Mondorf (2003). An opposing tendency is discussed in Szmrescanyi (2005: 95). In a multivariate corpus analysis he finds that "language users, [sic!] have a marked tendency to re-use chunks from previous discourse when they have a choice [...]." For instance, "[i]f a speaker uses the *V+inf.* patterns (as in *John began to wonder*) at one point, the odds that he or she will switch to the *V+ger.* pattern (as in *John started wondering*) at the next opportunity reduces substantially".

(28a) He told me (yesterday) that John had gone away.
(28b) He told me (yesterday) John had gone away. (Rohdenburg 1996: 160)

Note that for both of the examples above the same truth conditions hold and that (in line with what has been said about the interpretation of sentences in section 5.2.1) 'understanding' the sentences in this model means to assign the correct argument and participant roles to the constituents of the sentence. In the case of the examples above, we are, again, dealing with a ditransitive construction. *He* is the agent, *me* is the recipient and (*that*) *John had gone away* is the patient. The participant roles would be teller, tellee and told, respectively. Both examples (28a) and (28b), in the end, will result in the same analysis. It is important to note, though, that the realization of patients with the verb TELL is different from the usual ditransitive construction. While the vast majority of ditransitive (and also monotransitive) patients is realized by an NP, with TELL, patients are most frequently realized by clauses: Biber et al. (1999: 388), for instance, show the pattern 'SVOi + complement clause' to be the most frequent in the corpus underlying their grammar. Similarly, Mukherjee (2005: 127; table 3.7) reports that the direct object (i.e. the patient) is realized by a clause in more than half of all cases. In contrast, with the verb GIVE, almost 90% of all direct objects are NPs (Mukherjee 2005: 99; table 3.1). The verb TELL, we could say, has a pattern of connectivity in the network that is opposed to that of the ditransitive construction. Such expectations are represented in the network.

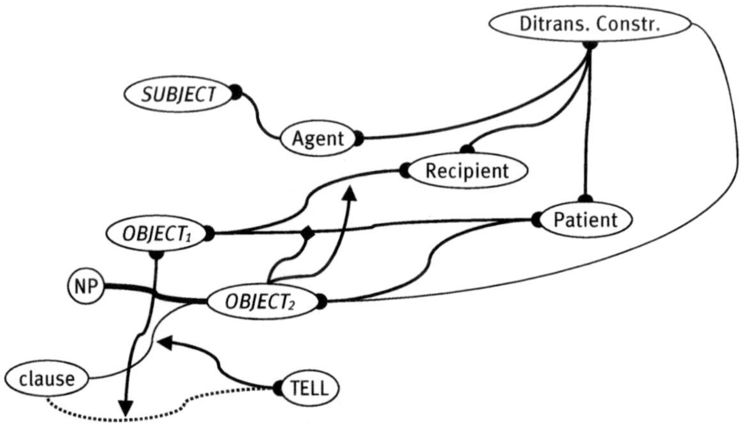

Figure 6.10: The preference of clausal indirect objects with the verb TELL in the network.

The preference of the verb TELL for clausal indirect objects is implemented by two excitatory connections (figure 6.10). One is very weak and leads from |TELL| to the node |clause|. When the former node is activated, it will start spreading this activation to the latter. This activation is boosted as soon as an indirect object has been identified, i.e. as soon as the node |*OBJECT*$_1$| is fully active. As a consequence, the processor is prepared to process clausal structures after the indirect object has been processed. In addition, the node |TELL| will also strengthen the connection between the node |clause| and the node |*OBJECT*$_2$|, which will further support the mapping of clausal structures onto the node |*OBJECT*$_2$| and then onto the node |*Patient*|.

If the node |TELL| activates the node |clause| anyway, what effect could the additional clause subordinator *that* have? According to Rohdenburg (1996), a possible advantage depends on the complexity of the structure as a whole. An increase in complexity may arise in different ways. Let us consider three aspects here: 1) intervening material between indirect and direct object, 2) the length of the indirect object, and 3) the length of the subject of the subordinate clause.

As to the first two, the increase in complexity is due to the distance of the verb and the clause which it governs. Recall from section 2.2.2.3 the discussion of activation decay, i.e. the fact that nodes will gradually lose their activation over time, if they do not become activated again. In the case above, the activation of the |TELL| node will also lead to an activation of the |clause| node, since that is the usual realization of the participant role 'told'. The active |clause| node will facilitate the processing of the object clause. It is reasonable to assume that this activation will decrease over time and eventually the facilitating effect will be lost. As a consequence, if too many words occur between one of the forms of TELL and the beginning of the patient clause, the activation of the node |clause| may not be strong enough to support the analysis of the patient clause. In that case, the occurrence of the explicit subordinator *that* will reactivate the |clause| node, and thus facilitate the processing of the patient clause.

A possible third source of complexity, according to Rohdenburg (1996), is the length of the subject of the subordinate clause: "While noun phrases favor the retention of *that*, personal pronouns disfavor it [...]" (163). This result cannot be accounted for by the distance of verb and patient clause. Nevertheless, the network is also able to provide an explanation here. Note that possible patients for the ditransitive construction are NPs and clauses. Note further that NPs are far more likely to be patients than clauses are. It is true that the activation of the node |TELL| spreads its activation to the |clause| node, but at the same time, NPs remain a valid realization of patients in ditransitive constructions. Note also that the subject NP (in many cases, such as *he told me the film was boring*) is a possible patient. Until the processor has encountered the verb of the object clause, the situation remains ambiguous, i.e. none of the two possible kinds of patients is preferred over the other – in our network this situation is represented by two nodes in the network that are activated to a similar degree. With a short subject, e.g. a pronoun, the verb will occur early in the object clause and resolve the ambiguity quickly. With a long subject NP, the verb occurs late in the clause and both the |clause| and the |NP| node remain at similar activation levels for a long time. In those cases, the introduction of the explicit subordinator *that* will facilitate processing, since the activation of the |*that*| node will lead to a higher activation of the |clause| node, which as we have seen before, supports the analysis of the object clause. In summary, the network model is also able to capture many of the findings that Rohdenburg discusses under the complexity principle.

6.4 A note on garden paths and related issues

Garden-path sentences are a phenomenon that has been discussed widely in linguistics and, more specifically, in literature on parsing. Even more, garden-path sentences appear to be a necessary condition for parsing models to be plausible: If parsers are not able to account for this phenomenon, then their corresponding models are basically considered useless. By way of the same argument, if the network model advocated here was able to account for garden-path effects, this would lend credibility to the approach it pursues.

Let us first consider the clause *I gave the letter to Frieda to Peter*. The problem here, obviously, is that the PP *to Frieda* first is understood as encoding the recipient of the 'giving event' instead of a postmodification of the NP head *letter*. Fodor and Frazier (1980) explain this preference of the human parser with what they call 'Minimal Attachment'. This principle states that

> an incoming word or phrase is to be attached into the phrase marker using the smallest possible number of nonterminal nodes linking it with the nodes that are already present. (Fodor & Frazier 1980: 426)

The PP *to Frieda* can be attached to the VP node of the whole clause (following the rule VP → V NP PP). Note that in this case, no additional nodes have to be created, since the PP node is already licensed by the VP node and the verb form *gave*. Alternatively, the PP *to Frieda* could be attached to the NP node *the letter* (following the rule NP → NP PP). In this case, however, a new NP node would have to be introduced into the parse tree alongside the NP node licensed by the verb. This is not in line with the principle of Minimal Attachment. It follows, on the basis of Minimal Attachment, that the first interpretation, i.e. *to Frieda* encoding the recipient, is preferred, which leads to the obvious garden-path effect.

Interestingly, in answering the question "*how* MA [minimal attachment] is imposed in practice on its [the human parsing mechanism's] operations" (434) the authors suggest:

> [T]he rules [...] are accessed in parallel and selected in terms of the outcome of a 'race' – the first rule or combination of rules that successfully relates the current lexical item to the phrase marker dominates subsequent processing. (Fodor & Frazier 1980: 434)

This explanation is in line with the spirit of the present network model. Section 2.2.2.5 has shown that the parallel processing of different analyses is a natural consequence of the layout of the network: As soon as a node is activated, it will spread its activation to all neighbouring nodes. The node |PP| which is activated by *to Frieda* will spread its activation both in the direction of the node |*ADVERBIAL*| of the prepositional construction and to the node |Postmod.|, which is connected to the node |NP|. This is equivalent to the idea that two analyses are pursued in parallel.

Which of the two alternatives wins? A look at different kinds of garden path sentences suggests that the higher-ranking structures win over lower-ranking

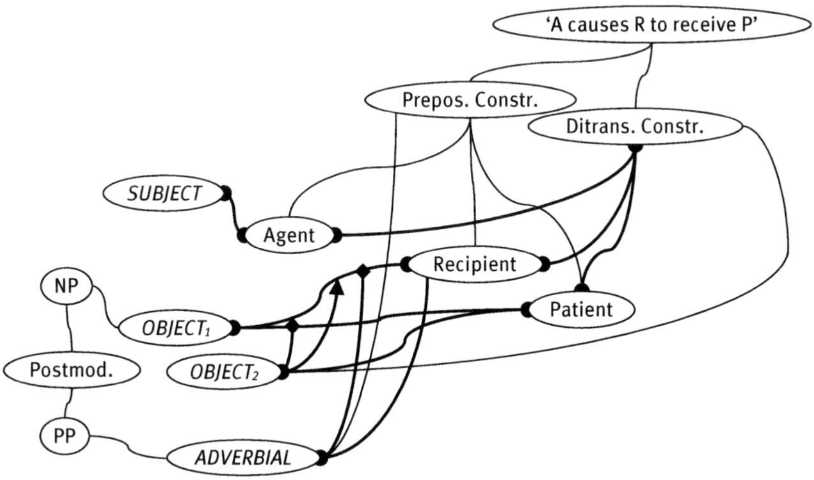

Figure 6.11: The PP as part of noun phrase postmodification or as adverbial.

ones. In the example above the PP *to Frieda* is analysed as being part of a higher-ranking structure (as recipient) rather than a lower-ranking one (as postmodification within an NP). Similarly, in the well-known example *the horse raced past the barn fell*, the garden-path effect is a consequence of treating *raced* as the main verb, although it could just as well be interpreted the beginning of a reduced relative clause. The garden-path effect seems to reside in treating (relatively) subordinate structures as superordinate. The processor thus seems to have a bias for superordinate structures. This bias can be implemented without any problems in the current network model, namely through the thresholds of individual nodes. For instance, the node representing the main verb in a clause has a lower threshold than that representing verbs in subordinate clauses. Accordingly, the main clause interpretation will win over the subordinate clause interpretation. Similarly, the activation threshold will be lower for argument role nodes than for postmodification nodes. Consequently, the first analysis of the processor will be biased towards mapping a possible postmodifying PP to the node |*ADVERBIAL*| of the prepositional construction, if this construction is licensed by the verb in the clause. In this way, the present network model also manages to account for a central phenomenon discussed in research on parsing models.

7 Outlook and conclusion

The idea to describe structures of knowledge with the help of network models is not new and has led to a number of accounts, most of all in the area of psycholinguistics. Most of these have been restricted to aspects of the mental lexicon and, accordingly, attempts to provide a comprehensive network model of language are rare, Lamb (1998) and Hudson (2007a) being the most notable exceptions. The present study, of course capitalising to a large extent on previous studies (both from psycholinguistics and linguistics in the stricter sense), understands itself as a contribution that is similar to those of Lamb and Hudson. It is guided by general assumptions concerning the nature of the mental grammar that can be taken for granted in cognitive linguistic circles. These include the view that "language can be seen as a complex adaptive system" (Bybee 2010:2), that competence is "a competence to perform" (Lamb 2000: 95), and that language "is not something a speaker *has*, but rather what he *does*" Langacker (1987: 382). The present model, in my view, departs from the works of Lamb and Hudson in that it interprets the concept of network models in a stricter way: not only does it follow Hudson's 'network postulate', i.e. the assumption that language is a conceptual network and nothing but a network, but it also subscribes to what has been termed the 'neurophysiological challenge':

> **The Neurophysiological Challenge**
> Language is nothing but a network. This network mirrors the neurophysiology of the brain in that the nodes and the connections are closely modelled on what we know from nerve cells and their connections.

In that, it follows Lakoff's (1990: 40) 'cognitive commitment' in a very strict fashion: "make one's account of human language accord with what is generally known about the mind and brain, from other disciplines."

As we have seen throughout the whole study, this reduction to the most primitive and basic descriptive apparatus has made the description of linguistic phenomena, units and structures a lot more difficult. Descriptions that are fairly simple and elegant with a 'machinery' that is only a little richer (as, for instance, in the models by Hudson and Lamb) become a daunting task if we follow the neurophysiological challenge. What then are the benefits, what are the advantages of and the insights gained from the present model? The answer is plain and simple: the present model demonstrates that it can be done! It has been shown that a large range of linguistic phenomena can be described in the present model and that it is able to account for a wide variety of findings in areas as distinct as traditional descriptive linguistics, corpus linguistics, construction grammar, prototype theory and language processing. Of course, it can be argued whether this result is worth the effort: after all, most of these phenomena are also described satisfactorily in other network models, and those that have not been described are in principle describable by them. As I see it, the major outcome of this study is not that the model presented here describes a similar range of phenomena in an arguably slightly more elegant way; the major outcome, in my view, lies in the fact that the study has succeeded to provide a descriptively adequate network model that is based on an extremely small set of assumptions that most linguists would subscribe to:

- the nodes and connections are modelled on what we know from the neurophysiology of the brain; this includes nodes with varying thresholds of activation, excitatory and inhibitory links between nodes as well as between nodes and links, the concept of spreading activation and parallel processing, the concept of competition
- the model follows the idea of entrenchment, i.e. processes that are exercised a lot are more readily available
- the model involves categorization, which is understood as their formation of classes on the basis of the perception of similarity
- the model involves association, i.e. linking hitherto unrelated events if they co-occur with sufficient frequency

Given that we can agree on the above assumptions, a number of important consequences arise. Some of these consequences are concerned with the nature of the network model itself. We have seen that the network model dispenses with the distinction of local and distributed storage of information; the nature of the network suggests that both happen, depending on the frequency of activation of particular network structures. Related to that, it was found that there is no need to make an *a priori* decision regarding real or virtual copying; the nature of the network suggests that both kinds of information storage have their place in the network. Some of these consequences concern the nature of the language system in a very general way. It has been shown, for instance, that many phenomena discussed or taken for granted in cognitive linguistic circles are motivated or can be explained by the way the network works. These include findings from prototype theory (e.g. the importance of basic level categories and the prototype or gradient structure of categories), but also aspects like the redundancy of storage or the fact that the language system contains structures at different levels of abstraction and specificity that transcend rank boundaries. It is important to emphasise, again, that these general features arise as a consequence of the nature of the network model, i.e. they are a consequence of the small set of assumptions mentioned above. This lends further credibility and plausibility to the model developed in this study. Finally, the nature of the network itself suggests answers to linguistic problems proper. With regard to the problem of gerunds, for instance, it was shown, that the present network model rules out a solution where an *–ing* form is classified as a verb and a noun at the same time. However, at the same time the present model does not deny the general possibility of the formation of an additional category *GERUND* that exists alongside the categories *VERB* and *NOUN*. As before, it is important to point out that the study (or its author) does not choose a particular representation of a linguistic feature. Rather, this view on gerunds follows as a consequence if we consider the assumptions underlying the network as valid.

The phenomena explored in the present study have necessarily been restricted and there are many that have not been discussed. However, the results so far are encouraging and lead us to hope that a fully comprehensive model of language can be devised on the basis of the network model advocated here.

In addition to a broader coverage of linguistic phenomena the model can be (and should be) extended in various directions. As remarked in section 2.2.1, the present model is understood to be usage-based in the sense that it is empiricist in nature. The structures presented in this study are to be taken as approximations of the strengths of nodes and connections within the network. A necessary next step is to extend the present model along the line of a 'Cognitive corpus linguistics' advocated in Grondelaers et al. (2007), thereby putting the network on a statistically sound corpus-based footing. First steps in that direction have been sketched out in the discussion of gradience in the network model. Here it was shown how corpus derived frequencies can be implemented. This, however, can only be a first step as a number of suggestions have been made to explore associations on different levels of linguistic description with the help of multifactorial statistics. For instance, Stefanowitsch and Gries's (e.g. 2003 and 2005) concepts of 'collostructional' and 'collexeme analysis' suggest ways of quantifying associations between lexicial units and constructions. Another example is Gries' (e.g. 2006) application of statistically based behavioural profiles to characterise the use of lexical units in authentic data. Such quantifications can easily be implemented in the present network and thus make the present model usage-based also in the sense that its structures are based on frequencies that are found in actual usage data.

Another prospect for future research concerns the application of the network model to diachronic data. In this way, diachronic processes could be observed from a new angle. Diachronic changes, in the network, would be mirrored by changes in the connections and in the nodes of the network. Given connections might be weakened and eventually be lost altogether, while new connections are established and strengthened through time. Similarly, existing nodes may be deleted from the network while new nodes may arise and thresholds of nodes will change, thereby increasing or decreasing the speed with which a node is activated. The advantage of the present network model to more traditional ways of representing diachronic change lies in the fact that the network model manages to portray simultaneously a large number of relations on different levels of linguistic description. Furthermore, since the present model is able to represent gradience, fuzziness and indeterminacy in the language system, it seems reasonable to assume that these areas are particularly susceptible to factors that induce change.

Finally, an important area for future research is the computational modelling of the present network model. More specifically, ways should be found to implement into computer routines what has been referred to here as the two fundamental cognitive mechanisms 'categorization based on similarity' and 'association of distinct events through repeated co-occurrence'. Then, the present network model would no longer be hand-wired but be truly self-organizing and thus still more cognitively plausible.

References

Aarts, B. 2007. *Syntactic gradience: The Nature of Grammatical Indeterminacy*. Oxford: Oxford University Press.

Aarts, B., D. Denison, E. Keizer & G. Popova (eds.). 2004. *Fuzzy Grammar: A Reader*. Oxford: Oxford University Press.

Abbot-Smith, K. & M. Tomasello. 2006. Exemplar-learning and schematization in a usage-based account of syntactic acquisition. *The Linguistic Review* 23. 275-290.

Aijmer, K. & B. Altenberg (eds.). 1991. *English Corpus Linguistics*: *Studies in Honour of Jan Svartvik*. London: Longman.

Alegre, M. & P. Gordon. 1999. Rule-based versus associative processes in derivational morphology. *Brain and Language* 68. 347-354.

Allerton, D.J. 1978. The notion of 'givenness' and its relations to presupposition and to theme. *Lingua* 44. 133-168.

Allerton, D.J., N. Nesselhauf & P. Skandera (eds.). 2004. *Phraseological Units: Basic Concepts and their Application*. Basel: Schwabe.

Altenberg, B. 1993. Recurrent verb-complement constructions in the London-Lund Corpus. In J. Aarts, P. de Haan & N. Oostdijk (eds.), *English Language Corpora: Design, Analysis and Exploitation*, 227-245. Amsterdam: Rodopi.

Altenberg, B. 1998. On the phraseology of spoken English. In Cowie (ed.), 101-122. Oxford: Oxford University Press.

Altenberg, B. & M. Eeg-Olofsson. 1990. Phraseology in English: Presentation of a project. In J. Aarts and W. Meijs (eds.), *Theory and Practice in Corpus Linguistics*, 1-26. Amsterdam: Rodopi.

Aristotle: Categories, *The Complete works of Aristotle. The Revised Oxford Translation*. In J. Barnes (ed.). 1984, 3-24. Princeton, NJ: Princeton University Press.

Armstrong, S.L., L. Gleitman & H. Gleitman. 1983. What some concepts might not be, *Cognition* 13. 263 – 308.

Arnold, J. E. & T. Wasow. 2000. Heaviness vs. newness: The effects of structural complexity and discourse status on constituent ordering, *Language* 76. 28-55.

Baayen, R.H. 2003. Probabilistic approaches to morphology. In Bod et al. (eds.), 229-287. Cambridge, MA: MIT Press.

Baayen, R.H., T. Dijkstra & R. Schreuder. 1997. Singulars and plurals in Dutch: Evidence for a parallel dual-route model. *Journal of Memory and Language* 37. 94-117.

Baayen, R.H. & A. Renouf. 1996. Chronicling the Times: productive lexical innovations in an English newspaper. *Language* 72. 69-96.

Baayen, R.H. & R. Schreuder. 1999. War and piece: morphemes and full forms in a noninteractive activation parallel dual-route model. *Brain and Language* 68. 27-32.

Baddeley, A.D., N. Thomson & M. Buchanan. 1975. Word length and the structure of short term memory. *Journal of Verbal Learning and Verbal Behavior* 14. 575-589.

Bardovi-Harlig, K. 2002. A new starting point? Investigating formulaic use and input in future expression. *Studies in Second Language Acquisition* 24. 189-198.

Barlow, M. 2000. Usage, blends and grammar. In Barlow & Kemmer (eds.), 315-345.

Barlow, M. & S. Kemmer. 1994. A schema-based approach to grammatical description. In Lima et al. (eds.), 19-42.

Barlow, M. & S. Kemmer (eds.). 2000. *Usage Based Models of Language*. Stanford: CSLI.

Bartlett, F.C. 1932. *Remembering*. Cambridge: CUP.

Bartsch, S. 2004. *Structural and Functional Properties of Collocations in English*. Tübingen: Narr.

Beaugrande, R.-A. de & W.U. Dressler. 1981. *Introduction to Text Linguistics*. London: Longman.

Beckwith, R., C. Fellbaum, D. Gross & G. A. Miller. 1991. WordNet: A lexical database organized on psycholinguistic principles. In U. Zernik. (ed.), *Lexical Acquisition. Exploiting Online Resources to Build a Lexicon*, 211-232. NJ: Erlbaum.

Behaghel, O. 1932. *Deutsche Syntax: Eine geschichtliche Darstellung: Band IV: Wortstellung: Periodenbau*. Heidelberg: Carl Winters Universitätsbuchhandlung.

Berg, T. & U. Schade. 1992. The role of inhibition in a spreading activation model of language production: The psycholinguistic perspective. *Journal of Psycholinguistics Research* 21. 405-434.

Bergen, B.K. & N. Chang. 2005. Embodied construction grammar in simulation-based language understanding. In Östman, J.-O. & M. Fried (eds.), 147-190.

Berlin, B. and P. Kay. 1969. *Basic Color Terms: Their Universality and Evolution*. Berkeley: University of California Press.

Bertram, R., R.H. Baayen & R. Schreuder. 2000. Effects of family size for complex words. *Journal of Memory and Language* 42. 390-405.

Bertram, R., R. Schreuder & R.H. Baayen. 2000. The balance of storage and computation in morphological processing: the role of word formation type, affixal homonymy, and productivity. *Journal of Experimental Psychology. Learning, Memory, and Cognition* 26. 489-511.

Biber, D., S. Conrad & V. Cortes. 2003. Lexical bundles in speech and writing: An initial taxonomy. In B. Lewandowska-Tomaszczyk & P.J. Melia, Peter Lang. (eds.), *Corpus Linguistics by the Lune: A Festschrift for Geoffrey Leech*, 71 – 92.

Biber, D., S. Conrad & V. Cortes. 2004. If you look at ...: Lexical bundles in university teaching and textbooks. *Applied Linguistics* 25. 371-405.

Biber, D., S. Johansson, G. Leech, S. Conrad & E. Finegan. 1999. *The Longman Grammar of Spoken and Written English*. Harlow: Pearson Education.

Bien, H., W.J.M. Levelt & R.H. Baayen. 2005. Frequency effects in compound production. *Proceedings of the National Academy Sciences* 102. 17876-17881.

Birbaumer, N. & R.F. Schmidt. ^{2}1991 [1990]. *Biologische Psychologie*. Berlin: Springer.

Birner, B.J. 1994. Information status and English inversion. *Language* 70. 233-259.

Birner, B.J. 1996. *The Discourse Function of Inversion in English*. New York & London: Garland.

Bley-Vroman, R. 2002. Frequency in production, comprehension, and acquisition. *Studies in Second Language Acquisition* 24. 209-213.

Bloomfield, L. 1933. *Language*. London: Allen & Unwin.

Bod, R. 1998. *Beyond Grammar: An Experience-Based Theory of Language*. Stanford: CSLI.

Bod, R., J. Hay & S. Jannedy. 2003. Introduction. In Bod et al. (eds.), 1-10.

Bod, R., J. Hay & S. Jannedy (eds.). 2003. *Probabilistic Linguistics*. Cambridge, MA: MIT Press.

Brown, E.K. 1991. Transformational-generative grammar. In K. Malmkjær (ed.), *The Linguistics Encyclopaedia*, 482-497. London: Routledge.

Brown, E.K. 2002. Transformational-generative grammar. In K. Malmkjær (ed.), *The Linguistics Encyclopaedia*, 171-192. London: Routledge.

Brugman, C. 1981 [1988]. *The Story of Over: Polysemy, Semantics, and the Structure of the Lexicon*. New York: Garland. [reprinted from: *Story of* Over. M. A. thesis, University of California, Berkeley.]

Brugman, C. & G. Lakoff. 2006 [1988]. Cognitive topology and lexical networks. In D. Geeraerts (ed.), *Cognitive Linguistics. Basic Readings*, 109-139. Berlin: Mouton, [reprinted from: S. L. Small, G. W. Cottrell & M. K. Tanenhaus (eds.), *Lexical Ambiguity Resolution: Perspectives from Psycholinguistics, Neuropsychology, and Artificial Intelligence*, 477-508. San Mateo, CA: Morgan Kaufmann.]

Bullinaria, J.A. 1997. Modeling reading, spelling, and past tense learning with artificial neural networks. *Brain and Language* 59. 236-266.

Bush, N. 2001 Frequency effect and word-boundary palatization. In Bybee & Hopper (eds.), 255-280.

Bussmann, H. 1996. *Routledge Dictionary of Language and Linguistics*. London: Routledge.

Butler, C.S. 1985. *Systemic Linguistics: Theory and Applications*. London: Batsford Academic and Educational.

Bybee, J.L. 1985. *Morphology: A Study of the Relation between Meaning and Form*. Amsterdam: John Benjamins.

Bybee, J.L. 2000. The phonology of the lexicon: Evidence from lexical diffusion. In M. Barlow & S. Kemmer (eds.), 65-85.

Bybee, J.L. 2001 *Phonology and Language Use*. Cambridge: CUP.

Bybee, J.L. 2002. Phonological evidence for exemplar storage of multiword sequences. *Studies in Second Language Acquisition* 24. 215-221.

Bybee, J.L. 2006. From usage to grammar: the mind's response to repetition. *Language* 82. 711-733.

Bybee, J.L. 2010. *Language, Usage and Cognition*. Cambridge: CUP.

Bybee, J.L. & P. Hopper (eds.). 2001. *Frequency and the Emergence of Linguistic Structure*. Amsterdam: John Benjamins.

Bybee, J.L. & C.L. Moder. 1983. Morphological classes as natural categories. *Language* 59. 251-270.

Bybee, J.L. & J. Scheibman. 1999. The effect of usage on degree of constituency: The reduction of *don't* in American English. *Linguistics* 37. 378-388.

Bybee, J.L. & S. Thompson. 1997. Three frequency effects in syntax. *Berkeley Linguistics Society* 23. 378-388.

Cazden, C.B. 1968. The acquisition of noun and verb inflections. *Child Development* 39. 433-448.

Chafe, W.L. 1974. Language and consciousness. *Language* 50. 111-133.

Chafe, W.L. 1976. Givenness, contrastiveness, definiteness, subjects, topics, and point of view. In C.N. Li (ed.), *Subject and Topic*, 25-55. New York: Academic Press.

Chafe, W.L. 1980. The deployment of consciousness in the production of a narrative. In W.L. Chafe (ed.), *The Pear Stories: Cognitive, Cultural, and Linguistic Aspects of Narrative Production*, 9-50. Norwood, NJ: Ablex.

Chafe, W.L. 1994. *Discourse, Consciousness, and Time: The Flow and Displacement of Conscious Experience in Speaking and Writing*. Chicago: Chicago University Press.

Chafe, W.L. 1996. Inferring identifiability and accessibility. In T. Fretheim & J.K. Gundel (eds.), *Reference and Referent Accessibility*, 37-46. Amsterdam: John Benjamins.

Childers, J.B. & M. Tomasello. 2001. The role of pronouns in young children's acquisition of the English transitive construction. *Developmental Psychology* 37. 739-748.

Chomsky, N. 1957. *Syntactic Structures*. The Hague: Mouton.

Chomsky, N. 1964. Current Issues in Linguistic Theory. In J.A. Fodor & J.J. Katz (eds.), *The Structure of Language: Readings in the Philosophy of Language*, 50-118, Englewood Cliffs, NJ: Prentice-Hall.

Chomsky, N. 1965. *Aspects of the Theory of Syntax*. Cambridge, MA: The M.I.T. Press.

Chomsky, N. 1970. Remarks on nominalization. In Waltham (ed.), *Readings in English Transformational Grammar*, 184-221. MA: Ginn.

Chomsky, N. 1975. *The Logical Structure of Linguistic Theory*. New York: Plenum.

Chomsky, N. 1995. *The Minimalist Program*. Cambridge, MA: The MIT Press.

Clahsen, H. 1999. Lexical entries and rules of language: a multidisciplinary study of German inflection. *Behavioral and Brain Sciences* 22. 991-1060.

Clark, B. 2005. On stochastic grammar. *Language* 81. 207-217.

Clark, E.V. & H.H. Clark. 1977. *Psychology and Language: An Introduction to Psycholinguistics*. New York: Harcourt, Brace, Jovanovich.

Clark, H.H. & S.E. Haviland. 1977. Comprehension and the given-new contract. In R.O. Freedle (ed.), *Discourse Production and Comprehension*, 1-40. Norwood: Ablex.

Collins, A.M., & E.F. Loftus. 1975. A spreading-activation theory of semantic processing. *Psychological Review* 82. 407-428.

Collins, A.M. & M.R. Quillian. 1969. Retrieval time from semantic memory. *Journal of Verbal Learning and Verbal Behavior* 8. 240-247.

Cook, V.J. & M. Newso. ^{2}1996 [1988]. *Chomsky's Universal Grammar: An Introduction*. Oxford: Blackwell.

Corbett, G., A. Hippisley, D. Brown & P. Marriott. 2001. Frequency, regularity and the paradigm: a perspective from Russian on a complex relation. In Bybee & Hopper (eds.), 201-226.

Coseriu, E. 1990. Semántica structural y semántica 'cognitiva'. In M. Alvar et al. (eds.), *Profesor Francisco Marsá: Jornadas de Filologia*, 239-282. Barcelona: Publicacions Universitat de Barcelona.

Cowan, N. 2001. The magical number 4 in short-term memory: A reconsideration of mental storage capacity. *Behavioral and Brain Sciences* 24. 87-185.

Cowan, N. 2005. *Working Memory Capacity*. New York, NY: Psychology Press.

Cowie, A.P (ed.). 1998. *Phraseology: Theory, Analysis, and Applications*. Oxford: Oxford University Press.

Craig, C.G. (ed.). 1986. *Noun Classes and Categorization: Proceedings of a Symposium on Categorization and Noun Classification, Eugene, Oregon, October 1983*. Amsterdam: John Benjamins.

Croft, W. 2001. *Radical Construction Grammar: Syntactic Theory in Typological Perspective*. Oxford: Oxford University Press.

Croft, W. & D.A. Cruse. 2004. *Cognitive Linguistics*. Cambridge: CUP.

Cruse, D. A. 1986. *Lexical Semantics*. Cambridge: Cambridge University Press.

Crystal, D. 1967. English. *Lingua* 17. 24-56.

Crystal, D. ^{4}1997, [1980]. *A Dictionary of Linguistics and Phonetics*. Oxford: Blackwell.

Cuyckens, H. & B. Zawada (eds.). 2001. *Polysemy in Cognitive Linguistics: Selected Papers from the Fifth International Cognitive Linguistics Association, Amsterdam, 1997*. Amsterdam: John Benjamins.

Dabrowska, E. 2004. *Language, Mind and Brain: Some Psychological and Neurological Constraints on Theories of Grammar*. Edinburgh: Edinburgh University Press.

Dabrowska, E. 2006. Low-level schemas or general rules? The role of diminutives in the acquisition of Polish case inflections. *Language Sciences* 28. 120-135.

Daneš, F. 1964. A three-level approach to syntax. *Travaux du Cercle Linguistique der Prague* 1. 225-240.

Daneš, F. 1974. Functional sentence perspective and the organization of the text. In F. Daneš (ed.), *Papers on Functional Sentence Perspective*, 106-128. The Hague: Mouton.

Daugherty, K.G. & M.S. Seidenberg. 1994. Beyond rules and exceptions: A connectionist approach to inflectional morphology. In Lima et al. (eds.), 353-388.

Deane, P. 1993. *Multimodal Spatial Representations: On the Semantic Unity of 'over' and other Polysemous Prepositions*. Duisburg: LAUD.

DeCarrico, J.S. & J.R. Nattinger. 1988. Lexical phrases for the comprehension of academic lectures. *English for Specific Purposes* 7. 91-102.

Dell, G.S. 1986. A spreading-activation theory of retrieval in sentence production. *Psychological Review* 93. 283-321.

Derwing, B.L. & R. Skousen. 1994. Productivity and the English past tense: Testing Skousen's Analogy Model. In Lima et al. (eds.), 193-218.

Detges, U. & R. Waltereit. 2002. Grammaticalization vs. reanalysis: a semantic-pragmatic account of functional change in grammar. *Zeitschrift für Sprachwissenschaft* 21. 151-195.

Dijk, T.A. van. 1977. *Text and Context: Explorations in the Semantics and Pragmatics of Discourse*. London: Longman.

Dijk, T.A. van. 1980. *Textwissenschaft: Eine Interdisziplinäre Einführung*. München: Deutscher Taschebuch Verlag.

Dik, Simon C. 1989. *The Theory of Functional Grammar. Part 1: The Structure of the Clause*. Dordrecht: Foris.

Dodson, K. & M. Tomasello. 1998. Acquiring the transitive construction in English: the role of animacy and pronoun. *Journal of Child Language* 25. 605-622.

Du Bois, J.W. 2003. Discourse and grammar. In: Tomasello (ed.), 47-87.

Dupoux, E. (ed.). 2001. *Language, Brain, and Cognitive Development: Essays in Honor of Jacques Mehler*. Cambridge, MA: MIT Press.

Eeg-Olofsson, M. & B. Altenberg. 1994. Discontinuous recurrent word combinations in the London-Lund Corpus. In U. Fries, G. Tottie & P. Schneider (eds.), *Creating and Using English Language Corpora*, 63-77. Amsterdam: Rodopi.

Eeg-Olofsson, M. & B. Altenberg. 1996. Recurrent word combinations in the London-Lund Corpus: Coverage and use for word-class tagging. In C.E. Percy, C.F. Meyer & I. Lancashire (eds.), *Synchronic Corpus Linguistics*, 97-107. Amsterdam: Rodopi.

Eggins, S. ^{2}2004 [1994]. *An Introduction to Systemic Functional Linguistics*. New York: Continuum.

Ellis, N.C. 2002. Frequency effects in language processing: A review with implications for theories of implicit and explicit language acquisition. *Studies in Second Language Acquisition* 24. 143-188.

Ellis, N. C. & R. Schmidt. 1998. Rules or associations in the acquisition of morphology? The frequency by regularity interaction in human and PDP learning of morphosyntax. *Language and Cognitive Processes* 13. 307-336.
Erman, B. & B. Warren. 2000. The idiom principle and the open choice principle. *Text* 20. 29-62.
Ernestus, M., M. Lahey, F. Verhees & R.H. Baayen. 2006. Lexical frequency and voice assimilation. *Journal of the Acoustic Society of America* 120. 1040-1051.
Esser, J. 1984. *Untersuchungen zum Gesprochenen Englisch*. Tübingen: Narr.
Esser, J. 1992. Neuere Tendenzen in der Grammatikschreibung des Englischen. *Zeitschrift für Anglistik und Amerikanistik* 40. 112-123.
Esser, J. 1998. Lexical items and medium-transferability in English and German. In Weigand (ed.), 173-186.
Esser, J. 1999. Collocation, colligation, semantic preference and semantic prosody. New developments in the study of syntagmatic word relations. In W. Faulkner & H.-J. Schmid (eds.), *Words, Lexeme, Concepts – Approaches to the Lexicon. Studies in Honour of Leonhard Lipka*, 155-165. Tübingen: Narr.
Esser, J. 2000a. Corpus linguistics and the linguistic sign. In C. Mair & M. Hundt (eds.), *Corpus Linguistics and Linguistic Theory. Papers from the Twentieth International Conference on English Language Research on Computerized Corpora (ICAME 20)*, 91-101. Amsterdam: Rodopi.
Esser, J. 2000b. Medium-transferability and presentation structure in speech and writing. *Journal of Pragmatics* 32. 1523-1538.
Esser, J. 2006. *Presentation in Language: Rethinking Speech and Writing*. Tübingen: Gunter Narr.
Eubank, L. & K.R. Gregg. 2002. News flash – Hume still dead. *Studies in Second Language Acquisition* 24. 237-247.
Evans, V. & M. Green. 2006. *Cognitive Linguistics: An Introduction*. Edinburgh: Edinburgh University Press.
Fellbaum, C. 1998. A semantic network of English: The mother of all WordNets. *Computers and the Humanities* 32. 209-220.
Fillmore, C.J. 1977. Topics in lexical semantics. *Current Issues in Linguistic Theory*. In P. Cole (ed.), 76-138. Bloomington: Indiana University Press.
Fillmore, C.J. 1982. Towards a descriptive framework for spatial deixis. In R. J. Jarvella & W. Klein (eds.), *Speech, Place, & Action: Studies in Deixis and Related Topics*, 31 – 59. Chichester: John Wiley.
Fillmore, C.J. 1985. Frames and the semantics of understanding. *Quaderni di Semantica* 6. 222-253.
Fillmore, C.J., P. Kay & M.C. O'Connor. 1988. Regularity and idiomaticity in grammatical constructions: The case of *let alone*. *Language* 64. 501-538.
Firbas, J. 1992. *Functional Sentence Perspective in Written and Spoken Communication*. Cambridge: CUP.
Firth, J.R. 1951. Modes of meaning: *Essays and Studies* 4. 118-149. [Repr. in: John Rupert Firth (1957): *Papers in Linguistics 1934 – 1951*. London: Oxford University Press. 190-215.]
Firth, J.R. 1968 [1957]. A synopsis of linguistic theory, 1930 – 55. In F.R. Palmer (ed.), *Selected Papers of J. R. Firth 1952 – 59*, 168-205. London: Longmans, Green and Co.

Fodor, J.D. & L. Frazier. 1980. Is the human sentence parsing mechanism and ATN? *Cognition* 8. 417-459.

Francis, G. 1993. A corpus-driven approach to grammar: Principles, methods and examples. In M. Baker, G. Francis & E. Tognini-Bonelli (eds.), *Text and Technology. In Honour of John Sinclair*, 137-156. Amsterdam: John Benjamins.

Francis, G., S. Huston & E. Manning. 1996. *Collins COBUILD Grammar Patterns 1: Verbs*. London: Harper Collins.

Frazier, L. 1985. Syntactic complexity. In L. Karttunen & A. M. Zwicky (eds.), *Natural Language Parsing. Psychological, Computational, and Theoretical Perspectives*, 129-189. Cambridge: CUP.

Frazier, L. & J. D. Fodor. 1978. The sausage machine: A new two-stage parsing model. *Cognition* 6. 291-325.

Fried, M. & J.-O. Östman. 2004. Construction Grammar: A thumbnail sketch. In Fried & Östman (eds.), 11-86.

Fried, M. & H.C. Boas (eds.). 2005. *Grammatical Constructions: Back to the Roots*. Amsterdam: John Benjamins.

Fried, M. & J.-O. Östman (eds.). 2004. *Construction Grammar in a Cross-Language Perspective*. Amsterdam: John Benjamins.

Fries, C.C. 1952. *The Structure of English: An Introduction to the Construction of English Sentences*. New York: Harcourt, Brace & Company.

Gabelentz, G. v.d. 1901, [1972 2nd imprint]. *Die Sprachwissenschaft, ihre Aufgaben, Methoden und bisherigen Ergebnisse*. Tübingen: TBL.

Garrett, M. 2001. Now you see it, now you don't: Frequency effects in language production. In Dupoux (ed.), 227-240.

Gass, S.M. & A. Mackey. 2002. Frequency effects and second language acquisition. *Studies in Second Language Acquisition* 24. 249-260.

Gasser, M. & L.B. Smith. 1998. Learning nouns and adjective. A connectionist account. *Language and Cognitive Processes* 13. 269-305.

Geeraerts, D. 1995. Representational formats in cognitive semantics. *Folia Linguistica* 29. 21-41.

Geeraerts, D. 1997. *Diachronic Prototype Semantics*. Oxford: Clarendon.

Geeraerts, D. (1999. Diachronic prototype semantics: A digest. In A. Blank & P. Koch (eds.), *Historical Semantics and Cognition*, 91-107. Berlin: Mouton de Gruyter.

Geeraerts, D. 2000. Salience phenomena in the lexicon: A typology. In L. Albertazzi (ed.), *Meaning and Cognition: A Multidisciplinary Approach*, 79-101. Amsterdam: John Benjamins.

Geeraerts, D. 1988 [2006]. Where does prototypicality come from. In Geeraerts (ed.), 27-47. [reprinted from: B. Rudzka-Ostyn (ed.), *Topics in Cognitive Linguistics*, 207-229. Amsterdam: John Benjamins].

Geeraerts, D. 1989 [2006]. Prospects and problems of prototype theory. In Geeraerts (ed.), 3-26. [reprinted from: *Linguistics* 27, 587-612].

Geeraerts, D. 1992 [2006]. The semantic structure of Dutch *over*. In Geeraerts (ed.), 48-73. [reprinted from: *Leuvense Bijdragen* 81, 205-230].

Geeraerts, D. 1993 [2006]. Vagueness's puzzles, polysemy's vagaries. In Geeraerts (ed.), 99-148. [reprinted from: *Cognitive Linguistics* 4, 223-272].

Geeraerts, D. (ed.). (2006) *Words and other Wonders. Papers on Lexical and Semantic Topics*, ed. by D. Geeraerts. Berlin: Mouton de Gruyter.

Geeraerts, D. & H. Cuyckens. (eds.). 2007. *The Oxford Handbook of Cognitive Linguistics*. Oxford: Oxford University Press.

Geeraerts, D., S. Gondelaers & P. Bakema. 1994. *The Structure of Lexical Variation. Meaning, Naming, and Context*. Berlin: Mouton de Gruyter.

Geurts, B. 2000. Explaining grammaticalization (the standard way). *Linguistics* 35. 781-788.

Gibson, E. & C.T. Schütze. 1999. Disambiguation preferences in noun phrase conjuncttion do not mirror corpus frequency. *Journal of Memory and Language* 40. 263-279.

Gibson, E., C.T. Schütze & A. Salomon. 1996. The relationship between the frequency and the processing complexity of linguistic structure. *Journal of Psycholinguistic Research* 25. 59-92.

Givón, T. 1985. Iconicity, isomorphism and non-arbitrary coding in syntax. In Haiman (ed.), 187-219.

Givón, T. 1986. Prototypes: Between Plato and Wittgenstein. In Craig (ed.), 77-102.

Givón, T. 1991a. Markedness in grammar. *Studies in Language* 15. 335-370.

Givón, T. 1991b. Isomorphism in the Grammatical Code. *Studies in Language* 15. 85-114.

Givón, T. 1995. *Functionalism and Grammar*. Amsterdam: John Benjamins.

Goldberg, A. 1995. *Constructions: A Construction Grammar Approach to Argument Structure*. Chicago: University of Chicago Press.

Goldberg, A. 1998. Patterns of Experience in Patterns of Language. In Tomasello (ed.), 203-219.

Goldberg, A. 2006. *Constructions at Work: The Nature of Generalization in English*. Oxford: OUP.

Gordon, P. & M. Alegre. 1999. Is there a dual system for regular inflections. *Brain and Language* 68. 212-217.

Granger, S. 1998. Prefabricated patterns in EFL writing. In Cowie (ed.), 145-60. Oxford: Oxford University Press.

Grice, P. 1975. Logic and conversation. In P. Cole & J. L. Morgan (eds.), *Syntax and Semantics, Vol. 3: Speech Acts*, 41-58. New York: Academic Press.

Gries, S.Th. 2002. Evidence in Linguistics: three approaches to genitives in English. In R. M. Brend, W. J. Sullivan, and A. R. Lommel (eds.), *LACUS Forum XXVIII: What Constitutes Evidence in Linguistics?*, 17-31. Fullerton, CA: LACUS.

Gries, S.Th. 2006. Corpus-based methods and cognitive semantics: the many senses of *to run*". In Gries & Stefanowitsch (eds.), 57-99.

Gries, S.Th. forthc. Phraseology and linguistic theory: a brief survey. In Granger & F. Meunier (eds.), *Phraseology: An Interdisciplinary Perspective*. Philadelphia: John Benjamins.

Gries, S.Th., B. Hampe & D. Schönefeld. 2005. Converging evidence. Bringing together experimental and corpus data on the association of verbs and constructions. *Cognitive Linguistics* 16. 635-676.

Gries, S.Th. & A. Stefanowitsch. 2004a. Extending collostructional analysis: A corpus-based perspective on 'alternations'. *International Journal of Corpus Linguistics* 9. 97-129.

Gries, S.Th. & A. Stefanowitsch. 2004b. Covarying collexemes in the into-causative. In M. Achard & S. Kemmer (eds.), *Language, Culture and Mind*, 225-36. Stanford, CA: CSLI.

Gries, S.Th. & A. Stefanowitsch (eds.). 2006. *Corpora in Cognitive Linguistics: Corpus-based Approaches to Syntax and Lexis*, Berlin: Mouton de Gruyter.

Grondelaers, S., D. Geeraerts & D. Speelman. 2007. A case for a Cognitive corpus linguistics. In M. Gonzalez-Marquez, I. Mittelberg, S. Coulson & M. J. Spivey (eds.), *Methods in Cognitive Linguistics*, 149-169. Amsterdam: John Benjamins.

Haegeman, L. 1991 [^{2}1994]. *Introduction to Government and Binding Theory*. Oxford: Blackwell.

Haiman, John (ed.). 1985. *Iconicity in Syntax*. Amsterdam: John Benjamins.

Halliday, M.A.K. 1961. Categories of the theory of grammar. *Word* 17. 241-292.

Halliday, M.A.K. 1966. Lexis as a linguistic level. *In Memory of J. R. Firth*. In C.E. Bazell et al. (eds.), 148-162. London: Longmans.

Halliday, M.A.K. 1967. Notes on transitivity and theme in English. Part 1. *Journal of Linguistics* 3. 37-81.

Halliday, M.A.K. 1970. Language structure and language function. In J. Lyons (ed.), *New Horizons in Linguistics*, 140-164. Harmondsworth: Penguin.

Halliday, M.A.K. 1985a. *An Introduction to Functional Grammar*. London: Arnold.

Halliday, M.A.K. 1985b. Systemic background. In J.D. Benson & W. S. Greaves (eds.), *Systemic Perspectives on Discourse, Vol. 1. Selected Theoretical Papers from the 9th International Systemic Workshop*, 1-15. Norwood, NJ: Ablex.

Halliday, M.A.K. 1985 [^{2}1989]. *Spoken and Written Language*. Oxford: OUP.

Halliday, M.A.K. 1991. Corpus studies and probabilistic grammar. In Aijmer & Altenberg (eds.), 30-43.

Halliday, M.A.K. 1992. Language as system and language as instance: The corpus as a theoretical construct. In J. Svartvik (ed.), *Directions in Corpus Linguistics. Proceedings of the Nobel Symposium 82, Stockholm 4-8 August 1991*, 61-77. Berlin: Mouton de Gruyter.

Halliday, M.A.K. and R. Hasan. 1976. *Cohesion in English*. London: Longman

Halliday, M.A.K., A. McIntosh and P. Strevens. 1964. *The Linguistic Sciences and Language Teaching*. London: Longmans.

Hare, M.L., M. Ford & W.D. Marslen-Wilson. 2001. Ambiguity and frequency effects in regular verb inflection. In Bybee & Hopper (eds.), 181-200.

Harris, Z.S. 1951. *Structural Linguistics*. Chicago: The University of Chicago Press.

Harris, Z.S. 1954. Distributional structure. *Word* 10. 146-162.

Hasan, R. 1987. The grammarian's dream: lexis as most delicate grammar. In M.A.K. Halliday & R. Fawcett (eds.), *New Developments in Systemic Linguistics. Volume 1: Theory and Description*, 184-211. London: Frances.

Haviland, S.E. & H.H. Clark. 1974. What's new? Acquiring new information as a process in comprehension. *Journal of Verbal Learning and Verbal Behaviour* 13. 512-521.

Hawkins, J.A. 1990. A parsing theory of word order universals. *Linguistic Inquiry* 21. 223-261.

Hawkins, J.A. 1993. Heads, parsing and word-order universals. In G. G. Corbett, N. M. Fraser & S. McGlashan (eds.), *Heads in Grammatical Theory*, 231-165. Cambridge: CUP.

Hawkins, J.A. 1994. *A Performance Theory of Order and Constituency*. Cambridge: Cambridge University Press.

Hawkins, J.A. 1998. Some issues in a performance theory of word order. In A. Siewierska (ed.), *Constituent Order in the Languages of Europe. Empirical Approaches to Lanugage Typology*, 729-780. Berlin: de Gruyter.

Hawkins, J.A. 1999a. Processing complexity and filler-gap dependencies across grammars. *Language* 75. 244-285.

Hawkins, J.A. 1999b. The relative order of prepositional phrases in English: Going beyond manner-place-time. *Language Variation and Change* 11. 231-266.

Hawkins, J.A. 2001a. Why are categories adjacent. *Journal of Linguistics* 37. 1-34.
Hawkins, J.A. 2001b. The role of processing principles in explaining language universals. In M. Haspelmath, E. König, W. Oesterreicher & W. Raible, *Language Typology and Language Universals: An International Handbook*: *Volume 1*, 360-269. Berlin: de Gruyter.
Hawkins, J.A. 2002a. Symmetries and asymmetries: Their grammar, typology and parsing. *Theoretical Linguistics* 28. 95-149.
Hawkins, J.A. 2002b. Issues at the performance-grammar interface: Some comments on the commentaries. *Theoretical Linguistics* 28. 211-227.
Hawkins, J.A. 2003. Why are zero-marked phrases close to their heads. In Rohdenburg & Mondorf (eds.), 175-204.
Hawkins, J.A. 2004. *Efficiency and Complexity in Grammars*. Oxford: Oxford University Press.
Hay, J. 2001. Lexical frequency in morphology: Is everything relative? *Linguistics* 39. 1041-1070.
Heider, E.R. 1972. Universals in color naming and memory. *Journal of Experimental Psychology* 93. 10-20.
Hellman, C. 1996. The 'price tag' on knowledge activation in discourse processing. In T. Fretheim & J.K. Gundel (eds.), *Reference and Referent Accessibility*, 193-211. Amsterdam: John Benjamins.
Herdan, G. 1956. *Language as Choice and Chance*. Groningen: P. Noordhoff N.V.
Hinrichs, L. & B. Szmrecsanyi. 2007. Recent changes in the function and frequency of standard English genitive constructions: a multivariate analysis of tagged corpora. *English Language and Linguistics* 11. 437-474.
Hjelmslev, L. ^{2}1961 [1943]. *Omkring sporgteoriens grundlæggelse* [Prolegomena to a Theory of Language]. Madison: The University of Wisconsin Press.
Hockett, C.F. 1954. Two models of grammatical description. *Word* 10. 210-234.
Hoey, M. 2005. *Lexical Priming: A New Theory of Words and Language*. Oxon: Routledge.
Hoey, M. 2006. Language as choice: what is chosen? In Geoff Thompson & Susan Hunston (eds.), *System and Corpus. Exploring Connections*, 37-54. London: Equinox.
Hoffmann, S. (2005): *Grammaticalization and English Complex Prepositions: A Corpus-based Study*. London: Routledge.
Hooper, J.B. 1976. Word frequency in lexical diffusion and the source of morphophonological change. In W. Christie (ed.), *Current Progress in Historical Linguistics*, 95-105. Amsterdam: North Holland.
Hornby, A.S. 1954. *A Guide to Patterns and Usage in English*. London: Oxford University Press.
Howarth, P. 1996. *Phraseology in English Academic Writing: Some Implications for Language Learning and Dictionary Making*. Tübingen: Max Niemeyer.
Howarth, P. 1998a. Phraseology and second language learning. *Applied Linguistics* 19. 24-44.
Howarth, P. 1998b. The phraseology of learner's academic writing. In Cowie (ed.), 161-186. Oxford: Oxford University Press.
Hudson, R. 2007a. *Language Networks*. Oxford: Oxford University Press.
Hudson, R. 2007b. Word grammar. In Geeraerts & Cuyckens (eds.), 509-539.
Hudson, R. 2008. Word grammar, cognitive linguistics, and second language learning and teaching. In P. Robinson & N. C. Ellis (eds.), *Handbook of Cognitive Linguistics and Second Language Acquisition*, 89-113. New York: Routledge.
Hulme, C., S. Roodenrys, G. Brown R. & Mercer. 1995. The role of long-term memory mechanisms in memory span. *British Journal of Psychology* 86. 527-536.

Hulstijn, J. 2002. Towards a unified account of the representation, processing and acquisition of second language knowledge. *Second Language Research* 18. 193-223.
Hunston, S. 2006. Phraseology and system: a contribution to the debate. In G. Thompson & S. Hunston (eds.), *System and Corpus: Exploring Connections*, 55-80. London: Equinox.
Hunston, S. & G. Francis. 2000. *Pattern Grammar: A Corpus-Driven Approach to the Lexical Grammar of English*. Amsterdam: John Benjamins.
Iwata, S. 2005. Verb meaning in locative alternations. In M. Fried & H. C. Boas (eds.), 101-118.
Jackendoff, R. 1977. *X' Syntax: A Study of Phrase Structure*. Cambridge, MA: The MIT Press.
Jackson, Howard 1980 [[2]1982]. *Analyzing English: An Introduction to Descriptive Linguistics.* Oxford: Pergamon Press.
Jager, Cornelis de. 1992. Adventures in science and cyclosophy. *Skeptical Inquirer* 16. 167-172.
Jespersen, O. 1917. *Negation in English and other Languages*. Copenhagen: Bianco Lunos Bogtrykkeri.
Jurafsky, D. 2003. Probabilistic modeling in psycholinguistics: Linguistic comprehension and production. In Bod et al. (eds), 39-95.
Jurafsky, D., A. Bell, M. Gregory & W.D. Raymond. 2001. Probabilistic relations between words: evidence from reduction in lexical production. In Bybee & Hopper (eds.), 229-254.
Kastovsky, D. 1982. *Wortbildung und Semantik.* Düsseldorf: Schwann-Bagel.
Katz, J.J. & J.A. Fodor. 1963. The structure of a semantic theory. *Language* 39. 170-210.
Kay, P. 2005. Argument structure constructions and the argument-adjunct distinction. In M. Fried & H. C. Boas (eds.), 71-98.
Kay, P. & C.J. Fillmore. 1999. Grammatical constructions and linguistic generalizations: The What's X doing Y? construction. *Language* 75. 1-33.
Kazdin, A.E. 2000. *Encyclopedia of Psychology*, vol 7. Oxford: Oxford University Press.
Kemmer, S. & M. Barlow. 2000. Introduction: A usage-based conception of language. In Barlow & Kemmer (eds.), vii -xxviii.
Kilgarriff, A. 1992. *Polysemy.* Brighton: University of Sussex dissertation.
Kimball, J. 1973. Seven principles of surface structure parsing in natural language. *Cognition* 2. 15-47.
Kjellmer, G. 1990. Patterns of collocability. In J. Aarts & W. Meijs (eds.), *Theory and Practice in Corpus Linguistics*, 163-173. Amsterdam: Rodopi.
Kjellmer, G. 1991. A mint of phrases. In Aijmer & Altenberg (eds.), 111-127.
Kleiber, G. 1993 [[2]1998]. *Prototypensemantik: Eine Einführung*. Tübingen: Narr.
Kreitzer, A. 1997. Multiple levels of schematization: A study in the conceptualization of space. *Cognitive Linguistics* 8. 291-325.
Kreyer, R. 2003. Genitive and *of*-construction in modern written English: Processability and human involvement. *International Journal of Corpus Linguistics* 8. 169-207.
Kreyer, R. 2006). *Inversion in Modern Written English: Syntactic Complexity, Information Status and the Creative Writer*. Tübingen: Narr.
Krug, M. 1998. String frequency. A cognitive motivating factor in coalescence, language processing, and linguistic change. *Journal of English Linguistics* 26. 286–320.
Krug, M. 2001. Frequency, iconicity, categorization: evidence from emerging modals. In Bybee & Hopper (eds.), 309-335.
Krug, M. 2003. Frequency as a determinant in grammatical variation and change In Rohdenburg & Mondorf (eds), 7-67.

Kuczaj, S.A.II. 1977. The acquisition of regular and irregular past tense forms. Journal of Verbal Learning and Verbal Behavior 16. 589-600.
Kuczaj, S.A.II. 1978. Children's judgments of grammatical and ungrammatical irregular past-tense verbs. *Child Development* 49. 319-326.
Labov, W. 1973. The boundaries of words and their meaning. In C.-J. Bailey & R.W. Shuy (eds.), *New Ways of Analyzing Variation in English*, 340-373. Washington, DC: Georgetown University Press.
Lakoff, G. 1970. A note on vagueness and ambiguity. *Linguistic Inquiry* 1. 357-359.
Lakoff, G. 1986. Classifiers as a reflection of mind. In Craig (ed.), 13-51.
Lakoff, G. 1987. *Women, Fire and Dangerous Things: What Categories Reveal about the Mind.* Chicago: Chicago University Press.
Lakoff, G. 1990. The invariance hypothesis: Is abstract reason based on image-schemas? *Cognitive Linguistics* 1. 39-74.
Lamb, S.M. 1966. *An Outline of Stratificational Grammar.* Washington, DC: Georgetown University Press.
Lamb, S.M. 1998. *Pathways of the Brain: The Neurocognitive Basis of Language.* Amsterdam: John Benjamins.
Lamb, S.M. 2000. Bidirectional processing in language and related cognitive systems. In Barlow & Kemmer (eds.), 87-119.
Lambrecht, K. 1994. *Information Structure and Sentence Form: Topic, Focus, and the Mental Representations of Discourse Referents.* Cambridge: CUP.
Langacker, R.W. 1987. *Foundations of Cognitive Grammar: Volume 1 Theoretical Prerequisites.* Stanford: Stanford University Press.
Langacker, R.W. 1988a. An overview of cognitive grammar. In B. Rudzka-Ostyn (ed.), *Topics in Cognitive Linguistics*, 3-48. Amsterdam: John Benjamins.
Langacker, R.W. 1988b. A usage-based model. In B. Rudzka-Ostyn (ed.), *Topics in Cognitive Linguistics*, 127-161. Amsterdam: John Benjamins.
Langacker, R.W. 1991. *Concept, Image, and Symbol: The Cognitive Basis of Grammar.* Berlin: Mouton de Gruyter.
Langacker, R.W. 2000a. *Grammar and Conceptualization.* Berlin: Mouton de Gruyter.
Langacker, R.W. 2000b. A dynamic usage-based model. In Barlow & Kemmer (eds.), *Usage-Based Models of Language*, 1-63.
Langacker, R.W. 2005. Integration, grammaticization, and constructional meaning. In Fried & Boas (eds.), 157-189.
Langacker, R.W. 2008. *Cognitive Grammar: A Basic Introduction.* Oxford: Oxford University Press.
Langlotz, A. 2005. Are constructions the basic units of grammar? The phraseology turn in linguistic theory. *Ranam* 38. 45- 63.
Larsen-Freeman, D. 2002. Making sense of frequency. *Studies in Second Language Acquisition* 24. 275-285.
Lasnik, H. & J. Uriagereka. 1988. *A Course in GB Syntax: Lectures on Binding and Empty Categories.* Cambridge, MA: MIT Press.
Lass, R. 1984. *An Introduction to Basic Concepts.* Cambridge: Cambridge University Press.
Lee, D. 2001. *Cognitive Linguistics: An Introduction.* Oxford: OUP.
Lee, C.-D. & M. Gasser. 1991. Learning morphophonemic processes without underlying representations and explicit rules. *Language Research* 27. 303-317.

Leech, G. 1983. *Principles of Pragmatics*. London: Longman.

Li, P. 2006. In search of meaning: The acquisition of semantic structures and morphological systems. In J. Luchjenbroers (ed.), *Cognitive Linguistics Investigations: Across Languages, Fields and Philosophical Boundaries*, 109-137. Amsterdam: John Benjamins.

Lima, S.D., R.L. Corrigan & G.K. Iverson (eds.). 1994. *The Reality of Linguistic Rules*. Amsterdam: John Benjamins.

Lipka, Leonhard 2002. *English Lexicology: Lexical Structure, Word Semantics and Word-Formation*. Tübingen: Narr.

Lockwood, D. G. 1972. *Introduction to Stratificational Linguistics*. New York: Harcourt Brace Jovanovich.

Lohse, B., J.A. Hawkins & T. Wasow. 2004. Domain minimization in English verb-particle constructions. *Language* 80. 238-261.

Louw, B. 1993. Irony in the text or insincerity of the writer? The diagnostic potential of semantic prosodies. In M. Baker, G. Franics & E. Tognini-Bonelli, *Text and Technology. In Honour of John Sinclair*, 157-176. Amsterdam: John Benjamins.

Luger, G: and W. Stubblefield. 1993. *Artificial Intelligence: Structures and Strategies for Complex Problem Solving*. New York: Benjamin Cummings.

Lyons, J. 1977. *Semantics*. Cambridge: CUP.

Lyons, J. 1981. *Language and Linguistics: An Introduction*. Cambridge: CUP.

MacDonald, M.C. 1994. Probabilistic constraints in syntactic ambiguity resolution. *Language and Cognitive Processes* 9. 157-201.

MacWhinney, B. 2000. Connectionism and language learning. In Barlow & Kemmer (eds.), 121-149.

MacWhinney, B. & J. Leinbach. 1991. Implementations are not conceptualizations: Revising the verb learning model. *Cognition* 40. 121-157.

MacWhinney, B., J. Leinbach, R. Taraban & J. McDonald. 1989. Language learning: Cues or rules? *Journal of Memory and Language* 28. 255-277.

Makkai, A. & D. G. Lockwood (eds.). 1973. *Readings in Stratificational Linguistics*. Alabama: University of Alabama Press.

Mangasser-Wahl M. 2000. Roschs Prototypentheory: Eine Entwicklung in drei Phasen. In Mangasser-Wahl (ed.), 15-31.

Mangasser-Wahl M. (ed.). 2000. *Prototypentheorie in der Linguistik: Anwendungsbeispiele – Methodenreflexion – Perspektiven*. Tübingen: Stauffenberg.

Mann, W.C., C. Matthiessen & S.A. Thompson. 1992. Rhetorical structure theory and text analysis. In W.C. Mann & S.A. Thompson, *Discourse Description: Diverse Linguistic Analyses of a Fund-raising Text*, 39-78. Amsterdam: John Benjamins.

Martinet, A. 1960 [1964]. *Eléments de Linguistique Générale* [Elements of General Linguistics]. London: Faber & Faber.

Mathesius, V. 1961 [1975]. In J. Vachek (ed.), *A Functional Analysis of Present Day English on a General Linguistic Basis*. The Hague: Mouton.

Matthews, P.H. 1997. *The Concise Oxford Dictionary of Linguistics*. Oxford: OUP.

Matthiessen, C. & S.A. Thompson. 1988. The structure of discourse and 'subordination'. In J. Haiman & S.A. Thompson (eds.), *Clause Combining in Grammar and Discourse*, 275-329. Amsterdam: John Benjamins.

McKoon, G. & R. Ratcliff. 1980. Priming in item recognition: The organization of propositions in memory for text. *Journal of Verbal Learning and Verbal Behavior* 19. 369-386.

Mervis, C.B. 1980. Category structure and the development of categorization. In R.J. Spiro, B.C. Bruce & W.F. Brewer (eds.), *Theoretical Issues in Reading Comprehension: Perspectives from Cognitive Psychology, Linguistics, Artificial Intelligence, and Education*, 279-307. Hillsdale, NJ: Lawrence Erlbaum.

Mervis, C.B. & E. Rosch. 1981. Categorization of natural objects. *Annual Review of Psychology* 32. 89-115.

Michaelis, L.A. 2005. Entity and event coercion in a symbolic theory of syntax. In Östman & Fried (eds.), 45-88.

Miller, G.A. 1956. The magical number seven, plus or minus two: Some limits on our capacity for processing information. *Psychological Review* 63. 81-97.

Miller, G.A. 1965. Introduction. In G.K. Zipf, *The Psycho-Biology of Language. An Introduction to Dynamic Philology*, v-x. Cambridge, MA: The M.I.T. Press.

Miller, G.A. & C. Fellbaum. 1991. Semantic networks of English. *Cognition* 41. 197-229.

Miller, G.A. & C. Fellbaum. 1992. WordNet and the organization of lexical memory. In M.L Swartz & M. Yazdani (eds.), *Intelligent Tutoring Systems for Foreign Language Learning*, 89-102. Berlin: Springer.

Miller, J. 1995. Does spoken language have sentences. In J. Lyons (ed.), *Grammar and Meaning*, 116-135. Cambridge: CUP.

Mindt, D. 2002. What is a grammatical rule? In L.E. Breivik & A. Hasselgren (eds.), *From the Colt's Mouth ... And Others': Language Corpora Studies in Honour of Anna-Brita Stenström*, 197-212. Amsterdam: Rodopi.

Minsky, M. 1975. A framework for representing knowledge. In P.H. Winston (ed.), *The Psychology of Computer Vision*, 211-277. New York: McGraw-Hill.

Mondorf, Britta 2003. Support for *more*-support. In Rohdenburg & Mondorf (eds.), 251-304.

Moon, R. 1998a. *Fixed Expressions in English: A Corpus-based Approach*. Oxford: Clarendon.

Moon, R. 1998b. Phrasal lexemes in English. In Cowie (ed.), 82-100. Oxford: Oxford University Press.

Mukherjee, J. 2005. *English Ditransitive Verbs: Aspects of Theory, Description and a Usage-based Model*. Amsterdam: Rodopi.

Nattinger, J.R. 1980. A lexical phrase grammar for ESL. *TESOL Quarterly* 14. 377-344.

Nattinger, J.R. 1988. Some current trends in vocabulary teaching. In R. Carter & M. McCarthy (eds.), *Vocabulary and Language Teaching*, New York: Longman.

Nattinger, J.R. & J.S. DeCarrico. 1989. Lexical phrases, speech acts and teaching conversation. *AILA Review 6: Vocabulary Acquisition*. 118-139.

Nattinger, J.R. & J.S. DeCarrico. 1992. *Lexical Phrases in Language Teaching*. Oxford: Oxford University Press.

Nehrlich, B., Z. Todd, V. Herman & D. D. Clarke (eds.). 2003. *Polysemy: Flexible Patterns of Meaning in Mind and Language*. Berlin: Mouton de Gruyter.

Nemoto, N. 2005. Verbal polysemy and Frame Semantics in Construction Grammar: Some observations on the locative alternation. In Fried & Boas (eds.), 119-136.

Nesselhauf, N. 2003. The use of collocations by advanced learners of English and some implications for teaching. *Applied Linguistics* 24. 223-242.

Nesselhauf, N. 2004. What are collocations? In Allerton et al. (eds), 1-21. Basel: Schwabe.

Nesselhauf, N. 2005. *Collocations in a Learner Corpus*. Amsterdam: John Benjamins.

Newmeyer, F.J. 1996. *Generative Linguistics. A Historical Perspective*. London: Routledge.

Newmeyer, F.J. 2003. Grammar is grammar and usage is usage. *Language* 79. 682-707.

Nikanne, U. 2005. Constructions in conceptual semantics. In: Östman & Fried (eds.), 191-242.
Nooteboom, S., F. Weerman & F. Wijnen. 2002. Minimising or maximising storage? An introduction. In Nooteboom et al. (eds.), 1-19.
Nooteboom, S, F. Weerman, F. Wijnen (eds.). 2002. *Storage and Computation in the Language Faculty*. Dordrecht: Kluwer.
Nunberg, G., I.A. Sag & T. Wasow. 1994. Idioms. *Language* 70. 491-538.
Östman, J.-O. & M. Fried. 2004. Historical and intellectual background of Construction Grammar. In Fried & Östman (eds.), 1-10.
Östman, J.-O. & M. Fried 2005. The cognitive grounding of construction grammar. In Östman & Fried (eds.), 1-13.
Östman, J.-O. & M. Fried (eds.). 2005. *Construction Grammars: Cognitive Grounding and Theoretical Extensions*. Amsterdam: John Benjamins.
Ouhalla, J. 1994. *Transformational Grammar: From Rules to Principles and Parameters*. London: Arnold.
Palmer, F. R. 1976 [[2]1981]. *Semantics*. Cambridge: Cambridge University Press.
Partington, A. 1998. *Patterns and Meanings: Using Corpora for English Language Research and Teaching*. Amsterdam: John Benjamins.
Partington, A. 2004. 'Utterly content in each other's company': Semantic prosody and semantic preference. *International Journal of Corpus Linguistics* 9. 131-156.
Pawley, A. & F.H. Syder. 1983. Two puzzles for linguistic theory: Nativelike selection and nativelike fluency. In J.C. Richards & R.W. Schmidt (eds.), *Language and Communication*, 191-226. London: Longman.
Phillips, B.S. 2001. Lexical diffusion, lexical frequency, and lexical analysis. In Bybee & Hopper (eds.), 123-136.
Pickering, M.J., M.J. Traxler & M.W. Crocker. 2000. Ambiguity resolution in sentence processing: evidence against frequency-based accounts. *Journal of Memory and Language* 43. 447-475.
Pierrehumbert, J.B. 2001. Exemplar dynamics: word frequency, lenition and contrast. In Bybee & Hopper (eds.), 137-157.
Pilch, H. 1964. *Phonemtheorie*. Basel: Karger.
Pinker, S. 1998. Words and rules. *Lingua* 106. 219-242.
Pinker, S. 2001. Four decades of rules and associations, or whatever happened to the past tense debate? In Dupoux (ed.), 157-179.
Pinker, S. & A. Prince. 1988. On language and connectionism: Analysis of a parallel distributed processing model of language acquisition. *Cognition* 28. 73-193.
Pinker, S. & A. Prince. 1994. Regular and irregular morphology and the psychological status of rules of grammar. In Lima et al. (eds.), 321-351.
Plag, I. 2003. *Word-formation in English*. Cambridge: Cambridge University Press.
Plag, I., C. Dalton-Puffer & R.H. Baayen. 1999. Morphological productivity across speech and writing. *English Language and Linguistics* 3. 209-228.
Plunkett, K. & V. Marchman. 1993. From rote learning to system building: acquiring verb morphology in children and connectionist nets. *Cognition* 48. 21-69.
Pluymaekers, M., M. Ernestus & R.H. Baayen. 2005. Lexical frequency and acoustic reduction in spoken Dutch. *Journal of the Acoustical Society of America* 118. 2561-2569.
Posner, M.I. 1986. Empirical studies of prototypes. In Craig (ed.), 53-61.

Prasada, S. & S. Pinker. 1993. Generalisation of regular and irregular morphological patterns. *Language and Cognitive Processes* 8. 1-56.

Prince, E.F. 1981. Toward a taxonomy of given-new information. In P. Cole (ed.), *Radical Pragmatics*, 223-255. New York: Academic Press.

Prince, E.F. 1992. The ZPG Letter: subjects, definiteness, and information-status. In W.C. Mann & S.A. Thompson (eds.), *Discourse Description. Diverse Linguistic Analyses of a Fund-raising Text*, 295-325. Amsterdam: John Benjamins.

Quine, W. V. O. 1960. *Word and Object*. Cambridge, Mass.: MIT Press.

Quirk, R. 1965. Descriptive statement and serial relationship. *Language* 41. 205-217.

Quirk, R., S. Greenbaum, G. Leech & J. Svartvik. 1985. A Comprehensive Grammar of the English Language. Harcourt: Longman.

Radford, A. 1988. *Transformational Grammar. A First Course*. Cambridge: Cambrige University Press.

Renouf, A. & J. Sinclair. 1991. Collocational frameworks in English. In Aijmer & Altenberg (eds.), 128-143.

Roelofs, A. 1997. The WEAVER model of word-form encoding in speech production. *Cognition* 64. 249-284.

Rohdenburg, G. 1995a. Betrachtungen zum Auf- und Abstieg präpositionaler Konstruktionen im Englischen. *North-Western Language Evolution* 26. 67-124.

Rohdenburg, G. 1995b. On the replacement of finite complement clauses by infinitives in English. *English Studies* 16. 367-388.

Rohdenburg, G. 1996. Syntactic complexity and increased grammatical explicitness in English. *Cognitive Linguistics* 7. 149-182.

Rohdenburg, G. 1998a. Clarifying structural relationships in cases of increased complexity in English. In R. Schulze (ed.), *Making Meaningful Choices in English*, 189-205. Tübingen: Narr.

Rohdenburg, G. 1998b. Syntactic complexity and the variable use of *to be* in 16th and 18th century English. *Arbeiten aus Anglistik und Amerikanistik* 23. 199-228.

Rohdenburg, G. 1999. Clausal complementation and cognitive complexity in English. In W. Neumann & S. Schülting (eds.), *Anglistentag Erfurt 1998*, 101-112. Trier: Wissenschaftlicher Verlag.

Rohdenburg, G. 2000. The complexity principle as a factor determining grammatical variation and change in English. In I. Plag & K.P. Schneider (eds.), *Language Use, Language Acquisition and Language History. (Mostly) Empirical Studies in the Honour of Rüdiger Zimmermann*, 25-44. Trier: Wissenschaftlicher Verlag.

Rohdenburg, G. 2002. Processing complexity and the variable use of prepositions in English. In H. Cuyckens & G. Radden (eds.), *Perspectives on Prepositions*, 79-100. Tübingen: Niemeyer.

Rohdenburg, G. 2003. Cognitive complexity and *horror aequi* as factors determining the use of interrogative clause linkers in English. In Rohdenburg & Mondorf (eds.), 205-249.

Rohdenburg, G. 2006. Processing complexity and competing sentential variant in present-day English. In W. Kürschner & R. Rapp (eds.), *Linguistik International: Festschrift für Heinrich Weber*, 51-67. Pabst Science Publishers.

Rohdenburg, G. 2007. Functional constraints in syntactic change. The rise and fall of prepositional constructions in Early and Late Modern English. *English Studies* 88. 217-233.

Rohdenburg, G. & B. Mondorf (eds.). 2003. *Determinants of Grammatical Variation*. Berlin: de Gruyter.

Rosch, E. 1973a. Natural categories. *Cognitive Psychology* 4. 328-350.

Rosch, E. 1973b. On the internal structure of perceptual and semantic categories. In T. Moore (ed.), *Cognitive Development and the Acquisition of Language*, 111-144. New York: Academic Press.

Rosch, E. 1978a. Cognitive representations of semantic categories. *Journal of Experimental Psychology: General* 104. 192-233.

Rosch, E. 1978b. Principles of Categorization. In E. Rosch & B.B. Lloyd (eds.), *Cognition and Categorization*, 28-48. Hillsdale, NJ: Lawrence Earlbaum.

Rosch, E. & C.B. Mervis. 1975. Family resemblances: Studies in the internal structure of categories. *Cognitive Psychology* 7. 573-605.

Rosch, E., C.B. Mervis, W.D. Gray, D.M. Johnson & P. Boyes-Braem. 1976. Basic objects in natural categories. *Cognitive Psychology* 8. 382-439.

Rosenbach, A. 2003. Aspects of iconicity and economy in the choice between the s-genitive and the of-genitive in English. In Rohdenburg & Mondorf (eds), 379-411.

Rosenbach, A. 2005. Animacy versus weight as determinants of grammatical variation in English. *Language* 81. 613-644.

Rosenzweig, M.R. & A.L. Leiman. 1982. *Physiological Psychology*. Lexington, Mass.: D.C. Heath.

Ross, J.R. 1973 [2004]. Nouniness. In Aarts et al. (eds.), 351-422. [reprinted from: *Three Dimensions of Linguistic Research*, ed. by O. Fujimura, Tokyo: TEC. 137-257.]

Roth, E.M. & E.J. Shoben. 1983. The effect of context on the structure of categories. *Cognitive Psychology* 15. 346-378.

Rudzka-Ostyn, B. 1989. Prototypes, schemas, and cross-category correspondences: the case of *ask*. *Linguistics* 27. 613-661.

Rumelhart, D.E. 1980. Schemata: The building blocks of cognition. In R. J. Spiro, B. C. Bruce & W. F. Brewer (eds.), *Theoretical Issues in Reading Comprehension: Perspectives from Cognitive Psychology, Linguistics, Artificial Intelligence, and Education*, 33-58. Hillsdale, NJ: Lawrence Erlbaum.

Rumelhart, D.E., G. Hinton & R. Williams. 1986. Learning internal representations by error propagation. In D. E. Rumelhart & J. L. McClelland (eds.), *Parallel Distributed Processing: Explorations in the Microstructure of Cognition Vol. 1*, 318-362. Cambridge, MA: MIT Press.

Rumelhart, D., and J. McClelland. 1986. On learning the past tenses of English verbs. In D. Rumelhart, J. McClelland & the PDP Research Group (eds.), *Parallel Distributed Processing: Explorations in the Microstructure of Cognition Vol. 2*, 216-271. Cambridge, Mass.: MIT Press.

Rumelhart, D.E. & A. Ortony. 1977. The representation of knowledge in memory. In R.C. Anderson, R.J. Spiro & W.E. Montague (eds.), *Schooling and the Acquisition of Knowledge*, 99 – 135. Hillsdale, NJ: Lawrence Erlbaum.

Sampson, G. 1970. *Stratificational Grammar: A Definition and an Example*. The Hague: Mouton.

Sánchez, M.A. 2006. *From Words to Lexical Units: A Corpus-driven Account of Collocation and Idiomatic Patterning in English and English-Spanish*. Frankfurt a. M.: Peter Lang.

Sandig, B. 2000. Text als prototypisches Konzept. In Mangasser-Wahl (ed.), 93-112.

Saussure, F. de. 1916 [1960]. *Course in General Linguistics*. London: Peter Owen Limited.

Say, T. & H. Clahsen. 2002. Words, rules and stems in the Italian mental lexicon. In Nooteboom et al. (eds.), 93-129.

Schank, R. 1975. The structure of episodes in memory. In D.G. Bobrow & A. Collins (eds.), *Representation and Understanding: Studies in Cognitive Science*, 237-272. New York: Academic Press.

Schank, R. & R. Abelson. 1977. *Scripts, Plans, Goals and Understanding: An Inquiry into Human Knowledge Structures*. Hillsdale, NJ: Lawrence Erlbaum.

Schmid, H. J. 1993. *Cottage und Co., idea, start vs. begin: Die Kategorisierung als Grundprinzip einer differenzierten Bedeutungsbeschreibung*. Tübingen: Niemeyer.

Schmid, H. J. 1996. Review of Geeraerts, Gondelaers, and Bakema 1994. *Lexicology* 2. 78-84.

Schmid, H. J. 2000. Methodik der Prototypentheory. In Mangasser-Wahl (ed.), 33-53.

Schmid, H. J. 2007. Entrenchment, salience and basic levels. In Geeraerts & Cuyckens (eds.), 117-138.

Schreuder, R. & R.H. Baayen. 1997. How complex simplex words can be. *Journal of Memory and Language* 37. 118-139.

Schreyer, R. 1977. *Stratifikationsgrammatik: Eine Einführung*. Tübingen: Niemeyer.

Sinclair, J. 1991. *Corpus, Concordance, Collocation*. Oxford: Oxford University Press.

Sinclair, J. 1996. The search for units of meaning. *Textus* 9. 75-106.

Sinclair, J. 1998. The lexical item. In Wiegand (ed.), *Contrastive Lexical Semantics*, 1-24.

Sinclair, J. & S. Jones. 1974. English lexical collocations: A study in computational linguistics. *Cahiers de Lexicologie* 24. 15-61.

Skandera, P. 2004. What are idioms? In Allerton et al. (eds), 23-35. Basel: Schwabe.

Slobin, D.I. 1985. The child as linguistic icon-maker. In Haiman (ed.), 221-248.

Stefanowitsch, A. & S.Th. Gries. 2003. Collostructions: Investigating the interaction of words and constructions. *International Journal of Corpus Linguistics* 8. 209-243.

Stefanowitsch, A. & S.Th. Gries. 2005. Covarying collexemes. *Corpuslinguistic Theory* 1. 1-43.

Stemberger, J.P. 1994. Rule-less morphology at the phonology-lexicon interface. In Lima et al. (eds.), 147-169.

Stemberger, J. P. & B. MacWhinney. 1988. Are inflected forms stored in the lexicon? In M. Hammon & M. Noonan (eds.), *Theoretical Morphology: Approaches in Modern Linguistics*, 101-116. San Diego: Academic Press.

Steyvers, M. & J.B. Tenenbaum. 2005. The large-scale structure of semantic networks: Statistical analyses and a model of semantic growth. *Cognitive Science* 29. 41-78.

Stubbs, M. 2002. Two quantitative methods of studying phraseology in English. *International Journal of Corpus Linguistics* 7. 215-244.

Stubbs, M. 2004. On very frequent phrases in English: Distributions, functions and structures. *Paper held at the 25th Conference of the International Archive of Modern and Medieval English (ICAME 25), Verona, 19-23 May, 2004.*

Stubbs, M. 2007. An example of frequent English phraseology: distributions, structures and functions. In R. Facchinetti (ed.), *Corpus Linguistics 25 Years on*, 89-105. Amsterdam: Rodopi.

Stubbs, M. & I. Barth. 2003. Using recurrent phrases as text-type discriminators: A quantitative method and some findings. *Functions of Language* 103. 61-104.

Szmrescanyi, B. 2005. Never change a winning chunk. *RANAM* 38. 85-98.

Szmrecsanyi, B. & L. Hinrichs. (forthc.) Probabilistic determinants of genitive variation in spoken and written English: a multivariate comparison across time, space, and genres. *Proceedings of 27th ICAME Conference, University of Helsinki.*

Tarone, E. 2002. Frequency effects, noticing, and creativity: Factors in a variationist interlanguage framework. *Studies in Second Language Acquisition* 24. 287-296.

Taylor, J. R. 1989. *Linguistic Categorization: Prototypes in Lingustic Theory*. Oxford: Clarendon.

Taylor, J. R. 1992. How many meanings does a word have. *Stellenbosch Papers in Linguistics* 25. 133-168.

Taylor, J. R. 1995. Models of word meaning in comparison: The two-level model (Manfred Bierwisch) and the network model (Ronald Langacker). In R. Dirven & J. Vanparys (eds.), *Current Approaches to the Lexicon*, 3-26. Frankfurt a. M.: Peter Lang.

Taylor, J. R. 1998. Syntactic constructions as prototype categories. In Tomasello (ed.), 177-202.

Taylor, J. R. 1999. Cognitive semantics and structural semantics. In A. Blank & P. Koch (eds.), *Historical Semantics and Cognition*, 17-48. Berlin: Mouton de Gruyter.

Taylor, J. R. 2002. *Cognitive Grammar*. Oxford: Oxford University Press.

Taylor, J. R. 2003. Polysemy's paradoxes. *Language Sciences* 25. 637–655.

Taylor, J. R. 2004. The ecology of constructions. In G. Radden & K.-U. Panther (eds.), *Studies in Linguistic Motivation*, 49-73. Berlin: Mouton de Gruyter.

Taylor, J. R. 2008. Prototypes in cognitive linguistics. In P. Robinson & N. C. Ellis (eds.), *Handbook of Cognitive Linguistics and Second Language Acquisition*, 39-65. New York: Routledge.

Taylor, J. R., H. Cuyckens & R. Dirven. 2003. Introduction: New directions in cognitive lexical semantic research. In H. Cuyckens, R. Dirven & J. R. Taylor *Cognitive Approaches to Lexical Semantics*, 1-28. Berlin: Mouton de Gruyter.

Thompson, S. A. 1995. The iconicity of 'dative shift' in English: Considerations from information flow in discourse. In M. E. Landsberg (ed.), *Syntactic Iconicity and Linguistic Freezes: The Human Dimension*, 155-175. Berlin: de Gruyter.

Thompson, S. A. & W. C. Mann. 1987. Rhetorical structure theory: A framework for the analysis of texts. *IPRA Papers in Pragmatics* 1. 79-105.

Tognini-Bonelli, E. 2001. *Corpus Linguistics at Work*. Amsterdam: John Benjamins.

Tognini-Bonelli, E. 2002. Functionally complete units of meaning across English and Italian: Towards a corpus-driven approach. In B. Altenberg & S. Granger (eds.), *Lexis in Contrast*, 73–95. Amsterdam: John Benjamins.

Tomasello, M. 2003a. *Constructing a Language: A Usage-based Theory of Language Acquisition*. Cambridge, MA: Harvard University Press.

Tomasello, M. 2003b. Introduction: some surprises for psychologists. In Tomasello (ed.), 1-14.

Tomasello, M. 2006. Acquiring linguistic constructions. In D. Kuhn & R. Siegler (eds.), *Handbook of Child Psychology*, 255-298. New York: Wiley.

Tomasello, M. (ed.). 1998. *The New Psychology of Language: Cognitive and Functional Approaches to Language Structure. Vol. 1.* Mahwah, NJ.: Lawrence Erlbaum.

Tomasello, M. (ed.). 2003. *The New Psychology of Language: Cognitive and Functional Approaches to Language Structure. Vol. 2.* Mahwah, NJ.: Lawrence Erlbaum.

Tomasello, M. & K. Abbot-Smith. 2002. A tale of two theories: response to Fisher. *Cognition* 83. 207-214.

Trask, R.L. 1993. *A Dictionary of Grammatical Terms in Linguistics*. London: Routledge

Trask, R.L. 1999. *Key Concepts in Language and Linguistics*. London: Routledge

Trubetzkoy, N.S. 1939. *Grundzüge der Phonologie*. Prag.
Tsohatzidis, S.L. (ed.). 1990. *Meanings and Prototypes: Studies on Linguistic Categorization*. Oxford: Routledge.
Tucker, G. 2006. Systemic incorporation: on the relationship between corpus and systemic functional grammar. In Geoff Thompson & Susan Hunston (eds.), *System and Corpus: Exploring Connections*, 81-102. London: Equinox.
Tuggy, D. 2005. Cognitive approach to word-formation. In P. Štekauer & R. Lieber (eds.), *Handbook of Word-Formation*, 233-265. Dordrecht: Springer.
Tuggy, D. 1993 [2006]. Ambiguity, polysemy, and vagueness. In D. Geeraerts (ed.), *Cognitive Linguistics. Basic Readings*, 167-184. Berlin: Mouton de Gruyter. [reprinted from: *Cognitive Linguistics* 4, 273-290].
Tuggy, D. 2007. Schematicity. In Geeraerts & Cuyckens (eds), 82-116.
Tversky, B. 1986. Components and categorization. In Craig (ed.), 63-75.
Tyler, A. & V. Evans. 2001 [2007]. Reconsidering prepositional polysemy networks: the case of *over*. In V. Evans, B. Bergen & J. Zinken (eds.), *The Cognitive Lingustics Reader*, 186-237. London: Equinox. [reprinted from: *Language* 77, 724-765].
Ungerer, F. & H.-J. Schmid. 1996. *An Introduction to Cognitive Linguistics*. London: Longman.
Vallduví, E. 1992. *The Informational Component*. New York & London: Garland.
Vallduví, E. & E. Engdahl. 1994. Information packaging and grammar architecture. *Proceedings of NELS* 25. 519-533.
Vallduví, E. & E. Engdahl. 1996. The linguistic realization of information packaging. *Linguistics* 34. 459-519.
Verhoeven, L., H. Baayen & R. Schreuder. 2004. Orthographic constraints and frequentcy effects in complex word identification. *Written Language and Literacy* 7. 49-59.
Viereck, W. 1989. Diachronic English morphology and the notion of frequency. In L.E. Breivik, A. Hille & S. Johansson (eds.), *Essays on English Language in Honour of Bertil Sundby*, 367-373. Oslo: Novus.
Vosberg, U. 2003. The role of extractions and *horror aequi* in the evolution of *–ing* complements in Modern English. In Rohdenburg & Mondorf (eds.), 305-327.
Vosberg, U. 2006. *Die Große Komplementverschiebung: Außersemantische Einflüsse auf die Entwicklung satzwertiger Ergänzungen im Neuenglischen*. Tübingen: Narr.
Wasow, T. 1997a. Remarks on grammatical weight. *Language Variation and Change* 9. 81-105.
Wasow, T. 1997b. End-weight from the speaker's perspective. *Journal of Psycholinguistic Research* 26. 347-361.
Wasow, T. 2001. Generative Grammar. In M. Aronoff & J. Rees-Miller (eds.), *The Handbook of Linguistics*, 295-328. Oxford: Blackwell.
Wasow, T. & J. Arnold. 2003. Post-verbal constituent ordering in English. In Rohdenburg & Mondorf (eds.), *Determinants of Grammatical Variation in English*, 119-154.
Weigand, E. (ed.). 1998. *Contrastive Lexical Semantics*. Amsterdam: John Benjamins.
Weil, H. 1844 [1978]. *The Order of Words in the Ancient Languages Compared with that of the Modern Languages*. Amsterdam: John Benjamins.
Wierzbicka, A. 1985. *Lexicography and Conceptual Analysis*. Ann Arbor: Karoma.
Wierzbicka, A. 1990. 'Prototypes save': On the uses and abuses of the notion of 'prototype' in linguistics and related fields. In Tsohatzidis (ed.), 347-367.
Wittek, A. & M. Tomasello. 2002. German children's productivity with tense morphology: the *Perfekt* (present perfect). *Journal of Child Language* 29. 567-589.

Wittgenstein, L. 1953 [2004]. *Philosophical Investigations*. In Bas Aarts et al. (eds.), 41-44.
Wray, A. 1999. Formulaic language in learners and native speakers. *Language Teaching* 32, 213-231.
Wray, A. 2000. Formulaic sequences in second language teaching: Principles and practice. *Applied Linguistics* 21. 463-489.
Wray, A. 2002a. *Formulaic Language and the Lexicon*. Cambridge: Cambridge University Press.
Wray, A. 2002b. Formulaicity in computer-supported communication: Theory meets reality. *Language Awareness* 11. 114-131.
Wray, A. & M.R. Perkins. 2000. The functions of formulaic language: An integrated model. *Language & Communication* 20. 1-28.
Yngve, V.H. 1960. A model and an hypothesis for language structure. *Proceedings of the American Philosophical Society* 104, 444-466.
Zipf, G.K. 1949. *Human Behavior and the Principle of Least Effort: An Introduction to Human Ecology*. New York: Hafner.
Zipf, G.K. 1935 [1965]. *The Psycho-Biology of Language: An Introduction to Dynamic Philology*. Cambridge, MA.: The M.I.T. Press.

Index

abstraction 63, 74–81, 105–109, 160
– scale of 81, 83
activation threshold 2, 25, 32–33, 63, 70, 147, 263
ambiguity 168
– in the network 134–42, 249–51
argument roles 71, 188–89, 191–96, 232, 240, 259
– and mapping on participant roles 191–93
association 2, 4–5, 30, 32, 64–69, 80, 165, 213, 226
– direct 64, 107
– indirect 107
– indirect 65–67
background knowledge and the network 233–45
basic level 14, 139
basic level categories
– in the network 231–32
categorization 3–5, 85–86, 99, 107–10, 165
class 17, 67, 75–76, 92, 96–99, 105
– and description 77–79
– in the network 79–80, 108–15
– *sensu* Halliday 76–77
clause structure in the network 147–51
co-activation 6, 46, 64–66, 80, 107, 113, 160, 174, 213, 217, 221, 249
cognitive commitment 3, 106
cognitive economy 229, 232
cognitive schemas 181–87
– in the network 188–205
colligation 87, 207
collocation 80, 205–7, 210–11, 213–16, 221–22, 235
collocational framework 209–11, 212
competition 34–44, 131, 134, 178, 194
complex VP in the network 151–58
Complexity Principle 256–61
composing complex word forms in the network 162–63
composition route 44, 163–67, 174
conditional probabilities in the network 188
connection
– excitatory 2–3, 33, 243, 260
– inhibitory 125, 149
– inhibitory 2, 35–50, 57, 70, 123–25, 200
– node-to-connection 70, 143, 163
– non-directional 69
– unidirectional 29
constituency 14, 83–84, 89, 95, 102, 252
construction 170, 177
– as schema 183–85
– di-transitive 184, 188–92, 197, 199, 232, 240, 241, 249, 255, 259, 261
– prepositional 196–98, 241, 255
– *sensu* Construction Grammar 183–85
– *sensu* Goldberg 226
– transitive 170
– *WXDY* 183
– *WXDY* in the network 199–201
Construction Grammar 183, 191
constructions
– and verbal preferences in the network 239–41, 259–61
core 13–14, 116
cue validity 116, 119, 120, 126
– in the network 230–32
decomposing word forms in the network 163–64
degree of representativity 100–101
– in the network 126
delicacy 14, 81–90, 95, 111, 139, 182, 231
description through classes 77–81, 88, 90, 104

distributed 6, 44–46, 113, 145, 164, 204, 237
distribution 74
ditransitive construction
– Goldberg 188
– Hudson 189–92
– in the network 188–97
Early Immediate Constituents 246–47
– and Minimize Domains 251–52
elements
– in structuralism 294–76
– interaction of 150
entrenchment 2, 11–12, 27–28, 30–31, 63, 67–68, 107–108, 140, 168, 173, 245
exclusionary fallacy 6, 9, 169
expectation in the network 233–45
extension 93, 102–3, 112
freedom of occurrence 74, 76
frequency 11–12, 28–30, 80, 125, 139, 165, 206, 210, 214, 216, 247
– and morphological productivity 177–80
– in the network 167–77, 236–45
– token ~ 177–80
– type ~ 177–80
fronting in the network 149
fuzzy boundaries 101
– in the network 126–28
garden path sentences 256
garden path sentences in the network 262–64
generalization 54, 96–99, 112
generative_transformational grammar 101–5
genre and the network 234–36
gerund 128–34
Gesetz der Wachsenden Glieder 246
gradience
– intersective 99, 128, 131, 134
– subsective 116, 125
hard-wired networks 3, 21, 24
hierarchy 14–16, 21, 51, 100, 112, 115
– in the network 46–52
idiom 211, 216
– in the network 222–26
idiom principle 222
– in the network 222–26
if not-then 34
if-then 33–34, 40–41, 43, 62, 150, 153, 158, 163, 175
indeterminacy 99–101
– in the network 115–34
inheritance 189–91
– multiple default ~ 130–31
inheritance of features 52–59
– complete 52
– normal 52
instantiation 83–84, 88–91, 95–98, 102, 111–13, 182, 185, 187, 204
intension 93, 112
inversion in the network 149
irregularity 98, 167, 169, 175
ISA 16, 20, 46–52, 54–55, 204
langue 238
learning in the network 24, 26–27, 30, 45, 55, 63–67, 169, 174
– regular past tense 26–27
least effort 229, 251
lexical bundle 209, 211
lexical phrase 209
lexicalized sentence stem 212
local representation 6, 44–46
Maximize On-line Processing (MaOP) 247
– in the network 253–56
Minimize Domains (MiD) 258
– in the network 251–53
Minimize Forms (MiF) 258
– in the network 247–51
morphological productivity
– and frequency 177–80
– in the network 177–80
multiple membership 101
– in the network 128–34
negative features in the network 58
Network Postulate 1, 20
Neurophysiological Challenge 2
neurophysiology 25–28
n-gram 208–11
non-algorithmic model 24
open-choice principle 222
overgeneralization in the network 164–67
overriding features 55–57

participant roles 148, 184, 259
– and mapping on argument roles 191–93
– in the network 188–89
past tense allomorphy 172, 177, 178
– and regularization 175–77
– in the network 158–67
pattern grammar 86
Pattern Grammar 186–87
– and the network 201–5
perceived world structure 108, 229
periphery 13–14, 122
p-frame 209–11
– in the network 217–18
polysemy
– in the network 134–42
polyword 209, 211
POS-gram 207–11, 227
– in the network 218–19
prepositional construction
– in the network 197–99, 262–64
processing principles in the network 245–61
prototypicality 66, 125, 140
radial network 136
rank 81–90, 182
rank-permeability 15, 182, 187, 194, 205
real copying 53, 55, 57, 112, 114
recurrent item strings 205–12
– in the network 212–26
recurrent word combinations 206
redundancy in the network 167–75
redundant storage 6, 9–11, 57
regularity 95, 98, 99, 238
regularization in the network 175–77
rule and instantiation in the network 167–75
rule/list fallacy 9, 169
rules in the network 158–67
scales-and-categories (Halliday) 74
schema 152, 234
self-organizing networks 21–24
semantic preference 208–11
semantic prosody 208–11
semantic roles 38–39, 150
sequence 59–63, 68, 252
– bottom-up 61–62
– fronting 83, 149
– in the network 142–58
– inversion 83, 149–150
– top-down 60–62
– within complex VP 151–58
spreading activation 30–33, 58, 69, 163
structure *sensu* Halliday 59, 75–76
system *sensu* Halliday 75
taxonomic structuralism 294
unit 75–76, 82–86, 89, 161, 164, 169, 179, 211, 216–17
– *sensu* Halliday 75
usage-based 8–9, 13, 105, 106
vagueness 248
– in the network 134–42, 249
virtual copying 6, 16, 52–53, 57, 112, 114
whole-word route 44, 165–67, 174, 178–79, 216
Word Grammar 190–191, 197
X-bar Theory 103–5